OXFORD MONOGRAPHS ON LABOUR LAW

General Editors: PAUL DAVIES, KEITH EWING,
MARK FREEDLAND

Bullying and Behavioural Conflict at Work

OXFORD MONOGRAPHS ON LABOUR LAW

General Editors: Paul Davies, emeritus Fellow of Jesus College and emeritus Allen and Overy Professor of Corporate Law in the University of Oxford; Keith Ewing, Professor of Public Law at King's College, London; and Mark Freedland, emeritus Research Fellow in Law at St John's College and emeritus Professor of Employment Law in the University of Oxford.

This series has come to represent a significant contribution to the literature of British, European, and international labour law. The series recognizes the arrival not only of a renewed interest in labour law generally, but also the need for fresh approaches to the study of labour law following a period of momentous change in the UK and Europe. The series is concerned with all aspects of labour law, including traditional subjects of study such as collective labour law and individual employment law. It also includes works that concentrate on the growing role of human rights and the combating of discrimination in employment, and others that examine the law and economics of the labour market and the impact of social security law and of national and supranational employment policies upon patterns of employment and the employment contract. Two of the contributing authors to the series, Lucy Vickers and Diamond Ashiagbor, have received awards from the Society of Legal Scholars in respect of their books.

TITLES PUBLISHED IN THE SERIES

The Concept of the Employer
Jeremias Prassl

The Labour Constitution
The Enduring Idea of Labour Law
Ruth Dukes

The Legal Construction of Personal Work Relations
Mark Freedland FBA and
Nicola Kountouris

A Right to Care?
Unpaid Work in European
Employment Law
Nicole Busby

Regulating Flexible Work
Deirdre McCann

Welfare to Work
Conditional Rights in Social Policy
Amir Paz-Fuchs

EU Intervention in Domestic Labour Law
Phil Syrpis

Towards a Flexible Labour Market
Labour Legislation and Regulation
since the 1990s
Paul Davies and Mark Freedland

The European Employment Strategy
Labour Market Regulation and
New Governance
Diamond Ashiagbor

The Law of the Labour Market
Industrialization, Employment, and
Legal Evolution
Simon Deakin and Frank Wilkinson

The Personal Employment Contract
Mark Freedland

International and European Protection of the Right to Strike
A Comparative Study of Standards
Set by the International Labour
Organization, the Council of Europe
and the European Union
Tonia Novitz

Freedom of Speech and Employment
Lucy Vickers

Women and the Law
Sandra Fredman

Just Wages for Women
Aileen McColgan

Bullying and Behavioural Conflict at Work

The Duality of Individual Rights

LIZZIE BARMES

Professor of Labour Law, Queen Mary University of London

OXFORD

UNIVERSITY PRESS

Great Clarendon Street, Oxford, OX2 6DP,
United Kingdom

Oxford University Press is a department of the University of Oxford.
It furthers the University's objective of excellence in research, scholarship,
and education by publishing worldwide. Oxford is a registered trade mark of
Oxford University Press in the UK and in certain other countries

© L Barmes 2016

The moral rights of the author have been asserted

First Edition published in 2016

Impression: 1

Crown copyright material is reproduced under Class Licence
Number C01P0000148 with the permission of OPSI
and the Queen's Printer for Scotland

Published in the United States of America by Oxford University Press
198 Madison Avenue, New York, NY 10016, United States of America

British Library Cataloguing in Publication Data
Data available

Library of Congress Control Number: 2015951317

ISBN 978–0–19–969137–1

Printed and bound by
CPI Group (UK) Ltd, Croydon, CR0 4YY

To Mark and the Oulivaz Gang

General Editors' Preface

We have many reasons to welcome this latest addition to the Oxford Monographs on Labour Law series. The subject matter of *Bullying and Behavioural Conflict at Work* is one that is long overdue for extended analysis. Even identifying the types of conduct that fall within the notion of bullying and related behaviour is challenging, since the law does not address it directly and, outside legal discourse, no single way of framing the issue has become accepted. Of course, no one is in favour of bullying, but what bullying consists of is a much-contested question. An important function discharged in the first chapters of this book is thus to bring conceptual clarity to both the legal and social discourses on bullying and, more generally, behavioural conflict at work.

Our second reason for welcoming this new book is its methodological inventiveness, which is itself a response to the imprecision, just noted, of the social and legal discourses. The relevant case law is exhaustively analysed, but with a view to asking a broad range of questions about it, extending well beyond, but including, those suggested by traditional doctrinal assessments. The results of this analysis are, we think, both novel and revealing. Those are supplemented and reinforced by the outputs from interviews with senior managers and lawyers who have had to deal professionally with behavioural issues at work or in the courts.

Finally, the policy implications of the book are that our approach to the use of the law to address inappropriate behaviour at work needs significant revision. Simply giving employees further individual rights against their employer, while possibly necessary, is by no means enough by itself. In part, this is because the source of the inappropriate behaviour may be other employees who are not in a superior position to the claimant. As the research underlying this book demonstrates, much more important are the complexities and discouraging features of the litigation process and the limitations of the remedies awardable by courts or tribunals. Legal rights and legal remedies may need to be supplemented, perhaps even replaced, by other approaches to dispute resolution. But the book does not underestimate the challenges faced by those who want to put such alternative structures in place. We greatly welcome this book into our series, to which we are fully confident that it will be regarded as a very worthy addition.

Paul Davies, Keith Ewing, and Mark Freedland

Acknowledgements

I have incurred a great many intellectual and personal debts in researching and writing this book. The project has its roots much further back than the five years it took to complete, and its ultimate shape and content are profoundly influenced by colleagues, collaborators, friends, and family, a happily overlapping set of categories.

My first thanks are to the lawyers and managers who agreed to be interviewed. My appreciation of their contribution is no less heartfelt for being unable to name the individuals concerned. Speaking to them was an education and their participation made the book possible.

There are several people whose guidance throughout has been central. Kate Malleson was at my side at every stage, questioning, commenting, and ultimately giving me the confidence to finish. Juliette Towhidi's expert advice about writing got me through many difficult moments. Discussions with Saphieh Ashtiany have been a constant backdrop to my thinking about how law and work interact. I had the extraordinary good fortune to have Niki Lacey as my undergraduate law tutor and her perceptive comments, thirty years later, on a near final draft only accentuated how much I owe her. Paul Davies and Mark Freedland have been my teachers for (a mere) two decades and their influence and encouragement are fundamental to this book, not least as General Editors with Keith Ewing.

I am grateful to many other colleagues. Particular thanks go to Micheál O'Floinn and Giulia Liberatore for inspired research assistance. I received valuable early bibliographical advice from Hugh Collins and Roger Cotterrell, while Hugh made helpful drafting suggestions at the very end. Alan Bogg was generosity itself as a reader. Diamond Ashiagbor and Jo Braithwaite responded to early versions of some chapters and gave vital moral support along the way. Claire Kilpatrick read later versions of several chapters and provided many critical de-briefing opportunities. Pointers about the Scottish court system were given by David Cabrelli, Ruth Dukes, and Douglas Brodie. I also learned from discussions with the London Labour Law Discussion Group and audiences at the autonomy of labour law conference in Oxford in July 2013 and the empirical labour law conference in Cambridge in April 2014.

I want also to thank colleagues at QMUL, including successive Heads of Department during this project, Peter Alldridge and Valsamis Mitsilegas, for creating and sustaining a stimulating, congenial, and supportive intellectual community. I am grateful to Mark Byrne for assistance in recent months with communicating my ideas to a wider audience. I have also greatly appreciated working with Natasha Flemming, Elinor Shields, Geetha Parakkat, and my copy-editor, all at or for OUP. They have steered me through the process of writing and publishing with kindness, tact, and efficiency.

On a more personal level, my London family has been a constant source of sustenance. Thank you to the Dales; the Solly-Towhidis; the Tickner-Bellaus; and to Laura and Zoe, who cross many boundaries. My family in Australia and Max in Tennessee provided crucial long-distance support, Davy spurred me on from around the globe and David and Suzanna are, quite simply, always there when you need them. Finally, my brother Mark and our Oulivaz Gang, headed by him, Gillian, Ashling, and Markie created a haven in Gryon where this book was almost entirely written. That gave me the emotional peace and mental space I needed to do this. The book is dedicated to them with love and gratitude.

Contents

Table of Cases   xv
Table of Statutes   xix
Table of Statutory Instruments   xxi
Table of European Legislation   xxiii
List of Abbreviations   xxv

1. Introduction   1
   1. Individual Labour and Equality Rights and Law's Duality   1
   2. Individual Labour and Equality Rights and Traditions
      of Labour Law Scholarship   3
   3. Individual Labour and Equality Rights
      and Legal Realist Methodology   4
   4. Individual Labour and Equality Rights
      and Behavioural Conflict at Work   6

2. The Empirical Background to Behavioural Conflict at Work   11
   1. Empirical Knowledge about Negative Behaviour at Work   12
      (1) Psychologists and workplace bullying   13
          (a) Conceptual and definitional approaches   13
          (b) Approaches to incidence   14
      (2) Sociologists and ill treatment at work   18
          (a) Conceptual and definitional approaches   18
          (b) Approaches to incidence   19
   2. Empirical Knowledge about Law and Legal Process   25
      (1) Procedural issues   26
          (a) ETs v ordinary courts   27
          (b) Costs and funding litigation   27
      (2) Socio-legal research into claiming behaviour by individuals 28
          (a) Approaches to claiming behaviour generally   28
          (b) Claiming behaviour about individual employment rights 31
      (3) Socio-legal research into litigation experience with individual labour
          and equality rights   38
      (4) Socio-legal research into organizational experience
          with individual labour and equality rights   48
   3. Conclusion   53
      (1) Bad workplace behaviour, unsolved problems,
          and suboptimal legal interventions   53
      (2) Misconceiving the law and legal influence   54
      (3) The collectivity of working life in the individualized discourse of rights 55

3. The Substantive Legal Background to Behavioural Conflict
   at Work from 1995 to 2015   59
   1. The Statutory Right not to be Unfairly Dismissed   62
      (1) Liability   63
      (2) Remedies   68

2. Statutory Wrongs of Discrimination 71
   (1) Liability I: Discriminatory harassment 'old style' 72
       (a) Racial or sexual harassment as direct discrimination 72
       (b) The 'old-style' requirement to show a 'detriment' 74
       (c) The ambit of employer responsibility 75
   (2) Liability II: Discriminatory harassment 'new style' 77
       (a) Dedicated definitions of discriminatory harassment enacted
           from 2003 to 2006 78
       (b) 2008 changes to the law on sexual harassment 81
       (c) The EqA 2010 on discriminatory harassment 81
   (3) Liability III: Direct discrimination and victimization
       in behavioural conflict cases 82
       (a) Non-harassing conduct as direct discrimination 82
       (b) Victimization 85
       (c) The EqA 2010 on direct discrimination and victimization 85
   (4) Remedies 87
       (a) Pre-EqA 2010 remedies 87
       (b) The EqA 2010 on remedies 89
3. Protection from Harassment Act 1997 89
   (1) Liability 89
   (2) Remedies 92
4. The Common Law of Contract and Tort 92
   (1) Liability 93
       (a) Torts of intention 93
       (b) Negligence in contract and tort 93
       (c) The contractual duty of mutual trust and confidence 97
   (2) Remedies 98
5. Conclusions 100

4. Factual Themes in Case Law about Behavioural Conflict at Work 103

   1. Introduction and Method for the Qualitative Analysis
      of Judgments 103
   2. Classic Litigation Stories about Behavioural Conflict at Work 106
   3. Complexity in Litigation Stories about Behavioural Conflict
      at Work 107
   4. Complexity about the Influence of Group Identity
      on Behavioural Conflict at Work 109
   5. Complexity about the Role of Colleagues and Management
      in Behavioural Conflict at Work 110
   6. Judicial Scrutiny of Behavioural Conflict at Work 112
   7. Behavioural Conflict at Work Lost in a Litigation Maze 115
   8. Conclusion 117

5. Legal Themes in Case Law about Behavioural Conflict at
   Work I: Overlapping Rights and the Snakes-and-Ladders Effect 119

   1. Snakes I: Pre- and Post-Dismissal Compensation 120
   2. Snakes II: Group Identity and Compensation
      for Personal Injury 122
   3. Snakes III: Litigation Strategies 124

4. Ladders I: Common Law 128
5. Ladders II: Statute 131
6. Conclusion 132

6. **Legal Themes in Case Law about Behavioural Conflict at Work II: Consistency in Applying Behaviour Rules** 139
   1. Statutory Unfair Dismissal 141
   2. Statutory Wrongs of Discrimination I: Discriminatory Harassment 142
      (1) Drawing behavioural lines in 'old-style' harassment cases 143
      (2) Drawing behavioural lines in 'new-style' harassment cases 146
   3. Statutory Wrongs of Discrimination II: General Discrimination Cases 148
   4. Breach of the Protection from Harassment Act 1997 151
   5. Unlawful Conduct in Contract and Tort 160
   6. Conclusion 167

7. **Legal Themes in Case Law about Behavioural Conflict at Work III: Consistency in Analysing Employer Responses** 169
   1. Statutory Unfair Dismissal 170
   2. Statutory Wrongs of Discrimination I: Discriminatory Harassment 173
   3. Statutory Wrongs of Discrimination II: General Discrimination Cases 174
   4. Unlawful Conduct in Contract and Tort 177
   5. Conclusion 180

8. **Senior Managers and Lawyers on Behavioural Conflict at Work and Legal Influence** 183
   1. Introduction and Interview Study Method 184
   2. Organizational Perceptions of Behavioural Conflict at Work 186
      (1) Contents 187
      (2) Quantification and impact 188
      (3) Emergence and escalation 190
         (a) Individual influences 190
         (b) Organizational influences 191
         (c) Proceduralization and formality 194
   3. The Influence of Law and Legal Process 197
      (1) Procedural influences 197
      (2) Substantive complexities 200
         (a) Prioritizing equality law rules about behaviour 201
         (b) Marginalizing behavioural rules of other types 202
         (c) Juxtaposing organizational and legal reasoning 204
   4. Summary and Discussion 207

9. **Senior Managers and Lawyers on Behavioural Conflict at Work and the Missing Collective Dimension** 215
   1. Organizational Approaches and the Impact of Individual Rights 218
      (1) Employer dominance 220
      (2) Unitarism 221
         (a) Flattened hierarchy 221
         (b) Commitment-style management 222

(3) Modern versions of pluralist collectivism 222
  (a) Deep down 222
  (b) Large scale 223
  (c) Non-union solidarity 224
(4) Managers at the sharp end 224
2. The Silencing and Constructing of Individual Complaints 227
  (1) General reluctance to complain 227
  (2) Constructing reluctance (and complaint): Organizational culture 228
  (3) Constructing reluctance: The costs of speaking out and litigating 231
  (4) Constructing claims: Being 'difficult' 234
3. Complex Unease about Legal Intervention 236
  (1) Dichotomizing enlightened management and law 237
  (2) Ambiguity about law's influence 239
4. Summary and Discussion 240

10. **Conclusions** 245
  1. Excavating the Two Faces of Law and Legal Process 245
    (1) The challenge of law 245
      (a) Enforcement 245
      (b) Implementation 247
    (2) The acquiescence of law 247
      (a) Enforcement 248
      (b) Implementation 248
    (3) General methodological and theoretical implications 250
  2. Individual Labour and Equality Rights and the Variety
     of Working Lives 253
    (1) Managerialist evasion, unitarist ambiguity, and pluralist struggles 253
    (2) Discursive obstructions to the emancipatory potential
       of individual labour and equality rights 256
    (3) The missing collective dimension and using law to relocate it 259
      (a) Normative accessibility as an emancipatory legal device 259
      (b) Widening participation in implementation and enforcement
         as an emancipatory legal device 261
      (c) Experimentation as an emancipatory legal device 264
  3. Individualism, Individualization, and Solidarity 265

Appendix 1: Sample of Judgments 1995 to 2010 (Chronological Order by Judgment) 267
Appendix 2: Research Interviews with People in Organizations 271
Index 275

Table of Cases

Abbey National plc v Fairbrother [2007] IRLR 320 (EAT) 60, 66–67, 110
Abbey National Plc v Robinson (EAT, 20 November 2000) 111, 124–25, 132, 141
Addis v Gramophone [1909] AC 488 (HL) 96, 98–99
Aberdeen CC v McNeill (EAT, 9 February 2010) 59, 141–42
Allen v LB of Southwark [2008] EWCA Civ 1478 91
Amnesty International v Ahmed [2009] ICR 1450 (EAT) 83, 85
Anyanwu v South Bank Student Union (Commission for Racial Equality intervening)
    [2001] ICR 391 (HL) 175
Autoclenz Ltd v Belcher [2011] UKSC 41, [2011] ICR 1157 63
Bahl v Law Society [2004] EWCA Civ 1070, [2004] IRLR 799 113
Banks v Ablex Ltd [2005] EWCA Civ 173, [2005] ICR 819 . . . . 91, 123, 151–52
Barber v Somerset CC [2004] UKHL 13, [2005] 1 WLR 1089 . . . . 94, 155
Barclays Bank plc v Kapur (no 2) [1995] IRLR 87 (CA) 75
Barlow v Broxbourne BC [2003] EWHC 50 (QB) 163
Bernard v Attorney General of Jamaica [2004] UKPC 47, [2005] IRLR 398 93
Birmingham CC v Samuels (EAT, 24 October 2007) 170
Blackburn with Darwen Borough Council v Stanley (EAT, 20 January 2005) 131–32, 134, 170–71, 181
Bournemouth University Higher Education Corporation v Buckland [2009] ICR 1042 (EAT) 65–67
Bournemouth University Higher Education Corporation v Buckland [2010] EWCA Civ 121 66–67
British Telecommunications v Williams [1997] IRLR 668 (EAT) 72–73
Brumfitt v MoD [2005] IRLR 4 (EAT) 126, 133
Burton v Rhule De Vere Hotels Ltd [1997] ICR 1 (EAT) 77
Canniffe v East Riding of Yorkshire Council [2000] IRLR 555 (EAT) 76
Cartamundi UK Ltd v Worboyes (EAT, 4 December 2009) 128
CC of West Yorkshire Police v Khan [2001] UKHL 48, [2001] ICR 1065 . . . . 74, 85
Chagger v Abbey National plc [2009] EWCA Civ 1202, [2010] ICR 397 88
Chan v Barts & the London NHS Trust [2007] EWHC 2914 (QB) 108, 115, 180
Cheltenham Borough Council v Laird [2009] EWHC 1253 (QB), [2009] IRLR 621 113–16
City of Edinburgh v Wood (EAT, 2 May 2008) 67
Claridge v Daler Rowney [2008] ICR 1267 (EAT) 67
Clark v CC of Essex [2006] EWHC 2290 (QB) 129, 133–34, 167
Cleveland Police Authority v Francis (EAT, 10 March 2010) 106, 122, 134
Clyde & Co LLP v Bates van Winkelhof [2014] UKSC 32, [2014] ICR 730 72
Coleman v Attridge Law [2008] ICR 1128 (ECJ) 80–81, 86
Commissioner of Police of the Metropolis v Shaw [2012] ICR 464 (EAT) 89
Connor v Surrey CC [2010] EWCA Civ 286, [2011] QB 429 167
Courtaulds Northern Textiles Ltd v Andrew [1979] IRLR 84 (EAT), 86 64
Coventry University v Mian [2014] EWCA Civ 1275, [2014] ELR 455 67
Croft v Royal Mail Group plc [2003] ICR 1425 (CA) 76
Crossland v Wilkinson Hardware Stores Ltd [2005] EWHC 481 (QB) 90, 113, 132, 136
Cumbria CC v Carlisle-Morgan [2007] IRLR 314 (EAT) 137
Cyprus Airways Ltd v Lambrou (EAT, 1 May 2007) 68
D Watt (Shetland) Ltd v Reid Appeal (EAT, 25 September 2001) 176
Da'Bell v National Society for the Prevention of Cruelty to Children [2010] IRLR 19 (EAT) 88
Daniels v Commissioner of Police for the Metropolis [2006] EWHC 1622 (QB) 124, 133
Daw v Intel Corp (UK) Ltd [2007] EWCA Civ 70, [2007] ICR 1318 . . . . 94, 129, 133–34, 135
Derby Specialist Fabrication v Burton [2001] ICR 833 (EAT) 111, 150
Dickie v Flexcon Glenrothes Ltd [2009] GWD 35-602 (Sheriff Court) 90, 92, 103, 155–58, 169
Dowson v CC of Northumbria Police [2009] EWHC 907 (EAT) 91, 155
Driskel v Peninsula Business Services Ltd [2000] IRLR 151 (EAT) 173
Dunnachie v Kingston upon Hull CC [2004] UKHL 36, [2005] 1 AC 226 . . . . . . 70, 111–12, 120–21
Eastwood v Magnox Electric plc & McCabe v Cornwall CC [2004] UKHL 35,
    [2005] 1 AC 503 . . . . .62, 70, 93–98, 119–22, 128–31, 134–35

Edwards v Chesterfield Royal Hospital NHS Foundation Trust & Botham v MoD [2011]
    UKSC 58, [2012] 2 WLR 55 . . . . 62, 95–101, 119
Ellis v Eagle Place Services Ltd [2002] EWHC 1201 (QB) 162–63
English v Thomas Sanderson Blinds Ltd [2008] EWCA Civ 1421, [2009] ICR 543 . . . . 81, 86
Essa v Laing Ltd [2004] EWCA Civ 2, [2004] ICR 746 . . . . .88, 119, 132, 134, 145–46
Ferguson v British Gas Trading Ltd [2009] EWCA Civ 46, [2010] 1 WLR 785 . . . . 91, 156
Fernandez v Office of the Parliamentary Commissioner for Administration and Health Service
    Commissioners (EAT, 15 February 2005) 116, 170
GAB Robins (UK) Ltd v Triggs [2008] EWCA Civ 17, [2008] ICR 529. . . . 62, 71, 97, 119, 121–22,
                                                                         124–25, 131–32, 134–35
Garrett v London Borough of Camden [2001] EWCA Civ 395 177–78
Geary v Amec Logistics & Support Services Ltd (EAT, 1 November 2007) 122, 172–73
GMB Trade Union v Brown (EAT, 16 October 2007) 62, 71, 97, 119, 121–22, 124–25,
                                                                          131–32, 134, 171–72
Gogay v Hertfordshire CC [2000] IRLR 703 (CA) 97
Goodman v Members of the Executive of Shropshire Unison (EAT, 11 March 2010) 68
Grant v HM Land Registry [2011] EWCA Civ 769, [2011] ICR 1390 79
Greater Manchester Passenger Transport Executive v Sands (EAT, 11 January 2001) 127
Green v DB Group Services [2006] EWHC 1898 (QB), [2006] IRLR 764 . . . . . 91, 93–94, 108, 129,
                                                                              132–35, 166–67
Hall v Bull [2013] UKSC 73, [2013] 1 WLR 3741 83
Hammond v International Network Services UK Ltd [2007] EWHC 2604 (QB) 116–17
Harris v The Post Office (Royal Mail) (EAT, 25 February 2000) 111, 126
Hartman v South Essex Mental Health & Community Care NHS Trust [2005]
    EWCA Civ 6, [2005] ICR 782 . . . . 94, 128
Harvest Press Ltd v McCaffrey [1999] IRLR 778 (EAT) 63
Hayes v Willoughby [2013] UKSC 17, [2013] 1 WLR 935 91
Hipgrave v Jones [2004] EWHC 2901 (QB), [2005] 2 FLR 174 92
Horkulak v Cantor FitzGerald International [2003] EWHC 1918 (QB),
    [2004] ICR 697. . . . . 107–108, 131–35, 164–66, 181
Horkulak v Cantor FitzGerald International [2004] EWCA Civ 1287, [2005] ICR 402 131
Iceland Frozen Foods Ltd v Jones [1983] ICR 17 (EAT) 66
Igen Ltd v Wong [2005] EWCA Civ142, [2005] ICR 931 84
Iqbal v Dean Manson Solicitors [2011] EWCA Civ 123, [2011] IRLR 428 91–92
Islamic Cultural Centre v Mahmoud (EAT, 27 June 2007) 128
Jivraj v Hashwani [2011] UKSC 40, [2011] ICR 1004. 72
Johnson v Bank of England (EAT, 10 April 2003). 124
Johnson v The Governing Body of Coopers Lane Primary School (EAT, 1 December 2009) 128
Johnson v Unisys Ltd [2001] UKHL, [2003] 1 AC 518 . . . . . 61–62, 70, 93–98, 119–21, 128–32, 134–35
Jones v ICS Cleaning Services Ltd (EAT, 11 April 2000). 107, 145
Jones v Ruth [2011] EWCA (Civ) 804, [2012] 1 WLR 1495 . . . . 92, 157
Jones v Tower Boot Co Ltd [1997] ICR 254 (CA) 7, 76, 143
Kelly v DPP [2002] EWHC Admin 1428 92
King v Great Britain-China Centre [1992] ICR 516 (CA) 84
Kircher v Hillingdon PCT [2006] EWHC 21 (QB), [2006] Lloyd's Rep Med 215 . . . . . 99–100, 180
Laing v Manchester CC [2006] ICR 1519 (EAT) 84, 126, 150
Lambeth LBC v Owolade (EAT, 30 November 2004) 176
Lau v Director of Public Prosecutions [2000] 1 FLR 799 (Div Ct) 91
LB of Hackney v Sivanandan [2013] EWCA Civ 22, [2013] ICR 672 75
Leavers v The Victoria University of Manchester (EAT, 21 February 2000) 125–26, 133
Lew v Board of Trustees on behalf of United Synagogue [2011] EWHC 1265 (QB),
    [2011] IRLR 664. 99
Lipscombe v The Forestry Commission [2008] EWHC 3342 (QB) 108–109
Long v Mercury Communications [2002] PIQR Q1 (QB). 7–8, 129–30, 134, 161
Lord Chancellor v Coker [2001] ICR 507 (EAT) 75
M and L Sheet Metals Ltd v Willis (EAT, 12 March 2010) 132–34

Maclellan v Co-operative Group (CWS) Ltd (EAT, 11 May 2006) 92
Madarassy v Nomura International Plc [2007] EWCA Civ 33, [2007] ICR 867 . . . . 84, 126
Majrowski v Guy's and St Thomas's NHS Trust [2006] UKHL 34,
   [2007] 1 AC 224 . . . . 89–91, 119, 135–37, 152–56
Malik v BCCI [1998] AC 20 (HL). 64–65, 67, 96–97, 99
Marinello v City of Edinburgh Council [2011] CSIH 33, [2011] IRLR 669. 92
McNeill v Aberdeen CC (No. 2) [2013] CSIH 102, [2014] IRLR 102 . . . . 59, 141
Merelie v Newcastle PCT (EAT, 26 August 2009) 114
Merelie v Newcastle PCT [2006] EWHC 1433 (Admin) 113–15, 178–79, 181
Metrobus Ltd v Unite the Union [2009] EWCA Civ 829, [2010] ICR 173 3
Mezey v South West London & St George's Mental Health NHS Trust [2007]
   EWHC 62 (QB), [2007] IRLR 237. 99
Mezey v South West London & St George's Mental Health NHS Trust [2010]
   EWCA Civ 293, [2010] IRLR 512 99
Miles v Gilbank [2006] EWCA Civ 543, [2006] ICR 1297 . . . . 75, 112, 175–76
MoD v Fletcher [2010] IRLR 25 (EAT). 89
Monk v Cann Hall Primary School [2013] EWCA Civ 826, [2013] IRLR 732. 95
Moore v Welwyn Components Ltd [2005] EWCA Civ 6, [2005] ICR 782. . . . . 128–29, 133–34
Mullins v Laughton [2002] EWHC 2761, [2003] Ch 250 166
Munchkins Restaurant Ltd v Karmazyn (EAT, 28 January 2010) 110, 147–48
National Probation Service for England and Wales (Cumbria Area) v Kirby & Holland
   [2006] IRLR 508 (EAT) 109–110
Nayif v High Commission of Brunei Darrusalam [2014] EWCA Civ 1521,
   [2015] IRLR 134. 123
Norton Tool Co Ltd v Tewson [1972] IRLR 86 (NIRC). 70
NURMT v Serco Ltd t/a Serco Docklands [2011] EWCA Civ 226, IRLR 399 3
NURMT v UK [2014] IRLR 467 (ECtHR) 3
Omilaju v Waltham Forest LBC [2004] EWCA Civ 1493, [2005] ICR 481 170
Ormsby v CC of Strathclyde Police [2009] CSOH 143, 2008 SCLR 783. 112
Pakenham-Walsh v Connell Residential [2006] EWCA Civ 90. 124
Parchment v The Secretary of State for Defence, QB, 23 February 1998. . . . . . . 122–25, 130–31, 133
Pearce v Governing Body of Mayfield School MacDonald v Advocate General for Scotland
   [2003] UKHL 34, [2003] ICR 937 . . . . 73–74, 76–77, 80, 82, 84, 109, 125–26, 133
Perkin v St George's Healthcare NHS Trust [2005] EWCA Civ 1174, [2006] ICR 617. . . . . 115, 141
Polkey v AE Dayton Services Ltd [1988] AC 344 (HL) 69
Porcelli v Strathclyde RC [1986] ICR 564 (CSIH) 73–74
Post Office v Foley HSBC Bank plc Madden [2000] ICR 1283 (CA) 66
Pratt v DPP [2001] EWHC Admin 483. 91–92
Prison Service v Johnson [1997] ICR 275 (EAT) 88, 111, 176
R (on the application of E) v Governing Body of JFS [2009] UKSC15, [2010] 2 AC 728 . . . . . 83, 85
R (on the application of EOC) v SS for Trade and Industry [2007] EWHC 483 (Admin),
   [2007] ICR 1234. . . . . 78, 80–81, 83
R (on the application of Shoesmith) v Ofsted [2011] EWCA Civ 642, [2011] ICR 1195 99
R v Sean Peter [2001] EWCA Crim 1251. 91
Rayment v MoD [2010] EWHC 218 (QB), [2010] IRLR 768. . . . . 91, 132, 133–35, 158–59
Reed & Bull Information Systems Ltd v Stedman [1999] IRLR 299 (EAT) 73, 109, 143–45
Riley v Nick Base t/a Gl1 Heating (EAT, 19 July 2005). 127
Robertson v The Scottish Ministers [2007] CSOH 186 . . . . 93, 155
Royal Bank of Scotland v McAdie [2007] EWCA Civ 806, [2008] ICR 1087. 124
Royal Mail Letters and others v Muhammad (EAT, 20 December 2007). 68
Saini v All Saints Haque Centre [2009] IRLR 74 (EAT) 80–81
Sainsbury's Supermarkets Ltd v Hitt [2002] EWCA Civ 1588, [2003] ICR 111 66
Sandwell MBC v Jones [2002] EWCA Civ 76, [2002] ICR 613 . . . . 94, 162
Sayers v Cambridgeshire CC [2006] EWHC 2029, [2007] IRLR 29 179–80
Scally v Southern Health and Social Services Board [1992] 1 AC 294 (HL) 64
Serco Ltd v Redfearn [2006] EWCA Civ 659, [2006] ICR 1367 . . . . 80–81, 83–84, 86

Shamoon v CC of the Royal Ulster Constabulary (Northern Ireland) [2003] UKHL 11,
    [2003] ICR 337. . . . . 74–75, 84
Sheffield CC v Norouzi [2011] IRLR 897 (EAT) 81
Sheriff v Klyne Tugs (Lowestoft) Ltd [1999] EWCA Civ 1663, [1999] ICR 1170. . . 88, 109, 123–25,
    127, 130–31, 133
Showboat Entertainment Centre v Owens [1984] 1 WLR 384 (EAT) 80, 83
Smith v Gardner Merchant Ltd [1999] ICR 134 (CA) 73
Smith v Martin & Co (Marine) Ltd (EAT, 4 June 2003). 162
Smith v Zeneca (Agrochemicals) Ltd [2000] ICR 800 (EAT) 173–74
Smiths Detection Watford Ltd v Berriman (EAT, 9 August 2005). 124, 173
South London Healthcare NHS Trust v Rubeyi (EAT, 2 March 2010) 110, 133, 176
Spencer v Primetime Recruitment Ltd (EAT, 2 March 2006) 126
Spring v Guardian Assurance Plc [1995] 2 AC 296 (HL) 93
Sutherland v Hatton [2002] EWCA Civ 76, [2002] IRLR 263. . . . . 94, 155, 162–63
Swift v CC of Wiltshire Constabulary [2004] ICR 909 (EAT) 127
Thomas v News Group Newspapers Limited [2001] EWCA Civ 1233 90
Thornett v Scope [2006] EWCA Civ 1600, [2007] ICR 236 170
Unwin v West Sussex CC, QB, 13 July 2001 . . . . 130, 161
Veakins v Kier Islington Ltd [2009] EWCA Civ 1288, [2010] IRLR 132. . . . . 7, 106–107,
    132–36, 155–56, 159
Vento v CC of West Yorkshire Police [2002] EWCA Civ 1871, [2003] ICR 318. . . . . 88–89, 174–76
Villalba v Merrill Lynch and Co Inc [2007] ICR 469 (EAT). 108, 132–35, 149–50
Walton v Image Creative Ltd (EAT, 16 August 2002) 108, 171
Waters v Commissioner of Police of The Metropolis [2000] UKHL 50,
    [2000] 1 WLR 1607 . . . . .94, 123, 130–31, 133, 177
Weathersfield Ltd v Sargent [1999] ICR 425 (CA) 80, 83
Webb v Emo Air Cargo [1994] QB 718 (ECJ) & [1995] 1 WLR 1454 (HL) 82
West Coast Trains Ltd v Tombling (EAT, 3 April 2009) 173
West London Mental Health NHS Trust v Chhabra [2013] UKSC 80, [2014] ICR 194. 99
Western Excavating (ECC) Ltd v Sharp [1978] QB 761 (CA) 64–65, 67
Wong v Parkside Health NHS Trust [2001] EWCA CIV 1721, [2003] 3 All ER 932 . . . . 93, 126
Yapp v Foreign & Commonwealth Office [2014] EWCA Civ 1512, [2015] IRLR 112. . . . 67, 94, 99
Yeboah v Crofton [2002] EWCA Civ 794, [2002] IRLR 634 113
Yellow Pages Limited v Garton (EAT, 13 March 2003) 124–25, 132

Table of Statutes

Black Act 2
Deregulation Act 2015
  s 2 89
Disability Discrimination Act 1995 . . . 66, 71–72,
           74–85, 87–89, 100–101, 109–10,
           115, 122–28, 130–35, 142–50, 167–68,
           173–76, 187–91, 196, 200–203,
           206–207, 210, 229, 231–34, 263
  s 3A(5) 83
  s 4 74
  s 49A 261
  s 55 85
  s 57 75
  s 58 75
  s 68(1) 72
Disability Discrimination Act 2005 261
Employers' Liability (Compulsory
  Insurance) Act 1969 93
Employment Act 2002 . . . . 26, 60, 68, 263
Employment Act 2008 . . . . 68–70, 263
  s 3 . . . . 70, 263
Employment Rights Act 1996 . . . . . 60–71, 141
  Pt X (on unfair dismissal) 26, 32, 41–42,
          48–50, 62–71 87, 93–97, 100–101,
          107, 114, 116, 119–22, 124–26,
          129, 131–37, 140–42, 162,
          170–73, 181, 198
  s 95(1)(c) 64–65
  s 98(1)–(2) 65
  s 98(3) 65
  s 98(4) 65–66
  s 98(6) 65
  ss 99–105 63
  s 100(1)(d) 63–64
  s 108 63
  s 123 69–70
  ss 230(1)–(2) 63
Enterprise and Regulatory Reform
    Act 2013 . . . . 26–28, 69–70, 100
  s 15 69
  s 16 . . . . 70, 262–63
  ss 17–20 100
  s 65 81
Equal Pay Act 1970 . . . . . . 3, 27, 42, 56, 68, 74,
                  130, 149, 194
Equality Act 2006 261
Equality Act 2010 . . . . 49–50, 61, 71–72, 76–78,
        81–82, 84–87, 89, 92, 100, 261–65
  Pt 5 Ch 1 74
  ss 5–12 85
  s 13 85

  s 13(3) 86
  s 13(4) 86
  s 17 85
  s 18 85
  s 23 86
  s 23(2) 86
  s 23(3) 86
  s 26 . . . . 78, 82
  s 27 87
  ss 39–40 74
  s 40 81
  s 83(2)–(4) 72
  s 109 75
  s 110 75
  s 124 89
  s 136 87
  s 149 . . . . 164–65, 201, 239,
                         261–62
  s 212(1), (5) 72, 77
Industrial Relations Act 1971 62
  s 116 70
Legal Aid, Sentencing and Punishment
    of Offenders Act 2012 27–28
  ss 8–10 27–28
  sch 1 27–28
Misrepresentation Act 1967 114
National Minimum Wage Act 1998 48
Protection from Harassment Act 1997 . . . . 7, 27,
        54, 59, 61, 69, 71, 89–93, 100–101,
        103, 114–16, 119–21, 123–27, 129,
        131–37, 139–41, 151–60,
        166–67, 169, 180–82, 240
  s 1 . . . . 90–92, 155
  s 2 . . . . 90–92, 156
  s 3 . . . . 90–92, 156
  s 4 . . . . 90, 92
  s 7(2), (3), (4) 90
Public Interest Disclosure
    Act 1998 . . . . 60, 100, 137
Race Relations Act 1976 . . . . 3, 42–47, 71–85,
        87–89, 100–101, 109–10, 122–28,
        130–35, 142–50, 167–68, 173–76,
        187–91, 194, 196, 200–203, 206–207,
        210, 216–17, 228–29, 231–34, 261, 263
  s 2 85
  s 4 74
  s 32 75
  s 33 75
  s 76 261
  s 78(1) 72
Race Relations (Amendment) Act 2000 261

Sex Discrimination Act 1975 . . . . .3, 43–44,
    71–85, 87–89, 100–101, 109–10, 122–28,
    130–35, 142–50, 167–68, 171, 173–76,
    187–91, 194, 196, 200–203, 206–207,
    216–17, 210, 229, 231–34, 263
s 1(1)(a) 73, 77
s 3A 83
s 4 85
s 5(3) 73
s 6 74
s 41 . . . . 75, 175
s 41(3) 174

s 42 175
s 42(1) 75
s 42(2) 75
s 76A 261
s 82(1) 72
Trade Union and Labour Relations
    (Consolidation) Act 1992
s 207A 70
Unfair Contract Terms Act 1977 . . . . 93, 95
ss 1(1) 93
s 2 93
sch 1 para 4 93

Table of Statutory Instruments

Disability Discrimination Act 1995
(Amendment) Regulations 2003
(SI 2003/1673) 77, 83
Employment Act 2002 (Dispute
Resolution) Regulations 2004
(SI 752/2004) 68
Employment Equality (Age) Regulations
2006 (SI 2006/1031) 71–72, 74–81,
83–85, 87–89, 100–101,109–10,
122–28, 142–43, 146–48, 167–68,
173–76, 187–91, 196, 200–203,
206–207, 210, 229, 231–34, 263
reg 2 72
reg 4 85
reg 7 74
reg 25 75
reg 26 75
Employment Equality (Religion or
Belief) Regulations 2003
(SI 2003/1660) 44–47, 68, 71–72,
74–85, 87–89, 100–101, 109–10,
122–28, 142–43, 146–50, 167–68,
173–76, 187–91, 196, 200–203,
206–207, 210, 229, 231–34, 263
reg 2 72
reg 4 85
reg 6 74
reg 22 75
reg 23 75
Employment Equality (Sex
Discrimination) Regulations 2005
(SI 2005/2467) 83
Employment Equality (Sexual
Orientation) Regulations 2003
(SI 2003/1661) 44–47, 71–72, 74–85,
87–89, 100–101,109–10, 122–28,
142–43, 146–50, 167–68, 173–76,
187–91, 196, 200–203, 206–207,
210, 229, 231–34, 263
reg 2 72
reg 4 85

reg 6 74
reg 22 75
reg 23 75
Employment Tribunals Extension of
Jurisdiction (England and Wales)
Order 1994 (SI 1994/1623). 62
reg 3 62
reg 4 62
reg 10 62
Equality Act 2010 (Commencement No 4,
Savings, Consequential, Transitional,
Transitory and Incidental Provisions
and Revocation) Order 2010
(SI 2010/2317) 78
Race Relations Act 1976 (Amendment)
Regulations 2003 (SI 2003/1626) 77
Sex Discrimination (Indirect
Discrimination and Burden of Proof)
Regulations 2001 (SI 2001/2660) 84
Sex Discrimination Act 1975
(Amendment) Regulations 2008
(SI 2008/656) 78, 81
reg 2 83
reg 3 81
Unfair Dismissal and Statement of Reasons
for Dismissal (Variation of Qualifying
Period) Order 1999 (SI 1999/1436). . . .63
Unfair Dismissal and Statement of Reasons
for Dismissal (Variation of Qualifying
Period) Order 2012 (SI 2012/989). 63
Unfair Dismissal (Variation of the Limit
of Compensatory Award) Order
2013 (SI 2013/1949). 69
Working Time Regulations 1998
(SI 1998/1833) 48

Table of European Legislation

DIRECTIVES

Directive 97/80/EC of 15 December 1997
  on the burden of proof in cases of
  discrimination based on sex 84
Directive 2000/43/EC of 29 June 2000
  implementing the principle of
  equal treatment between persons
  irrespective of racial or ethnic
  origin 71, 77
  Art 2(3) 78
Directive 2000/78/EC of 27 November
  2000 establishing a general
  framework for equal treatment in
  employment and occupation 71, 77–78
  Art 2(3) 78

Directive 2002/73/EC of 23 September
  2002 on the implementation of
  the principle of equal treatment for
  men and women as regards access to
  employment, vocational training and
  promotion, and working
  conditions 71, 77–81
Directive 2006/54/EC of 5 July 2006 on
  the implementation of the principle
  of equal opportunities and equal
  treatment of men and women in
  matters of employment and
  occupation 71

List of Abbreviations

ACAS	Advisory, Conciliation and Arbitration Service
Am J Sociol	American Journal of Sociology
BIS	Department for Business, Innovation and Skills
BWBS	British Workplace Behaviour Survey
CA	Court of Appeal
CAB	Citizens Advice Bureau
CSIH	Court of Session, Inner House
CSJPS	Civil and Social Justice Panel Survey
CSJS	Civil and Social Justice Survey
CSOH	Court of Session, Outer House
DDA	Disability Discrimination Act
DDAAR	Disability Discrimination Act 1995 (Amendment) Regulations 2003
EA	Employment Act
EAT	Employment Appeal Tribunal
ECJ	European Court of Justice
EEAR	Employment Equality (Age) Regulations
EERBR	Employment Equality of Religion or Belief Regulations
EESOR	Employment Equality (Sexual Orientation) Regulations
EHRC	Equality and Human Rights Commission
EMAR	Employment Market Analysis and Research
EPA	Equal Pay Act
EqA	Equality Act
ERA	Employment Rights Act
ESRC	Economic and Social Research Council
ET	Employment Tribunal
ETD	Equal Treatment Directive
ETS	Employment Tribunals Service
Eur J Work Organ Psy	European Journal of Work and Organizational Psychology
FTWS	Fair Treatment at Work Survey
GEO	Government Equalities Office
HC	High Court
HL	House of Lords
HR	human resources
IT	Industrial Tribunal
Law and Soc'y Rev	Law and Society Review
NAQ	Negative Acts Questionnaire
NHS	National Health Service
PHA	Protection from Harrassment Act
PIDA	Public Interest Disclosure Act
PSED	Public Sector Equality Duty
RRA	Race Relations Act
SC	Supreme Court
SDA	Sex Discrimination Act
SETA	Surveys of Employment Tribunal Applications
UMIST	University of Manchester Institute of Science and Technology
WERS	Workplace Employment Relations Surveys

1

Introduction

The central finding of this study is that individual labour and equality rights, as currently legislated, implemented, and enforced in the UK, overall enhance the status quo by supporting traditional workplace hierarchy and marginalizing more plural, collective workplace ways of being. This is rooted in a paradox whereby individual rights are quite easily minimized, sidelined, and defused in employer-dominated environments, while more receptive organizations are at particular risk of damaging and disruptive individualized conflict. The broad context is the growing power of liberal individualist ideology, often based on a narrow, negative understanding of liberty, and the associated experience of deepening inequality. Ideological struggle surrounding the related move from collective to individual regulation at work and the consequent individualization of employment relations, have left a massive and growing number of working people to cope on their own with workplace problems and a tiny proportion to find their way through the alienating, often unsatisfying ordeal of litigation. Yet, while managers are in theory beneficiaries of the shift in workplace power this entails, and are often responsible for problems working people encounter, they can face parallel isolation as 'shock absorbers' for conflict between collective employer power and individual employee interests.

It seems forlorn to hope for purposeful attempts to change these patterns when national governments appear complicit, quiescent, or powerless before modern re-orderings of working life. Nonetheless, this state of affairs calls for a redesign of labour and equality rights to stimulate the expression and reconciliation of different points of view in their implementation and enforcement. Without such innovation, the use of law to emancipate at work must represent an ongoing loss, not only for people and organizations directly affected by problems and conflict at work, but for society as a whole and the many who hope for more just distributions of power in working life and beyond.

1. Individual Labour and Equality Rights and Law's Duality

At the broadest level this book is a legal account of individualization, reflecting wider developments towards individualism and away from collective understandings of how society in general, and working life in particular, ought to be structured. The particular context is that legal intervention at work in the UK has since the 1960s increasingly taken the form of individual rights. This trend gathered pace from the mid-1990s and the most legally favoured working people now have a significant catalogue of entitlements. Some of these rights have their origins in EU law. Often, however, they stemmed from domestic initiatives by governments across the political spectrum. This form of law thereby evokes the softer face of wider individualist trends by explicitly promoting justice norms in keeping with the global spread of legalized human rights discourse. In a variety of ways contemporary individual entitlements at work pursue the flattening of hierarchies and the equalization of societal goods in a crucial site for the distribution of power and wealth.

Despite their overt aims, however, individual labour and equality rights have not stood in the way of enduring, sometimes worsening, systemic inequality in the UK that echoes experience elsewhere.[1] This intervention has not translated in the hands of working people, either individually or as a group, into reliable and consistent tools for ameliorating their position, much as enshrining the pursuit of fairer, more just working lives into law has legitimated established power structures. The net effect is for this legally inspired process of individualization simultaneously to advance socially transformative goals and to support, even extend, existing hierarchies and ways of being. This narrative is accordingly emblematic of how society's increasing concentration on individuals intertwines the pursuit of liberal individualist ideology with the experience of resilient and often worsening structural inequality.

Regrettable as aspects of this complex reality are, research can at least illuminate the distinctive part law plays in producing and shaping it. The duality in how individual rights at work function arguably instantiates a deep truth about the nature of law: that it is fated simultaneously to challenge and to sustain the status quo. That law has this Janus-like quality has been contended by scholars as disparate as Kimberlé Crenshaw writing about anti-discrimination law in the modern USA,[2] and EP Thompson[3] in his famous work on the eighteenth-century Black Act in England.[4] That insight, however, remains to be tested in many contexts and little has been done to map the precise mechanisms by which law produces its contradictory outcomes.

This book undertakes those tasks in relation to UK individual labour and equality rights, elucidating how law functions along three axes. First, it considers the impact of centering emancipatory legal intervention on individuals.[5] Second, like Crenshaw's study, the focus is on whether law stabilizes social structures even where the intention is apparently to subvert them. This is the other side of the coin to the arguably more familiar dynamic, at least since Thompson exposed it, of law shoring up existing power relations by restraining authoritarian uses of power. Third, the operation of this form of law is examined in the particular context of work, paying attention to the variety of experiences and influences this brings into play.

---

[1] Evidence of this abounds and seems continually to increase. For some useful overviews from the UK, including some comparative material, see T Phillips, R Kerslake, and J Mayhew Jonas, *Fairness and Freedom: The Final Report of the Equalities Review* (HMSO, 2007); Strategy Unit, *Getting on, getting ahead, A discussion paper: analyzing the trends and drivers of social mobility* (Cabinet Office, Nov 2008); J Hills, M Brewer, S Jenkins, R Lister, R Lupton, S Machin, C Mills, T Modood, T Rees, and S Riddell, *An Anatomy of Economic Inequality in the UK: Report of the National Equality Panel* (Centre for Analysis of Social Exclusion, LSE, 2010); J Hills, F Bastagli, F Cowell, H Glennerster, E Karagiannaki, and A McKnight, *Wealth in the UK: Distribution, Accumulation, and Policy* (OUP, 2013).

[2] K Crenshaw, 'Race, Retrenchment and Reform: Transformation and Legitimation in Anti-Discrimination Law' (1988) 101 Harvard Law Review 1331.

[3] EP Thompson, *Whigs and Hunters: The Origin of the Black Act* (Pantheon, 1975).

[4] See more generally on the duality of law in liberal and Marxist thought, A Hunt, 'Dichotomy and Contradiction in the Sociology of Law' (1981) 8 Brit JLS 47.

[5] The work as a whole considers the UK, while the doctrinal exposition in Ch 3 concentrates on England and Wales.

2. Individual Labour and Equality Rights and Traditions of Labour Law Scholarship

Writing about UK labour law scholarship in 2005, Dickens and Hall commented that '[t]here is generally less attention …to how the law is used …[to] how people come to accommodate and live with it…'.[6] This perfectly captures what I have sought to achieve, mapping how judges work with individual labour and equality rights in adjudicating concrete situations, and, investigating organizational responses to law and legal process. This provides an evidence base for theorizing law, both generally and with regard to the current regime of UK individual labour and equality rights, while additionally suggesting ways that legal intervention in the workplace might be redesigned to improve the delivery of justice goals.

In particular, this book fills gaps in scant existing knowledge about the operation of laws about work. This paucity endures, and not only in the UK, despite examples over the years of relevant empirical investigation by lawyers,[7] more recent developments in the literature,[8] and important and growing sociological contributions.[9] The dearth in recent decades of empirical investigation in the field is arguably explained by major twentieth-century shifts in how law has been used to regulate work and the response of scholars. The move to legislating individual rights is one aspect of the regulatory change. The other started with the concerted campaign from 1979 to 1997 to reduce legal support for widespread collective bargaining and to enact legislation that was purposefully designed to undermine trade unionism. In turn, one of the most remarkable features of the Labour administrations of 1997–2010 was how many of these restrictive legal measures they retained.[10] It is true that Labour governments made some concessions to trade unions and that they enhanced the potential for countervailing constitutional developments deriving from UK membership of the Council of Europe[11] and the European Union.[12] Even so, domestic legislation remained significantly inhospitable to collective regulation of workplaces.[13] The election in 2010 of a Conservative/Liberal Democrat

---

[6] L Dickens and M Hall, 'The Impact of Employment Legislation: Reviewing the Research' in L Dickens, M Hall, and S Wood, *Review of Research into the Impact of Employment Legislation* (DTI, ERRS 45, Oct 2005), 32.

[7] See in the UK, eg, AM Leonard, *Judging Inequality: The Effectiveness of the Industrial Tribunal System in Sex Discrimination and Equal Pay Cases* (Cobden Trust, 1987); C McCrudden, D Smith, and C Brown, *Racial Justice at Work: The Enforcement of the 1976 Race Relations Act in Employment* (Policy Studies Institute, 1991); C McCrudden, R Ford, and A Heath, 'Legal Regulation of Affirmative Action in Northern Ireland: An Empirical Assessment' (2004) 24 OJLS 363. The US empirical literature is more established, discussed further below.

[8] See S Deakin, 'Labor and Employment Laws', in P Cane and H Kritzer (eds), *Oxford Handbook of Empirical Legal Research* (OUP, 2010), 326; A Blackham and A Ludlow (eds), *New Frontiers in Empirical Labour Law Research* (Hart, 2015).

[9] See Ch 2 on socio-legal investigations and overviews in W Brown, A Bryson, J Forth, and K Whitfield, *The Evolution of the Modern Workplace* (CUP, 2009) and L Dickens (ed), *Making Employment Rights Effective, Issues of Enforcement and Compliance* (Hart, 2012). See also R Saundry, P Latreille, L Dickens, C Irvine, P Teague, P Urwin, and G Wibberley, *Reframing Resolution: Managing Conflict and Resolving Individual Employment Disputes in the Contemporary Workplace* (ACAS, 2014), reporting on the ESRC Seminar Series in 2012–13 on this subject matter.

[10] See generally AJS Colvin, (2011) 49 BJIR583.

[11] Consider, eg, KD Ewing and J Hendy, 'The Dramatic Implications of Demir and Baykara' (2010) 39 ILJ2, although the decisions of the UK CA in *Metrobus Ltd v Unite the Union* [2009] EWCA Civ 829, [2010] ICR 173, *NURMT v Serco Ltd t/a Serco Docklands* [2011] EWCA Civ 226, IRLR 399, and of the ECtHR sitting as a Chamber in *NURMT v UK* [2014] IRLR 467 (ECtHR) all demonstrate the limitations of Council of Europe protections.

[12] The EU record is variable and recent developments make this route to enhancing trade union protections notably uncertain. See M Freedland and J Prassl, *Viking, Laval and Beyond* (Hart, 2014).

[13] See generally A Bogg, *The Democratic Aspects of Trade Union Recognition* (Hart, 2009).

coalition government deepened these alterations to the labour law landscape, election in 2015 of a fully Conservative administration is taking them further and the EU seems increasingly to be moving in the same broad direction.

Allied to this twin movement away from a legally tolerant, even supportive stance towards trades unions, and in favour of enacting individual labour and equality rights, there exists a powerful tradition of interdisciplinary labour law scholarship. However, the British roots of the kind of methodological openness which exists in this field lie deep in the experience of collective regulation of work. It was famously Kahn-Freund's fresh sociological approach which enabled him, starting in the second half of the twentieth century, both to document and to theorize the relationship between law and workplace collectivism.[14] Analysis of the few individual rights that then existed tended to be left to more classical doctrinal treatment.

My contention is that this methodological split remained even as individual labour and equality rights burgeoned through the late twentieth century and into the twenty-first. One way of characterizing my project, therefore, is as taking inspiration from the interdisciplinary tradition in labour law scholarship, and especially its sociological manifestations, in order to investigate how law is interacting with working lives in an individualized legal environment. Further, while in earlier times the data required for sociological analysis of the relationship between law and work may have been available from classical industrial relations (IR) enquiry, the increase in individual rights makes an enhanced legal dimension necessary for equivalent analyses now. This makes growing interest in the IR community in individual rights very welcome and also calls for more direct collaboration between the disciplines.[15] In any event, a vital line of enquiry, as shown by this study, is the connection between the experience of legally induced individualization and the idea and practice of collectivism at work.

3. Individual Labour and Equality Rights and Legal Realist Methodology

The specific research design reflects my understanding of law as sustaining the dominant forces in society at the same time as it challenges them.[16] Even if existing power is likely to be reinforced by law, both primary legal sources and associated processes have 'real-life' effects, not least where laws are on their face designed to pursue justice goals. This points to the tantalizing possibility that, however supportive law is of existing social structures, it can also be an engine for worthwhile change. The challenge is to discover ways of shifting the balance of legal effects, never losing sight that even a recast law will, to some extent, uphold current distributional patterns.

The initial need, therefore, is to work out the mechanisms by which law achieves its paradoxical feat. Much as some of these may be easy to spot, this cannot generally be

---

[14] See O Kahn-Freund, 'Intergroup Conflicts and their Settlement' (1954) 5 British Journal of Sociology 193, 'Legal Framework' in A Flanders and HA Clegg (eds), *The System of Industrial Relations in Great Britain* (Basil Blackwell, 1954), and 'Labour Law' in M Ginsberg (ed), *Law and Opinion in England* (Stevens, 1959).

[15] See n 9.

[16] See Thompson (n 3), eg at 265: 'The rhetoric and the rules of a society are something a great deal more than sham. In the same moment they may modify, in profound ways, the behaviour of the powerful, and mystify the powerless. They may disguise the true realities of power, but, at the same time, they may curb that power and check its intrusions. And it is often from within that very rhetoric that a radical critique of the practice of the society is developed'.

true as that would mean law is easily manipulable in the hands of those seeking change. Rather, it must be that law's effects are often realized by unpredictable, uneven, sometimes invisible and ideological means. What is needed, therefore, is painstakingly, piece by piece, to build a detailed picture of how law functions.

I turned to early American Legal Realism for inspiration in embarking on this task, in particular since my project evokes the central theoretical concern of Realists with documenting and explaining the relationship between law 'on the books' and in practice.[17] The idea of combining analysis of legal sources with qualitative interviewing was further influenced by the developing New Legal Realist literature in the US.[18]

It is important, however, to emphasize that these influences were mainly methodological, seeking to modernize 'old' Realism's sociological investigation of adjudication[19] and to learn from US scholars' innovative deployment of social science tools to elucidate how modern law about work functions.[20] It is striking that the case law element of my project led me back to mid-twentieth-century research experimentation by Llewellyn.[21] This evinces that empirical research in law has tended not to delve into the substance of law and legal decision-making, as opposed to the processes, structures, and institutions of this world.[22] Indeed, the methodological split in labour law scholarship exemplifies that tendency.

I did not rely on detailed substantive conclusions in the US literature about how law and legal process have worked there. This is the case in respect of earlier Realist scholarship, such work that is associated with the Critical Legal Studies movement,[23] and the ongoing resurgence of related lines of enquiry.[24] Rather, I took guidance at a

[17] See generally W Twining, *Karl Llewellyn and the Realist Movement* (2nd edn, CUP, 2012).

[18] See generally VE Nourse and GC Shaffer, 'Varieties of New Legal Realism: Can a New World Order Prompt a New Legal Theory?' (2009) 95 Cornell Law Review 61.

[19] See F Schauer, 'Foreword' in Twining (n 17), xi–xii and xv–xvii.

[20] See in particular, S Sturm, 'Race, Gender, and the Law in the Twenty-First Century Workplace: Some Preliminary Observations' (1997) 1 UPaJLab and EmpL 639; 'Second Generation Employment Discrimination: A Structural Approach' (2001) 101 ColumLRev 458; 'Gender Equity Regimes and the Architecture of Learning' in G de Búrca and J Scott (eds), *Law and New Governance in the EU and the US* (Hart, 2006); 'The Architecture of Inclusion: Advancing Workplace Equity in Higher Education' Columbia Law School, Public Law and Legal Theory Working Paper Group, 06-114; 'Law, Norms and Complex Discrimination' in C Estlund and B Bercusson (eds), *Regulating Labour in the Wake of Globalization, New Challenges, New Institutions* (CUP, 2008). See also the more institutionalist work of LB Edelman and collaborators: LB Edelman, 'Legal Ambiguity and Symbolic Structures: Organizational Mediation of Civil Rights Law' (1992) 97 Am J Sociol 1531; LB Edelman, SE Abraham, and HS Erlanger, 'Professional Construction of Law: The Inflated Threat of Wrongful Discharge' (1992) 26 Law and Society Review 47; LB Edelman, HS Erlanger, and J Lande, 'Internal Dispute Resolution: The Transformation of Civil Rights in the Workplace' (1993) 27 Law and Soc'y Rev 497; LB Edelman and MC Suchman, 'When the "Haves" Hold Court: Speculations on the Organizational Internalization of Laws' (1999) 33 Law and Soc'y Rev 941; LB Edelman, C Uggen, and HS Erlanger, 'The Endogeneity of Legal Regulation: Grievance Procedures as Rational Myth' (1999) 105 Am J Sociol 406; LB Edelman, S Riggs Fuller, and I Mara-Drita, 'Diversity Rhetoric and the Managerialization of Law' (2001) 106 Am J Sociol 1589; MC Suchman and LB Edelman, 'Legal Rational Myths: New Institutionalism and the Law and Society Tradition (1996) 21 Law and Soc Inquiry 903.

[21] See especially K Llewellyn, *The Common Law Tradition—Deciding Appeals* (Little, Brown and Company, 1960).

[22] See S Roach Anleu, *Law and Social Change* (2nd edn, Sage, 2010), 247–52.

[23] In any event there was less emphasis on empirical work in this movement, on which see C McCrudden, 'Legal Research and the Social Sciences' (2006) 122 LQR 632, 638. See also Twining (n 17), 315 about 'old' Realists not in fact carrying out much empirical work.

[24] See, first, B Leiter, *Naturalizing Jurisprudence, Essays on American Legal Realism and Naturalism in Legal Philosophy* (OUP, 2007) for an overarching interpretation of American Legal Realism and a 'reconstruction' of its philosophical components, and second, so-called New Legal Realist empirical studies in the employment and equality field at n 20 above.

general level from the theorizing of law outlined earlier while contending that accurate mapping of how law operates in a given area depends on close and contextualized observation.[25] It follows in particular that space should be left for the effects of local variation to emerge.[26] I therefore return in Chapter 10 to how my findings relate to analogous US investigations and how my conclusions might be useful to researchers elsewhere.

4. Individual Labour and Equality Rights and Behavioural Conflict at Work

I focus on behavioural conflicts at work, by which I mean disputes about how colleagues have behaved towards one another, whether in vertical or horizontal work relationships, and whether or not there was also conflict about a particular workplace practice or decision. The book is therefore *not* organized around a traditional legal category. No general conception of prohibited (or required) workplace behaviour is the foundation for a single cause of action, nor is any such idea traditionally used by lawyers to make sense of legal intervention at work. Yet, first, there are many legal rules, all in the form of individual rights, that regulate conduct at work; second, conflict about behaviour is important, perhaps increasingly, to the lived reality of working lives, and third, there has been considerable non-legal and socio-legal research about negative workplace behaviour and related engagement with law. The coincidence of these factors created significant potential for learning from observing individual rights in operation through the lens of this practically significant, knotty set of workplace conflicts. In classic American Legal Realist style, therefore, the research tracked the application of law to a particular type of dispute, instead of taking its steer from how legal sources and reasoning chop up reality.[27]

The framing I developed enabled me to isolate and investigate a stable category of workplace conflicts regulated by all sorts of individual labour and equality rights and illuminated by several useful research literatures. The range of situations and rights covered in this book further means the findings have wide implications. The tendency to diffuseness of the rules and conflicts I studied calls for particular care, however, in relating my conclusions to highly determinate, 'bright line' legal regulation, for example, about hours or deductions from pay.

Not limiting my enquiry according to technical legal categories (like harassment), or contested non-legal concepts (like bullying), was also practically necessary to capturing similar conflicts however they were legally analysed or described by those involved. While, therefore, increase in the use of the word 'bullying' in connection with work was helpful in finding judgments about behavioural conflicts, I went beyond this language both in assembling my case law sample and in interviews. It will be seen from Chapters 4–8 that this threw up a wide range of situations, ranging from the apparently trivial to the very serious. These involved allegations about the conduct of hierarchically

[25] See H Kritzer, 'Claiming Behaviour as Legal Mobilization' in Cane and Kritzer (eds) (n 8), 281.

[26] My approach in this regard is strongly supported by Deakin (n 8), 326–27, that: 'The new literature stresses that the effects of labour laws ... depend on the interaction of legal rules with a number of national, regional and industry-specific conditions and with complementary institutions in capital markets and product markets. This implies a need for better and more reliable data on the content of the law, on modes of operation, and on the context in which legal rules are applied.' See also RA Kagan, *Adversarial Legalism* (Harvard University Press, 2001) on the exceptionalism of the US approach, especially at 6–14.

[27] See Twining (n 17), 133 and 136–37.

superior and inferior colleagues as well as of peers, covered criticism of organizational reactions, including by those complained about, and even sometimes entailed employers suing their employees.

In order to be sure that readers have a clear sense of this subject matter from the start, I include some vignettes from the sample of judgments. For example, *Veakins v Kier Islington Ltd*[28] did not relate a severe or extreme instance of behavioural conflict, but it did exemplify the less dramatic battles recounted in the case law. The case comprised a claim by an electrician that her employer was vicariously liable under the Protection from Harassment Act (PHA) 1997 for behaviour by the supervisor, Mrs Lavy. The action was ultimately successful in the Court of Appeal (CA), which reported the factual account in Bristol County Court that was said to have been essentially unchallenged:

The problem was in the period from July to September 2005 … Miss Veakins said that Mrs Lavy clearly did not like her. They had an initial dispute over a wages problem, of a kind which is perfectly common in the workplace, leading to a possibly embarrassing 'telling-off' (that was Miss Veakins' phrase) in front of others. Miss Veakins said that she felt Mrs Lavy persistently picked on her, singling her out from her fellow employees for no reason at all. There were further disputes about time-keeping and about Mrs Lavy requiring the claimant for a time to sign an In and Out register every day. Miss Veakins complained that Mrs Lavy changed the existing practice about Miss Veakins being picked up on the way to a particular job by other workmen. There was also a complaint about Mrs Lavy on one occasion telling her to 'fuck off', although Miss Veakins acknowledged that that word was not in itself unusual in this work environment. There was also a complaint about Mrs Lavy ripping up in front of Miss Veakins a letter of complaint that Miss Veakins had written.[29]

In some ways the situation described comes across as trivial, even childish, but the consequences described for Miss Veakins were not. She was on sick leave with depression from September 2005 until July 2006, at which point her employment with Kier Islington ended. She said of her situation that '[a]part from Mrs Lavy the job was perfect for me. I had worked hard for the company for two years and eight months had been spent working without pay. I did not want this taken away just because someone did not like me.'

An example of more serious conduct was in the successful, doctrinally important, discrimination case of *Jones v Tower Boot Co Ltd*.[30] Waite LJ explained what had happened as follows:

In April 1992 a 16 year-old boy started work at the employers' shoe factory as a last operative. He was of mixed ethnic parentage and was joining a workforce which had not previously employed anyone of ethnic minority origin. From the outset he was subjected by fellow employees to harassment of the gravest kind. He was called by such racially offensive names as 'chimp' and 'monkey.' A notice had been stuck on his back reading 'Chipmunks are go.' Two employees whipped him on the legs with a piece of welt and threw metal bolts at his head. One of them burnt his arm with a hot screwdriver and later the same two seized his arm again and tried to put it in a lasting machine where the burn was caught and started to bleed again. Unable to endure this treatment the boy left the job after four weeks.[31]

Another more serious case was related in the successful tort action of *Long v Mercury Communications*.[32] The negative behaviour was described as continuing for just under two years and as involving, first, a 'vendetta'[33] by Mr Long's superior and, second, ill treatment more generally that culminated in redundancy. The judge said of the effects: 'I think

---

[28] [2009] EWCA Civ 1288, [2010] IRLR 132.   [29] ibid, [2].
[30] [1997] ICR 254 (CA).   [31] ibid, 259.   [32] [2002] PIQR Q1 (QB).
[33] ibid, Q2, [5].

it is probably true to say that the treatment he had received resulted in [Mr Long] being a broken man.'[34]

That begins to set the scene for the primary research in the book, which Chapters 2 and 3 place in full empirical and legal context. Chapter 2 surveys and analyses existing empirical evidence, particularly in the UK, about first, experience of, and attitudes to, negative behaviour at work, and second, complaining practice and engagement with relevant law. Chapter 3 outlines the legal rules as they developed from 1995 to the present day. In contrast to the external, non-doctrinal analysis of adjudicative practice that follows, this gives a largely internal, technical account of the legislative rules and major case law developments. The intention in doing so is to give readers sufficient background to make doctrinal sense of my data about adjudicative patterns and the reception of law into organizations.

The case law primary research, reported in Chapters 4–7, involved qualitative analysis of authoritative UK judgments about behavioural conflict at work from 1995 to 2010. The focus was on the way workplace 'stories' were presented to courts and retold by judges and on decision-making approaches to working out the concrete implications of the rights that litigants invoked. The judgments considered, while not all doctrinally striking, together recounted the day-to-day, case-by-case engagement by courts both with behavioural problems at work and with the impact of individual legal entitlements. Analysing the judgments as records of judges 'working' on a given category of workplace interactions made it possible to fill in an important part of how individual labour and equality rights are actually functioning.[35]

The interview study, reported in Chapters 8 and 9, used semi-structured interviews with senior managers and senior lawyers to explore the influence of law and legal process on behavioural conflict at work. Senior lawyers were included to permit comparison between what was said by, on the one hand, organizational insiders (some with legal training and experience), who had a more external perspective on law, and, on the other hand, lawyers who, while to some extent still moving between organizational and legal worlds, are very much 'legal insiders'. Both sets of interviews investigated, first, how people in organizations are affected by law and legal process when either they are involved in, or required to respond to, behavioural conflict at work, and second, what causes such conflict to become litigious at all and to different degrees.

Several analytical points about the relation between law and practice are threaded through what follows. First, *there is the distance between overarching norms that inspire, motivate, and are found within legal interventions, and the specificity of how legal texts are written, implemented, and enforced.* In noticing this gap I do not mean to pretend that the high-level normative implications of law in general, and certainly of UK individual labour and equality rights in particular, are clear, uncontestable, or generally agreed. Indeed, I have spent a good part of my life decoding various areas of law to uncover their meaning. The contention rather, especially investigated in Chapters 3, 6, and 7, is that somewhat general ideals of workplace fairness, reasonableness, and egalitarianism are immanent in the legal sources in this area. It is vital however that even if this is true, it in no sense guarantees that these ideas get through to regulated spaces, nor that they alter what happens there in easily predictable directions.

Second, *there are the varied means by which law exerts influence within and beyond workplaces, with differences not least deriving from the variety of individuals and groups who*

---

[34] ibid, Q5, [21].
[35] See Twining (n 17), 246–48, 264–66, and 411 on the untapped potential of case reports.

engage with law. Discursive influences, operating at the level of ideology, are undoubtedly as important as law's direct impact on particular practices and situations. By this I mean the manifold ways that law and legal process structure thinking and communication and, in turn, influence private, public, and political debate.[36] Building an accurate empirical picture of how law works imperatively requires this complex set of effects to be related to the specifics of when organizations come to implement legal standards, when individuals attempt to enforce their rights, and when rulings are made in courts.

Third, *there are the differences in the structural positions of the cast of actors to whom the law is directed and who engage with it.* Within workplaces, these range from individual workers with minimal labour market power to large, well-funded organizations, with endless gradations, variations, and contrasts of power and resources in between. Outsiders can additionally alter the stakes—for example, trades unions, civil society organizations, lawyers, politicians, and indeed, society more widely. Representing law in practice requires that this variety be encompassed and that its multiple effects be brought into focus.

Finally, to fill out the sketch of my conclusions given at the start, the picture painted by my data depicts law's dual nature in operation to an almost uncanny degree, showing individual labour and equality rights simultaneously challenging and supporting established allocations of power in a wide range of ways. That aspect of my findings and analysis has general resonance for understanding law, whatever its subject matter and form, while some of the mechanisms I documented in operation have a generic quality. It is also evident that these patterns could not be seen from a purely internal perspective, both reinforcing the case for empirical study of law and emphasizing the ultimate responsibility of the political sphere for the balance struck by legal intervention.

More specifically, my data lead me to theorize that the undoubtedly significant normative challenge from individual labour and equality rights in the UK, including that which comes through from the judgments, is most felt in organizations that are anyway committed to workplace fairness, reasonableness, and equality. At the same time, I documented various devices that systematically undercut law's emancipatory influence. These were, first, considerable patchiness in the legal standards that got through to organizations; second, many depictions of procedural legal influence impeding problem solving within workplaces, and specifically problem-solving that is rooted in respect for fundamental justice precepts; third, disjuncture between employers' motivations for settling claims and concern to resolve underlying problems, let alone by applying legally inspired fairness, reasonableness, and equality norms; fourth, fragmentation and variety in law and legal process producing arbitrariness and artificiality in the handling of individual claims; and fifth, judgments having minimal, if any, impact at work. These factors, considered against the options that individual working people realistically have, resulted in support from individual rights for workplace justice being easily neutralized in more 'managerialist' organizations, and their ameliorative effects being undermined even in more hospitable environments.

Adding to the duality, my data posit that employers who more readily espouse the standards set by individual labour and equality rights are at particular risk of destructive, individualized legal conflict. This tendency is particularly connected to the difficulty

---

[36] See Thompson (n 3), 260–61 and 267, the latter where it was observed that: '[T]he rules and categories of law penetrate every level of society, effect vertical as well as horizontal definitions of men's rights and status, and contribute to men's self-definition or sense of identity. As such law has not only been imposed *upon* men from above: it has also been a medium within which other social conflicts have been fought out.' (italics in the original)

of accommodating the individual frame of legal complaints within organizational approaches that vindicate the essentially communal, collective nature of working life. The upshot is that the move in the UK to regulating working life through individual rights has in many ways supported traditional workplace hierarchy, while along the way legitimating managerial dominance that survives the challenge of emancipatory legal regulation. Equally, so far as such rights are most easily managed in more authoritarian workplaces and fit uneasily with collective regulation, they arguably constitute a spur to all organizations moving in that hierarchical direction.

This pattern does not, however, emerge as costless to anyone, even for organizations in which law's emancipatory capacity is stringently undermined. Workplace problems and unease, as well as the damage these cause, do not disappear because they are suppressed and marginalized. Furthermore, there is the waste inherent in suboptimal, at times dysfunctional, deployment of law and legal process. Perhaps most importantly, a great many UK citizens, including amongst managers, are committed to decent, even high, labour standards.

Be that as it may, there are a range of discursive effects surrounding these developments that operate ideologically to undercut the chances that individual labour and equality rights will have much socially transformative effect. In particular, these make it highly unlikely that any UK political party will make serious efforts to reorient legal regulation governing working life. Equally, the risk is accumulating that individualization at work, and the ascendance of liberal individualist ideology, will prevent working people conceiving of and deploying collective means to bring about change, whether through trades unions or other forms.

The only possibility I see for altering these patterns is for pluralist, collective involvement within workplaces to be built into the implementation and enforcement of individual rights. This would confront such regulation being sidelined by employer dominance and seek constructively to integrate collective and individualized means of ordering working lives, building on how more enlightened organizations already work with legal standards. My two specific ideas for doing so are, first, to make the basic normative messages that individualized legal regulation means to convey more usable in the hands of the range of people and institutions to whom they are addressed, and second, for legislative design to widen involvement in implementation and enforcement, including at the remedial stage.

I put forward these suggestions, however, fully cognizant that my other conclusions indicate that it is unlikely that any UK government will take them forward. That leads to my final suggestion, that those engaging with existing legal sources might usefully be guided by what I have found in the law. People and groups within and outside organizations might already extract the basic normative implications of individual labour and equality rights and strategically deploy these in the organizational and wider pursuit, even through litigation, of better implementation of, and dispute resolution about, individual workplace entitlements. One corollary is that the findings of this project, and the empirical research agendas it highlights for the UK and elsewhere, may have direct, 'on the ground' utility to inform and ground such experimentation.

2

The Empirical Background
to Behavioural Conflict at Work

This chapter brings together knowledge in the United Kingdom about working people's experiences and perceptions of bad behaviour at work, their responses to this, their use of law, what happens in the small subset of situations that result in litigation, and about the legal environment of organizations. The purpose is both to enrich the conclusions that may be drawn from my data and to show how this work addresses knowledge gaps and misconceptions about the interactions between law and working life. The central messages are that reports of negative conduct at work are widespread, working people often try to do something internally about problems but very often fail to get anywhere, only a tiny proportion litigate with very mixed effects, and there are uneasy interactions all the way through between the collectivity or working life and the increasing individualization of law and legal process.

The starting point that I would argue cannot be emphasized enough is that a great many people who experience problems at work, whether about behaviour or other things, do not turn to law and lawyers. While the majority reacts in some way, what they do often does not invoke law and there is a non-negligible minority who do nothing at all. This has been a clear and consistent pattern in large-scale, representative, and longitudinal data, particularly from the UK, yet public and press discussions about working life routinely ignore this reality. Instead, prevailing narratives incorrectly characterize working people as easily turning not only to law but even to the courts.

This misleading tendency is not a feature only of sensationalist media discussion, but also of debate in political, policy, and legal circles.[1] Arguably its most problematic aspect is that it engenders simplistic assumptions that law has clear, direct, organizational effects.[2] Noticing the vast number of situations in which individuals do little or nothing about legally regulated problems instead shows that law's influence at work may be unexpected, minimal, or even counterproductive. Critically this is the case as much for rules which are apparently worker-protective, like individual labour and equality rights, as for any others.

It is necessary, therefore, to be alert to law's influence beyond the immediate outcomes of individual enforcement action to encompass, first, the indirect, systemic effects

---

[1] See eg H Kritzer, 'Claiming Behaviour as Legal Mobilization' in P Cane and H Kritzer (eds), *Oxford Handbook of Empirical Legal Research* (OUP, 2010), 276 and S Lee and D McCann, 'The Impact of Labour Regulations: Measuring the Effectiveness of Legal Norms in a Developing Country' in S Lee and D McCann, *Regulating for Decent Work: New Directions in Labour Market Regulation* (Palgrave MacMillan and ILO, 2011), 291–97 and 307–09.

[2] See on the complexity of tracing this impact, MC Suchman and LB Edelman, 'Legal Rational Myths: New Institutionalism and the Law and Society Tradition' (1996) 21 Law and Soc Inquiry 903, and L Dickens and M Hall, 'Legal Regulation and the Changing Workplace' in W Brown, A Bryson, J Forth, and K Whitfield (eds), *The Evolution of the Modern Workplace* (CUP, 2009), 344–47 specifically on the difficulty of pinning down even the influence of the 1979–97 UK legislative onslaught on trade unions.

of some individuals asserting legal rights, and second, organizational responses independently of enforcement attempts. My qualitative analysis of judgments and my interview study directly investigated the possibilities by examining the operation in practice of employment rights adjudication and the reception of law into organizations. The research that follows sets the scene for those enquiries, adding the perspective of employees and claimants which my primary research only indirectly examined.

1. Empirical Knowledge about Negative Behaviour at Work

It is extraordinarily challenging to devise reliable ways of investigating the incidence of, and circumstances surrounding, bad behaviour at work. There is no single definition capable of distinguishing acceptable from unacceptable conduct for all workplaces, all working people, and across all times. What is regarded as unacceptable differs with context, sometimes widely; individuals have different reactions and ways of being; attitudes and perceptions change, both generally as to acceptable workplace behaviour and specifically about particular interactions.

This evokes the challenge I faced in defining my field of study. Ultimately, however, my project did not require that I grapple with defining negative workplace behaviour because my concern is with understanding how relevant law operates in the myriad situations with which it engages. Observing how law deals with divergent and even tenuous subjective viewpoints about workplace conduct is, in truth, necessary to achieving that aim.

Definitional considerations are, however, a major concern for research into the incidence of poor workplace conduct. If behaviour is ruled in or out of being unacceptable because of subjective views, this will deliver unreliable findings so far as those perceptions are contestable. At the same time, an objective approach that does not recognize bad behaviour in unusual forms will deliver prevalence rates that underestimate the problem. This makes it important to approach quantitative empirical investigations in this field with caution. Further, the more that data are drawn from non-representative samples and self-report questionnaire studies, the more caution is required given the particular risks that these design features produce distortions in the data.

This is particularly true for evidence about workplace bullying emanating from organizational and social psychology that is discussed in section (1) below.[3] While methodological weaknesses in such studies are increasingly being acknowledged,[4] I feel able to draw on this research only in quite circumscribed ways. Its usefulness is that, first, psychologically inspired approaches to unacceptable workplace behaviour give a sense

[3] See S Einarsen, H Hoel, D Zapf, and CL Cooper in 'The Concept of Bullying and Harassment at Work: The European Tradition' in the same authors' (eds), *Bullying and Harassment in the Workplace, Developments in Theory, Research and Practice* (2nd edn, CRC Press, 2011), 3, 16 on the dominance of self-report studies in this literature, and L Barmes, 'Worlds Colliding: Legal Regulation and Psychologists' Evidence About Workplace Bullying' in B Brooks-Gordon and M Freeman (eds), 9 CLI *Law and Psychology* (OUP, 2006) about methodological issues.
[4] See eg I Coyne, P Smith-Lee Chong, E Seigne, and P Randall, 'Self and Peer Nominations of Bullying: An Analysis of Incident Rates, Individual Differences and Perceptions of the Working Environment' (2003) 12 Eur J Work Organ Psy 209; MB Nielsen, SB Matthiesen, and S Einarsen, 'The Impact of Methodological Moderators on Prevalence Rates of Workplace Bullying. A Meta-Analysis' (2010) 83 Journal of Occupational and Organizational Psychology 955; and MB Nielsen, G Notelaers, and S Einarsen, 'Measuring Exposure to Workplace Bullying' in Einarsen, et al, ibid, 149.

of the kinds of conduct working people view as unacceptable.[5] Second, psychologists' quantitative empirical data to some degree map perceptions of negative behaviour at work in the UK, providing a backdrop to more recent findings discussed in section (2).

The other body of work on which I draw in section (2) is more sociological in orientation. This has addressed some limitations in the bullying literature, adding to knowledge about behavioural problems in UK workplaces. The tighter research design also makes it possible to draw on broader arguments from the data about systemic influences on what was found.

(1) Psychologists and workplace bullying

This literature originated in research by psychologists in Scandinavia in the early 1990s and now spans several disciplines and countries. The object of study is mostly called bullying, often used interchangeably with harassment, and the equivalent term in some countries is mobbing. In spite of methodological concerns this line of research has been influential, the major recent UK study of 'trouble at work' characterizing bullying as having become 'the dominant way of conceptualizing workplace troubles'.[6]

(a) Conceptual and definitional approaches

Catalogues of 'negative acts' have been compiled for use in survey studies. The most widely adopted is the negative acts questionnaire (NAQ),[7] which continues to be developed,[8] including for use in different countries.[9] The behaviours listed do not use the word 'bullying', but rather comprise actions found by qualitative research to come within this label. These range from personal attacks, such as 'having insulting or offensive remarks made about your person (i.e. habits and background), your attitudes or your private life', to work-related matters, for example, 'persistent criticism of work and effort'.[10]

Alongside this questionnaire, various narrative definitions of bullying have been coined. The most internationally influential is set out in successive reviews of the field:

Bullying at work means harassing, offending, or socially excluding someone or negatively affecting someone's work. In order for the label *bullying* (or *mobbing*) to be applied to a particular activity, interaction or process, the bullying behaviour has to occur repeatedly and regularly (e.g., weekly) and over a period of time (e.g., about six months). Bullying is an escalating process in the course of which the person confronted ends up in an inferior position and becomes the target of systematic

---

[5] See also A Liefooghe and K Mackenzie Davey, 'The Language and Organization of Bullying at Work' (2010) 32 Administrative Theory and Praxis 71, 81–82 on this perspective feeding into organizational discourse.

[6] R Fevre, D Lewis, A Robinson, and T Jones, *Trouble at Work* (Bloomsbury, 2012), 7.

[7] See S Einarsen and BI Raknes, 'Harassment in the Workplace and the Victimization of Men' (1997) 12 Violence and Victims 247, and Nielsen, Notelaers, and Einarsen, (n 4), 154–59 for other examples.

[8] S Einarsen, H Hoel, G Notelaers 'Measuring Exposure to Bullying and Harassment At Work: Validity, Factor Structure and Psychometric Properties of the Negative Acts Questionnaire—Revised' (2009) 23 Work and Stress 24.

[9] See, eg, K Tsuno, N Kawakami, A Inoue, and K Abe, 'Measuring Workplace Bullying: Reliability and Validity of the Japanese Version of the Negative Acts Questionnaire' (2010) 52 Journal of Occupational Health 216.

[10] See H Hoel and CL Cooper, *Destructive Conflict and Bullying at Work*, (2000) School of Management, University of Manchester, Institute of Science and Technology (unpublished report), 27 and App II.

negative social acts. A conflict cannot be called bullying if the incident is an isolated event or if two parties of approximately equal strength are in conflict.[11]

UK studies in this tradition have used a variation of this definition.[12] Other definitions, however, have appeared in trade union or activist literature, for example describing workplace bullying as:

Persistent, offensive, abusive, intimidating, malicious or insulting behaviour, abuse of power or unfair penal sanctions, which make the recipient feel upset, threatened, humiliated or vulnerable, which undermine their self-confidence and which may cause them to suffer stress.

Definitions of this kind have in turn been adopted by some researchers.[13]

Both the questionnaire and narrative definitional approaches are striking for their approach to subjectivity and, in tension with this, for being highly prescriptive. The narratives tend to conceive of behaviour as bullying because of how it was experienced by the person reporting it, while the categories in NAQ-type instruments describe conduct as seen from a recipient's point of view. At the same time, the frequency and duration criteria included in some definitions, and which are often used to analyse reports of negative acts, are arguably arbitrary. The idea that negative conduct should only be labelled as bullying if experienced weekly for six months seems to me particularly contestable, not least from my reading of judgments.[14]

(b) Approaches to incidence

The two definitional approaches give rise to two ways of measuring incidence. According to the 'behavioural experience' method, the responses of working people to instruments like the NAQ are used to categorize them as bullied or not. It is here that frequency and duration criteria are often applied. More recently, however, a statistical method called 'latent class cluster analysis' has been used to unpack the data in a less binary way.[15] The second methodology involves 'self-labelling', whereby surveys ask if respondents have been bullied, sometimes presenting a definition. Other aspects of researchers'

---

[11] See Einarsen et al, (n 3), 22. This definition is very slightly different to that in the earlier edition of this book, but in ways that do not alter the meaning.
[12] See in particular H Hoel, C Cooper, and B Faragher, 'The Experience of Bullying in Great Britain: The Impact of Organizational Status' (2001) 10(4) Eur J Work Organ Psy 443, 447 reporting on Hoel and Cooper, (n 10).
[13] This was the definition used in L Quine, 'Workplace Bullying, Psychological Distress and Job Satisfaction in Junior Doctors' (2003) 12 Cambridge Quarterly of Healthcare Ethics 91, and in Coyne et al (n 4), although citing, respectively, R Lyons, H Tivey, and C Ball, *Bullying at Work: How to Tackle It. A Guide for MSF Representatives and Members* (MSF, 1995), and Fire Brigades Union, *Bullying at Work: How to Tackle It* (FBU, 1997).
[14] This criterion seems to have originated with the pioneer of this literature, Heinz Leymann. See H Leymann, 'Mobbing and Psychological Terror at Workplaces' [1990] 5 Violence and Victims 119, at 120: 'This definition eliminates temporary conflicts and focuses on the transition zone where the psychosocial situation starts to result in psychiatric and/or psychosomatic pathological states.' See also Einarsen et al (n 3), 16–18 where they link individual perceptions creating difficulties for subjective conceptions with their arguments, first, that single occurrences do not constitute bullying, and second, that conceiving of bullying as a process makes it an observable, objective stressor. See the text to ns 25, 28–30 and 35–37 in Ch 6 for examples of single incidents leading to legal liability.
[15] G Notelaers, S Einarsen, H De Witte, and JK Vermunt, 'Measuring Exposure to Bullying at Work: The Validity and Advantages of the Latent Class Cluster Approach' (2006) 20 Work and Stress 289, and see the use of this method in MB Nielsen, A Skogstad, SB Matthiesen, L Glaso, MS Aasland, G Notelaers, and S Einarsen, 'Prevalence of Workplace Bullying in Norway: Comparisons across Time and Estimation Methods' (2009) 18 Eur J Work Organ Psy 81.

conceptions might then be probed with questions regarding, for example, the frequency of conduct.

The difference between the two methods is that the 'behavioural experience' approach tends to categorize people as either bullied or not irrespective of how they see their treatment[16] and according to contestable criteria. The self-labelling method, on the other hand, classes people as bullied when others would not regard them as being so and leaves out those who put up uncomplainingly with harsh treatment.[17] Unsurprisingly therefore the different methods deliver consistently different findings. A recent meta-analysis across various countries found that:

[w]ith an overall rate of about 11%, the results show that studies using the self-labelling with defi-nition method provide the lowest estimate of bullying. When using the behavioural experience method, the prevalence is somewhat higher with rates about 15%, whereas the self-labelling with-out definition method yields the highest estimates with overall rates of 18%. Hence, compared to studies using self-labelling with definition, the prevalence rates of this latter approach are almost twice as high. With regard to sampling technique, the findings show that non-random samples at an average yield 8.7% point higher estimates of workplace bullying than do random samples.[18]

I would argue that this variety is the inevitable effect of the difficulty, probably the impossibility, of reliably capturing what bad behaviour at work comprises. A recent exploratory interview study by Fevre and colleagues supported this analysis. The aim was to work out why higher numbers consistently report negative acts that researchers classify as bullying, than themselves label their experiences in this way if presented with a definition. It was found that:

there were major problems with providing a comprehensive yet clear definition of 'workplace bullying' that was interpreted in similar ways by different groups of respondents ... When asked to define bullying, a wide variety of examples were given ... Many interviewees felt that all of the NAQ items might be considered 'bullying' depending on the circumstances in which they occurred... The perception of an overlap between bullying and ill treatment, not only varied between individuals but also changed for the same individual, depending on the circumstances.[19]

Coyne and colleagues demonstrated a variation on this theme, showing that survey respondents' categorizations varied according to whether they were answering questions about either themselves or their peers.[20] These findings confirm the need for caution in relation to quantitative data on bullying[21] and reinforce my conclusion that its empirical usefulness lies in what it shows about the attitudes of working people, not what it says about the incidence of bullying.

In terms of UK findings, the largest study was done at the University of Manchester Institute of Science and Technology (UMIST) and dates from 1999. This indicated quite high levels of dissatisfaction with workplace behaviour amongst a non-representative

---

[16] APD Liefooghe and R Olafsson, 'Scientists and Amateurs: Mapping the Bullying Domain' (1999) 20 (1/2) Int J Manpower 39, 40.
[17] ibid.   [18] Nielsen, Matthiesen, and Einarsen, (n 4), 967.
[19] Fevre et al, *Trouble at Work* (n 6), 27–28. See also P Saunders, A Huynh, and J Goodman-Delahunty, 'Defining Workplace Bullying Behaviour: Professional Lay Definitions of Workplace Bullying' (2007) 30 International Journal of Law and Psychiatry 340, demonstrating variation in understandings of bullying in an international sample of 1,095 individuals.
[20] Coyne et al (n 4).
[21] See for trenchant criticism of the underlying science from within the psychological litera-ture: Liefooghe and Mackenzie Davey, 'Language and Organization' (n 5), 82. Similar concerns from outside the discipline are explained in R Fevre, A Robinson, T Jones, and D Lewis, 'Researching Workplace Bullying: The Benefits of Taking an Integrated Approach' (2010) 13 International Journal of Social Research Methodology 71.

sample, based both on self-labelling according to a variation of the main psychological definition above and on the 'behavioural experience' approach using an adapted NAQ questionnaire.[22] According to Hoel and colleagues:

With 10.6 % of respondents reporting having been bullied within the last 6 months, a figure which rises to 24.7 % for bullying within the last 5 years, the present study confirms that workplace bullying is a major social problem in Great Britain. Taking into account that 46.5 % reported having witnessed bullying within the last 5 years, it is possible to conclude that a majority of employees will have some experience of bullying either directly or indirectly as a witness or observer of bullying.[23]

Somewhat astonishingly, moreover, up to 38 per cent of respondents were found to fall into the 'bullied' category on the 'behavioural experience' approach.[24] Other UK studies in this tradition have also found very high prevalence rates.[25]

Investigations by psychologists into the attitudes behind these findings, however, gave early indications that workers deploy a variety of interpretative frameworks in defining bullying and applying this label. Liefooghe and Olafsson observed university staff and students choosing between various explanatory models in accounting for experiences they saw as bullying.[26] Liefooghe and Mackenzie Davey found similar flexibility in other settings.[27] They also observed workers moving easily between individualistic and organizational accounts of bullying, sometimes using the term for work systems, appraisal and sickness policies, pay negotiations, and generalized threats to jobs, including where collective bargaining was in place.

More illuminating than quantitative work in this tradition, however, are qualitative investigations into how people respond to finding themselves the subject of workplace bullying. A small-scale study by Niedl in Austria found a complex set of responses. The only uniform pattern was that individuals tried several strategies for coping before withdrawing organizational commitment.[28] Zapf and Gross observed victims of bullying generally to start with constructive conflict-solving strategies, after which their approach changed several times until they often left. Many, however, recommended that others simply leave the organization. Successful copers tended to be better at recognizing and avoiding escalating behaviours and also took sickness absence less often. Victims who fought for justice were perceived frequently to contribute to the problem escalating.[29] A study with a representative Danish sample found that individuals who reported repeated negative behaviour made lesser use than others of problem-solving strategies.[30]

[22] Hoel and Cooper, (n 10).   [23] Hoel, Cooper, and Faragher, (n 12), 457.
[24] Hoel and Cooper, (n 10), 25.
[25] See eg, L Quine, 'Workplace Bullying in NHS Community Trust: Staff Questionnaire Survey' (1999) 318 BMJ 228, L Quine, 'Workplace Bullying in Nurses' (2001) 6 Journal of Health Psychology 73 and Quine, (n 13).
[26] Liefooghe and Olafsson (n 16).
[27] APD Liefooghe and K Mackenzie Davey, 'Accounts of Workplace Bullying: The Role of the Organization' (2001) 10 Eur J Work Organ Psy 375, and APD Liefooghe and K Mackenzie Davey, 'Explaining Bullying at Work: Why Should We Listen to Employee Accounts?' in S Einarsen, H Hoel, D Zapf, and CL Cooper (eds), *Bullying and Emotional Abuse in the Workplace, International Perspectives in Research and Practice* (Taylor and Francis, 2003), 219.
[28] K Niedl, 'Mobbing and Well-Being: Economic and Personnel Development Implications' (1996) 5 Eur J Work Organ Psy 203.
[29] D Zapf and C Gross, 'Conflict Escalation and Coping with Workplace Bullying: A Replication and Extension' (2001) 10 Eur J Work Organ Psy 497.
[30] A Hogh and A Dofradottir, 'Coping with Bullying in the Workplace' (2001) 10 Eur J Work Organ Psy 485.

In terms of UK evidence of this kind, an exploratory interview study[31] with a small sample of ten British women, all public sector professionals who reported bullying at work, suggested that working people do not easily label interpersonal conduct as bullying. Minimizing incidents and being reluctant to perceive a pattern were instead part of how interviewees initially coped with treatment they later saw as bullying. The process by which their attitudes changed was complicated. Naming what had happened appeared to help individuals to confront their situation at the same time as it carried significant risks. These included damage to the participants' sense of themselves as successful, resilient professionals and to their beliefs in their employers. The damage extended to their working situations when managers, colleagues, and trade unions reacted in unhelpful ways.

Further analysis of the same data by Lewis and Orford[32] illustrated means by which organizational and trade union actors avoided dealing with complaints, including denial that a problem existed and attributing difficulties that could not be denied to the person making the complaint. The forlorn position of study participants was also apparent from reports of negative effects on their home life and other relationships. Again this showed the organizational nature of the problem, the writers concluding that 'prevention of bullying is rarely a feasible individual responsibility, since recognition and prevention may challenge organizational structures, values and practices'.[33]

Qualitative work specifically about sexual harassment resulted in uncannily similar findings. A small-scale study of women workers conducted by Handy in New Zealand[34] documented, first, women minimizing what had happened, and second, various managerial means of denying that there was a problem. She also observed interpretive processes operating as a means of coping. Women in very different workplaces developed taxonomies of sexually harassing behaviour as, sometimes, 'normal' and, at other times, deviant and upsetting. This lead Handy to conclude that '[w]hile these shared understandings normalized and implicitly legitimized some forms of harassment, they also helped women cope by supplying informal guidelines for interpreting different behaviour.'[35] Blackstone and colleagues made analogous observations of co-workers collaborating to avoid sexually harassing behaviours, influencing one another regarding whether to view a given situation as serious and about how to respond, and finally, deploying a range of informal strategies, again including ignoring behaviour in order to cope.[36]

Finally, an unusual exploratory study[37] shed light on the experiences of those on the other side of bullying complaints. Thirty managers were surveyed and twenty-four were interviewed about the impact of being accused of bullying behaviour and their perceptions of whether this was handled fairly. Survey responses indicated a range of negative health effects irrespective of whether complaints were upheld. Most participants also expressed concerns about the conduct of the investigation regardless of outcome, several going on to sue their employers either for unfair termination or injury compensation.

[31] SE Lewis, 'Recognition of Workplace Bullying: A Qualitative Study of Women Targets in the Public Sector' (2006) 16 Journal of Community and Applied Social Psychology 119.

[32] SE Lewis and J Orford, 'Women's Experiences of Workplace Bullying: Changes in Social Relationships' (2005) 15 Journal of Community and Applied Social Psychology 29.

[33] ibid, 43.

[34] J Handy, 'Sexual Harassment in Small Town New Zealand: A Qualitative Study of Three Contrasting Organizations' (2006) 13 Gender Work and Organization 1.

[35] ibid, 20.

[36] A Blackstone, C Uggen, and H McLaughlin, 'Legal Consciousness and Responses to Sexual Harassment' (2009) 43 Law and Soc'y Rev 631, especially at 655–61.

[37] M Jenkins, H Winefield, and A Sarris, 'Consequences of Being Accused of Workplace Bullying: An Exploratory Study' (2011) 4 International Journal of Workplace Health Management 33.

Twenty-five per cent left work, again not confined to those found to have bullied. Those who stayed reported lost confidence and insufficient workplace support.

(2) Sociologists and ill treatment at work

(a) Conceptual and definitional approaches

The UK government has commissioned successive studies into good and bad treatment at work, the most recent taking place in 2008. The latest series is known as the Fair Treatment at Work Survey (FTWS), involving a face-to-face questionnaire study of a representative sample of people in work in Great Britain in the preceding two years.[38] The 2008 version investigated awareness of employment rights as well as experience of a wide range of problems. The latter covered problems 'related to specific employment rights alongside questions about sex-based harassment, other forms of bullying and harassment, other serious problems and an expanded set of questions on unfair treatment and discrimination'.[39]

Respondents were told that 'sex-based harassment at work is any unwelcome sex or gender related behaviour that creates a hostile working environment', and were asked: 'In the last TWO years, have you experienced sex-based harassment at work? This could be sexual in nature or be related to the fact you are a man/woman.' They were then immediately asked about 'other forms of bullying and harassment that create a hostile working environment.'[40] Psychological approaches were additionally drawn upon through inclusion of questions about seven of the negative behaviours typically listed in bullying surveys. The first three questions related to 'unreasonable management', the next three to 'personal attack', and the last to 'violence at work'.

The second recent large-scale study, also led by Fevre, was funded by the Economic and Social Research Council and is known as the British Workplace Behaviour Survey (BWBS). It comprised, first, a nationally representative quantitative survey, with data gathered in face-to-face interviews in 2007–08, and, second, an associated qualitative study of four organizations. No overarching definition of bad behaviour was used, with the focus conceived as ill treatment at work. This was investigated through questioning about categories of conduct developed from psychologists' lists of negative acts.[41] The quantitative survey also asked about the perpetrator of reported behaviour, but this aspect of the questionnaire was only directed to respondents in 'the troubled minority', namely those who had reported three or more out of the twenty-one listed forms of ill treatment.

The research report of the BWBS was explicit that its underlying thinking differed to that in bullying investigations. It put at the centre Wright Mills' idea that the job of sociology is to explain the structural causes behind private troubles.[42] Fevre and colleagues perceived their research to have revealed workers' values being threatened, which Wright Mills argued 'could form the seed of the public issue that sociology could help people to fashion from their private troubles'.[43] The bullying concept was seen as inappropriate to expose this precisely because it rules situations in and out of consideration without catering for the many ways working people characterize their experiences.[44]

---

[38] R Fevre, T Nichols, G Prior, and I Rutherford, *Fair Treatment at Work Report: Findings from the 2008 Survey* (BIS, ERRS 108, Sept 2009), combining the issues dealt with in several earlier government funded studies.

[39] Fevre et al, ibid, 52.   [40] ibid, 74–75.

[41] See further about this process in Fevre et al (n 21).

[42] Fevre et al, *Trouble at Work*, (n 6), 4.   [43] ibid, 5.   [44] ibid, 5–6 and 7.

(b) Approaches to incidence

In both the FTWS and the BWBS evidence was gathered about who reported certain experiences, with statistical operations digging into this data to find, for example, over-representations of certain groups. Again, therefore, it needs to be borne in mind that the findings came from self-reports. At least, however, these were from large representative samples, face-to-face interviews took place, and there was some mixing of methods in the BWBS survey.

The FTWS 2008 asked respondents if they labelled themselves as either being bullied or sexual harassed, presenting a minimalist definition. In the BWBS, survey respondents were asked about experiences from an adapted NAQ-type list. The responses were not, however, presented as enabling the researchers to measure the incidence of a predefined behavioural construct, but rather as analyses of self-reports of certain experiences recognizing that responses are influenced by individuals' interpretive frames. Compared to the psychological research, therefore, the numbers produced were more transparently only a record of the attitudes of working people. Still, it will be seen below that there was some slippage into describing self-reports as if they necessarily corresponded to incidence of the behaviour reported and I have sought to guard against myself making this assumption.

In the FTWS 2008, one-third of respondents said they had experienced problems at work, widely conceived, in the last five years. More specifically, and in relation to the previous two years only, 13 per cent reported unfair treatment, 7 per cent discrimination, and 7 per cent bullying and harassment. The 7 per cent bullying rate was evidently lower than in the psychological studies, and the researchers observed that it accorded better with figures 'in the specialist European literature where studies with representative samples have been a little more frequent'.[45] The same pattern of lower incidence rates was reflected in answers to questions about conduct; for example, 5 per cent reporting having been 'humiliated or ridiculed in connection with your work', 'now and then' in the last two years, as opposed to 25.4 per cent in the UMIST study for the previous six months.[46]

Around one in six reported more than one category of problem, and over half who reported any problem described more than one type.[47] The mean number of employment rights problems was significantly higher for those who described either discrimination or bullying/harassment.[48] The researchers observed, however, that most of the reported unfair treatment and discrimination was not encompassed by either the current anti-discrimination legislation or the employment rights framework.[49] They meant by this, however, only the framework of statutory employment rights, not including other relevant statutory and common law wrongs that will be outlined in Chapter 3.

Members of several identity groups, including ones protected by anti-discrimination legislation, were over-represented amongst those reporting bullying and harassment. These groups included trade union members, women, those with disabilities and also gay, lesbian, and bisexual people.[50] Putting aside pay issues, respondents were more likely to identify their most serious problem as being about unfair treatment, bullying, and

---

[45] ibid, 76.   [46] ibid, 78.   [47] ibid, 53.   [48] ibid, 55–56.

[49] ibid, 67 and 72, especially at 67: '[J]ust as for unfair treatment, the equality grounds are not what the majority think of when they are asked for a reason why they might have suffered discrimination.' See further K Perren, S Roberts, B Stafford, D Hirsch, and M Padley, *Report 3—Disputes and Challenges* (GEO, 2012), 6 and 11, that 41 out of 171 reported disputes in the previous three years about unequal treatment or discrimination were said not to have been about a protected characteristic.

[50] Fevre et al, *Trouble at Work* (n 6), 112.

harassment, other serious problems affecting health/well-being and discrimination.[51] The researchers concluded that 'it was the problems which were less easily identified with specific employment rights that were the things that respondents were most likely to choose when they told us what their most serious problem looked like'.[52]

The BWBS analysis of answers to the adapted twenty-one-item NAQ-type list led the researchers to posit the existence of three categories of ill treatment, namely 'unreasonable treatment', 'incivility and disrespect', and 'violence and injury', corresponding to different groupings of the listed behaviours.[53] The researchers saw these as relating to distinct experiences, while acknowledging that which category an item fell into was not always obvious. In relation to ambiguous items, they allocated an item 'based not only on an empirical but also a conceptual framework', although without further explaining their thinking in this regard.[54]

Aside from large proportions reporting the three kinds of ill treatment, the data gathered showed considerable overlap in reported experiences, paralleling the blurring in legal claims of complaints about behaviour alone and about the handling of particular work issues.[55] Most who reported ill treatment to the BWBS reported more than one type, with 33 per cent of the whole sample indicating both unreasonable treatment and incivility and disrespect.[56] Everyone who reported violence or injury reported one of the other kinds of ill treatment. Conspicuously, all members of this group were in the 'troubled minority'.[57] The researchers additionally observed a 'high degree of overlap between experiencing, witnessing and perpetrating trouble at work'.[58] They took support from this for their central argument that 'it is the characteristics of troubled workplaces ... rather than of people ... that will provide the best explanations of ill-treatment at work.'[59]

The numbers reporting the various categories of experience were very large, in some sense going back to those found in the earlier, non-representative bullying studies considered earlier. In terms of unreasonable treatment, half of all respondents reported experiencing this in the previous two years. Close to one-quarter reported three or more different kinds and 10 per cent five kinds or more.[60] Employees with either impairments or long-term serious health conditions stood out as far more likely to report unreasonable treatment, with the situation much worse for those with psychological problems and learning difficulties. Both effects were supported after controlling for other factors.[61] There were less strong associations between reports of unreasonable treatment and being white, younger, having a higher income, having managerial or supervisory responsibilities, and being subject to certain kinds of organizational change, particularly reduced control over their work, undertaking intense work, and working outside London.[62] Further analysis confirmed that reports of unreasonable treatment were not particularly a feature of obvious vulnerability.[63]

General attitudes to work were probed by asking respondents if they agreed that, first, 'where I work, the needs of the organization always come before the needs of people', second, 'where I work, you have to compromise your principles', and third, 'where I work, people are treated as individuals'. The researchers called these the 'FARE' questions and

[51] ibid, 79.   [52] ibid, 80.   [53] ibid, 31–32.   [54] ibid, 33.
[55] See also the qualitative analysis, ibid at 113, and p 6 in Ch 1, p 103 in Ch 4 and p 181 in Ch 8 on my research design.
[56] Fevre et al, *Trouble at Work* (n 6), 34.   [57] ibid, 86.   [58] ibid.
[59] ibid, 35 and 65–66.   [60] ibid, 37.
[61] ibid, 44–46. See further R Fevre, A Robinson, D Lewis, and T Jones, 'The ill-treatment of employees with disabilities in British workplaces' (2013) 27 Work, Employment and Society 288 for further discussion of this phenomenon.
[62] Fevre et al, *Trouble at Work* (n 6), 48–52 and 54–55.   [63] ibid, 59.

suggested that answers to them may be a better guide than conventional measures of whether or not workplaces are troubled.[64] The view that people were not treated as individuals was the strongest predictor of reports of unreasonable treatment, while responses generally to the FARE questions were at least as important as more directly relevant questions at predicting a high incidence of reports of incivility and disrespect.

Fevre and colleagues in turn concluded from reports of incivility and disrespect that this is 'a malaise of highly visible organizations with HR functions, union recognition and highly skilled, well paid workforces',[65] also noticing that it is more frequently reported in the public sector owing to greater exposure to the public (notwithstanding the growth in the private service sector). Overall, 40 per cent of the sample reported the relevant cluster of experiences in the past two years, nearly one-quarter of three or more kinds of ill treatment, and just over 10 per cent of five or more kinds. Generally this type of behaviour was reported happening less frequently than once a month, but for nearly all types at least 20 per cent said it had happened once a week or daily.[66] In contrast to the FTWS 2008, however, unreasonable treatment was more likely to be said to have had the greatest impact, notwithstanding reports also of significant effects from incivility and disrespect.[67]

The single most important group identified by the 'troubled minority' as the source of incivility and disrespect was management. Of 2,600 incidents reported, 40 per cent were attributed to managers and about 25 per cent to co-workers and customers/clients. Subordinates were less often identified as responsible.[68] As for unfair treatment, however, men were more likely to be identified, linked to their over-representation amongst management.[69] Reports of having witnessed incivility and disrespect were nearly as common as having experienced it.[70]

There were no longer associations between reporting those experiences and higher income, having managerial responsibilities, change in the nature of work and region, but there were to being gay or lesbian. Lessened control over work, 'super intense work', being younger, not having an Asian background,[71] having disabilities, especially psychological and learning disabilities, and being in the public sector, were all important.[72] Some explanation of the regional and sectoral patterns emerged: customers and clients accounted for a good deal of incivility and disrespect and there is a higher proportion of service-oriented work in London and in the public sector.[73]

Once they controlled for various factors, researchers said that '[t]he increased [reported] exposure to incivility and disrespect experienced by employees with psychological/learning disabilities was extreme.'[74] Managers may not have been as responsible for this, in comparison with customers, clients, and co-workers. The over-representation of gay and lesbian people was almost as marked.[75] Neither religion, place of birth, nor

---

[64] ibid, 52–54 and 74–75. Note Fevre and colleagues' speculation at 54 that accounts of unreasonable treatment absent these views related to situations in which 'more individual, psychological or clinical models of bullying and/or stress might apply', as opposed to what they saw as the more common phenomenon of such reports indicating that workplaces were troubled in a more general way.

[65] ibid, 79.   [66] ibid, 61.   [67] ibid, 62.   [68] ibid, 63–64.

[69] ibid.   [70] ibid.

[71] But see ibid, 77, that within the 'troubled minority' there were associations with being BME (and the case-study evidence, discussed at 198, of ill treatment of Asians elsewhere), giving some support to the possibility advanced by the researchers that Asians are, for some reason, less likely to work in 'troubled workplaces'.

[72] ibid, 66–67.   [73] ibid, 54–55, 67, and 76.   [74] ibid, 69.

[75] See also ibid, 96 about the greater likelihood within the 'troubled minority' of gays, lesbians, and bisexuals reporting violence.

gender,[76] however, showed up in significant correlations and all job types were equally exposed.

It was notable too that 'violence or injury' were far more frequently reported to be perpetrated by non-employees, while the closest links between such conduct and incivility and disrespect were amongst employees. Moreover, 'this [reported] pattern of abusive and violent relationships between employees was more common in the private ... than the public sector.'[77] Aside from there again being a significantly higher incidence of people with psychological and learning disabilities reporting workplace violence,[78] the researchers' general conclusion was that it was the work context that was key, with a critical variable being whether work was public-facing.[79] Indeed 79 per cent of incidents of violence or injury were reported to have been perpetrated by customers, clients, or members of the general public, thereby creating a particular vulnerability in the public sector.[80]

Finally, the qualitative aspects of the study[81] gave texture to the quantitative findings. This investigated four British organizations, one a National Health Service (NHS) public sector entity. The aim was to help answer questions raised by the BWBS, in particular 'why some workplaces are more troubled than others and what can be done to reduce trouble at work'.[82] There were over 100 interviews, mostly with employees recruited in various ways, but also with 'key informants' from, for example, management, human resources, and trade unions. Each of the organizations studied 'had been able to rely upon an extraordinarily high level of commitment from their employees and had enviable public reputations'.[83] The researchers, however, found this had not wholly insulated these organizations either from instances of 'trouble at work' or from the risk of becoming 'troubled workplaces' more generally.

First, interviewees' strong commitment to their work, as well as their faith in their organizations, came across powerfully. Fevre and colleagues documented this in a range of ways.[84] The data painted a nuanced picture of 'management' and 'labour' having overlapping interests, concerns, and motivations. Much as there was evidence of employees not complaining or speaking up for negative reasons, like mistrust of the impartiality of processes and fear of victimization,[85] the data also demonstrated reticence being rooted in positive feelings towards work.[86] Perhaps the clearest manifestation of this was in reports of stoical and tolerant reactions to even quite serious incivility and violence from members of the public.[87] In turn, criticism of management was not evidently self-serving; for example, some respondents deplored failures to advance organizational goals due to management being too lenient in the face of poor performance.[88] There

[76] But see ibid, that there were correlations within the 'troubled minority' with being female and being, insulted (77), unfairly treated (56), and working in places associated with the most extreme problems (98). The researchers observed that, first, these kinds of effects did not emerge in the national sample because of the significance of there being some workplaces that were so much more prone to ill treatment, and second, that therefore non-representative samples may give a misleading picture.

[77] ibid, 87 and discussed further at 88–89 and 99–101.   [78] ibid, 93.

[79] ibid, 93–94 and 97–99.   [80] ibid, 86.   [81] See generally ibid, 103–07.

[82] ibid, 105.   [83] ibid, 106.   [84] ibid, 121–22, 132, 141, 148, 152, and 167–68.

[85] ibid, 138, 143–45, 192, 195, and 220–21.

[86] ibid, 141, 162, 169, 170–71, although there was real complexity here as to why people would not object to certain things, and very disquieting accounts at 171–73 of sexist and racist behaviour and of people feeling they must keep quiet.

[87] ibid, 90, 157, and 166.

[88] ibid, 122, 128, 175, and 207. A complex variation to this concerned reports in one case study that others were not 'called' on disciplinary matters because they were from an ethnic minority and managers feared allegations of racism, mentioned at 115, 118, and 120.

were also repeated instances of employees being slow to attribute ill treatment to a feature of their own identity, instead putting forward multi-layered hypotheses about why the behaviour had occurred.[89] Corollaries to all this were observations, on the one hand, that stark instances of poor conduct could tip employees into viewing treatment as discriminatory[90] and, on the other, that many interviewees who had spoken out perceived their strength and assertiveness as important to having done so.[91]

Fevre and colleagues drew on this aspect of the qualitative data to explain the quantitative finding that unreasonable treatment was more often reported than other kinds of negative behaviour as having the biggest impact on respondents:

Finding that there is no rhyme or reason to decisions, that counterproductive behaviour is rife, that money, time and effort are frittered away, is not what people are meant to find. But when people do begin to believe that they have been unreasonably treated, this is the territory they find themselves in—a strange and unsettling world in which markets and professional managers and public oversight to not apparently make organizations behave rationally—and they often find it both frustrating and upsetting. Most often, they also believe there is nothing that can do to change this. Their frustration at seeing the wrong things done or the right things omitted—service worse than necessary, equipment or talent going to waste—is made keener by their impotence.[92]

In this way, the sting in unreasonable treatment was not the affront, nor even the injury, to affected individuals, but instead it was in the way this undermined strong and resilient expectations of rational workplace behaviour in pursuit of shared goals. This exemplified how individual problems may in current conditions be the vehicle for the expression of discontent that is in truth about the collective construction of working life.

Second, the centrality of management was clear.[93] This came across both in the sense that so much ill treatment was seen as originating from this group, but also in the importance attributed to managers being driven professionally and in turn driving others, often in response to the pressure they were subject to.[94] In a sense, this again depicted blurred boundaries between 'management' and 'labour', employers and employees, collective and individual interests. The repeated impression the research offered was that managers were embodying all of these perspectives, sometimes trying to reconcile them, sometimes trying to assert one over the other.[95]

Finally, attitudes to process emerged as significant. While established procedures to deal with workplace difficulties were regarded as important, frustration was expressed about how these worked. Respondents' concern seemed to be that they stopped people sorting problems out and instead channelled difficulties into unproductive bureaucracy.[96] A notable consequent conclusion was that policies and practices that are not explicitly about interpersonal behaviour (eg about sickness and disability) may be more important than workplace measures that specifically address

---

[89] See ibid 46–48, 92, 97, 157–58, and 216–17, but also 160 for the comment about the NHS case study that people were more ready to see behaviour they had witnessed, as opposed to being subject to, as discriminatory. See also R Fevre, H Grainger, and R Brewer, 'Discrimination and Unfair Treatment in the Workplace' (2011) 49 BJIR 207 about how beliefs in instrumental rationality arguably reduce the reporting of discrimination.
[90] Fevre et al, *Trouble at Work* (n 6), 120.   [91] ibid, 121, 140–41, and 153.   [92] ibid, 40.
[93] ibid, 106.   [94] ibid, 119–20, 139–40, 142–43, 153–57, 161–62, and 178–80.
[95] ibid, 223–24. There were also interesting observations at 225–26 of very different points of view regarding individualism and collectivism between white- and blue-collar employees and also internationally, including about one case study finding that '[w]e have noted at several points how these [white collar] employees seemed to value the team-working, and continuous team-building ... What we failed to emphasize is how little this team-working had in common with not only traditional collectivism but also conventional informal social ties.'
[96] ibid, 106, 123–24, 162–63, 165, and 194–96.

conduct. If an underlying problem is a broader, less individualized conflict, it follows that a broader solution is needed.[97]

Fevre and his colleagues' overall conclusions offered greater specificity to their argument that it is workplaces rather than individual characteristics that affect 'trouble at work' most. From their quantitative and qualitative data, they extrapolated that the two workplace characteristics most strongly associated with trouble at work are first, conflict with employees over workplace norms, and second, the ill treatment of those who provide public services to members of the public.[98] It is the former that has most direct relevance to this study, while the second is important to making sense of my data about lawyers' perceptions of public sector experience. Fevre and colleagues developed their point in relation to findings on reduced control and 'super intense work', arguing in relation to the former that:

[t]he turning of a difference of opinion into actual conflict was marked by the occurrence of ill-treatment. This ill-treatment might reside in the tactics employers used to force through the changes they wanted to make, or employees might simply see the accomplishment of these changes as constituting ill-treatment. At Banco, for example, the field force of financial advisors complained both that their loss of autonomy amounted to unreasonable treatment and that their managers were treating them with incivility and disrespect as a tactic to achieve the changes they wanted.[99]

This again showed collective and individual disputes intermingling, while the researchers further took support for their argument here from strong associations between answers to the FARE questions and reports of ill treatment.[100]

Findings about worker commitment were central to the analysis, the researchers explaining that many interviewees described themselves as 'model employees' who felt they had learned through unreasonable treatment, incivility, and disrespect that they were no longer viewed positively. Where ill treatment was associated with managerial attempts to bring about change the researchers argued that it was:

[a] marker for a fundamental disagreement between employer and employee about the nature of valued work … No matter how steadfastly the employee held to the view that they ha[d] been a good and valuable employee, they now knew that their employer thought they were deluded. It was this slur on their integrity … that had such a great impact on so many of the employees in our study.[101]

This raised the possibility that such effects on employees may be 'a price employers are willing to pay when they view change as essential to the progress of the business'. Having this effect may in fact be part of the employers' objective, 'inherent in the change they want to bring about'.[102] This brought Fevre and colleagues' analysis to a central issue within collective systems for regulating work of where the balance should be struck when employers' and employees' interests cease to align. The implication is that in modern industrial relations in the UK, contestation about this essentially collective issue will express itself in more individualized discontent and conflict.[103]

----

[97] ibid, 119–22. This supports that the law relevant to behavioural conflict implicates many aspects of working life, as discussed at p 6 in Ch 1, pp 60, 65 and 104–105 in Ch 3, pp 187–88 in Ch 8 and pp 245–46 in Ch 10.

[98] ibid, 201.   [99] ibid, 206.   [100] ibid, 208.

[101] ibid, 203.   [102] ibid, 204.

[103] See their final paragraph at 230 that '[i]n collective times, conflicts over workplace norms did not get framed as unreasonable treatment but as issues for collective bargaining. Any incivility and disrespect that arose could also be dealt with by collective response … but companies that go down the individualized route … dispense with the possibility of collective solutions. Trouble at work is not only an expression of industrial relations problems … but is also an outcome of the transformation

It is also in this area that the research made its most significant theoretical suggestion, arguing that a cause of modern day difficulties may be uneven adaptation by employers to the move away from collectivism to individualism. While enthusiastically embracing the freedom that more 'one by one' relationships with employees provides, the argument was that employers have not made the parallel transition to dealing effectively with new ways that employee demands emerge in this changed environment. Aside from recognizing the likelihood that employers sometimes, directly or indirectly, seek 'trouble at work',[104] Fevre and his researchers floated the possibility that:

[w]ith the addition of our idea of an imperfect adjustment to individualized employment relations, this looks like employers were using the old-fashioned tactics that might be employed when fighting a powerful trade union rather than acting as the trustworthy partner in an individualized employment relationships. It is as if these employers embraced the easy part of the new relationship, the change in the nature and aspirations of their employees, without doing the harder part of shaping their own behaviour to match the change.[105]

Interestingly for the purposes of this project, they also speculated that in hard economic times there may be a lesser market punishment to employers who fail to make this adjustment, and that current reductions in employment rights 'could be seen as a way of extending further those mitigating conditions into the recovery'.[106]

To me, this is striking because the latter observation makes the sort of assumption about the direct impact of law that I deplored at the opening of this chapter, taking it as read that individual rights mitigate employer domination of an individualized working relationship. There were similar tendencies in Liefooghe and MacKenzie-Davey's work. Having shown that bullying discourses provide new means of contestation about basic conflicts of interests at work,[107] they extrapolated that moves in Europe towards legal regulation of workplace bullying should be resisted because this would 'render one discourse fixed'. This again makes unwarranted assumptions about how law works in practice, in this context that it necessarily entrenches a discourse that influenced legal development.

2. Empirical Knowledge about Law and Legal Process

There is some overlap in the questions investigated by research considered in this section regarding how people respond to problems at work. The focus in the research surveyed here, however, is on how law and litigation figure. As noted earlier, this makes clear that any idea that working people easily turn to law, lawyers, and courts is profoundly misguided.[108] The critical questions become accordingly first, whether the subset of cases that are litigated, or in which law is at least invoked, have a wider

---

of industrial relations with uncertain, and often unhappy, consequences for all involved.' See also H Hoel and D Beale, 'Workplace Bullying, Psychological Perspectives and Industrial Relations: Towards a Contextualized and Interdisciplinary Approach' (2006) 44 BJIR 239, 251.

[104] See also D Beale and H Hoel, 'Workplace Bullying and the Employment Relationship: Exploring Questions of Prevention, Control and Context' (2011) 25 Work Employment and Society 5, 7, 9–11, and 13.

[105] Fevre et al, *Trouble at Work* (n 6), 227 and more generally at 226–28 and 229–30.

[106] ibid.

[107] Liefooghe and Mackenzie Davey, 'Language and Organization' (n 5).

[108] See H Genn with National Centre for Social Research, *Paths to Justice, What People Do and Think About Going to Law* (Hart Publishing, 1999), 254 for the conclusion: 'When faced with a justiciable event, most people simply want to solve the problem or to obtain compensation for harm and loss ... In seeking these solutions there is little evidence from this study of any "rush" to law.'

influence, and second, what effect law has irrespective of individual behaviour with regard to raising issues at work and external enforcement.

(1) Procedural issues

It is convenient briefly to sketch the central procedural issues for those contemplating litigation. It will be seen from Chapter 3 that procedural matters sometimes have substantive effects. Equally it is not always easy to categorize a legal measure as purely either procedural or substantive, with, for example, the changes to unfair dismissal law in the Employment Act (EA) 2002 arguably on the cusp between the two. Accordingly, I deal here only with the most basic procedural concerns relevant to litigation about work.

These matter because procedural issues may be what dissuade someone from either turning to law or carrying on with a claim. Potential litigants being put off by procedural issues is, moreover, increasingly to be expected, not least because of recent changes to the Employment Tribunal (ET) system by governments of varying political hues. In an arguably curious reaction to rising claim rates, changes have been made to discourage working people from bringing or proceeding with actions. This is despite, first, the same governments enacting and implementing new individual employment rights that are subject to ET enforcement. Second, the fluctuations in claims' rates have been attributed to varied causes, some of which are unlikely to have been affected by the new rules.[109]

What is clear, nonetheless, is that the practical impact of adjustments to the ET system has exponentially increased with a raft of measures by the UK Coalition government from 2010 to 2015. Highly significant in procedural terms are the introduction of hefty fees for instituting and pursuing ET claims and compulsory early conciliation by the Advisory, Conciliation and Arbitration Service (ACAS). The latter might have something positive to contribute, albeit within the somewhat narrow and unambitious frame of avoiding hearings.[110] Overall, however, the long list of changes was about deterring employees from making external legal challenges to what they see as unfair or wrongful acts at work. Moreover, the government seems finally to have achieved this aim, with dramatic recent falls in both single and group-type claims to the ET.[111]

These latest developments came after the period from which my selection of judgments was taken and during which my interviews were conducted. They are important to interpretation of my data, however, because the upshot is that there are now greater procedural obstacles in the way of individuals taking complaints beyond the workplace and into the courts. The economic climate has also both increased worker vulnerability and decreased the sources of help for taking action.[112] Putting all this together, the

---

[109] See GS Morris, 'The Development of Statutory Employment Rights in Britain and Enforcement Mechanisms' in L Dickens (ed), *Making Employment Rights Effective, Issues of Enforcement and Compliance* (Hart, 2012) on the evolution of the system and fluctuations in ET claims to 2011 and G Dix, K Sisson, and J Forth, 'Conflict at Work: The Changing Pattern of Disputes' in Brown et al (eds) (n 2), 183–85 and 190–91 on the increase in ET claims from 1972–2006.

[110] See OM Fiss, 'Against Settlement' (1984) 93 Yale LJ 1073 for a classic cautionary note about settlement, in particular that background inequalities structure how this turns out, detaching underlying justice norms in the application of law to concrete situations and, further, M Galanter, 'Why the Haves Come Out Ahead' (1974) 9 Law and Society Review 1, 34, 53, and 55.

[111] See B Hepple, 'Back to the Future: Employment Law Under the Coalition Government' (2013) 24 ILJ 203 generally on the coalition government changes and Ministry of Justice, Tribunal and Gender Recognition Certificate Statistics Quarterly, Jul–Sept 2014, 4, and 6–8, and *Senior President of Tribunals' Annual Report* (Senior President of Tribunals, Feb 2015), 70, 73–74, and 82–84 on the steep, ongoing decline in ET claims (and appeals) after the introduction of fees.

[112] See A Pollert, 'The Unorganized Worker: The Decline in Collectivism and New Hurdles to Individual Employment Rights' (2005) 34 ILJ 217 about the then obstacles to enforcement for

reluctance of working people to take legal action appears now more deeply entrenched than ever.

(a) ETs v ordinary courts

Keeping that important background in mind, the first major procedural decision for a would-be litigant, in theory at least, may be whether to sue in the ET or the ordinary courts. Another odd feature of political debate, guidance, research,[113] and legislative initiatives[114] is, however, that this typically ignores the possibility of employment claims in the ordinary courts. This is despite the fact that, while ETs have exclusive jurisdiction over many statutory claims, a good many actions can only be brought in the ordinary courts. This includes many in contract and all tort and Protection from Harassment Act (PHA) 1997 claims. Moreover, the jurisdictions of ETs and ordinary courts overlap for claims in contract about termination and regarding equal pay.

That makes differences in the organization of ETs and ordinary courts pertinent. First, procedure in ordinary courts is generally more formal, technical, and complicated. The relevance of this should not, however, be overstated in that the value of many employment cases would put them in the highly informal Small Claims Court. Second, adjudication in ordinary courts is exclusively by legally qualified judges who are unlikely to be specialists in labour and equality law. In the ET system, by contrast, the usual approach, at least until the coalition government reduced the participation of lay judges, was for cases to be decided by tripartite courts comprising a legally qualified chair plus two, lay, 'wing members'. Legally qualified ET judges are specialists in the field while lay members bring employers' and employees' experience of working life. The initial stage of appeals from ETs is to the Employment Appeal Tribunal (EAT), whose full panels were similarly structured until Coalition government changes reduced lay involvement there as well.

(b) Costs and funding litigation

The second major procedural consideration for claimants is costs. The rules differ significantly between ETs and ordinary courts. In general, costs are not recoverable in an ET, even if a claim is successfully brought or defended. In ordinary courts and on appeal from either an ET or court, costs typically follow the event, except that the usual costs rule for the Small Claims Court is the same as for ETs. While in England and Wales there was until recently some provision for legal aid to cover advice and assistance in employment and equality cases, and for representation on appeal, the Legal Aid, Sentencing and Punishment of Offenders Act 2012[115] has limited this to discrimination

workers who were not trade union members nor covered by a collective agreement. More recently see N Busby, M McDermont, E Rose, and A Sales (eds), *Access to Justice in Employment Disputes: Surveying the Terrain* (Institute of Employment Rights, 2013), and S Tailby, A Pollert, S Warren, A Danford, and N Wilton, 'Underfunded and Overwhelmed: The Voluntary Sector as Worker Representation in Britain's Individualized Industrial Relations Systems' (2011) 42 Industrial Relations Journal 273.

[113] See, amongst many examples, Dix et al (n 109), 177–78 and D Lucy and A Broughton, *Understanding the Decision-making of Employees in Disputes and Conflicts at Work* (BIS, ERRS 119, May 2011). In fact, I am not sure I have *ever* read either research or policy guidance by a non-lawyer that acknowledges that employment litigation occurs outside ETs.

[114] See L Dickens, 'Fairer Workplaces: Making Employment Rights Effective' in Dickens (ed) (n 109), 206, criticizing the focus on the ET system from a different point of view, arguing there is a need to consider enforcement more generally.

[115] Ss 8–10 and Sched 1. For a helpful explanation of the changes in employment cases, see Bar Council Remuneration Committee's Civil (Public) Panel, *Changes to Civil Legal Aid, Practical Guidance for the Bar* (Bar Council, 2013), 36–38.

cases and some exceptional funding possibilities, for example in respect of human rights breaches. The position in Scotland is different.[116] For some time now there has also been the possibility of conditional fee agreements and insurance can potentially be taken out to cover the risk of having to pay the other side's costs.[117] Other external sources of support for claimants are legal expenses insurance, the legal services provided by trades unions or, in a few cases, legal support from the Equality and Human Rights Commission and its predecessors. The options for respondents for external support to cover their costs are fewer, with the taking out of legal expenses insurance perhaps the most likely.

Arguably relevant also is where the money comes from to pay settlements and compensation awards. Little is known about the availability and take-up of employers' insurance to cover liability for breaches of labour and equality law. Cursory searches on the Internet suggest that this kind of insurance is available, but none of my interviewees mentioned it and I have not found systematic research on this topic.[118] It is, however, compulsory for employers to have liability insurance for negligently caused personal injury or death. This difference explains distinct ways that organizations deal with various categories of claim, often handling proceedings about employment and equality law themselves, even if personal injury is alleged, while personal injury actions in the ordinary courts are handed over to their insurers, whose internal or external lawyers then run the litigation. The implications of these practicalities are illuminated by my case law analysis and interviews.

There have also been changes over the years in costs rules, directed especially toward discouraging weak claims. These are again currently being taken further, not least through the new ET fees regime. It is particularly odd in this regard that policy makers seem to have ignored the possibility of some employment claims being made in the ordinary courts, since a rational reaction to the ET changes would be for claims to be redirected to the ordinary courts where possible. Not only are fees modest there but the fact that many employment claims would be suitable for the informal small claims court means the default rule would remain that costs did not follow the event.[119]

(2) Socio-legal research into claiming behaviour by individuals

(a) Approaches to claiming behaviour generally

Influential theoretical work[120] has posited three stages in the process by which individuals seek legal redress: 'naming, blaming, and claiming'. In this strand of research the word 'claiming', however, does not signify litigating, but instead means confronting the alleged wrongdoer. Some people will choose instead to 'lump it', while disputes can at any stage be resolved or abandoned. Only a few individuals will move from 'claiming'

---

[116] See on Scotland and also generally about the availability of legal aid, Morris (n 109), 13. Morris also adverts to a possible requirement for legal aid in cases involving EU law.

[117] See R Moorhead and R Cumming, *Something for Nothing? Employment Tribunal Claimants' Perspectives on Legal Funding* (BIS, 2009, ERRS 101) and R Moorhead, 'An American Future? Contingency Fees Claims Explosions and Evidence from Employment Tribunals' (2010) 73 MLR 752.

[118] See n 232 below for a rare example of relevant data.

[119] See K Hall, 'Employment claimants go forum shopping' LS Gaz, 9 June 2014, quoting employment solicitor, Richard Fox, that low value claims 'for things like the non-payment of wages and breach of contracts where the cost of the [ET fee] renders the claim uneconomic' are being taken to the county courts.

[120] WLF Felstiner, RL Abel, and A Sarat, 'The Emergence and Transformation of Disputes: Naming, Blaming, Claiming' (1980–81) 15 Law and Soc'y Rev 631.

to litigation. Still, despite the logical appeal of this model, reality seems to be less linear and ordered. Lloyd-Bostock's survey of plaintiffs in personal injury actions, for example, showed that law may explain where individuals place blame rather than this stage preceding the turn to law.[121]

In terms of large-scale empirical investigations into claiming behaviour, the modern approach, pioneered by Genn in England and Wales in *Paths to Justice*,[122] is to investigate 'justiciable problems' using face-to-face interviews with representative national samples. Genn defined a 'justiciable event' as 'a matter experienced by a respondent which raised legal issues, whether or not it was recognized by the respondent as being "legal",[123] and whether or not any action taken by the respondent to deal with the event used any part of the civil justice system'.[124] Studies based on this approach identify categories and sub-categories of justiciable event for investigation, with employment being one such and comprising a range of workplace experiences.

Genn's initial work involved a national study of how individuals respond to justiciable events, swiftly repeated in Scotland[125] and continuously adapted and rerun since, both within and beyond the UK. The fieldwork for Genn's English and Welsh study was in 1997–98, close to the start of the period from which my sample of judgments was taken. I particularly rely on this to set the socio-legal scene, also highlighting differences in the Scottish data. I rely less on later iterations[126] because they focused on the earlier phases in which individuals react to a justiciable problem and provide less disaggregated employment data.[127]

It is important again to bear in mind that these were self-report studies. This makes it significant that they were of large representative samples and there was some probing of the data in qualitative interviews.[128] It is also worth noting the conceptual difference to sociological investigations of workplace behaviour, that the experiences surveyed were

---

[121] S Lloyd-Bostock, 'Fault and Liability for Accidents: The Accident Victim's Perspective' in D Harris, M Maclean, H Genn, P Fenn, S Lloyd-Bostock, P Corfield, and Y Brittan, *Compensation and Support for Illness and Injury* (OUP, 1984). See also Lucy and Broughton (n 113), 30 on US evidence suggesting a complicated relationship between blaming and claiming, and Blackstone et al (n 36) on complex influences on whether, and how, legal consciousness develops about sexually harassing behaviour.

[122] Genn et al (n 108).

[123] See P Pleasence, N Balmer, A Patel, A Cleary, T Huskinson, and T Cotton, *Civil Justice in England and Wales, Report of Wave 1 of the Civil and Social Justice Panel Survey* (CSJPS) (Legal Services Commission and Ipsos MORI, 2011), ii and 37 that fewer than 10 per cent of problems reported were characterized as 'legal'.

[124] Genn et al (n 108), 12.

[125] H Genn and A Paterson, with National Centre for Social Research, *Paths to Justice, Scotland, What People in Scotland Do and Think About Going to Law* (Hart Publishing, 2001).

[126] The successive English and Welsh studies that have built on Genn's method are reported in P Pleasence, A Buck, NJ Balmer, A O'Grady, H Genn, and M Smith, *Causes of Action* (1st edn, TSO, 2004); P Pleasence, *Causes of Action: Civil Law and Social Justice* (CSJS) (2nd edn, TSO, 2006); P Pleasence, N Balmer, A Patel, and C Denvir, *Civil Justice in England and Wales 2009, Report of the 2006–2009 English and Welsh Civil and Social Justice Survey* (Legal Services Commission, 2010); P Pleasence et al (n 123), and N Balmer, *English and Welsh Civil Social Justice Panel Survey Wave 2* (Legal Services Commission, 2013). Significantly, the latest version has a longitudinal design.

[127] Pleasence (2006), ibid, 6, explained that the CSJS in 2001 'substantially shifted the focus of questions away from rare events (such as the use of formal process) towards early stage decision-making' and that in 2004 'continued the process of shifting the focus of questions towards early stage decision-making'. Pleasence et al (2010), ibid, 2 indicated that this shift in emphasis carried through to the continuous survey in 2006–09.

[128] See Pleasence (2006), ibid, 22–23 on methodology, and A Pollert and A Charlwood, 'The Vulnerable Worker in Britain and Problems at Work' (2009) 23 Work, Employment and Society 343, 346 regarding cognitive testing for their study that 'the threshold for registering workplace experiences as "problems" can be high, especially at the lower end of the labour market', echoing similar findings about bad behaviour at work mentioned in the text to ns 31 and 34–36 above and in n 263 below.

ones with necessary legal implications. This does not, however, make much difference in that so many of the events investigated in the sociological studies in fact raise legal issues. More distinctive, however, is that *Paths to Justice* asked interviewees about their experiences as both plaintiffs and defendants.

To look at the general picture before turning in the next section to the data specifically about employment problems, people were asked whether they had any problems or disputes that were difficult to solve, with some reports investigated further.[129] Initial questions were about all justiciable events, some of which were subsequently excluded on various measures of seriousness. At the first stage about 40 per cent of respondents in England and Wales reported one or more justiciable problem in the past five years,[130] with some indications of problems multiplying and clustering.[131]

There was one arresting difference in the Scottish study, however, in that the equivalent figure was only 26 per cent.[132] Genn and Paterson argued that this most likely represented differences in reporting between the two regions. They speculated that lower rates might particularly be explained, first, by a greater sense of fatalism or powerlessness in segments of the Scottish population. This was supported by respondents who reported problems being significantly more educated and younger than those who did not. Second, the researchers thought underreporting might be because the strong socialist tradition in Scotland had made the population 'more community-oriented than the English, and thus less likely to perceive disputes as being individual matters rather than collective problems'.[133]

As regards the composition of the smaller group who survived application of the triviality threshold in England and Wales, there was a broad similarity with the general population. This replicated consistent findings within and across countries that individual characteristics 'are relatively weak predictors of individual claiming behaviour (where they predict it at all)'.[134] Rather, the dominant factor, confirmed in Genn's studies,[135] is the type of issue in dispute.

More detailed evidence was obtained in England and Wales from a subset of 1,134 respondents, again across all problem categories, who had experienced one or more problem for which a legal remedy existed and who had either taken action or not for a reason other than the triviality of the problem.[136] In general, the data showed the 'overwhelming majority' tried to resolve the issue by contacting the person or institution concerned. Even those who took advice did so only after trying to sort the matter out

[129] Genn et al (n 108), 291.

[130] The equivalent percentages in the CSJS in 2001, 2004, and 2006–09, were 36, 33, and 35 per cent respectively, but regarding the previous three-and-a-half years only. The methodological differences between these and *Paths to Justice* probably account for the change from 1997 and 2001: see Pleasence (2006) (n 126), 15–16 and Pleasence et al (2010) (n 126), 10. The equivalent finding for the CSJPS in 2011 was 33 per cent over the previous 18 months, and that in 2013 was 32 per cent for the same time interval: see, respectively Pleasence et al (2011) (n 123), 8 (and at 39 that this survey included problems that were not 'difficult to solve'), and Balmer (2013) (n 126), 9.

[131] Genn et al (n 108), 30, 31–36 and 65–66, and see further the later studies in England and Wales (ns 123 and 126) and specifically P Pleasence, NJ Balmer, A Buck, A O'Grady, and H Genn, 'Multiple Justiciable Problems: Common Clusters and Their Social and Demographic Indicators' (2004) 1 Journal of Empirical Legal Studies 301.

[132] Genn and Paterson (n 125), 34.   [133] ibid, 82.

[134] Kritzer (n 1), 279. Consider however the associations found between reporting of justiciable problems and various social and demographic characteristics reported in Pleasence (2006) (n 126), 18–23, and 74–76.

[135] Eg Genn et al (n 108), at 105, 135, 253, and generally in Chapters 4 and 5.

[136] ibid, 269–71.

themselves. Only 5 per cent did nothing and Genn noted that, aside from being unlikely to have sought advice in the past, this group:

also disproportionately comprised people on low incomes, with little education, living in rented accommodation. Reasons for failure to take any action at all reflected a sense of powerlessness, fear of becoming involved in acrimony and concern about the cost of taking formal action.[137]

Around one-third tried to sort the problem out themselves, many giving up without seeking outside assistance. There were various reasons for failing to get advice, especially practical barriers to accessing advice agencies, fear of costs, and negative past experiences or beliefs about legal advisers and the legal system.[138] Finally, about three in five individuals obtained advice with about one-quarter at some point going to a solicitor.[139]

Thirty-five per cent of the justiciable problems surveyed in more depth were resolved by agreement, about 3 per cent after legal proceedings were commenced.[140] For about one-half of this category of problem, however, there had been neither agreement nor a court decision by the time of the interview. The numbers achieving a resolution barely differed between those who sought advice and did not, while the former had generally first tried to sort out the problem themselves.[141] For some people the problem ended anyway; for example, this occurred for 7 per cent of these respondents when they moved to another job. Still, that left many with an ongoing, non-trivial problem, more than half of whom had given up trying to find a solution.[142] Genn concluded, however, that avoidance of legal proceedings required some interpretation:

Most people *do* try to press their claims or defend their position, presumably by some reference to rights that have moral or legal force. Many express a strong sense of injustice and unfairness about the problem with which they have been faced. It is not the law that is remote from attempts to resolve justiciable problems, but rather it is formal legal proceedings that are largely remote from the resolution of many day to day justiciable problems.[143] (italics in the original)

(b) Claiming behaviour about individual employment rights

The Department for Business, Innovation and Skills (BIS) recently commissioned a review of literature on 'the factors that may influence the behaviour of employees who are involved in a conflict or dispute at work', in order to 'inform the debate about how to encourage parties to resolve such problems earlier and more informally'.[144] Much of

---

[137] ibid, 101.

[138] See ibid and also 142–43 reporting that some demographic associations were found with not seeking advice; namely, having the lowest educational levels and incomes, being younger, and being a man. Even so patterns of advice-seeking were still largely explained by problem type. Genn consequently observed at 143 that 'those members of the public with low levels of competence in terms of education, income, confidence, verbal skill, literacy skill and emotional fortitude are likely to need some help in resolving justiciable problems no matter what the importance of the problem and no matter how intransigent or accommodating the opposition, although this need will increase as problem severity and opponent intransigence increases.' See further Pleasence (2006) (n 126), 81–86 and 129–30 about varied reasons for inaction amongst those reporting justiciable problems in 2001 and 2004 and also confirming the importance of problem type.

[139] Genn et al (n 108), 101.   [140] ibid, 148.

[141] ibid, 176. Some were discouraged from proceeding and generally accepted this advice, but Genn observed at 177 that 'the relatively low level of advice to abandon cases that was actually given by advisers ... suggests that those taking the step of seeking advice had persevered with some justification.'

[142] ibid, 148–49.   [143] ibid, 245.

[144] B Wells, Director Labour Market Analysis and Minimum Wage Team, BIS, in the Foreword to Lucy and Broughton (n 113). Both the Foreword and the report, at 9, illustrate the common tendency to ignore the possibility of employment actions in the ordinary courts.

the literature reviewed came from the United States and did not relate to workplaces. Still, there were some interesting suggestions made. It is easy to see how psychological theorizing and experimentation about attribution errors might explain some litigation decisions. The 'fundamental attribution error' posits a tendency to attribute the conduct of others to disposition rather than situation, while the 'actor-observer' bias suggests people, in contrast, emphasize situational constraints to explain their own harmful acts. The BIS report also referred to US evidence that escalating a conflict is more likely where, first, responsibility has been attributed,[145] second, organizational norms of justice have been violated, and third, individuals are of certain personality types.[146]

The Genn study in 1997–98 also provided useful data specifically about employment problems in England and Wales. Interviewees were shown a card listing the kinds of problems that might arise in the employment category. What was on the cards included losing a job, (eg unfair dismissal) and disputes about a redundancy package, getting pay or a pension, other rights at work (eg maternity leave, sickness pay, holiday entitlement), working hours, changes to terms and conditions, unsatisfactory or dangerous working conditions, harassment, and unfair disciplinary procedures.[147] There was the same approach for two other potentially relevant categories, namely, '[i]njuries and health problems arising from accidents or poor working conditions requiring medical treatment', and '[p]roblems with discrimination in relation to sex/race/disability'.[148] My focus is on the employment category because the other two included so many non-employment situations. Still, the evidence does not precisely map either onto the range of potential employment problems or the particular focus of this work. The data is nonetheless informative about individual experiences of, and responses to, employment problems, and there is a degree of updating from subsequent adaptations of Genn's survey.

Amongst the matters most frequently reported in *Paths to Justice* in England and Wales, with similar patterns in Scotland,[149] were 6 per cent of employment problems[150] and 8 per cent for injuries/health problems resulting from accidents or poor working conditions.[151] Only a maximum of 1 per cent of reports were about discrimination problems.[152] Once the initial triviality threshold was applied, the reporting of employment problems stayed static at 6 per cent and that for injuries and the like went down to 5 per cent. The ill-health reduction was out of line with the others in that 37 per cent took no action, generally because they thought either that no-one was to blame or that

---

[145] But cf K Harlos, 'If you build a remedial voice mechanism, will they come? Determinants of voicing interpersonal mistreatment at work' (2010) 63 Human Relations 311, 321, and 325 that intent attribution did not appear to increase the likelihood of going to an internal mediator about interpersonal mistreatment.

[146] Lucy and Broughton (n 113), 26–27. See also further about organizational justice at 36–37.

[147] Genn et al (n 108), 21–22.   [148] ibid.

[149] Genn and Paterson (n 125), 55–57.

[150] In the 2001 CSJS the percentage was again 6, and in 2004 it was 5, while for discrimination the respective figures were 1.4 per cent and 2.2 per cent: see Pleasence (2006) (n 126), 27. In 2006–09 the number was 4.9 per cent for employment and 2 per cent for discrimination: see Pleasence et al (2010) (n 126), 11. In 2011 it was 5.5 per cent for employment and, while discrimination was not separately investigated, in 8.1 per cent of situations it was said the problem also involved discrimination, rising to about 18 per cent in relation to employment problems: see Pleasence et al (2011) (n 123), 8–9. In 2013, 6.4 per cent, of problems were reported to be about employment, with 8.5 per cent of problems overall being perceived also to involve discrimination, rising to 20 per cent for employment problems: see Balmer (2013) (n 126), 10–11.

[151] Genn et al (n 108), 23.

[152] ibid, 53. Other data about this category tended to be aggregated in the report.

the incident had not been important enough.[153] The figure representing those who did nothing about discrimination problems was second highest at 35 per cent, and next was that for employment problems at 16 per cent.[154]

Regarding employment problems, 14 per cent of all reports were about harassment (which I calculate at around 1 per cent of the whole sample).[155] About three-quarters said they had taken some action, most commonly by 'seeking advice' (56 per cent) and 'talking or writing to the other side' (52 per cent). Fourteen per cent indicated threatening legal action. This activity was, however, balanced by the relatively large group who reported doing nothing. The largest subset (around a third) said this was because they did not think anything could be done, while about a quarter thought the other side was in the right. Smaller numbers said they had done nothing because they did not think the problem was very important (13 per cent), they were too scared (5 per cent), they thought it would take too much time (4 per cent), they thought it would damage their relationship with the other side (2 per cent), and they thought it would cost too much (2 per cent).

The analogous, although not fully comparable, figures in the 2006–09 Civil and Social Justice Survey (CSJS) for those reporting employment problems indicated that 53.3 per cent obtained advice, 29.6 per cent handled their problem alone, 6.6 per cent tried and failed to obtain advice and went on to handle the problem themselves, 1.1 per cent tried and failed to obtain advice and did nothing further, and 9.4 per cent did nothing.[156] In the 2010 panel wave 1 survey, which notably did not ask only about 'difficult to solve' problems (unlike Genn and the CSJS), 43.4 per cent reported obtaining advice, 7 per cent said they had handled their problem with informal advice, 31.1 per cent that they handled it alone, and 18.4 per cent that they did nothing.[157] In the wave 2 survey, the equivalent figures were 39.6 per cent who obtained advice, 8.4 per cent who sought informal help, 26.7 per cent who dealt with the situation alone, and 25.3 per cent who did nothing.[158]

As regards the more in-depth investigation included in *Paths to Justice* in England and Wales, 107 individuals reported employment problems. Compared to the larger sample, this group was slightly younger, comprised more men than women (where the opposite was true for the whole sample),[159] far fewer had incomes below £10,000, and they had somewhat higher levels of both education and home ownership. Most of the reported employment problems were with the employer, although about 10 per cent concerned colleagues.

In this subset, there were about 7 per cent of 'lumpers' (people who took no action). The reasons most often given for this were that they had left the job in question, that pursuing the matter would not be worth the trouble, that they believed nothing could be done and that they were worried about cost. There was also some indication amongst this group of respondents that they did not want to cause

---

[153] ibid, 36–38.
[154] ibid, 38.
[155] ibid, 42–43. Methodological issues about self-reports are arguably especially relevant regarding harassment given the particular importance of perception and interpretation to whether conduct is characterized in that way. See on this Kritzer (n 1), 267.
[156] Pleasence et al (2010) (n 126), 53.   [157] Pleasence et al (2011) (n 123), 43.
[158] Balmer (2013) (n 126), 47.
[159] See Pleasence (2006) (n 126), Ch 2, generally, for associations in the 2001 and 2004 CSJS samples between problem reporting and demographic etc characteristics (including having a long-standing illness or disability) and specifically 34–35, that men were more likely to report employment problems (although there was gender parity overall).

trouble.[160] In relation to these more serious employment problems, however, there were only about 15 per cent 'self-helpers'.[161] That left nearly eight out of ten individuals[162] who obtained advice, mostly after they themselves had tried to solve the issue directly. This was a relatively large percentage compared to other categories and multiple regression analysis showed employment problems to be associated with an increased likelihood that advice would be obtained.[163] Still, only around one-third with non-trivial employment problems obtained legal advice at some point either from solicitors or law centre-type organizations,[164] despite many wanting this kind of help.[165]

Involvement in formal legal proceedings was reported in respect of about 21 per cent of these more serious employment problems,[166] one-third in the County courts.[167] This looks a large number given other findings cited here. Also, the equivalent figure in Scotland was only 11 per cent.[168] It is also worth recalling that these percentages refer to involvement both as a plaintiff and a defendant, and a court or tribunal decision was far more likely where someone reported being a defendant.

In terms of outcome, aside from the 7 per cent reporting that they took no action, 27 per cent said that they reached agreement, and 14 per cent that there was a court decision or order that had been made. Problems in respect of which advice was obtained were in fact more likely to result in a hearing than an agreement, and as many as 60 per cent of respondents then reported winning. Most strikingly perhaps, reflecting the position with the sample as a whole, 52 per cent with non-trivial justiciable employment problems, all of whom had tried to do something, reported that no resolution had been attained. For the vast majority in this group, the problem was continuing at the time of the research with no prospect of being resolved.[169] This bleak picture was reinforced by even higher rates of non-resolution in Scotland, where 68 per cent of those reporting non-trivial employment problems said that they achieved no agreement or formal resolution, and 5 per cent said they took no action at all.[170]

Multiple regression analysis in the England and Wales study showed that the subset of participants who reported non-trivial employment problems were about one-third less likely to achieve a resolution than participants overall.[171] This was particularly the case where the respondent either did not obtain advice, or obtained 'other' advice (eg from a Citizens Advice Bureau (CAB), where no active assistance was provided.[172] If, however, someone obtained advice from a solicitor or law centre, or from somewhere like a CAB with active assistance given, they had similar chances of achieving a resolution to respondents to the study as a whole.[173]

---

[160] Genn et al (n 108), 109–10.

[161] ibid, 111.   [162] On this group see ibid, 111–13.

[163] ibid, 135 and 140–41. Note that the same was true also for those suffering from accidental injury or work-related illness.

[164] ibid, 112, but compare Genn and Paterson et al (n 125), 119 and 137 that respondents were significantly less likely than in England and Wales to go to solicitors (although based on a rather small sample). Pleasence (2006) (n 126), 115, however found that people will very likely have received advice about law from other institutions like 'advice agencies, trade unions and the police in particular'.

[165] Genn et al (n 108), 113. See also NJ Balmer, A Buck, A Patel, C Denvir, and P Pleasance, 'Knowledge, Capability and the Experience of Rights Problems' (Legal Services Research Centre, 2010) about the phenomenon of people not acting although they wanted to.

[166] Genn et al (n 108), 150–53.   [167] ibid, 157.

[168] Genn and Paterson et al (n 125), 158–59.

[169] See Genn et al (n 108), 158, that only 6 per cent reported that the problem had resolved itself.

[170] Genn and Paterson et al (n 125), 164–65.   [171] Genn et al (n 108), 171.

[172] ibid, 174.   [173] ibid, 175 and 252.

A relatively large proportion (80 per cent) reported finding the experience of sorting their problem out stressful and those with employment problems were amongst the groups reporting the most negative effects.[174] Those who reported employment problems were also one of the subsets of participants in the survey that was least likely to say they had achieved their objectives. Of these objectives, a change in behaviour in the other party (22 per cent) and a job-related aim (14 per cent) were particularly unlikely outcomes.[175] In addition, respondents with employment problems were some of the most pessimistic about achieving their aim, 40 per cent thinking this unlikely or very unlikely.[176] Forty-eight per cent of these individuals said they thought agreements reached were unfair, significantly more than in respect of other problem types.[177]

Turning to the FTWS 2008,[178] this arguably provides the most relevant recent evidence of how working people respond to workplace problems. It is true that it investigated reports of particular workplace experiences in the previous two years rather than justiciable problems. Still, as seen earlier, it disaggregated data about specific employment rights, as well as unfair treatment, discrimination, bullying, and harassment, each of which is legally regulated. The evidence about how people responded is therefore indicative of their reaction to justiciable problems of these types. This survey was also undertaken towards the end of the period from which my sample of judgments was taken, when Genn's study was towards the beginning.

Confirming *Paths to Justice*, nearly three-quarters (72 per cent) of all respondents sought some kind of advice or information in relation to the most serious problem that they reported, a significant increase from 53 per cent for the 2005 FTWS.[179] Most commonly, in 66 per cent of all situations people discussed the matter with their employer while 52 per cent tried to resolve the problem informally. Least common was to make an application to the ET which happened only in 3 per cent of cases.[180] Eleven per cent did absolutely nothing, while another 7 per cent sought information and advice but took no action.[181]

The researchers reached the stark conclusion that '[i]ncreased confidence in knowledge of employment rights has increased the likelihood of employees asking for help and advice but there is no evidence this has brought about a higher proportion of positive outcomes.'[182] This was despite around two-thirds reporting that their most serious problem was over or 'most likely over' by the time of the interview (a similar percentage as had reported the same in 2005).[183] Eighteen per cent overall were found to have left their jobs as a direct result of the issue, rising to 24 per cent of those who left despite resolution of the problem.[184] The analysis suggested that there were overall positive outcomes in only 52 per cent of the situations investigated and negative ones in 47 per cent,[185] leading to the following observation:

There is some evidence here of people not behaving exactly in the way the employment rights framework assumes they will. With the help of managers and local trade union representatives,

---

[174] ibid, 193–94. See further on the very significant, absolutely, and relatively, adverse consequences from employment problems reported in the CSJS in 2001, 2004, and 2006–09 and the CSJPS in 2011 in Pleasence (2006) (n 126), 61–62 and 64–65, Pleasence et al (2010) (n 126), 38–40, Pleasence et al (2011) (n 123), 32, and Balmer (2013) (n 126), 35.

[175] Genn et al (n 108), 197.   [176] ibid, 199.

[177] ibid, 200. They were also one of the groups most likely to express regrets about the way they had handled the situation, 204.

[178] Fevre et al, *Fair Treatment at Work Report 2008* (n 38).

[179] ibid, 2, 126–27, and 150.   [180] ibid, 2, 136, and 150–51.

[181] ibid, 2, 140, and 151.   [182] ibid, 158 and 163.   [183] ibid, 2, 114, and 125.

[184] ibid, 118 and 125.   [185] ibid, 120.

employees are achieving positive results not so much by applying knowledge but by getting others to fix their problems. But perhaps one lesson to be learned for dispute resolution and for wider industrial relations is that positive outcomes are more likely when managers and trade union representatives are involved. No matter how knowledgeable they might be, expert sources do not appear to be effective substitutes. An employee who is forced to rely on these sources—for example because they think that their manager is causing the problem they are experiencing or because there is no trade union representative in the workplace—is at a disadvantage.[186]

There could be no more eloquent contradiction of the commonplace notion that working people easily turn to lawyers and courts to assert legal entitlements. Individuals may well take steps to try to resolve a problem but they are frequently reliant on managers and local trade union representatives to get anywhere.[187]

Work by Pollert has provided insight into the experiences and reactions of more vulnerable workers. In 2004 she conducted a telephone survey with Charlwood, the Unrepresented Worker Survey (URWS), of 501 non-unionized and low-paid people. This explored experience of problems over the previous three years.[188] Women were significantly more likely to report these, reflecting their over-representation amongst vulnerable workers. Workers from ethnic minority communities were also over-represented, and were so beyond their proportion in this work group. This suggested either a higher occurrence of problems or of reporting. The same was also true of workers in medium-sized workplaces (comprising 50 to 249 workers), full-time workers, those with less than six-months' tenure in their jobs, and temporary and agency workers.[189]

Problems with work relations, such as stress and bullying, were the second highest category of reported problems (after pay), comprising 36.7 per cent overall, 34.3 per cent in the respondent's main job, and 15.2 per cent of respondents' main problems, defined in the survey as the one they pushed hardest to solve. All respondents, however, reported multiple issues. Eighty-six per cent reported taking some action, 61 per cent after taking advice. Amongst the 14 per cent who did nothing, pessimism and fear were the main themes in their reported reasons.[190]

People reported trying a range of things, often more than one, with the highest number, 69.3 per cent, indicating they had made an informal approach to their manager and an intriguing 24.2 per cent that they had joined with others to take action. This generally only comprised a discussion about what to do, yet 19 per cent reported going to management as a group. Only 11.6 per cent said they used a formal complaints procedure and only 2 per cent that they brought an ET claim.[191]

The reported outcomes were depressing. Of the people who took action, 47 per cent said there was no result, good or bad. While for 38 per cent there was a conclusion, this translated to only 16 per cent of the sample overall achieving an outcome with which they were satisfied. Many nonetheless remained in their jobs in that only 40 per cent took action and left.[192]

---

[186] ibid, 157.
[187] Contrast, however, the more positive picture from interviews with the most senior person responsible for staff or personnel issues as regards complaints about unequal treatment and discrimination, reported at Perren et al, *Disputes and Challenges* (n 49), 12. See also there at 14 that only one-quarter of respondents who had resolved disputes said they had responded by modifying their practices or procedures.
[188] See Pollert et al (n 128).   [189] ibid, 348–49.   [190] ibid, 350.
[191] ibid, 351.   [192] ibid, 352–53.

It is hard to dissent from Pollert and Charlwood's conclusion that their data indicated 'the current system of individual workplace problem resolution is not delivering fairness at work'.[193] This is made all the more vivid by qualitative evidence gathered by Pollert in telephone interviews with fifty people with problems at work who approached CABs.[194] She summarized stories by workers in small workplaces: 'Each of these narratives illustrated how "abuse" was not a single legal breach, but an ensemble of poor and unfair employment practices, which culminated in dismissal or resignation.'[195] The complexity of what had occurred was palpable, including descriptions of convoluted and sometimes protracted attempts to find a solution[196] and of initial problems in large organizations being compounded by human resources and organizational reactions.[197] From a legal point of view there were recurrent reports of advisers not wanting to pursue constructive dismissal cases, particularly because they were seen as difficult to prove given the need to rely on employees' evidence.[198]

These accounts also added evidence about the myriad reasons people either give up trying to resolve a work problem or never attempt to deal with it in the first place. The lasting impression was that it is surprising that people do as much as they do. Pollert, however, did not find her interviewees' experiences had led them to become socially and politically engaged, concluding instead that 'respondents were cut off from civic society, were not coping with representation at work on their own, turned to an external support … as a last resort, were generally disillusioned and knew nothing about unions or were deterred from seeking them through fear.'[199]

Pollert extrapolated what seem to me two important general points. First, commenting on the inadequacy of external help for problems suggested by her study and echoing the comments above from the FTWS 2008, she contended that poor outcomes were 'fundamentally [due] to the intrinsic weakness of external, remedial support which cannot "shadow" a problem as it unfolds in the complexities of the workplace'.[200] Leading on from this point, she argued that this role 'can only be performed from within, by workplace representation, with enforcement backed by the threat of collective power'. Second, Pollert pointed to the relationship between her respondents' experiences, de-unionization over time, external enforcement of individual rights, and the political popularity of individualized employment regulation. On the one hand, the picture she saw was of 'worker vulnerability associated with a workplace culture in which there has been no challenge to managerial prerogative for over two decades'.[201] On the other hand, while regarding the enforcement of individual rights as vital, she argued that 'doing so with external bodies alone reinforces the individual nature of the problem—which is arguably the reason a neoliberal policy paradigm places its emphasis on them'. Again, this led her to a trade-union-focused prescription, namely that there should be more attention to using individual grievances as the vehicle for union mobilization amongst vulnerable workers.[202] It is interesting to juxtapose this with Genn's finding that where there is recourse to law, it is either legal advice or active help from elsewhere that makes a difference.

---

[193] ibid, 358.
[194] A Pollert, 'The Lived Experience of Isolation for Vulnerable Workers Facing Workplace Grievances in 21st Century Britain' (2010) (31) Economic and Industrial Democracy 62.
[195] ibid, 71.   [196] ibid, generally and in particular at 72, 73, and 76.
[197] ibid, 71–76.   [198] ibid, 71 and 73.   [199] ibid, 79.
[200] ibid, 80. See also T Colling, 'Trade Union Roles in Making Employment Rights Effective' in Dickens (ed) (n 109), 195.
[201] ibid, 82.   [202] ibid.

(3) Socio-legal research into litigation experience with individual labour and equality rights

One of the most remarkable things about the evidence considered so far is how unsatisfyingly things turn out for people who try to resolve a problem at work, whether or not they invoke the law. The focus here is on the experience of the tiny subset who litigate and the even tinier group who reach the stage of a hearing. In principle, this should be the zenith of the system in terms of delivering legal solutions; again, the reality appears much messier.

Before turning to the evidence to this effect, it is important to point out a major gap in the research: I found no systematic enquiry into experience of non-ET employment litigation. This appears to be the corollary of the policy debate ignoring that this kind of litigation exists. A rare nugget of data is Genn's finding that about one-third of respondents to *Paths to Justice* who were involved in employment litigation, whether as claimant or defendant, said this took place in the county courts. What lies behind that number is not clear, however, in that Genn was sceptical about respondents' reliability in identifying different courts.[203]

Another research gap is that the growing body of literature regarding how judges work—sometimes conceived as 'judgecraft'—tends to deal only with the day-to-day practice of adjudication rather than with substantive legal reasoning. It also concentrates on criminal litigation to such an extent that I struggled to find any coverage of employment cases.[204] Indeed, this absence partly explains the design of this project to include investigation of substantive decision-making.

The lack of specific evidence about non-ET employment litigation means that only general findings about civil litigation as a whole may be drawn upon. A striking observation by Genn regarding England and Wales was that in cases involving money (about one-third),[205] the sum claimed more than half of the time was the survey respondent's own calculation of their entitlement. Only 7 per cent reported that a figure had been suggested by a solicitor, and 3 per cent cited media reports as influential.[206] Equally, the amount at stake was generally modest, 90 per cent involving £5,000 or less.[207] Finally, it was notable that perceptions of fairness were most closely associated with respondents who expressed confidence in the judicial system.[208] A specific employment finding, however, was that nearly three-quarters of respondents in England and Wales who had gone through adjudication reported thinking the decision arrived at was fair, often correlated to whether they had won their case or not.[209]

More generally, however, Genn found rather negative attitudes about the justice system in Britain, also reflected in more detailed qualitative interviews.[210] She observed:

Respondents' views about the legal system often conveyed a sense of alienation from the institutions and processes of the law, despite the fact that the courts are regarded as important and that they would be used if something terrible occurred. There is a lack of sympathy with the jargon of the law, the mystifying procedures of the courts, the closed world of the profession, and what is seen as a worrying camaraderie between opposing advocates. Fears about the cost of embarking on legal proceedings and a belief that resources are crucially important to the outcome of litigation lead many people to feel that the courts are largely irrelevant to their lives and the

---

[203] Genn et al (n 108), 151 and 222–23 and also see Genn and Paterson (n 125), 158–59.
[204] See generally S Roach Anleu and K Mack, 'Trial Courts and Adjudication' in Cane and Kritzer (eds) (n 1), 545.
[205] Genn et al (n 108), 186.   [206] ibid, 187–88.   [207] ibid, 187.
[208] ibid, 214.   [209] ibid, 202–04.
[210] ibid, 226 (and 273 about the selection process etc for further qualitative interviewing).

resolution of their problems. The view of judges as inconsistent, old and remote is simply part of this picture.[211]

Even so, reflecting the finding on responses to adjudication of employment cases, she generally found actual experience of the courts etc in England and Wales to have been broadly positive.[212] This contrasted with the finding in Scotland that only 45 per cent of all individuals who had gone through adjudication felt the ultimate decision was fair.[213] The England and Wales finding was also contradicted by the Civil and Social Justice Survey (CSJS) in 2006–09 which observed greater negativity about the prospects of a fair hearing among those who had attended court,[214] as did the two Civil and Social Justice Panel Survey (CSJPS) surveys.[215]

Turning more specifically to employment litigation, there is considerable research available about the ET system. This has been provided in particular by successive government-commissioned Surveys of Employment Tribunal Applications (SETA) conducted in 1987, 1992, 1998, 2003, 2008, and, most recently, in 2013. I primarily draw on the report of the research conducted into cases completed from February 2007 to January 2008 because this is towards the end of the period from which my sample of judgments was taken. I have, however, added some updating in respect of cases completed from January 2012 to January 2013. Both research reports to some extent compared earlier findings, while the latter one provided useful context by starting to track the likely effect of the introduction of ET fees. The results are based on random samples of completed single cases in Great Britain in the respective periods, leading to representative findings about such cases.[216] Computer-assisted telephone interviews took place and were split roughly half and half between claimants and employers. Again, therefore, these are self-report studies but are more reliable than other research of this type because they involved large representative samples and covered claimants and employers in order to garner varied perspectives.

Men and those over forty-five years were found to be over-represented among claimants in both 2008 and 2013, reflecting earlier findings.[217] Also in keeping with earlier data, small employers (with one to twenty-four employees) were over-represented amongst respondents. In 2008, 72 per cent of cases came from the private sector (compared to 82 per cent in 2003), 19 per cent from the public sector (compared to 12 per cent in 2003), and 8 per cent from the non-profit sector (compared to 6 per cent in 2003). These proportions were broadly consistent in the data

---

[211] ibid, 247.   [212] ibid, 246.

[213] Genn and Paterson (n 125), 201–03 and 208. See also 201 and 254 that 57 per cent who settled employment claims saw the agreements reached as unfair, and the higher proportions than in England and Wales who attributed settlement to avoiding 'more bother, trouble, and inconvenience' (58 per cent) and to a general sense of powerlessness (23 per cent).

[214] Pleasence et al (2010) (n 126), 64.

[215] Pleasence et al (2011) (n 123), 53 and Balmer (2013) (n 126), 61.

[216] See M Peters, K Seeds, C Harding, and E Garnett, *Findings from the Survey of Employment Tribunal Applications 2008* (BIS, ERRS No 107, March 2010), 2–4 and C Harding, S Ghezelayagh, A Busby, and N Coleman, *Findings from the Survey of Employment Tribunal Applications 2013* (BIS, Research Series No 177, June 2014), 16–17. The term 'single claims' means they are brought by one person, not that they allege only one wrong. Government statisticians treat these differently to what they call 'multiple claims', in which more than one person sues about the same situation albeit again perhaps alleging more than one cause of action. I could not find where this was spelled out in SETA 2008, although it was implicit, but see 17 in SETA 2013.

[217] The data reported in this paragraph come from the executive summaries of Peters et al (2008) and Harding et al (2013), (both at n 216), with more detailed analyses contained in the body of the reports.

from 2013 and showed a slight over-representation of the private sector in the claims rate. Interestingly, specific over-represented sectors differed in the 2008 study compared with that of 2013: in 2008 this comprised people working in hotels, restaurants, and finance (with under-representation in wholesale and retail, transport, communication, utilities and other services, and public administration). In 2013, over-represented sectors were construction, administrative and support service activities, and human health and social work activities.

In both the 2008 and 2013 studies, many more employers than claimants reported both that they had given their employees statutory statements of terms and conditions of employment and that there were written grievance and disciplinary procedures at their workplaces. Claimant success in the ET was associated in 2008 and 2013 with reports by both claimants and employers of statutory statements not having been given by the employer, with more varied findings about the relationship between claimant success and responses about whether written procedures were followed. In both surveys there were more likely to be reports of documentation and of procedures being followed by large employers than small, and by those in the public and non-profit sectors as opposed to workplaces in the private sector.[218]

In 2008 and 2013, representation was reported more frequently by employers than claimants, and far more before hearings, with legal representation being the most common type.[219] In 2008, 40 per cent of claimants said that they had received neither representation nor advice (up from 34 per cent in 2003), while in 2013 the comparable figure seems to have dropped back to 27 per cent.[220] In 2008, trade union advice or representation was reported for 9 per cent of claimants (rising to 13 per cent in discrimination claims) representing 31 per cent of respondents who were trade union members. The comparable figures from 2003 had, respectively, been 13 per cent and 49 per cent[221] and, perhaps in a sign of the times, I could not find the equivalent data in the 2013 report.[222] The 2013 report did, however, provide an early indication that the introduction of ET fees would have a dramatic impact in that 49 per cent of claimants said their decision to go to the ET would have been influenced even by the initial fee of £250 for more complex claims.[223]

There was differing satisfaction with ET hearings and the system as a whole, often related to outcome. Even so, in 2008, reflecting both Genn's finding and those in SETA 2013, nearly three-quarters of claimants (71 per cent) and employers (73 per cent) who had gone through an ET hearing believed that it gave both sides a fair chance to make their case, while 74 per cent of claimants were satisfied with the workings of the ET system in general. This number, however, fell to 65 per cent for employers.[224] In terms of outcome, there was broad similarity to the findings in 2003, with about three-fifths of all claims settled (39 per cent through the Advisory, Conciliation and Arbitration Service (ACAS) and 19 per cent privately), 12 per cent of claimants successful following a hearing and 8 per cent unsuccessful, 15 per cent of cases withdrawn and the remaining

---

[218] Peters et al (2008), 28–33 and Harding et al (2013), 31–33, (both at n 216).

[219] ibid, 2008, xxii–xxiii and 45–48, and 2013, 6–7 and 42–46.

[220] ibid, 2008, xvi, xxii, 48 and152, Table 5.8, 152, and 2013, 45 and 126, Flowchart 3.1 (combining those who nominated a representative at the start but then had no day to day advice or other representation, with those who never nominated a representative).

[221] ibid, 2008, 54.

[222] But see Harding et al (2013) (n 216), 129, Table 3.12 about the proportions who received different kinds of advice and representation from trade unions.

[223] ibid, 5 and 38–39.

[224] Peters et al (2008) (n 216), xxv and 69–72, and ibid, 12–13 and 80–81.

8 per cent dismissed, disposed of, or with another outcome.[225] Fourteen per cent of the cases that had gone to a full hearing went on to appeal to the EAT, but the numbers were so small that this figure is indicative only.[226]

In both 2008 and 2013, claimants gave a range of reasons for withdrawing, as did employers for settling, 51 per cent of employers saying that settlement was to keep costs down. The vast majority of settlements and tribunal awards included payments of money. In 2008, the mean amount for settlements was £5,431 and the median £2,000, while equivalent figures for tribunal awards were £12,052 and £2,163 (reflecting some very high numbers at the top end).[227] The median numbers corresponded to those for claimants' financial expectations, while the means were inflated by some people giving very high figures.[228] The median for claimant expectations was also not that far from figures cited by employers as the amounts they would settle for, while there was a big disparity in the mean.[229] By 2013, while there were similar patterns overall, there was more disparity in that even the median for claimants' initial hopes was £4,000 when the median award was £3,000.[230]

In 2008, SETA evaluated respondents' satisfaction with the outcome of their case, 59 per cent of claimants and 69 per cent of employers reporting they were satisfied, often again correlated to the outcome.[231] There were also some indications of employers changing policy both in 2008 and in 2013, in particular to ensure existing policies were adhered to and associated with smaller employers.[232] There were at the same time reports in both surveys of various non-financial costs of taking claims, with 36 per cent of claimants in 2008 reporting this had caused stress and depression and, even more strikingly, 63 per cent in 2013 mentioning stress, depression, or being emotionally drained.[233] In 2008, 65 per cent had found new work or become self-employed since the case and 8 per cent were still with the employer against whom the claim was brought. Only 63 per cent of participants involved in discrimination cases, however, were in work.[234] In 2013, of those who had left the employer against whom they were claiming, 76 per cent reported having found a new job, while 8 per cent were still with the respondent employer rising to 16 per cent for discrimination claimants. Again, however, discrimination claimants were overall more likely to be out of work than was the average for all claimants.[235]

An interesting set of issues concerns the nature of disputes that are brought to ETs and in particular how they relate to collective disputes, especially historically given the upward trajectory until recently in individual claims to ETs and the decline in collective conflict that is expressed through industrial action.[236] Many more claims now involve more than one ET jurisdiction (eg claiming both unfair dismissal and unlawful discrimination) and there had until recently been an increase in multiple claims. These group claims to some extent suggest collective issues have been taken up through individual rights litigation. Dix and colleagues, however, rejected the idea that ET claims are 'a new manifestation of the conflict that was previously voiced through collective

---

[225] ibid, 2008, xxv and 78–79. That the percentages come to 101 is presumably because of rounding issues.
[226] ibid, 77. But see Morris (n 109), 19 on the small proportion of EAT appeals that progress.
[227] Peters et al (2008), xxvi and 82–84, and Harding et al (2013), 7, 51–53, and 57 (both n 216). Note that in 2013 the median final offer to settle was £2,500.
[228] ibid, 2008, 85.   [229] ibid, 2008, 86.   [230] Harding et al (2013) (n 216), 66–68.
[231] Peters et al (2008) (n 216), xxvi and 82–89.
[232] ibid, xxvi and 89 (and see at 90 that 8 per cent had taken out insurance against further claims, 17 per cent amongst smaller employers) and see Harding et al (2013) (n 216), 12 and 77.
[233] ibid, 2008, xxvii and 96–97, and 2013, 11, 75, and 217, Table 6.12.
[234] ibid, 2008, 98.   [235] Harding et al (2013) (n 216), 75–76 and 219, Table 6.14.
[236] See generally Dix et al (n 109) and at 185–88.

action':[237] not only are the actors different but also collective action has tended to be about ongoing workplace issues, whereas ET litigation has focused on discrete problems like under-payment of wages, dismissal, and discrimination, often in respect of an employment relationship that has ended. They noted, however, that the rise in multiple claims may herald a change. Further, they saw trade union collectivism and ET litigation as linked on the basis of evidence that, while workplaces with representative voice arrangements involving trade unions report much higher levels of collective disputes and grievances, the average rate of ET claims per 1,000 employees is much lower.[238]

This is an area in which juxtaposing different sources of evidence complicates the matter in that the qualitative analyses from organizational psychologists about bullying,[239] as well as Fevre and colleagues' study of 'trouble at work'[240] all pointed to collective conceptions and concerns being bound up in problems that are articulated in superficially individual terms. This suggests the existence of interactions between individual and collective grievances even if previously collective disputes have not metamorphosed into ET claims. The point is that the same dissent may now be framed differently, such that what is expressed in individualist terms might previously have been raised and dealt with collectively. This would be unsurprising in circumstances where there is no collective outlet for so many working people, and individualism and individual labour rights provide means, discursively and practically, to assert workplace entitlements. It also raises the possibility, explored further in my interview study and overall conclusions, that organizational adaptation to individual labour and equality rights may interfere with remaining collective systems for dealing with employee relations.

Beyond these systemic overviews of ET litigation, an unusual study was commissioned by the government qualitatively to analyse judgments in race discrimination claims.[241] The sample was gathered with the assistance of the Employment Tribunals Service (ETS) and Employment Market Analysis and Research (EMAR), the research division within the employment relations section of the then Department of Trade and Industry. While not a fully randomized sample, there was random selection of cases.[242]

The main aim was 'to identify any persistent patterns in the written judgments of Race Relations Act ... cases that might explain why these claims are relatively unlikely to succeed at Tribunal'.[243] This was done by coding for themes drawn from earlier research as potential reasons for claims failing.[244] The overall finding was that there were no clear patterns. Factors confirmed to be key to success or failure were the nature of evidence presented, the location of the burden of proof, the weight given by ETs to judgments of credibility, and the relationship between discrimination and unfair dismissal claims. While these extrapolations from the case law seem pretty self-evident, it is perhaps more interesting that no significance was found to attach, first, to the relationships between

[237] ibid, 187.
[238] ibid, 197–98. See also L Dickens and M Hall, 'The Impact of Employment Legislation: Reviewing the Research' in L Dickens, M Hall, and S Wood, *Review of Research into the Impact of Employment Legislation* (DTI, ERRS 45, Oct 2005), 31.
[239] See text to ns 26–27.   [240] See text to ns 92–95, 99–100, and 103.
[241] A Brown, A Erskine, and D Littlejohn, *Review of Judgments in Race Discrimination Employment Tribunal Cases* (DTI, ERRS 64, 2006).
[242] ibid, 11 and 22–24.   [243] ibid, 10.
[244] ibid, 24–27. The potential reasons for race claims disproportionately failing were particularly drawn from the studies of the operation of the ET system in, respectively, race and sex discrimination cases, in AM Leonard, *Judging Inequality: The Effectiveness of the Industrial Tribunal System in Sex Discrimination and Equal Pay Cases* (Cobden Trust, 1987), and C McCrudden, D Smith, and C Brown, *Racial Justice at Work: The Enforcement of the 1976 Race Relations Act in Employment* (Policy Studies Institute, 1991).

criteria of direct and indirect discrimination and between racial and any other forms of discrimination; second, to how the tribunal interpreted the justifiability of indirect discrimination; third, to references by the tribunal to the intention and motivation of alleged discriminators; fourth, to the type of representation and the tribunal's interaction with unrepresented complainants; or fifth, to the ability of complainants to obtain relevant information from respondents.[245]

There were more interesting findings in a recent study involving statistical analysis of 22 per cent of sexual harassment claims that had gone to hearing before the ET in the period from 1995–2005.[246] The final sample was chosen from a random selection because the case data were complete, but it was also ensured that there was no weighting towards successful or unsuccessful claims.[247] The writers developed a series of hypotheses about what might determine success or failure, particularly based on preconceptions ETs might be expected to have about sexual harassment, factors that would be anticipated to influence whether claimants were believed and the effect of having women judges.[248]

The majority of hypotheses were not supported. Those that straightforwardly received no support and gave rise to no other findings were, first, that people (the vast majority of claimants being women) who had resigned prior to the claim rather than being sacked would be more likely to succeed; second, that the same would be true of those alleging sexual harassment by colleagues above them in the organizational hierarchy rather than on the same level; third, that cases about either sexual coercion or unwanted sexual attention would have a greater chance of succeeding than those about gender harassment more generally; fourth, that allegations of a higher number of incidents over time would be associated with winning; fifth, that the rate of success would increase over the years of the study; and, finally, that the presence and number of women on the judging panel would be positively associated with claimants succeeding.[249]

The researchers had also hypothesized that claimants from professional and managerial occupations would be more likely to be successful. This was also not supported, but it was found that those in elementary occupations, like cleaning and labouring, were eight times less likely to win than claimants in sales and customer service occupations.[250] In a result that will be no surprise to lawyers but that contradicted the researchers' hypotheses, the fewer claims brought in addition to that for sexual harassment, the more likely the claimant was to win. In fact, each additional claim reduced the odds of success in the sexual harassment claim by 50 per cent.[251] At the same time, it was confirmed that a claimant's initial response was important, with those who 'sought emotional support through friends and relatives but took no assertive steps within the organization to stop the behaviour' disadvantaged: such claimants were 92 per cent less likely to have won their case compared to those who had confronted their employer.[252] Where the respondent but not the claimant was represented, the claim was also significantly more likely to lose than if neither were represented.[253]

These results are, like the study of judgments of race discrimination cases, as interesting for what they *did not* confirm as for what they did, reassuringly suggesting that ideas about ET preconceptions may not be borne out in practice. The fact that the presence of women on the judging panel made no difference is also notable.[254] In some ways this general picture makes it more disturbing that a passive reaction by a sexual harassment

[245] Brown et al (n 241), 43.
[246] P Rosenthal and A Budjanovcanin, 'Sexual Harassment Judgments by British Employment Tribunals 1995–2005: Implications for Claimants and their Advocates' (2011) 49 BJIR 236–57.
[247] ibid, 245–46.   [248] ibid, 239–45.   [249] ibid, 250.   [250] ibid, 248.
[251] ibid, 250.   [252] ibid, 248–50.   [253] ibid, 250.   [254] ibid, 245.

claimant was found to be associated with losing. The worry is that this common response by working women to sexual harassment, as suggested also by qualitative evidence surveyed earlier, is being misconceived by ETs as undermining their credibility.[255] More detailed investigation is necessary, however, to find out whether this really is the case,[256] as well as to learn what is what is behind the failure rate for some low-skilled claimants compared to those from certain other occupations.[257]

Another useful strain of research about ET litigation comes from two qualitative studies about claimants' experiences in ET discrimination cases.[258] The first concerned race discrimination and involved forty in-depth interviews with people who had, on the one hand, settled or withdrawn claims at various stages and, on the other hand, gone through to a full hearing, both successfully and unsuccessfully. The second involved similar interviews with fifteen claimants from each category who had litigated, again to various stages, about first, sexual orientation discrimination, and second, religion or belief discrimination. The samples were constructed to represent a range of litigation experiences and to include interviewees with a variety of social and demographic identities.[259] The participants came from many social groups and had widely differing life experiences.[260] The studies naturally did not claim to be representative and only reported claimants' sides of the stories. They provide a valuable perspective, however, not least because my interviews did not directly obtain claimants' points of view.

The regularity with which certain themes emerged in the data, often in both studies, was noticeable.[261] There was frequently great complexity in the descriptions of the antecedents to claims, often spanning an extended period of time. This covered the behaviour at issue, managerial reactions, claimants' attempts to secure internal resolution, and the ultimate triggers for ET proceedings, which were often perceived as a last resort. The researchers in the race study concluded:

The common theme is that challenging the behaviour of others, especially those in a more senior position, damages the employment relationship to a significant degree. At this point, employer and employee take up their positions, and become increasingly entrenched in them. It appears that a 'line in the sand' is drawn when an individual tells their employer they feel they are being discriminated against. Both sides believe that they are right, and the conflict builds, so that it cannot be resolved within the organization, even with use of the grievance procedure. In fact, on occasion, the disciplinary procedure is used against the individual. (notes omitted)[262]

---

[255] ibid, 251.

[256] Other factors might independently have determined failure, meaning this result is suggestive of causation but cannot prove it. Detailed analysis of the judgments would be necessary to know for sure and the researchers noted at 254 that this is needed as a complement to their work.

[257] The researchers' analysis of what might lie behind this was at 250–51.

[258] J Aston, D Hill, and ND Tackey, *The Experience of Claimants in Race Discrimination Employment Tribunal Claims* (DTI, ERRS 55, 2006), and A Denvir, A Broughton, J Gifford, and D Hill, *The Experiences of Sexual Orientation and Religion or Belief Employment Tribunal Claimants* (ACAS, 2007).

[259] Aston et al, ibid, 1–2 and 4, and Denvir et al, ibid, 12.

[260] Aston et al, ibid, 4–6, and Denvir et al, ibid, 12–14.

[261] See also the echo of a number of these in qualitative evidence about judicial mediation of ET discrimination cases in A Boon, P Urwin, and V Karuk, 'What Difference Does It Make? Facilitative Judicial Mediation of Discrimination Cases in Employment Tribunals' (2011) 40 ILJ 45, namely at 55 and 57 about the impact of claimants' emotional and psychological health, at 55 and 60 on some judicial mediators perceiving respondents to make cynical use of the mediation process, eg to assess the claimant, and at 68–69 and 71 on claimants' ambivalent feelings about outcomes and significantly fewer expressing satisfaction than amongst employers in the study.

[262] Aston et al (n 258), 135 and more generally at 130 and 134–37. There was notably comment at 134 and 137 about the complexity and variety of thought processes regarding whether race was behind treatment and whether to speak out, including because of difficulty in interpreting what had happened.

Certainly there were frequent indications of missed opportunities to resolve a difficulty, of unconstructive managerial reactions, including avoiding the problem and characterizing the complainant as the trouble-maker, and of internal procedures that claimants perceived as ineffective and as causing the situation to deteriorate.[263] Reminiscent of Fevre and colleagues' more recent findings, bullying and harassment were a particular issue in respect of sexual orientation claims,[264] with reports of grievances about these ignored in parallel disciplinary procedures. The researchers speculated that a key characteristic of these claims may explain this, in that interviewees 'had tolerated, or put up with, a degree of discrimination or bullying or harassment in the workplace for an extended period of time'.[265] This was gloomily suggestive of the finding cited earlier that passive reactions to sexual harassment, however common and understandable, might make an eventual legal challenge more difficult to win. Amidst all this, rare accounts stood out of situations being constructively tackled.[266]

The research also described highly nuanced reasoning and reflection about whether to take ET proceedings, with a strong emphasis on seeking justice rather than money. The sense claimants had of the justice of their cause seemed to give them optimism about the outcome of litigating.[267] This made their narratives of how they experienced proceedings even more perturbing. Many accounts conveyed how bewildering, frightening, alienating, disappointing, and stressful claimants found bringing a case, and this was apparent through all stages of the litigation.[268] One comment suffices:

A Black Caribbean male claimant argued that the process needed to be less formal, less reliant on complex legal terms and on adversarial principles. He felt that an inquisitorial rather than adversarial process would better serve claimants taking ET cases against employers. He said: 'Explain it in layman's terms; don't put us up to be slaughtered. We're made to look a fool. The initial act of discrimination may not have been enough to cause mental damage, it's the battle after that compounds and destroys the individual.' (Settled case)[269]

General as the problems were, there were especially worrying descriptions in the race study of the difficulty, often impossibility, of finding representation, of struggling to cope with preliminary and final hearings, and of being overwhelmed in settlement negotiations and discussions about withdrawing from proceedings. Disquieting reports were also given of race claimants feeling their deteriorating health had given them no option but settlement.[270]

[263] Aston et al, ibid, Ch 2 generally and 124–25 and Denvir et al (n 258), Chs 5 and 6 generally, 149, and 156–57. See also the qualitative US study of organizational experience with sexual harassment grievances and their effect on understandings of legality reported in AM Marshall, 'Idle rights: Employees' Rights Consciousness and the Construction of Sexual Harassment Policies' (2005) 39 Law and Soc'y Rev 83. This comprised interviews in one organization with women reporting experience of 'unwanted sexual attention in the workplace' and a randomized survey of other women from the same workplace. The subjects' reports about their reactions resonated with findings reported at the text to notes 34–36 above, and those about the operation of grievance procedures with what was reported here. Marshall extrapolated that in enacting grievance procedures, women and supervisors constructed an internal legality that offered only limited protection to women's rights. Despite adoption of an open-textured, broad, and flexible organizational policy about sexual harassment, supervisors were said to operate this restrictively and adversarially, eg taking sides with the alleged harasser, reading non-existent requirements into the document and restrictively interpreting the conduct covered. The respondents in turn reacted by 'lumping' many situations, sometimes 'self-helping' and complaining only about the most severe or troubling forms of sexual conduct.
[264] Denvir et al, ibid, 51–53, 62–63, and 155–56.   [265] ibid, 67.
[266] Aston et al (n 258), 68–69, 74–75, and 121.
[267] ibid, Ch 3 generally and 125–26 and 145.
[268] ibid, Chs 3–6 generally and 126–28, and Denvir et al (n 258), Chs 7 and 8 generally and 157.
[269] Aston et al (n 258), 115.   [270] ibid, 70–71 and 90–91.

The multilayered reasoning that led people to litigate was also reflected in complicated retrospective feelings regardless of whether they had won or lost. Frequent expressions of regret at how things had turned out were sometimes mixed with more positive feelings about, for example, taking a stand.[271] In the sexual orientation and religion or belief study it was observed that '[a]lthough many claimants regretted settling and had misgivings over the outcomes of their claims, it is an important finding that only one claimant regretted pursuing a claim against their employer. For many, the employment tribunal system allowed an important and symbolic action against unchecked and unresolved discrimination.'[272] Nonetheless a combination of negative and positive came across in what these claimants said about whether they would litigate again and how they would advise others faced with analogous situations.[273]

A major theme in discussions of what claimants had endured was the central importance of having good legal representation, both to navigate the ET system and to meet their respondent on some kind of equal footing. In the race study this echoed strong feelings that power imbalance between claimants and employers was built into the system, allied to concerns about the homogeneous group composition of judging panels[274] and for some a more general loss of trust.[275] There were similar concerns about lack of legal representation and imbalance of power among sexual orientation and religion or belief claimants,[276] with some doubting the appropriateness of panel composition.[277]

Finally, accounts of ongoing negative consequences to claimants, whatever the legal outcome, were harrowing.[278] It was not always possible to ascertain whether these flowed from either the original experience or the litigation, while bad consequences could be leavened by positive ones, as explained above. Still, it was evident that many felt they had paid a very high price for bringing their case. The complexity of claimants' situations was eloquently expressed in the following from the race study:

She felt that despite winning her case she had suffered both financially and emotionally but that it was important to make a stand to try and change things in the future: 'If you feel strongly and you want justice and you've been through all the different various stages of trying to sort the problem out then you will never ever have peace until you get what you're working for. If it's something that will happen to other people like racism, then you have to make a stand and the cost to you comes second to what you hope to achieve for the people following you. The fact that I don't feel that I've been able to achieve much is not from the lack of fighting or still fighting for it.'[279]

At the same time, the sexual orientation and religion or belief study concluded that '[a]lthough examples of despair were evident in the experiences of both sexual orientation and religion or belief claimants, those that took claims based on sexual orientation discrimination seemed to be particularly devastated by the experience.'[280]

---

[271] ibid, 72–76, 85–86, 90–92, and 127–28.
[272] Denvir et al (n 258), 157, and further on this aspect of the study at 141–44.
[273] Aston et al (n 258), 116–20, and also ibid, 145–46.
[274] Aston et al (n 258), 86–88, 128, and 149–50.
[275] ibid, 114–15. See also Denvir et al (n 258), 159.   [276] Denvir et al (n 258), 129–31.
[277] ibid, 122 and 126. Note however that there was little scope for such views here, only 1 sexual orientation claimant (118), and 2 religion or belief claimants (124), having gone to a full hearing. Comments therefore were mostly about preliminary hearings.
[278] Aston et al (n 258), Ch 8 generally and 129, and also ibid, Ch 9 generally and 158–60.
[279] Aston et al (n 258), 118.   [280] Denvir et al (n 258), 158.

Perhaps most strikingly of all was the sense of ET litigation having imposed significant harms even where people had won and in some instances recovered substantial sums.[281]

The researchers in the race study persuasively analysed the phenomena of disappointment despite winning, as related to claimants' understanding of the justice they had sought:

> To many of these claimants, the concept of justice meant their employer being publicly reprimanded and being made to change their practices. Their employer had seemingly not been prevented from acting in the same way again towards them or others. Claimants were particularly aggrieved when despite having won their cases, individual perpetrators remained unpunished, and continued to work in the same position and with the same responsibilities for the employer. In essence, it seems that the Employment Tribunal is simply not equipped to bring about the kinds of judgments that claimants were hoping for. As a result, even when claimants won at Tribunal, they did not always feel that justice had been done.[282]

The researchers also perceived claimants' feeling that an appropriate resolution had not been achieved as retrospectively influencing how they viewed the entire process and the fairness of the system. This was arguably confirmed in the sexual orientation and religion or belief study by the emphasis participants put on justice rather than financial compensation, and the interrelation this had with feelings of regret about settlements. The following comment about the sexual orientation sample voices this well: 'Without exception, claimants were dismayed that money became a focus rather than justice and disdainful about the language of money overtaking the language of right and wrong.'[283] A further depressing postscript comes from recent qualitative BIS research showing that only 49 per cent of ET claimants awarded compensation received the full sum, 35 per cent receiving nothing at all.[284]

There were also consistent findings in a recent interview study tracking the experiences of ET claimants helped by a CAB.[285] This was a pilot study for a larger ongoing project[286] and difficulties in recruitment meant there were only ten participants. The individuals came from the group that the researchers saw as likely to find the ET system most problematic in neither being able to afford legal representation nor having access to trade union help.[287] They drew the following from what they were told by these vulnerable workers:

> They see highly formalised, court-like procedures that discourage participation. Facing legal teams of well-financed employers, such workers experience ... ETs as *barriers* to justice. Settlements reached pre-Tribunal leave them without jobs, inadequately compensated and often traumatised by the experience. (emphasis in the original; notes omitted)[288]

---

281 See the example given of this phenomenon at Aston et al (n 258), 104.

282 ibid, 148. See very similarly in Boon et al (n 261), at 71.

283 Denvir et al (n 258), 142 and more generally at 142–44.

284 IFF Research, *Payment of Employment Tribunal Awards* (BIS, Nov 2013), 6 and 27 ,and the discussion by the President of ETs in Scotland, Shona Simon, at *Senior President of Tribunals' Annual Report* (n 111), 83–84, in particular noting that the combined effect of non-recovery and ET fees may be further to deter claims.

285 N Busby and M McDermont, 'Workers' Marginalized Voices and the ET System: Some Preliminary Findings' (2012) 41 ILJ 166.

286 The overall project is called 'Advice Agencies: New Sites of Legal Consciousness', one strand of which is on 'Citizens Advice Bureaux and Employment Disputes'. See further <http://www.bristol.ac.uk/law/research/centres-themes/aanslc/cab-project/> (last visited 28 April 2015).

287 N Busby and M McDermont (n 285), 170–71.   288 ibid, 167.

(4) Socio-legal research into organizational experience with individual labour and equality rights

The evidence surveyed has considered the impact of litigation but little has been said about organizational reactions. In general it is important to keep in mind lessons from US explorations of the translation of legal norms into organizations. These have demonstrated several means by which worker-protective rules can be reconfigured, for example through internal dispute resolution procedures, to fit organizational ways of being and to advance managerial goals.[289] There have also been investigations of the extent to which lawyers, HR professionals, and others mediate organizational reactions to law, and the subsequent feedback of such influence into the law itself through adjudication and legislation. A particularly apposite example is the work of Dobbin and Kelly,[290] which found that personnel specialists had been more influential than lawyers on organizational responses to developments in sexual harassment law, notwithstanding the shaky foundations (including legally) of their prescriptions. This lead to widespread organizational adoption of training schemes and formal processes, despite it being wholly unclear that these offered any legal protection, and that grievance procedures in fact created legal risks. Later case law developments, however, came to recognize that formal procedures could in certain circumstances shield employers from liability.

Edelman derived her theory of legal endogeneity from the observation of such patterns in the US. Recognizing that law neither straightforwardly produces organizational responses, nor that organizations construct future enactments, she suggested that legal rules and organizational practices rather 'emerge in tandem', with the boundaries between the two worlds becoming 'increasingly ambiguous' as common underlying belief systems permeate both.[291] In Edelman's account this is explained by ideas of rationality, morality, and legality flowing freely between the overlapping socio-legal field and that of regulated organizations. Practices in the legal field thereby help to constitute ideas of legitimacy in the organizational field and vice versa. Consequently she argued that this 'dynamic interplay ... gives rise to socially constructed legalities in both arenas'.[292]

As to the influence of law more generally on organizational life, there is a relative dearth in the UK of empirical research to which this study in part responds.[293] The legal rules administered by the ordinary courts in particular are pretty much entirely ignored. Still, there is useful work, not least by Dickens and Hall in the 2005 review of knowledge about the impact of New Labour's changes to employment.[294] This reported a series of effects from interventions including the National Minimum Wage Act 1998 and the EU-inspired Working Time Regulations 1998. Earlier research on unfair dismissal and successive Workplace Employment Relations Surveys (WERS) had already

---

[289] See eg LB Edelman, HS Erlanger, and J Lande, 'Internal Dispute Resolution: The Transformation of Civil Rights in the Workplace' (1993) 27 Law and Soc'y Rev 497 and LB Edelman, S Riggs Fuller, and I Mara-Drita, 'Diversity Rhetoric and the Managerialization of Law' (2001) 106 Am J Sociol 1589.

[290] F Dobbin and EL Kelly, 'How to Stop Harassment: Professional Construction of Legal Compliance in Organizations' (2007) 112 Am J Sociol 1203. See also LB Edelman, SE Abraham, and HS Erlanger, 'Professional Construction of Law: The Inflated Threat of Wrongful Discharge' (1992) 26 Law and Society Review 47 and LB Edelman, C Uggen, and HS Erlanger, 'The Endogeneity of Legal Regulation: Grievance Procedures as Rational Myth' (1999) 105 Am J Sociol 406.

[291] LB Edelman and MC Suchman, 'The Legal Environments of Organizations' (1997) 23 Annual Review of Sociology 479, 502.

[292] ibid.   [293] Dickens and Hall (n 238).

[294] This did not however cover post-1997 changes to the law on industrial action and internal union affairs, ibid, 10.

demonstrated 'the formalisation of workplace discipline, with a growth in disciplinary and grievance procedures following the introduction of unfair dismissal legislation'.[295] As regards equality legislation, while noting the limited direct use of the law, Dickens and Hall pointed out that survey evidence suggested various indirect effects, for example on the existence and coverage of equal opportunities policies.[296] Their sobering overall conclusion was, however, that '[e]vidence of continuing segregation and disadvantage in employment ... suggests that ... the impact of the legislation has been limited in terms of changing distributional outcomes.'[297]

The Government Equality Office (GEO) recently commissioned research into the organizational impact of equality law and particularly the Equality Act 2010.[298] This consisted of telephone interviews with the most senior person responsible for staff or personnel issues in 1,811 organizations in England, Scotland, and Wales, with the final dataset weighted to reflect the geographical distribution of workplaces. The study confirmed widespread adoption of formal equality policies, but in a recurrent pattern in which the overlapping categories of micro-firms (two to nine employees) and the private sector reported similar and lower levels of attention to equality and equality legislation.[299] The adoption of formal policies, as well as having a conscious approach to equality, was said by over 90 per cent of those interviewed to have been in part a response to legislation, and by similar proportions to have been influenced by owners' and managers' moral views. By contrast, only 11 per cent of respondents identified staff and trade union pressure as influential.[300]

There was considerable backing for equality legislation with 89 per cent of respondents expressing support to some extent.[301] In contrast, the law was perceived to have less relevance to respondents' own organizations, especially amongst those from micro-employers and the private sector.[302] Legislation in relation to some groups, including the disabled, attracted lower levels of support. These differences were found across the board but were particularly marked for those from micro-employers and the private sector.[303]

These data were further linked to patchy evidence of the Equality Act (EqA) 2010 having made an impact in the year or so after it was enacted, with increased awareness of and information-seeking about the legislation related to organization size and being in the public sector.[304] This led the researchers to observe that: 'the widening scope of

---

[295] ibid, 19. Dickens led the important early study in which this effect was observed and analysed, reported in L Dickens, *A Study of Unfair Dismissal and the Industrial Tribunal System* (Blackwell, 1985), especially at Chapter 8. Compare the US-focused overview of evidence about grievance procedure adoption in AJS Colvin, 'Grievance Procedures in Non-Union Firms' in WK Roche, P Teague, and AJS Colvin (eds), *The Oxford Handbook of Conflict Management in Organizations* (OUP, 2014).

[296] Dickens and Hall (n 238), 22.   [297] ibid.

[298] K Perren, S Roberts, B Stafford, and D Hirsch, *Evaluation of the Implementation of the Equality Act 2010, Report 1, Organizational Approaches to Equality* (GEO, 2012), *Report 2, Awareness and Impact of the Equality Act* (GEO, 2012) and K Perren et al, *Disputes and Challenges* (n 49).

[299] Perren et al, *Organizational Approaches*, ibid, 6, 10, 24, 26, and 28. See here that 48 per cent of micro employers and 53 per cent of private employers reported having a written policy on equality issues as opposed to 96 per cent of larger organizations, 89 per cent in civil society, and 86 per cent in the public sector. Further, there are more micro organizations in the private than the public sector.

[300] ibid, 7, 14–15, and 26–27. See that again the outliers for reporting of trade union or staff influence were large and public sector organizations at, respectively, 26 per cent and 18 per cent, of workplaces, when the equivalent figures for other categories hovered around 10 per cent.

[301] ibid, 21–22. See also Perren et al, *Awareness and Impact* (n 298), 7 and 13.

[302] Perren et al, *Organizational Approaches* (n 299), 23.

[303] Perren et al, *Awareness and Impact* (n 298), 14–18.

[304] ibid, Perren et al, *Organizational Approaches* (n 299), 7, 19–20, and 24 (but see there that multivariate analysis showed information seeking behaviour was not significantly linked to being in the

equality legislation may have had most impact on those with the highest prior level of engagement'.[305] Even so, they also observed that 'the link between size and action seems to be weaker than the link between size and awareness. This may imply that within firms there is a degree of risk aversion to being more active about promoting equality.'[306] There were also data which indicated startlingly poor knowledge of the Act and its implications, for example about the aspects of identity that are covered[307] and the areas of organizational life affected by it. While nearly half of all respondents saw the law's relevance to recruitment, 24 per cent were unable to think of any situations to which it applied.[308] Indeed, 34 per cent of respondents had never heard of the Act and another 32 per cent said they knew nothing about it.[309] This perhaps makes it less surprising that 84 per cent felt that the Act had not raised the importance of equality matters in their organization and 77 per cent that it had not affected their operations or practices. The limited response to the Act evidenced by these findings is somewhat astounding, and it appears even more so when it is recalled that this is the picture of organizational engagement with law that comes from the most senior people with responsibility for personnel and human resources.

More generally, Dickens has theorized[310] that greater effects are to be expected from laws that require proactive, collective, structural change from employers. That said, she observed that UK law imposes largely passive and individualized obligations, compliance with which requires little of employers.[311] Her conclusion is that law often provides a weak lever for organizational change, reinforced by the fact that even losing an ET claim frequently has no wider effect even on the employers immediately concerned.[312] She has contended that this general approach is potentially counterproductive to employers, however, in that they may only be alerted to a problem when they become embroiled in proceedings. At that point the focus will not be on 'exploring and addressing underlying workplace practice issues'.[313] Even the formalization effect observed regarding unfair dismissal and equality law has not clearly been associated to changes in practice, instead often resulting in a gap between the existence of policies and their use.[314]

Dickens and Hall also related causes for the variation observed in the impact of law.[315] Naturally legal interventions interact with a range of internal and external influences on employers, as the US evidence about competing HR and legal advice demonstrated. Purcell has illuminated the different approaches that can be taken by organizations.[316] His starting point was the inevitability that setting and achieving business goals will be prioritized. The effect is that protecting labour rights is rarely given much attention and certainly not for its intrinsic value. The increase in businesses that

---

public sector as opposed to being large). Note also at 13 and 27 that there was some evidence of policies being updated in response to the EqA 2010, but not that the legislation had led to adoption.

[305] ibid, 7 and 27.   [306] Perren et al, *Awareness and Impact* (n 298), 9 and further at 29.
[307] Perren et al, *Organizational Approaches* (n 299), 17 and 27.   [308] ibid, 18 and 27.
[309] Perren et al, *Awareness and Impact* (n 298), 19.
[310] Dickens, 'Fairer Workplaces' (n 114), 211–15.
[311] See L Barmes and K Malleson, 'The Legal Profession as Gatekeeper to the Judiciary: Design Faults in Measures to Enhance Diversity' (2011) 74 MLR 245–71 for the argument that even equality law only asks 'tempered passivity' of employers (and others).
[312] Dickens, 'Fairer Workplaces' (n 114), 213 and see above at pp 35 and 41.
[313] ibid, 212. See also C Rayner and K McIvor, *Research Report on the Dignity at Work Project* (Univ of Portsmouth, 2008), 84 on employers reporting various ways that legal advice had prevented them taking the initiative in addressing bullying and harassment.
[314] Dickens, 'Fairer Workplaces' (n 114), 214–15.
[315] Dickens and Hall (n 238), 29–31.
[316] J Purcell, 'Management and Employment Rights' in Dickens (ed) (n 109).

rely on financial rather than central control, influenced by the growth of private equity companies, has moreover tended to marginalize labour standards further.[317] Against this background Purcell argued that four strategic HR goals influence the stance taken at the top level: achieving cost-effective labour, organizational flexibility, social legitimacy, and preserving managerial prerogative. The social legitimacy goal is arguably the counterweight to the others. Pressures towards this include but are not limited to law. Purcell made what seems to me an important point that other 'normative' pressures:

affect, and are influenced by, the way members of society think and behave. Managers are no different from others in being citizens, consumers and parents save, perhaps, that in larger companies with graduate recruitment programmes they can be expected to have a higher level of education and greater awareness of societal issues.[318]

In terms of structural features affecting organizational reactions to employment rights, Purcell related first, that size is important. In spite of the SETA findings about small employers attracting more claims, longitudinal WERS data have shown that medium-sized firms over time have disproportionately faced ETs. This belies stereotypical ideas about the approach of micro and small firms to employment rights[319] and may to some extent be explained by the transition from the intimacy and informality of some small firms to the formal systems associated with larger firms. Second, as noted regarding ET litigation, the presence of trade unions matters. Active trade union presence has been found significantly to affect compliance by employers with individual employment rights and to aid internal resolution.[320] Colling describes this as 'organic enforcement' in which trade unions actively communicate and interpret statutory rights within workplaces, at least initially without the involvement of formal legal institutions.[321] Ironically, however, this is associated with more complaints, disputes, and more negative subjective perceptions of working relationships by managers and employees. This makes unsurprising Purcell's observation that '[traditional pluralist acceptance of trade unions] is profoundly out of fashion with most, but not all, top managers in the private sector, including many of those in HR where the current, unitarist rhetoric is "engagement" ... and the shades of paternalism it implies'.[322] Third, high labour turnover is linked to less regard for employment rights. This may not matter much to some employers and pressure on retention will weaken generally in poor economic conditions. Still, there are employers, perhaps increasingly, that have business reasons to avoid labour turnover, for example because workers have valuable skills and experience and exercise considerable discretion. Finally, the use of outsourcing and offshoring is important. As the trend grows to reduce the core of workers and increase those on the periphery, whether in private or public employment, there is a linked bifurcation between good practice for some workers and the transfer of responsibility to third parties for others.[323]

---

[317] See further E Applebaum, R Batt, and I Clark, 'Implications of Financial Capitalism for Employment Relations Research: Evidence from Breach of Trust and Implicit Contracts in Private Equity Buy Outs' (2013) 51 BJIR 498, and E Applebaum and R Batt, *Private Equity at Work: When Wall Street Manages Main Street* (Russell Sage Foundation, 2014).

[318] Purcell (n 316), 164.

[319] See generally P Edwards, 'Employment Rights in Small Firms' in Dickens (ed) (n 109), particularly 146–47 about the approach of small firms to employment rights and 147–51 on variations between ideal types.

[320] W Brown, S Deakin, D Nash, and S Oxenbridge, 'The Employment Contract: From Collective Procedures to Individual Rights' (2000) 38 BJIR 611, and T Colling, 'Trade Union Roles in Making Employment Rights Effective' in L Dickens (ed) (n 109).

[321] ibid, Colling, 194–95.   [322] Purcell (n 316), 166 (notes omitted).

[323] ibid, 168.

These different background considerations coalesce in different management styles, with 'commitment' or 'relational' approaches directed at establishing long-term, high-trust working relationships, and 'command and control' stances more short-term and directional. Neither model favours collectivism for an increasing number of employers, whether through trade union or other entities. Even so, there remain workplaces with both commitment styles of management and cooperative relationships with collective representatives, in which most concern may be expected for the procedural, distributive, and interactional justice of decision-making about employment rights.

The role of line managers regarding employment rights has grown in importance since the 1990s and raises various questions.[324] An effect is that line managers' actions are frequently implicated in problems escalating. Typical issues include managers being overloaded with work, HR-related tasks being neglected and given low priority, and managers feeling unsupported in this aspect of their jobs, especially where the law is involved. This has been reflected in recent findings that line managers often receive neither relevant training nor appraisal about the people-oriented features of their jobs. Much in this regard would seem to depend on whether HR staff take either a positive 'custodian of best practice' approach to employment rights (and more generally) or whether they act defensively as 'gatekeepers', with their main aim being reactively to protect the organization. The former is more associated with larger, better-run firms, likely to have commitment-style management and perhaps sophisticated collective relationships. The latter suggests an HR function without the standing and authority to do more.

Very recent government-commissioned research has specifically investigated private sector employers' accounts of the impact of employment regulation[325] through in-depth qualitative interviewing within forty organizations spread across a range of industries and locations.[326] This made interesting and perhaps unexpected findings, at least for successive governments engaged in complicated, allegedly de-regulatory, legal interventions.[327] Those interviewed indicated that employment regulation had little effect on HR practices and that generally HR staff did what they saw as best for their businesses.[328] Employment regulation was, however, viewed as necessary to ensuring that employees were treated fairly,[329] with legal complexity appearing significantly to account for such negative attitudes as were expressed.

The researchers did report that for some employers, especially amongst micro-, small-, and medium-sized private sector firms, informal practices and a lack of internal HR expertise led to anxiety. It was this which caused a perception of regulation as burdensome, notwithstanding reports of its minimal day-to-day impact.[330] At the same time, beliefs amongst smaller businesses that law was too complex and fluid for them to understand reinforced passivity towards it.[331]

---

[324] See further P Teague and W Roche, 'Line Managers and the Management of Workplace Conflict: Evidence from Ireland' (2012) 22 Human Resource Management Journal 235, and J Purcell, 'Line Managers and Workplace Conflict' in Roche et al (eds) (n 295), 233.

[325] E Jordan, AP Thomas, JW Kitching, and RA Blackburn, *Employer Perceptions and the Impact of Employment Regulation* (BIS, ERRS 123, March 2013).

[326] ibid, 7–9.

[327] This is fully demonstrated by the review of relevant substantive law in Ch 3 and see also Dickens, 'Fairer Workplaces' (n 114), 210 for the comment that '[i]ronically, some of the complexity, frequent changes and other problems for employers arise through what have purported to be 'business friendly' legislative actions by successive governments.'

[328] Jordan et al (n 325), 17, and Ch 3 generally.   [329] ibid, 34–35.

[330] ibid, 17, Ch 3 generally and 35–37.

[331] ibid, 17 and 34–38. See the interesting observation at 37 that '[g]overnment policy has been to reduce [the] burden on small and micro employers, however, this research indicates the impact may be

More specific findings of particular relevance here were, on the one hand, that larger employers reported being affected by equality law in taking measures to show their recruitment choices were not discriminatory[332] and, on the other hand, that regulation was said more generally to have very little impact on working practices when managing staff.[333] The adoption of various policies was also reported by larger organizations, but also that complying with regulation was a secondary reason for doing so. The primary reasons given were transparency and consistency.[334] Some micro and small businesses, however, reported both greater informality and not wanting to depart from this because it enabled them to respond flexibly to individual employees.[335]

Regulation was said nonetheless to be a primary driver in what respondents did regarding dismissal.[336] There were also anxieties that ET proceedings were costly in various ways, too easy for claimants to initiate, and that procedures would be found unfair because of the subjectivity of elements in the ACAS Code. Some respondents reported seeing settlement as the safest response to a claim irrespective of whether an employer had acted fairly.[337] This was in a context of some misconception about the law, for example unawareness of the increased length of the qualifying period for most unfair dismissal rights and beliefs that procedural steps were mandatory.[338]

3. Conclusion

Bringing together these sources is instructive in itself for contrasting different approaches to understanding the working world and for exposing interrelations and gaps in the data. I return in Chapters 4 to 10 to specific conceptions and findings that assist in the interpretation of my qualitative evidence and in developing my conclusions. At this stage I extract three clusters of ideas from the data that frame the argument in the rest of the book.

(1) Bad workplace behaviour, unsolved problems, and suboptimal legal interventions

The psychological and sociological literatures, backed up by the literature on 'claiming', show beyond doubt that in the eyes of many working people, individual British labour and equality rights have not prevented unacceptable conduct, whether this is conceived as bullying, harassment, incivility, disrespect, or simply unfairness. Accounts of being on the receiving end of questionable behaviour also come disproportionately from particular identity groups, especially sexual minorities and those with health issues. It is also clear from the socio-legal literature that half of the considerable majority of

---

limited as micro employers have a poor understanding of their obligations in any case. The root cause of their difficulties concerning regulation was a lack of understanding and reluctance to deal with HR issues formally.'

[332] ibid, 19 and 22.   [333] ibid, 24.

[334] ibid. See also 25–26 on the influences on formalization, including that for smaller employers this was sometimes triggered by an ET claim (with the finding at 19 that for medium-sized ones an ET claim sometimes led to a comprehensive review of working practices by an external HR expert) and 37 on the confidence formalization gave managers.

[335] ibid, 24–25 and see text to n 319 above.   [336] ibid, 17 and 30–33.

[337] ibid, 32.   [338] ibid, 29–30.

people who try to do something about non-trivial employment problems get nowhere. If we add the significant minority who do nothing, that translates to a great many employment problems, whether about behaviour or other things, which are going unaddressed. This makes research into what is occurring in relation to these problems vital to understanding the part law plays at work. This was quickly confirmed during my interview study, the data from which have troubling implications as to the capacity for some employers to silence and marginalize dissent and the wide-ranging harms that individualized conflict can inflict, including perhaps being more damaging for well-intentioned employers.

The empirical evidence about litigation experience is undoubtedly bleak. Knowledge is missing about what happens in the ordinary courts, but the tiny proportion that pursues ET litigation faces an alienating, lonely, often harmful experience, with uncertain results, limited gains, and outcomes that can substantially depart from what claimants hope to achieve. The narratives of discrimination claimants were by turns heart-rending, depressing, and uplifting, a far cry from the stories of self-serving, money-grabbing, and heedless litigants often portrayed in public and media discussion.

This did not, however, correlate to positive accounts of organizational experience, with recent BIS research among private employers documenting a curious combination in some instances of anxiety and passivity and more general indications of variable and uncertain responses to law. While the complexity of law was deprecated, stereotypical attitudes often attributed to employers were absent. Instead, legal intervention was described as necessary to ensure that employees are treated fairly. Combining this with the individual point of view from the claiming and litigation data, a picture emerges of considerable societal effort being expended on legal interventions that function suboptimally to solve workplace problems. My analyses of both judgments and interview data strongly support this impression while documenting specific means by which this state of affairs is brought about.

(2) Misconceiving the law and legal influence

It seems that preconceptions, assumptions, and omissions regarding the content and operation of law extend beyond public discourse to sophisticated research literatures. The wholesale avoidance of employment adjudication in the ordinary courts is remarkably odd. As Chapter 3 makes plain, some of the most innovative and important legal norms governing working life, including those regarding behaviour, emanate from the common law of contract and tort and may well be litigated outside ETs. Equally, the Protection from Harassment Act (PHA) 1997 has obvious relevance and can only be litigated in the ordinary courts. Finally, ordinary court litigation is likely to increase as ETs become more inhospitable.

Just as notable was the fact that research studies that were not specifically about legal effects said little or nothing about law and made simplistic assumptions about its impact so far as it was mentioned.[339] The chapters that follow, both in outlining the relevant law and through qualitative analysis, develop the argument that much more comprehensive, nuanced, and consistent account needs to be taken of the range of legal sources, how they are deployed in litigation, and how far, if at all, they penetrate organizational lives.

---

[339] See p 25 above.

(3) The collectivity of working life in the individualized discourse of rights

What is most powerful in the evidence is the way it repeatedly documented tensions between the essentially collective nature of most work and the assertion of individual claims and entitlements.[340] I take from this that individualization generally, and in the form of individual employment rights specifically, is forcing working people to assert workplace claims in ways that are fundamentally at odds with how work is organized, experienced, and undertaken. The shift to this mode of expressing discontent is in turn interacting with the changed ideological and industrial relations landscape in damaging ways for workers, organizations, and society, not least by failing effectively to use law to realize greater fairness, reasonableness, and equality at work.

The growing influence of liberal individualist ideas has arguably translated at work into a notably ironic kind of power imbalance, in which organizations continue largely to function, in a sense, as collectives, while workers must increasingly fend for themselves. My point goes beyond noticing this, however, to contend that friction arises in and of itself from the mismatch between collective understandings of working life, whether constructed by employers, unions, or indeed individuals, and workplace demands being presented in individualized terms. As more law and legal process is framed in this way, it should be anticipated that tension between the innate collectivity of working life and the pursuit by employees of their interests will often be played out in relation to individual rights. Employer dominance of the communal space of work is, however, likely to deliver two responses: the silencing and marginalizing of individual workplace challenges, and organizations finding conflicts that do emerge difficult to manage, such that the risk of individual and organizational harm is increased and the potential value of legal intervention diminished.

That does not, however, suggest that employers will necessarily be dismissive of legal obligations, whether or not in the form of individual rights: there is plainly great variety in that regard and even the most recalcitrant employer is likely to respond in some way. Still, a corollary is that employer perspectives increasingly determine what is done about implementation, crowding out divergent views on what the organizational response ought to be.

The diminution of institutionalized means, like collective representation and bargaining, is important to this line of reasoning. These means are better placed to deal with tensions between different perspectives on working life, precisely for providing for negotiation and dispute resolution within a collectivist frame: the employers' construction of working life is matched and challenged by those of unions and, it is to be hoped, their members, with the position of individuals balanced against those points of view. Of course, the fact that such systems embed challenge to employer domination explains in large part why traditional collective institutions are 'profoundly out of fashion'.[341] There is an obvious appeal from an employer perspective in taking the chance offered by the ideology of individualism and the process of individualizing employment relationships, including legally, to impose its idea of the organizational good, to marginalize dissension, and to adhere only to a thin account of individuals' stake in working life. Still, experience of collective dispute resolution further illustrates the poor fit between the inherent collectivity of work and individualization, including in the form of many

---

[340] See the text to n 133 above for Genn and Paterson's idea that lesser reporting of justiciable problems in Scotland may result from a collectivist mindset preventing issues from being seen as individual ones.
[341] See text to n 322 above.

modern employment rights: compromise and trade-off is the life-blood of the former and frequently anathema to the latter.

This last point undoubtedly highlights technical challenges in incorporating any kind of collective dimension to the implementation and enforcement of individual rights. Even still, it is important that the data surveyed in this chapter suggest that the move by employers away from participative arrangements is not proving costless. Many workplace problems may not be fully articulated but this does not mean they disappear; instead they are left quietly to cause opportunity costs and positive harm. When problems escalate this is liable, as noted earlier, to be significantly damaging and unconstructive. Indeed, it seems likely that management trends about 'engagement' in part seek to mitigate those features of a more individualized employment relations settlement.

In terms of specific support for this reasoning from the evidence, Fevre and colleagues' study about 'trouble at work' documented the complexity that arises from the dichotomy between work frequently combining the effort and contributions of many and it giving rise to myriad individual interests, like developing a sense of self, promoting well-being, earning a living, and potentially prospering. This came across, first, in interviewees' deep, organizationally minded commitment to their jobs and their corresponding profound sense of being personally let down if they came to feel ill treated. Second, it was apparent in the contradictory pressures that managers struggled to balance and arguably even embodied between managerial reasoning and divergent perspectives and needs.

Fevre and colleagues' overall conclusion reflected these findings, speculating that trouble at work might result from employers struggling to adapt to modern employee expectations and expressions of dissatisfaction that derive from relationships being conducted on a more individual basis. I extrapolate the idea that wholesale individualizing of employment relations only works from an employer's perspective, and then imperfectly, so far as what it really delivers is a distortion of individualist ideology in which (collective) employers dominate over mostly weaker (individual) employees. So far as this way of constructing employment relationships leads to assertions, legally or in other ways, of individual claims, interests, needs, expectations, and rights, organizations may be expected to struggle with the challenges to workplace regimes these entail in the absence of embedded, participative structures for doing so. Further, individual claims that in truth reflect collective disagreements are likely to be especially problematic: issues that call for negotiation, trade-offs, and compromise will be much harder, perhaps impossible, to resolve if forced into individualist, winner-takes-all, and adversarial forms of dispute resolution, as recent experience of mass equal-pay litigation has demonstrated.[342]

The psychological evidence is worth considering in this light. Fevre and colleagues observed:

It has been argued that the bullying concept has been widely adopted precisely because it fails to turn private workplace troubles into public issues in a convincing way ... In effect, the concept of workplace bullying did not attempt to generalize from the individual experience and therefore, could only propose individual solutions to the issues it raised. As a result, private troubles stayed private and did not become public issues.[343]

---

[342] L. Hayes, 'Women's Voice and Equal Pay: Judicial Regard for the Gendering of Collective Bargaining' in A Bogg and T Novitz (eds), *Voices at Work* (OUP, 2014) and C McLaughlin, 'Equal Pay, Litigation and Reflexive Regulation: The Case of the UK Local Authority Sector' (2014) 43 ILJ 1.
[343] Fevre et al, *Trouble at Work* (n 6), 21–22.

The premise seems to be that employers are drawn to the psychologically inspired concept of bullying, because their greater (collective) power makes it easier for them to control how problems unfold given the underlying individualist ideology of psychological conceptions of bullying. According to my analysis, however, there is as great a potential for employers to struggle to adapt to challenges that are put in these terms, since they still oppose group and individual interests at work. Furthermore, this is precisely a context in which qualitative findings showed research subjects smuggling collective understandings of working life back into ideas about bullying. Whatever the prevailing discourse, the suggestion is that the inherently group experience of most work will somehow be reasserted. If that dimension is not then incorporated into the search for resolution, ongoing difficulty may be anticipated.

If the bullying conception is individualistic, the same is undoubtedly true of the range of individual employment rights now on the statute book, including those regarding behaviour that Chapter 3 outlines. It is surely right, as Pollert indicated,[344] that the casting of new employment rights in this form has been one contribution by successive governments to shifting UK employment relationships in this direction. Yet, the argument pursued here suggests that whatever the form in which claims about work emerge, struggles over who gets to participate in constructing working lives are, to a greater or lesser degree, always implicated. So it may not be that the same issues are litigated as would previously have led to collective conflict, as Dix and colleagues argued,[345] but that does not mean that collective concerns are absent from individualized legal disputes.

It follows from my reasoning that the more employment protections and associated processes are individualized, the more difficulty workplace conflict may be expected to provoke. The individual orientation of challenges based on such laws creates an inherent risk that those making them, irrespective of the justice or potential organizational (and wider) utility of their points, will be cast as outsiders, disrupting the smooth, harmonious functioning of the workplace and, in some sense, 'letting the side down'. Equally, this feeling is liable not only to come from management, who anyway will most likely be employees,[346] but also from any colleagues, lay trade union representatives included, who are battling to hold organizational loyalty in balance with the vindication of their own and others' individual interests. Indeed, my interview study suggests such difficulties also amongst trade unions.[347] Various findings that employees can be slow to characterize issues at work as problematic are also suggestive that the move to articulating events as appropriate for individual, internal complaint provokes similar conflict in those who take this step. The FTWS 2008 conclusion that people who achieve a good solution internally, often do so because either a manager or a local trade union representative has assisted them,[348] also suggests that it is this kind of constructive reaction that is lacking where complaints founder. Remembering the growing imbalance of power at work and taking account of how UK law currently and increasingly deters ET claims, it appears that individual enforcement of employment laws as currently designed cannot be expected to be much of an engine for beneficial change at work.

This is clearly reflected in the evidence about claiming behaviour and litigation mentioned earlier. It becomes wholly unsurprising that so many people are passive in the face of difficulties at work once their initial attempts at resolution fail, that litigation is such

---

[344] See text to n 202.   [345] See text to n 237.

[346] Perren et al, *Awareness and Impact* (n 298), 26 about ideas about fairness coinciding as between owners and senior employees with responsibility for human resources.

[347] See p 17 above and pp 219 and 234-36 in Ch 9.   [348] See p 36 above.

a vexed experience for the few who engage in it, and that there is so little organizational adaptation even to successful ET actions.

The upshot is that it is in large measure the experiences of the large proportion of working people who do little or nothing, and of employers irrespective of what individual employees do, that hold the key to how individual employment rights work in practice and what effects, for good or ill, they have on working life. It is equally clear that any possibility for such laws to work better resides in finding ways to ensure that individual and organizational responses to them deliver more benefits and pose fewer risks. Pollert's answer was greater trade union involvement and I am convinced that a collective dimension to securing respect for individual rights is critical. At the same time, it seems to me highly unlikely that this would help much if provision for broader involvement is confined to trade unions because they are now absent from such vast tracts of the UK labour market. Instead innovation is needed, in keeping with Dickens' analysis,[349] to improve the functioning of the law, including through participatory mechanisms with wider application.[350] It is necessary though to move beyond Dickens' prescription that law should insist on more active engagement by employers. Returning to the theorization of law on which this project tests, the dark side of law makes it as important to look for ways of inoculating emancipatory legal innovation against being undermined from within.

[349] See text to ns 310–14.
[350] See Colvin (n 295) on the importance in practice of non-union grievance procedures in the US for analogous reasons.

3

The Substantive Legal Background to Behavioural Conflict at Work from 1995 to 2015

This chapter provides the substantive legal background to the qualitative analyses that follow, adding to the empirical context provided by Chapter 2. It is mainly concerned, therefore, with explaining the individual labour and equality rights that are typically deployed in claims about behavioural conflict at work in both Employment Tribunals (ETs) and the ordinary courts. As such it traces the development of the rules from 1995 to 2010, the period during which the judgments in my sample were decided, and explains major developments to date. The focus is on England and Wales, given that much of the law in this area is common to Northern Ireland and Scotland. This is not to deny that there are differences, however, some of which are noted here and discussed further in Chapters 4 to 7.[1]

The purpose of the chapter is to give enough legal description and analysis for readers to make sense of the doctrinal aspects of my primary findings. I therefore use a different methodology for analysing legal sources to that employed later in this book. Here I take the classic, internal legal approach according to which legislation, statutory interpretation, and common law reasoning are scoured to piece together the rules and principles governing a given aspect of social life. Further, there is a historical dimension in that I record how the law has developed over the last two decades. This contrasts with the reporting in Chapters 4–6 of my coding of a subset of authoritative judgments about behavioural conflict at work. The aim in those chapters is to answer my overall research question for that aspect of the work, namely: *How does law about behavioural conflict at work operate through authoritative adjudication?* That means the later chapters do not focus on the content of the law but instead on how it was presented to and handled by higher courts. Chapters 8 and 9 are equally not about the doctrine itself but about how organizations deal with situations to which it relates and respond to legal intervention.

This means the internal legal analysis in this chapter is in the service of external evaluation. As a corollary, the chapter does not seek to accomplish, nor purport to have achieved, a complete internal critique. There is much more that could be said on that score. The point of this book, however, is not classic doctrinal scrutiny. It is through varied external evaluations to develop understanding of how law functions, the wider meaning this has, and its implications, including for how law's emancipatory potential might better be realized.

---

[1] Eg there are differences in the protection provided by the PHA 1997 and in contract law. The latter was important to the EAT judgment in *Aberdeen CC v McNeill*, one of my sample, on which see H Collins, 'Constructive Dismissal and the West Lothian Question' (2011) 40 ILJ439. A further appeal to the CSIH was reported as *McNeill v Aberdeen CC (No. 2)* [2013] CSIH 102, [2014] IRLR 102 and discussed in D Brodie, 'Common Law Remedies and Relational Contracting' (2014) 43 ILJ 170.

Even so, it is notable that so far as overall criticism of the framework of rules emerges from this chapter, it has an external flavour. This is because the evolution of law relevant to behavioural conflict demonstrates that, regardless of the internal logic or philosophical merits of individual elements, the combination is inaccessible, confusing, and makes it difficult to extract overarching norms with which to guide workplace conduct and organizational arrangements. This is in part the result of ceaseless change. It might also be that the convolution is worse because the rules engage with diffuse aspects of working life. Whatever the reasons, these features of the law are a significant concern, not least because so much of the UK framework of individual labour and equality rights is implicated and such a wide array of workplace situations is liable to be affected.[2]

The chapter proceeds by setting out the main ways that a claim about behavioural conflict might be put, with Table 3.1 offering a quick guide to the options. It will be seen that the various possibilities are directly concerned with behavioural standards to variable degrees. In all cases, however, the sources regulate more than workplace behaviour: they are either about more than just work, or more than just conduct.

There is inevitably some overlap in the cases considered with those discussed in Chapters 4–6. This is because legal points of general importance were sometimes determined in judgments from the sample on which I have undertaken non-doctrinal qualitative analysis. I have dealt with this by saying the least possible about those cases here. Also, this chapter does not cover the legal background to some claims that appear only rarely in the case law, in particular under the Public Interest Disclosure Act (PIDA) 1998, in the tort of defamation, or that draw on health and safety regulation. This adverts to there being yet further litigation possibilities out there, although exposition of the law surrounding them was unnecessary to meet the aim of the chapter.

Finally, I have included significant legal changes that came and went in the period studied because even short-lived developments influenced adjudication. Notable amongst these was the dispute resolution provisions in the Employment Act (EA) 2002 and case law controversy about the statutory concept of constructive dismissal started in *Abbey National plc v Fairbrother*, one of my sample of judgments.[3]

Structurally, it is important that my account of the law separates liability and remedial rules. This is fundamental to clarifying the overlapping legal sources in this area in that it is this distinction that makes the law as convoluted as it is. In particular, separating liability and remedial rules is the technical means by which legislators have provided for adjudication of causes of action in different courts to have divergent potential outcomes. In other words, ETs and ordinary courts have both been given power to decide certain categories of case and yet different remedial options if the claimant wins.

This is what explains the odd jurisdictional position of claims for breaches of contracts of employment. When this cause of action is pursued in the ordinary court system, the potential remedies include injunctions and common law damages, albeit subject in recent years to compensation limits for breaches related to dismissal. At the same time, common law contract claims may be brought in the ET provided they are associated with dismissal. If a litigant takes this option, however, she must accept that ETs have no jurisdiction to give injunctions and more limited powers to compensate. To complicate matters, the employee might additionally have an ET claim for statutory unfair dismissal that alleges constructive dismissal. Because the courts have ruled that the unfair dismissal legislation imported the common law notion of

---

[2] See p 6 in Ch 1, pp 23–24 in Ch 2, pp 187–88 in Ch 8 and pp 245–46 in Ch 10.
[3] [2007] IRLR 320 (EAT).

Table 3.1 Brief guide to the main ways of putting a legal claim arising from behavioural conflict at work

General Legal Regime	Statutory			Common Law	
Specific Legal Regime	Unfair Dismissal Law (Employment Rights Act 1996)	Equality Law (Predecessor statutes and regulations and the Equality Act 2010)	Law on Non-Discriminatory Harassment (Protection from Harassment Act 1997)	Contract Law	Tort Law
ET or ordinary courts?	ET	ET (although in some instances claims can also be made in the ordinary courts)	Ordinary courts	Ordinary courts and ETs (the latter only if connected to termination)	Ordinary courts
Legal wrongs (with brief, simplified overviews of what these entail)	Unfair dismissal ie either (1) dismissing for an automatically unfair reason, or (2) dismissing for a potentially fair reason when this was, in all the circumstances, either procedurally or substantively unreasonable. N.B. dismissal covers (1) straight contractual termination, (2) expiration of a fixed-term contract, and (3) constructive dismissal (further explanation, see*).	Direct discrimination ie treating someone less favourably than their comparator because of a protected group identity (with protective coverage extended over the years). Victimization ie penalizing someone for using equality law. Discriminatory harassment (from 2003 onwards) ie unwanted conduct related to a protected group identity with either the purpose or effect of either violating someone's dignity or creating an intimidating, hostile, degrading, humiliating, or offensive environment for them.	Harassment ie pursuing an oppressive and unacceptable course of conduct (involving at least two incidents) targeted at an individual, that is calculated to alarm them or cause them distress. Speech is specifically covered.	Breach of contract ie breaching the express or implied terms of an employee's contract. The main relevant implied terms impose duties (1) not, without reasonable and proper cause, to act in a manner calculated or likely to destroy or seriously damage the relationship of confidence and trust between the parties, and (2) to take reasonable care not reasonably to cause harm. N.B. breach of contract by the employer in attempting to terminate an employment contract is typically called wrongful dismissal. Repudiatory breach of contract by the employer followed by acceptance by the employee is called constructive dismissal* (which will always also be contractually wrongful, and, in my view, vice versa).	Torts of intention, like the intentional infliction of physical or psychiatric harm. Negligence ie the duty to take reasonable care not to cause reasonably foreseeable harm
Usual remedies	Compensation (partly formulaic; partly compensatory; usually subject to multiple statutory limits) N.B. consider *Johnson* effects.	Compensation (normally compensatory; available for injury to feelings; unlimited)	Compensation (normally compensatory; available for injury to feelings; unlimited) Injunction possibility	Ordinary courts: Compensation (usually compensatory and unlimited) Injunctions possibility N.B. consider *Johnson* etc effects. ETs: Compensation (compensatory and subject to limits).	Compensation (usually compensatory and unlimited) Injunctions possibility NB: consider *Johnson* etc effects

constructive dismissal, the law governing liability in such a claim significantly over-laps with that regarding breach of contract, although the similarity has been lessened by recent court decisions excluding liability for some common law claims related to dismissal. At the remedial stage, however, the statutory unfair dismissal regime contains a dedicated reinstatement and re-engagement remedy and particular statutory compensation rules.

The liability/remedies distinction is in turn critical to the distinctly peculiar ways that judges have in recent years developed the law on the common law/statutory boundary. This notably occurred in *Johnson v Unisys Ltd*,[4] *Eastwood v Magnox Electric plc & McCabe v Cornwall CC*,[5] *GMB Trade Union v Brown*,[6] *GAB Robins (UK) Ltd v Triggs*,[7] and *Edwards v Chesterfield Royal Hospital NHS Foundation Trust & Botham v MoD*,[8] the last of which post-dated the period from which my sample of judgments was taken. Constitutional reasoning led new rules (either of common law or as a result of statutory interpretation) to be created about the scope of, and remedies for, overlapping common law and statutory causes of action. These rules were, however, in addition to the traditional means by which boundary issues between causes of action are reconciled: namely, the general principle that regardless of how many ways a person establishes that conduct was legally wrongful, the same loss can never be compensated twice.

1. The Statutory Right not to be Unfairly Dismissed

The modern statutory right not to be unfairly dismissed, now contained in Part X of the Employment Rights Act (ERA) 1996, has its origins in the Industrial Relations Act 1971. It is a resilient survivor of the failed attempt in that Act to regulate the UK system of collective industrial relations more directly. Over forty years later, the modern legislation grants rights, enforceable only in the ET, to a subset of working people who have been dismissed on notice or summarily, had renewal of their fixed term contract refused, or been forced out of work by their employer's repudiatory breach of contract. Under the statutory regime, the ETs have some jurisdiction to deal with contract claims associated with dismissal.[9] The most significant limits on this are first, that ETs do not have power to give injunctions; second, they cannot award common law damages for personal injury, and third, common law compensation is subject to a £25,000 limit.[10]

The essential elements of the statutory right not to be unfairly dismissed are that some reasons for dismissal (like being pregnant or being a member of a trade union) are automatically unfair, and others (like lack of capability, misconduct, and redundancy), while recognized as potentially fair, must not unreasonably be relied on as reasons to dismiss. In that second class of cases, however, statutory unfairness will only be found, either in respect of the actual dismissal or of the procedure leading to it, where no reasonable employer would in all the circumstances have seen the employer's conduct as a reasonable response to what had occurred. If unfair dismissal is proven, the remedy is generally an award of compensation. Available compensation is capped in a variety of ways and is, anyway, typically modest.

---

[4] [2001] UKHL, [2003] 1 AC 518.   [5] [2004] UKHL 35, [2005] 1 AC 503.
[6] EAT, 16 October 2007.   [7] [2008] EWCA Civ 17, [2008] ICR 529.
[8] [2011] UKSC 58, [2012] 2 WLR 55.
[9] Employment Tribunals Extension of Jurisdiction (England and Wales) Order 1994 SI 1994/1623.
[10] ibid, regs 3, 4, and 10.

(1) Liability

It is important that not all working people have the statutory right not to be unfairly dismissed. The requirement most likely to exclude a person from protection is that they must have worked under either a contract of employment or of apprenticeship. Since contracts of apprenticeship are relatively unusual, it is the contract of employment condition that most limits the protective ambit of the legislation.

A 'contract of employment' is specified by the ERA 1996 to refer to the common law notion of a contract of service.[11] Case law over the years has distinguished between contracts *of* service, work under which renders someone an employee, and contracts *for* services, work under which the law categorizes as self-employment. The relevant common law rules have perennially given rise to controversy about arrangements that do not obviously constitute contracts of employment. The latest in a long line of litigation battles is about agency workers. On the case law analysis prevailing through the period from which my sample of judgments was taken, individuals working in this way would frequently not be categorized as employees of anyone, irrespective of how long they had worked, either through the same agency or on the same assignment.[12]

The other significant general limit on protection is the requirement for continuous employment, as defined in the ERA 1996, before an employee gains the full right not to be unfairly dismissed. For the first few years in which judgments in my sample were delivered the requirement was for two years of continuous employment. This was reduced to one year for dismissals occurring on or after 1 June 1999.[13] In the latest swing in the political pendulum, the Coalition government that was elected in 2010 re-extended the limit to two years from April 2012.[14]

Still, there are exceptions. This is usually the case where the reason for dismissal was automatically unfair, in respect of which there is protection from 'day one'.[15] A case in my sample, *Harvest Press Ltd v McCaffrey*,[16] illustrated this possibility. It concerned a single incident in the course of which the ET found Mr McCaffrey to have been subjected to abusive behaviour by a younger colleague. This occurred some two-and-a-half months into Mr McCaffrey's employment and he reacted by leaving work in fear for his safety. The ET found that Mr McCaffrey had contacted senior colleagues when he reached home to explain his absence and indicated that he would only return to work on receipt of certain assurances. However, the employer accepted the colleague's different version of events and told Mr McCaffrey his employment was at an end because they viewed his departure from work as a resignation.

In Mr McCaffrey's action for unfair dismissal the ET held that there had been an automatically unfair dismissal under section 100(1)(d) ERA 1996. This applies if the reason for dismissal was that 'in circumstances of danger which the employee reasonably believed to be serious and imminent and which he could not reasonably have been expected to avert, he left (or proposed to leave) or (while the danger persisted) refused

[11] ERA 1996, s 230(1)-(2).
[12] See further L Barmes, 'Learning from Case Law Accounts of Marginalized Working' in J Fudge, S McCrystal, and K Sankaran (eds), *Regulating Legal Work: Challenging Legal Boundaries* (Hart, 2012) and *Autoclenz Ltd v Belcher* [2011] UKSC 41, [2011] ICR 1157, which significantly liberalized the law on the employment status of anyone working under an allegedly sham work contract, agency workers included.
[13] The Unfair Dismissal and Statement of Reasons for Dismissal (Variation of Qualifying Period) Order 1999, SI 1999/1436.
[14] The Unfair Dismissal and Statement of Reasons for Dismissal (Variation of Qualifying Period) Order 2012, SI 2012/989.
[15] See ERA 1996, ss 99–105 and 108.   [16] [1999] IRLR 778 (EAT).

to return to his place of work or any dangerous part of his place of work'. It is unusual for employees either to invoke this provision (and others about automatic unfairness) or to do so successfully, yet the Employment Appeal Tribunal (EAT) held that the dangerous circumstances referred to in the section were not limited to those generated by the workplace itself. Rather, it was found that the legislation clearly covered danger owing to the presence or absence of a colleague.

It is necessary also to emphasize that it is employers who are potentially liable for the statutory wrong of unfair dismissal, even though it may have been conduct by managers or peers that gave rise to unlawful dismissal. This is the legal consequence of Part X of the ERA 1996 specifying that an employee who terminates their contract of employment, with or without notice, will be treated as having been dismissed if they did so in circumstances where they were 'entitled to terminate [the contract] without notice by reason of the employer's conduct'.[17] An important decision came soon after this sub-section was added to the legislation in 1974. It was held in *Western Excavating (ECC) Ltd v Sharp*[18] that the common law test for constructive dismissal governed whether an employee had been so dismissed. In other words, to come within the statutory provision, an employee must establish that their employer had committed a repudiatory breach of contract in response to which the employee either left work or, as specified in the statute, gave notice.

The idea this decision imported from the common law is that an employee has the legal option to treat their contract as no longer binding where it is flouted by their employer's conduct. The common law has long recognized that such situations in practice amount to the employer forcing someone to leave. Still, the employer's breach of contract must be fundamental to entitle an employee to regard it as, in effect, a dismissal. Equally, at common law an employee who delays risks losing the opportunity the law gives them to walk out. In that situation, as well as when the employee deliberately elects to stay at work, the law views the employee as affirming the contract such that no termination occurs. In such circumstances, the only contractual possibility for legal redress is a claim in the ordinary courts for breach of contract, although this is only an option where continuing at work is not taken also to have waived the breach.

In a paradigmatic example of interconnections in this field between statutory and common law developments, the decision in *Western Excavating* provoked formulation in later decisions of a common law contractual duty of mutual trust and confidence. This is a set of obligations that the common law presumes to be implied in all contracts of service (or employment) as 'necessary incident[s] of a definable category of contractual relationship'.[19] It is a mutual obligation, meaning employees are equally bound. Its novel feature when it emerged, however, was that it articulated diffuse obligations that contract law presumes to be on employers. These were given an influential narrative formulation in the early case of *Courtaulds Northern Textiles Ltd v Andrew*. This remains the authoritative abstract account of the duty, as follows:

that the employers would not, without reasonable and proper cause conduct themselves in a manner calculated or likely to destroy or seriously damage the relationship of confidence and trust between the parties.[20]

The House of Lords (HL) first approved the duty in *Malik v BCCI*[21] (also known as *Mahmud v BCCI*).

---

[17] ERA 1996, s 95(1)(c).   [18] [1978] QB 761 (CA).
[19] *Scally v Southern Health and Social Services Board* [1992] 1 AC 294 (HL), 307.
[20] [1979] IRLR 84 (EAT), 86.   [21] [1998] AC 20 (HL).

The sense in which *Western Excavating* explains the 'discovery' of the mutual contractual duty of trust and confidence[22] was that ETs had previously not always required employees to show a fundamental breach of contract to prove dismissal under the then equivalent of section 95(1)(c) ERA 1996.[23] After *Western Excavating*, ideas that ETs had been formulating about how employers should behave seem simply to have been recast as a contractual term implied by law, breach of which would give rise to a common law constructive dismissal and hence to a likely finding of statutory unfair dismissal. Through the newly formulated implied term, therefore, ETs were able still to find that disregard by employers of a range of implicit workplace obligations constituted the statutory wrong of unfair dismissal.[24]

At the same time, however, recognition of the mutual trust and confidence term was a major development in the common law of the contract of employment, the effects of which are still being worked through today. Certainly, lawyers tend to see this as a highly significant aspect of modern employment law, particularly in that it imposes day-to-day obligations on employers in relation to pretty much everything they or their employees do, behaviour included. That is a large part of what makes it so very odd that the research about employment litigation surveyed in Chapter 2 largely ignores ordinary court litigation, since this is where major cases about mutual trust and confidence may well be pursued, as indeed occurred in *Malik*.[25]

Another noteworthy feature of the statutory, unfair dismissal side of the story is that it is technically possible, if unlikely, for a constructive dismissal to be lawful under the ERA 1996. Proving dismissal is only an initial stage in this kind of claim. The decision as to whether or not dismissal was in fact fair or unfair generally depends, first, on the employer proving that it had one of the specified potentially fair reasons for dismissal, as well as there being no finding by the ET that the actual reason for dismissal was automatically unfair.[26] Second, assuming that first stage is passed and leaving aside certain exceptional categories,[27] the statute sets out that:

the determination of the question whether the dismissal is fair or unfair (having regard to the reason shown by the employer)—(a) depends on whether in the circumstances (including the size and administrative resources of the employer's undertaking) the employer acted reasonably or unreasonably in treating it as a sufficient reason for dismissing the employee and (b) shall be determined in accordance with equity and the substantial merits of the case.[28]

For many years that statutory test has been applied according to the following judicial interpretation:

We consider that the authorities establish that in law the current approach for the [employment] tribunal to adopt in answering the question posed by s [98(4)] is as follows: (1) the starting point should always be the words of [the subsection] themselves; (2) in applying the [sub]section an [employment] tribunal must consider the reasonableness of the employer's conduct, not simply whether they (the members of the [employment] tribunal) consider the dismissal to be fair; (3) in

[22] See in particular MRF Freedland, *The Personal Employment Contract* (OUP, 2003), 155 and the ensuing account of the emergence of the implied duty of mutual trust and confidence.
[23] See, eg, *Bournemouth University Higher Education Corporation v Buckland* [2009] ICR 1042 (EAT) at [28].
[24] See Freedland (n 22),156 that '[the implied term] represented a general behavioural standard for judging whether the conduct of one of the parties had left an employment relationship in a condition of viable continuance or placed it in a state of breakdown.'
[25] See p 38 in Ch 2.   [26] ERA 1996, s 98(1)–(2), (3), and (6).
[27] There were, eg, for a time particular rules regarding dismissal because someone had reached retirement age.
[28] ERA 1996, s 98(4).

judging the reasonableness of the employer's conduct an [employment] tribunal must not substitute its decision as to what was the right course to adopt for that of the employer; (4) in many, though not all, cases there is a band of reasonable responses to the employee's conduct within which one employer might take one view, another may quite reasonably take another; (5) the function of the [employment] tribunal, as an industrial jury, is to determine whether in the particular circumstances of each case the decision to dismiss the employee fell within the band of reasonable responses which a reasonable employer might have adopted. If the dismissal falls within the band dismissal is fair; if the dismissal falls outside the band it is unfair.[29]

As mentioned earlier, this approach will be used to decide the fairness both of the decision to dismiss and of the procedure by which that decision was reached.[30] In considering the fairness of the procedure, however, ETs are required to have regard to the contents of the Advisory, Conciliation and Arbitration Service (ACAS) Code of Practice on Disciplinary Procedures and Grievances, while not being bound to follow its recommendations.

Applying this general approach to claims for constructive unfair dismissal, it is conceivable that an employer could establish that the employer had a potentially fair reason for the conduct that resulted in constructive dismissal and, in turn, for the ET to find that the dismissal itself passed the sub-section 98(4) hurdle. Still, the unmindful way that constructive dismissals typically unfold makes this unusual.[31]

In a further example of the complex interconnections between common law and statute, however, comparison between the fairness enquiry in constructive dismissal cases and in respect of other kinds of dismissals led to case law controversy about how ETs should determine whether breach of the implied duty of mutual trust and confidence (and arguably other breaches) gave rise to a constructive dismissal. The hare was set running, so to speak, in *Abbey National plc v Fairbrother*.[32] The ET found that the employer's handling of a grievance had so breached the mutual duty of trust and confidence as to give rise to a constructive unfair dismissal. On the employer's successful appeal to the EAT, both against this aspect of the ET's decision and against its upholding of the claimant's Disability Discrimination Act (DDA) 1995 claim, it was argued that the approach in the ET to constructive dismissal was wrong because 'employers should be in no worse a position regarding the standards of reasonableness which they were expected to achieve in a case of constructive dismissal following a grievance procedure than in a case where an employee claims that he has been unfairly dismissed after having been disciplined for misconduct'.[33]

Responding to the employer's contentions, Lady Smith concluded that, although whether there had been a constructive dismissal depended on the common law of the contract of employment and the precise terms of the implied contractual duty of mutual trust and confidence, the enquiry into the reasonableness of the employer's actions was in substance the same as in respect of other kinds of dismissals and, in particular, depended on the 'range of reasonableness responses test' enunciated above. She described how she saw this working as follows:

Accordingly, in a constructive dismissal case involving resignation in the context of a grievance procedure, when asking ... 'did the employer have reasonable and proper cause for that conduct?' it seems to us that it is not only appropriate but necessary to ask whether the employer's conduct

[29] *Iceland Frozen Foods Ltd v Jones* [1983] ICR 17 (EAT), 24–25 and *Post Office v Foley HSBC Bank plc Madden* [2000] ICR 1283 (CA).
[30] *Sainsbury's Supermarkets Ltd v Hitt* [2002] EWCA Civ 1588, [2003] ICR 111.
[31] See on this point Sedley LJ, with the agreement of Carnwath and Jacob LJJ, in *Bournemouth University Higher Education Corporation v Buckland* [2010] EWCA Civ 121, [29]–[30], and [95]–[98].
[32] *Abbey National* (n 3).   [33] *Bournemouth University* (n 23), [28].

of the grievance procedure was within the band or range of reasonable responses to the grievance presented by the employee ... Just as happens when the conduct of a disciplinary procedure falls to be considered, the conduct of a grievance procedure requires to be looked at as a whole. Only if it has been conducted in a manner in which no reasonable employer would have conducted it can it be said that he did not have reasonable and proper cause for his conduct.[34]

This approach, if ultimately authoritative, would have ensured that a constructive unfair dismissal would only be found for breach of the trust and confidence term where the employer had gone outside the 'range of reasonable responses', bringing ET decisions in such cases into line with those in other unfair dismissal scenarios. At the same time, since the implied duty of mutual trust and confidence is part of the common law of the contract of employment, it would likely also have recast what is now an important element of that body of law.

What in fact happened, however, is that there was case law debate on the point from when the EAT decided *Abbey National v Fairbrother* in January 2007, until February 2010 when the Court of Appeal (CA) definitively confirmed in *Buckland v Bournemouth University* that the pre-*Abbey National* position was, after all, still the law.[35] In between, in July 2008 the EAT in *Claridge v Daler Rowney*[36] agreed with the broad thrust of Lady Smith's reasoning but differed on the detail,[37] and in May 2009 a different division of the EAT, deciding the first appeal stage of *Buckland*, stuck to the orthodox approach. The CA in *Buckland* went on to endorse that division of the EAT's reasoning and conclusion.

The CA found that the *Abbey National* and *Claridge* approaches were, first, in conflict with the rule, confirmed in *Malik*, that whether or not there has been a fundamental breach of contract, and in particular of the implied duty of mutual trust and confidence, is to be judged objectively. Second, those decisions could not stand with the authority of *Western Excavating* in which the CA had 'counterposed the objective test and the unreasonableness test of constructive dismissal and held in clear terms that the former was the correct one'.[38]

Some litigants inevitably became trapped in these legal eddies, conceivably either losing or winning according to when their case happened to be decided. A judgment from my sample, *The City of Edinburgh v Wood*,[39] was a case in point. The ET's finding that Mr Wood was constructively unfairly dismissed was overturned by the EAT because the *Abbey National v Fairbrother* test was not applied. Fortunately the ultimate outcome was probably not affected, however, as a successful perversity appeal independently led the EAT to dismiss Mr Wood's claim.

[34] ibid, [36].
[35] *Bournemouth University* (n 31), especially in Sedley LJ's speech at [22], with which Carnwath and Jacob LJJ both agreed.
[36] [2008] ICR 1267 (EAT).   [37] ibid, [27]–[39].
[38] ibid, [27]. See, however, that a new version of this debate might be re-emerging on notably dubious doctrinal terms, not least for ignoring this line of authority. In a very curiously reasoned decision, the CA in *Coventry University v Mian* [2014] EWCA Civ 1275, [2014] ELR 455, seems uncritically to have accepted the parties' agreement that employer liability in negligence regarding the institution of disciplinary proceedings depended on whether it had acted 'outside the range of reasonable responses open to an employer in the circumstances' (at [23], [30], and [41]–[42]) and, further, hinted that this was the test for contractual liability for breach of the duty of mutual trust and confidence ([20]). In turn, the CA in *Yapp v Foreign & Commonwealth Office* [2014] EWCA Civ 1512, [2015] IRLR 112 adverted to this view of negligence liability without comment, stating that the trial judge in *Yapp* had effectively applied such a test ([61]). In addition, while it was accepted that the formal analysis differs as between 'a breach of the common law duty of care and a breach of another contractual duty—most obviously the *Malik* term but perhaps also an express term', Underhill LJ for the CA observed that 'further thought [may] need to be given to whether the *Malik* term really has any separate role to play in this area' ([120]).
[39] EAT, 2 May 2008.

Another legal escapade in recent times was more long-lived and disruptive. This time it was the responsibility of Parliament in the form of the dispute resolution provisions of the EA 2002. These made large changes to unfair dismissal law. There was perhaps a clue that the new law was not going to work well in the fact that regulations to fill in the detail were not made until late 2004.[40] In the event, only four years later, the EA 2008 repealed all these 'reforms' and legislated new, scaled-down provisions. The latter were brought into force from April 2009 and yet further changes concerned with employment disputing and ET litigation have since been made by the Coalition government that was elected in 2010.[41]

The stated aim of the EA 2002 amendments to the ERA 1996 was to aid the resolution of employment disputes. An independent review in March 2007 found the new law had done the opposite, however, encouraging formalism and channelling disputes towards ETs.[42] The individual focus of the underlying model seemed also to have caused problems because of the increasing volume of group-like claims at the time, especially for equal pay in the public sector.[43] In light of this report and two further consultation exercises,[44] the then Prime Minister, Gordon Brown, announced in July 2007 that the statutory dispute resolution provisions would be repealed.

This was a shockingly wasteful legislative misstep which graphically illustrated how difficult it is for law to influence the detail of what goes on in workplaces. Some of the negative individual effects were felt in cases considered in my sample, a proportion of which effectively disappeared down a procedural black hole. I would certainly not dissent, including from experience of teaching this area of law, from Underhill J's description of the rules as 'rebarbative', cited with approval by Judge McMullen in *Cyprus Airways Ltd v Lambrou*.[45]

Royal Mail Letters and others v Muhammad[46] is a good example of the mischief created by implementation of these rules. The EAT held that Mr Muhammad's claim against his employer (as opposed to colleagues) could not be adjudicated because his explanation of the problem had not spelled out that he was alleging discrimination on grounds of race and religion. Moreover, this was the outcome despite Judge Pugsley noticing the frequent factual overlap between unfair dismissal and unlawful discrimination allegations. As Judge Pugsley said: 'The reality is that the findings of tribunals that lead it to determine that an employee has been unfairly dismissed in many cases would also provide a factual matrix from which an inference of discrimination could be drawn.'[47]

(2) Remedies

It was originally intended that reinstatement or re-engagement would be the primary remedy for unfair dismissal. These remedies are, however, ordered in a tiny minority of cases. This makes it possible to interpret judgments about behavioural conflicts with

---

[40] The Employment Act 2002 (Dispute Resolution) Regulations 2004, SI 752/2004.
[41] See p 26 in Ch 2.
[42] M Gibbons, *A Review of Employment Dispute Resolution in Great Britain* (DTI, March 2007), Executive Summary and paras. 2.7–2.19.
[43] ibid, paras 1.26 and 2.18. See pp 41–42 in Ch 2.
[44] See DTI, *Success at Work, Resolving disputes in the workplace, A consultation* (March 2007), and DTI, *Supplementary review of options for the law relating to procedural fairness in unfair dismissal* (2007).
[45] EAT, 1 May 2007, [1].   [46] EAT, 20 December 2007.
[47] See also *Goodman v Members of the Executive of Shropshire Unison* (EAT, 11 March 2010) on the sheer technicality implementation of the rules gave rise to.

only a background awareness of those possibilities. Deeper knowledge of recoverable compensation is, however, necessary.

This understanding is needed even though many judgments say nothing about damages. This silence is because claimants who win at trial often agree compensation instead of going back to the ET. The only sorts of compensation issues that tend to require a hearing are where the award is liable to be reduced because a claimant either contributed to the dismissal by their own fault or should have mitigated their loss better. Generally, however, the framework of rules makes it quite easy to work out the range within which an ET award would fall.

First, successful unfair dismissal claimants generally receive a 'basic award'. This reflects an employee's job tenure in that it is calculated by multiplying a claimant's net weekly pay by their years of service, with some extra weeks' pay added with seniority. The maximum claimable net weekly wages is also specified in legislation and updated yearly. Consequently, the maximum basic award is thirty weeks multiplied by the highest allowable figure for net weekly earnings. From October 2009, for example, the maximum basic award was £11,900, while from April 2014 it was £14,250.[48]

Second, the non-formulaic, compensatory award for unfair dismissal is normally subject to a statutory cap,[49] unlike compensation for unlawful discrimination, under the Protection from Harassment Act (PHA) 1997 or at common law. The significance in practice of the statutory cap, however, should not be overstated: in the vast majority of cases unfair dismissal compensatory awards get nowhere near it. Moreover, the Enterprise and Regulatory Reform Act 2013 introduced a further change, such that from 29 July 2013 the compensatory award will be the lesser of twelve months gross pay and the statutory cap.[50]

The legislative provision that governs the compensatory award is section 123 of the ERA 1996. This provides for the award of 'such amount as the tribunal considers just and equitable in all the circumstances having regard to the loss sustained by the complainant in consequence of the dismissal in so far as that loss is attributable to action taken by the employer'. It specifies that the concept of loss includes expenses reasonably incurred as a consequence of the dismissal, and benefits foregone that the claimant would reasonably have expected had the dismissal not occurred. Claimants are put under the common law duty to mitigate their loss, meaning, broadly speaking, that they must act reasonably to reduce loss caused by the dismissal. Awards are also liable to be reduced to the extent that the claimant caused or contributed to the dismissal.[51]

Beyond this, first, case law has given rise to another possible reduction. This is where there was technically an unfair dismissal because the employer followed an unreasonable procedure, but a lawful procedure would have made no difference given that the employee was in fact at fault. While there will still be a finding of unfair dismissal, the compensatory award should reflect the factual findings.[52] Second, the EA 2008

---

[48] Note also that there is provision sometimes for a minimum basic award and for an additional award if a reinstatement or re-engagement ordered is not complied with.

[49] The maximum compensatory award took a leap from £12,000 to £50,000 on 25 October 1999 and has been automatically uprated each year since (eg it reached £66,200 from February 2009 and £78,335 from April 2015). Unlimited compensation is potentially payable for health and safety and whistle-blowing dismissals.

[50] See s 15 and the Unfair Dismissal (Variation of the Limit of Compensatory Award) Order 2013, SI 2013/1949.

[51] See also in s 123 on third party pressure on employers and avoiding various possible instances of double recovery.

[52] *Polkey v AE Dayton Services Ltd* [1988] AC 344 (HL).

provided for unfair dismissal (and other statutory) damages to be increased or decreased by up to 25 per cent where the ET judges thought it 'just and equitable in all the circumstances' to do so because of, respectively, the employer or employee's unreasonable failures to comply with a relevant Code of Practice dealing, either exclusively or primarily, with dispute resolution.[53] The Enterprise and Regulatory Reform Act 2013 has made further innovations by giving ETs the power to impose a financial penalty, payable to the Secretary of State, when an employer is found to have breached the claimant's rights and 'aggravating features' are present.[54]

Finally, section 123 ERA 1996 has long been interpreted to mean that only pecuniary (or financial) losses and expenses are recoverable in an action for unfair dismissal. This was established by the National Industrial Relations Court in *Norton Tool Co Ltd v Tewson*, interpreting section 116 of the Industrial Relations Act 1971, the legislative predecessor to section 123 ERA 1996.[55]

This outcome was reaffirmed in 2004 by a unanimous HL in *Dunnachie v Kingston upon Hull CC*,[56] also a judgment in my sample, following another confusing flurry of judicial activity. That had resulted from the HL decision in *Johnson v Unisys Ltd*[57] (upheld and taken forward in *Eastwood v Magnox Electric plc & McCabe v Cornwall CC*, another behavioural conflict case).[58] That was the case in which the HL created new rules about the overlap between common law and statutory claims about dismissal. The basis of the *Johnson* decision was that Parliament had by its unfair dismissal legislation implicitly limited judicial power to alter common law rules about dismissal. Since Parliament is constitutionally superior, this was taken to mean that judges must make no change that would cut across Parliament's will as expressed in the dismissal legislation. Combining the decisions in *Johnson* and *Eastwood*, the net effect, which I expand on later in this chapter, was that first, in certain circumstances there can be no common law challenge to the lawfulness of a dismissal that was allegedly in breach of contract, and second, loss caused by dismissal consequent on some breaches of contract is not recoverable at common law. In reaching the decision in *Johnson v Unisys*, however, Lord Hoffmann made this *obiter* comment (in a speech with which two other Law Lords agreed)[59] about unfair dismissal compensation:

> I know that in the early days of the National Industrial Relations Court it was laid down that only financial loss could be compensated: see *Norton Tool Co Ltd v Tewson* ... *Wellman Alloys Ltd v Russell* ... It was said that the word 'loss' can only mean financial loss. But I think that is too narrow a construction. The emphasis is upon the tribunal awarding such compensation as it thinks just and equitable. So I see no reason why in an appropriate case it should not include compensation for distress, humiliation, damage to reputation in the community or to family life.

Some ETs reacted by relying on Lord Hoffmann's dictum to award unfair dismissal compensation for injury to feelings.

This, however, turned out to be a legal mistake, since the HL in *Dunnachie* unanimously confirmed that non-pecuniary loss is not recoverable in a claim for unfair dismissal. It is important still to remember that *Dunnachie* had no implications for the recoverability of *financial* (or pecuniary) losses caused by unfair dismissal (including where such losses arise from personal injury). Such losses remain recoverable, as they always have been.

---

[53] See TULR(C)A 1992, s 207A, inserted by EA 2008, s 3. Note that this replaced provisions about adjusting compensation in the EA 2002.
[54] See s 16 which was brought into force from 6 April 2014.
[55] [1972] IRLR 86 (NIRC).   [56] [2004] UKHL 36, [2005] 1 AC 226.
[57] *Johnson* (n 4).   [58] *Eastwood* (n 5).
[59] Lord Bingham and Lord Millett, the latter also giving a separate opinion.

The final twist in the tale is discussed further in Chapter 6 because it occurred in another two cases about behavioural conflict, *GMB Trade Union v Brown*[60] and *GAB Robins (UK) Ltd v Triggs*.[61] These found there was an unfair dismissal corollary to the restrictions on damages for non-dismissal breaches of contract in the ordinary courts. The effect is that compensation is not recoverable in an unfair dismissal case for losses and expenses caused by breaches of contract prior to dismissal even if, as is frequently the case in constructive dismissal situations, the former caused the latter. Damages for such losses must be pursued, if at all, some other way, most likely in a common law action in the ordinary courts.

2. Statutory Wrongs of Discrimination

UK anti-discrimination law underwent many changes from 1995 to 2010. These resulted, first, from enactment of new laws to prohibit discrimination related to a wider range of identities than sex, race, and disability. This was prompted by the EU Employment Directive of 2000 about discrimination on grounds of age, disability, religion or belief, and sexual orientation.[62] Second, there were manifold case law and legislative developments relating to particular wrongs, some also initiated by EU Directives.[63] The culmination of this period of change came with enactment of the Equality Act (EqA) 2010 just before the Labour Party lost the election. This was very late in the period from which cases were taken for my sample and its influence was consequently slight, if present at all. The new law was, however, well in place by the time my interviews were undertaken. The Coalition government has also continued the process of change, with some amendments even to the EqA 2010 having already been made.

Starting with a backward glance, I begin with liability rules that governed discriminatory harassment claims before dedicated definitions of this wrong started to be enacted in 2003. Before then, discrimination liability for harassing conduct was possible only in respect of disability, racial, or sexual harassment, and only if use could be made of an existing prohibition.[64] Case law developments occurred in litigation about direct race and sex discrimination which were important for anti-discrimination law in general and behavioural conflict in particular.

Next, I explain the specific wrongs of discriminatory harassment that were enacted from 2003 to 2006 during implementation of various EU Directives. These required, first, changes to the existing law on disability, race, and sex discrimination, and second, the extension of protection to those discriminated against on grounds of age, sexual orientation, and religion or belief. In each case a legislative prohibition of discriminatory harassment was part of the package. The EqA 2010 in turn codified the law on this topic.

I then deal with the law regarding discrimination claims that do not directly allege harassment, since claims of this kind arise in behavioural conflict litigation. Typically such actions have been for direct discrimination and victimization, the law on which has

---

[60] *GMB* (n 6).   [61] *GAB Robins* (n 7).

[62] Directive 2000/78/EC of 27 November 2000 on age, disability, religion or belief, and sexual orientation.

[63] See Directive 2000/43/EC of 29 June 2000 on race and ethnic origin, Directive 2002/73/EC of 23 September 2002 on sex, gender reassignment, and marital status discrimination, and Directive 2006/54/EC of 5 July 2006 which consolidated several directives related to equal treatment and some case law developments.

[64] Harassing conduct at work might of course have been unlawful as another kind of legal wrong, eg, at common law or under the PHA 1997.

tended to be more stable. It is in this context that 'old-style' discriminatory harassment cases may still be influential, since courts may regard themselves as bound by those decisions when interpreting the wrongs of direct discrimination in the EqA 2010.

Finally, I explain the central points on remedies for unlawful discrimination, in relation to which there has been reasonable continuity. This is, incidentally, also the case regarding which working people qualify for anti-discrimination rights. None of the pre-EqA 2010 anti-discrimination legislation contained a general qualifying period of employment before rights accrued and protection extended to people employed under contracts of service, of apprenticeship and 'personally to do work'. That formulation goes well beyond the 'employee' category.[65] At the margins nonetheless, some working people are still excluded, typically because of an insufficiently personal element to their work obligation,[66] and this aspect of the law has been retained in the EqA 2010.[67] In reading what follows it is important to remember that the ETs have exclusive jurisdiction in the discrimination actions described.

(1) Liability I: Discriminatory harassment 'old style'

The liability rules explored here are those governing whether harassing conduct was unlawful as direct race and sex discrimination prior to the EqA 2010. Chapter 4 shows that claims were still at times being put this way after specific wrongs of discriminatory harassment were enacted. This is hard to understand in legal terms, since it is technically more difficult to establish direct discrimination than 'new-style' discriminatory harassment. Interestingly, that possibility has specifically been curtailed in the EqA 2010, which seeks to channel those with a discriminatory harassment claim into framing their case in that way rather than as direct discrimination.[68]

I should point out that I do not cover how a harassment claim might have been put under the DDA 1995. While this was a conceivable way of framing some disability claims, it did not emerge as significant in the case law.

(a) Racial or sexual harassment as direct discrimination

The term 'sexual harassment' was coined in the United States in the 1970s in studies of workplace behaviour.[69] The notion gained currency and over time was absorbed into US law.[70] This was the result especially of existing wrongs of sex discrimination being interpreted to proscribe a version of sexual harassment. There were analogous developments in the United Kingdom in the 1980s when the concept of direct sex discrimination was, with some strain, adapted to prohibit conduct described as sexual harassment. The equivalence in the wording of the Race Relations Act (RRA) 1976 further meant racial harassment was encompassed by this development.

---

[65] Sex Discrimination Act (SDA) 1975, s 82(1); Race Relations Act (RRA) 1976, s 78(1); Disability Discrimination Act (DDA) 1995, s 68(1); Employment Equality (Religion or Belief) Regulations (EERBR) 2003; SI 2003/1660, reg 2; Employment Equality (Sexual Orientation) Regulations (EESOR) 2003; SI 2003/1661, reg 2; Employment Equality (Age) Regulations (EEAR) 2006; SI 2006/1031 reg 2.

[66] See Freedland (n 22), 23–26 and important recent case law developments, particularly, in *Jivraj v Hashwani* [2011] UKSC 40, [2011] ICR 1004 and *Clyde & Co LLP v Bates van Winkelhof* [2014] UKSC 32, [2014] ICR 730.

[67] EqA 2010, s 83(2)–(4).   [68] See EqA 2010, ss 212(1) and (5).

[69] See L Farley, *Sexual Shakedown: The Sexual Harassment of Women on the Job* (New York, 1978).

[70] C MacKinnon, *Sexual Harassment of Working Women: A Case of Sex Discrimination* (New Haven, 1979) was particularly influential in this regard.

The critical decision in the UK was *Porcelli v Strathclyde RC*[71] in 1986. The case was brought under section 1(1)(a) of the Sex Discrimination Act (SDA) 1975, which provided there was direct discrimination against a woman if she was, 'on the grounds of her sex', treated less favourably than an actual or hypothetical male comparator would have been treated. The same definition applied, appropriately adjusted, to discrimination against a man. Section 5(3) specified that the comparison between a man and a woman must be such that the relevant circumstances of each were either the same or not materially different.

The evidence in *Porcelli v Strathclyde RC* was that the claimant had been subjected by two male colleagues to sexual insults and to physical intimidation intended to force her to apply for a transfer. It was found, however, that there was no objection to Ms Porcelli as a woman, only to anyone, male or female, being in her post. On this basis the employer argued that direct sex discrimination was not established because Ms Porcelli was treated no worse than her hypothetical male comparator would have been.

This argument was rejected by the Inner House of the Court of Session (CSIH), holding that part of the behaviour towards Ms Porcelli was linked to her sex and was not of a kind that would have been used against a man. The Lord President said:

In my opinion this particular part of the campaign was plainly adopted against the applicant because she was a woman. It was a particular kind of weapon, based upon the sex of the victim, which, as the [employment] tribunal recognized, would not have been used against an equally disliked man.[72]

The implication was that not only was Ms Porcelli's treatment sex based, but it was also for that reason 'less favourable' than would have been meted out to an equivalent male.

Following on from this a good number of cases found conduct described as racial and sexual harassment to constitute unlawful direct discrimination. There were also judicial interpretations of *Porcelli* to the effect that harassing conduct which referred to race or sex was directly discriminatory with no need to consider how an appropriate comparator either had been, or would have been, treated.[73] It also tended to be taken as read that such behaviour had been on a proscribed ground. Much as this view of the law was disapproved in the CA in 1998,[74] it continued to be influential.[75] In fact it appeared in general EAT guidance in 1999 in *Reed & Bull Information Systems Ltd v Stedman*.[76] Only in *Pearce v Governing Body of Mayfield School and MacDonald v Advocate General for Scotland*[77] was this legal analysis discredited at the highest level. Accordingly, this was another technical legal detour that occurred during the period from which my sample of judgments was taken.

The HL in *Pearce* required courts to stick to the exact wording of the legislative provisions on direct discrimination. The general legal importance of the decision makes it necessary to describe briefly here, while it is discussed further later in this work because the facts involved behavioural conflict. In brief, these were unsuccessful claims for direct discrimination under the SDA 1975 by, respectively, a gay man and a lesbian in respect of unpleasant behaviour to which each was subjected at work. In Mr MacDonald's case,

---

[71] [1986] ICR 564 (CSIH).   [72] ibid, 569.

[73] See especially Morison J's comments in *British Telecommunications v Williams* [1997] IRLR 668, particularly at 669 (EAT).

[74] See especially Ward LJ's comments in *Smith v Gardner Merchant Ltd* [1999] ICR 134 (CA), at 148.

[75] Including on the government, on which see L Barmes, 'Constitutional and Conceptual Complexities in UK Implementation of the EU Harassment Provisions' (2007) 36 *ILJ* 446, 448–51.

[76] [1999] IRLR 299 (EAT). See pp 143–45 in Ch 6.

[77] [2003] UKHL 34, [2003] ICR 937. Their Lordships gave separate speeches but two agreed with Lord Nicholls' opinion and three with Lord Rodgers.

the conduct was by his employers, and in Ms Pearce's case by pupils of the school where she taught, with separate allegations about her employer's reaction.

An important aspect of the HL decision was the unanimous finding that the conduct in question was not prohibited by the SDA 1975 because it had not been on grounds of sex, instead being explained by the claimants' sexual orientations.[78] This was found further to entail that Mr MacDonald's and Ms Pearce's comparators were, respectively, a lesbian and a gay man. That view of the law separately ensured their claims failed, since the factual findings were that these comparators would have been treated equally badly.[79]

Crucial general statements were made in the judgments about the circumstances in which sexual harassment is capable of being direct discrimination.[80] It was made clear that first, a claimant must demonstrate that their comparator had either not been, or would not have been, subjected to equivalently bad treatment. Even where the treatment of the comparator was not gender-specific, it was reasoned by the HL that their actual experience might nonetheless be either equivalent to or worse than that of the claimant. Second, a claimant must additionally show that any less favourable treatment was on the ground of his or her sex. These pronouncements were authoritative also for interpretation of the equivalent RRA 1976 provision.

The HL explicitly disapproved interpretations of *Porcelli v Strathclyde RC*[81] to the effect that no comparison was necessary in cases of gender- or race-specific harassment. It was incorrect to say either that gender-specific harassment of itself indicated a claimant had been less favourably treated than his or her comparator, or that such behaviour was on the ground of sex.[82] It was possible for the *mode or form* of harassment to refer to a target's sex, while the *ground or reason* for it was something unrelated.[83]

(b) The 'old-style' requirement to show a 'detriment'

The ongoing practice in anti-discrimination law is to specify workplace actions (and omissions) in the undertaking of which discrimination is prohibited.[84] That ceased to cause technical problems in identity-based harassment claims once this conduct was specifically outlawed. However, it was necessary in 'old-style' harassment actions to show that what was done fell into a category of workplace conduct in respect of which unlawful discrimination was prohibited. This increased the importance of judicial interpretation of the requirement that employers not discriminate by subjecting those they employed to 'any other detriment'.

The meaning of this phrase was settled by the HL in *CC of West Yorkshire Police v Khan*[85] and *Shamoon v CC of the Royal Ulster Constabulary (Northern Ireland)*.[86] The

---

[78] ibid, Lord Nicholls [7], Lord Hope [59], where he reported that this was conceded by Counsel for Mr MacDonald, Lord Hobhouse [107], Lord Scott [113]–[115], Lord Rodger [148].

[79] ibid, Lord Nicholls [9], Lord Hope [61]–[66], with further explanation from [67]–[84], Lord Hobhouse [109], Lord Rodger [153]–[158], with further explanation from [164]–[175].

[80] ibid, Lord Nicholls [14]–[20], Lord Hope [94]–[95], Lord Hobhouse [110], Lord Scott [116]–[119], Lord Rodger [183]–[184] and [194].

[81] *Porcelli* (n 71).

[82] *Pearce* (n 77), Lord Nicholls [16]–[17] and [30], Lord Hope [86]–[93] and [98], Lord Hobhouse [105] and [110], Lord Rodger [185]–[193].

[83] Lord Hobhouse put this point most directly at [110].

[84] SDA 1975, s 6; RRA 1976, s 4; DDA 1995 s 4; EERBR 2003, reg 6; EESOR 2003, reg 6 (and see the Equal Pay Act (EPA) 1970 regarding discrimination in contractual terms); EEAR 2006, reg 7; and now see EqA 2010, ss 39–40 (and the rest of Part 5 Ch 1 of the EqA 2010 for some specific workplaces).

[85] [2001] UKHL 48, [2001] ICR 1065, Lord Nicholls [14], Lord Mackay [37], and Lord Hoffmann, [53].

[86] [2003] UKHL 11.

clearest exposition was in the second case placing great reliance on the first. To qualify as a detriment, a disadvantage must have arisen in the employment field[87] and the treatment must have been such that a reasonable worker would or might take the view, in all the circumstances, that it was to his or her detriment.[88] An unjustified sense of grievance could not amount to a detriment[89] while a claimant need not demonstrate physical or economic damage.[90] Note, however, that Lord Scott thought reasonableness should be judged from the perspective of the target, hence he said: 'If the victim's opinion that the treatment was to his or her detriment is a reasonable one to hold, that ought, in my opinion, to suffice.'[91]

(c) The ambit of employer responsibility

An important set of issues about the ambit of employer's liability for unlawful discrimination were also raised by 'old-style' discriminatory harassment cases. Anti-discrimination law, past and present, has provided for primary liability of employers and colleagues.[92] In practice, however, vicarious liability is by far the most important kind and absolutely central in harassment cases. Hence the interpretation of the legislative provisions on vicarious liability was again crucial: a narrow approach would have stopped developments regarding harassment in their tracks. A broad approach, however, was by no means inevitable in that it is commonplace for harassment to entail conduct that many would regard as taking the harasser well beyond what they were employed to do and arguably, therefore, outside the ambit of their employer's responsibility.

The various pre-EqA 2010 anti-discrimination statutes provided that employers are vicariously liable for anything done by their employees 'in the course of their employment', with actions by an employee treated 'as done by his employer as well as by him, whether or not it was done with the employer's knowledge or approval'. A potential defence to vicarious liability was, however, included. This operated where the employer was able to show that it 'took such steps as were reasonably practicable to prevent the employee' from doing the prohibited act, or from doing acts of its type, in the course of employment.[93] Section 109 of the EqA 2010 adopts the same framework and retains the same essential phrases, with some updating of the language. As such, it may be predicted that the pre-EqA 2010 law will continue to apply.

---

[87] ibid, per Lord Hope, with whom Lord Hutton and Lord Scott (and arguably also Lord Rodger) agreed on this issue, [34].

[88] ibid, [35].   [89] ibid, citing *Barclays Bank plc v Kapur (no 2)* [1995] IRLR 87 (CA).

[90] ibid, disapproving on this point *Lord Chancellor v Coker* [2001] ICR 507 (EAT).

[91] ibid, [105].

[92] Note that the pre-EqA 2010 law governing the liability of colleagues was remarkably convoluted. The practice was for anti-discrimination legislation to deem employees to have 'aided' an employer's unlawful act. In the SDA 1975, eg, s 42(1) provided for a person who knowingly aided an unlawful act to be treated as having done the act. S 42(2) then deemed an employee who had done something for which his employer was vicariously liable (or would have been but for the defence) as having aided the commission of that act. This odd arrangement was repeated in RRA 1976, s 33; DDA 1995 s 57; EERBR 2003, reg 23; EESOR 2003, reg 23; EEAR 2006, reg 26. See further pp 175–76 in Ch 7 on *Miles v Gilbank* [2006] EWCA Civ 543, [2006] ICR 1297. The EqA 2010 has now arguably simplified the language in s 110 while retaining the same overall approach, such that the pre-EqA 2010 interpretations should hold good. See also *LB of Hackney v Sivanandan* [2013] EWCA Civ 22, [2013] ICR 672, that multiple respondents liable for the same act of discrimination are jointly and severally liable (ie each is liable for the whole loss and required to recover any contribution due from others if action is pursued against them alone).

[93] SDA 1975, s 41; RRA 1976, s 32; DDA 1995, s 58; EERBR 2003, reg 22; EESOR 2003, reg 22; EEAR 2006, reg 25.

The critical decision interpreting the phrase 'in the course of their employment' was, in fact, a harassment case in my sample, *Jones v Tower Boot Co Ltd*.[94] The CA's determination that anti-discrimination legislation gives a wide ambit to vicarious liability was highly significant for the whole of UK anti-discrimination law. Indeed, it went on to influence the common law to adopt a similarly expansive notion of employer responsibility.

In reaching its conclusion the CA specifically rejected the argument that the then rather limited common law concept of vicarious liability should be imported. Rather, it held that the statutory language should be given its natural meaning. Waite LJ, with the agreement of Potter LJ, was bolstered in this conclusion by a purposive approach to construction. By this he meant the principle that 'a statute is to be construed according to its legislative purpose, with due regard to the result which it is the stated or presumed intention of Parliament to achieve and the means provided for achieving it'.[95] Beyond this, he rejected entirely the view that Parliament must have intended to limit an employer's potential liability by ensuring that the more heinous the act of discrimination, the less it would attract vicariously liability. In his view such a reading would cut across the whole legislative scheme and the underlying policy of the vicarious liability provisions in the RRA 1976 and the SDA 1975. Waite LJ observed that racial and sexual harassment in the workplace were to be deterred through a widening of the net of responsibility beyond the 'guilty employees' themselves. This approach was additionally reflected in the legislation including a defence that both rewarded conscientious employers who used their best endeavours to prevent discrimination and encouraged others to take equivalent steps.[96]

The defence to a claim of vicarious liability was itself explored in further cases that often dealt with harassment. The EAT in *Canniffe v East Riding of Yorkshire Council*[97] described a two-stage test. First, it was necessary to identify whether the employer had taken any steps to prevent its employee from doing the acts complained of in the course of employment. Second, there should be consideration of whether any further steps were reasonably practicable.[98] A distinction was drawn between cases where the employer had no particular knowledge of a risk of harassment and where there was such knowledge. In the former case, an adequately publicized sexual harassment policy might be sufficient. In the latter, other possibilities should be considered.[99]

It was pointed out that the defence could not be made out if reasonably practicable steps should have been taken, even if taking them would have made no difference to how its employee acted. The likely success of a measure might, however, go to its reasonable practicability.[100] In *Croft v Royal Mail Group plc* Lord Justice Pill, with the agreement of Jonathan Parker and Keene LJJ, also found that the concept of reasonable practicability entitled the employer to consider whether the time, effort, and expense of the suggested measures were disproportionate to the likely result.[101]

Finally, there is a further case law detour to explain, addressed in the EqA 2010 but now again under review. The issue was the scope of employer responsibility for third party harassment. The HL chose in *Pearce* to clear up what it regarded as another case law mistake.[102] The point arose on the facts (although decision on it was not required) because Ms Pearce had been harassed by school pupils. This meant her employer was not

---

[94] [1997] ICR 254 (CA).   [95] ibid, 261–62.   [96] ibid, 263–64.
[97] [2000] IRLR 555 (EAT).   [98] ibid, 558.   [99] ibid, 559.
[100] ibid, 558 and 559.   [101] [2003] ICR 1425 (CA), 1447.
[102] *Pearce* (n 77), Lord Nicholls [26]–[37], Lord Hope [96]–[103], Lord Hobhouse [105], Lord Scott [120]–[122], Lord Rodger [201]–[205].

vicariously liable for the harassment itself. Instead, the school's responsibility under the SDA 1975 depended on whether it was primarily liable for how it responded.

On this point, the HL again required strict adherence to the wording of the statute. To establish that an employer was itself liable for direct discrimination it must be shown, first, that the employer's response to the third party behaviour amounted to less favourable treatment than was, or would have been, afforded to the claimant's comparator. Second, the less favourable treatment must have been by reason of the claimant's sex. This interpretation furnished another basis on which Ms Pearce's claim failed, since it was held that her employer would have reacted in the same way to equivalent treatment of a gay male teacher.

This reasoning also led the HL to overrule the EAT in *Burton v Rhule De Vere Hotels Ltd*.[103] There it had been found sufficient to establish liability that the employer was in a position to control the third party. In the period when that case was authoritative from 1997 until 2003, courts had not concerned themselves in relevant cases with whether an employer had itself breached section 1(1)(a) and its equivalent in the RRA 1976. This is another vagary in the case law, therefore, that affected the handling of some behavioural conflict cases from 1995 until 2010. Further, more recent developments on this point are explained below.

(2) Liability II: Discriminatory harassment 'new style'

The amount of legislation on discriminatory harassment in the period from 2003 until 2010 was disconcerting. In the mass of changes, however, there are three main points to retain. First, the basic liability model was significantly uniform. Second, many elements in the various new laws were continuous with what had gone before. In particular, the initial definitions of discriminatory harassment, and now those in the EqA 2010, essentially retained the earlier approach to primary and vicarious liability. Third, the new definitions contained important simplifications. Most importantly, they dispensed with the requirement to show less favourable treatment than a comparator and with claimants having separately to establish that harassing conduct subjected them to a 'detriment'.[104]

It is helpful even so to have a chronology of when dedicated definitions of discriminatory harassment were enacted for each of the groups protected by UK anti-discrimination law and of when the EqA 2010 intervened. Specific prohibition of harassment was required in respect of race by the Race Directive of 2000, for gender by the amended Equal Treatment Directive (ETD) of 2002, and for the other grounds by the Employment Directive of 2000. This was legislated in the UK as follows:

(1) The RRA 1976 was amended by 2003 Regulations which came into force in time for the Race Directive's implementation deadline of 19 July 2003.[105]

(2) Regulations to alter the DDA1995 were laid in July 2003 to come into force on 1 October 2004.[106]

---

[103] [1997] ICR 1 (EAT).

[104] But see s 212(5) EqA 2010 providing that harassing conduct outside the dedicated definition can be challenged as direct discrimination (which s 212(1) otherwise excludes). See the text to n 68 above.

[105] The Race Relations Act 1976 (Amendment) Regulations 2003, SI 2003/1626. Note that the 2003 law on racial harassment applied only in relation to race, ethnic, and national origins, while colour and nationality discrimination continued to be covered by existing interpretations of the RRA 1976.

[106] The Disability Discrimination Act 1995 (Amendment) Regulations (DDAAR) 2003, SI 2003/1673.

(3) Regulations on religion or belief and sexual orientation came into force in December 2003.[107]

(4) The first harassment changes to the SDA 1975 were made by Regulations that came into force in October 2005.[108]

(5) Regulations on age came into force on 1 October 2006.[109]

(6) The 2005 changes to the SDA 1975 were later modified because of a successful judicial review challenge to the previous amendments in *R (EOC) v SS for Trade and Industry*.[110] The further changes were effected in Regulations that came into force in April 2008.[111]

(7) Finally the EqA 2010 rationalized the position by applying a core definition of discriminatory harassment at work across the board, although excepting conduct related to marriage, civil partnership, pregnancy or maternity. There are also two additional forms of sexual harassment only, as required by the 2002 and 2006 Equal Treatment Directives.[112] The harassment elements of the legislation were brought into force in October 2010.[113]

In view of this timeline it makes sense to divide this topic into, first, the concepts of discriminatory harassment that were successively introduced from 2003 until 2006, second, the changes to sexual harassment law in 2008, and third, the new law on discriminatory harassment in the EqA 2010.

(a) Dedicated definitions of discriminatory harassment enacted from 2003 to 2006

The new definitions of age, disability, race, religion or belief, and sexual orientation harassment remained in place from the date they were each enacted until the EqA 2010 harassment provisions came into force. Only the provisions on sexual harassment had to be legislatively altered in between. In each case there was a core concept of discriminatory harassment, with the 2002 Equal Treatment Directive requiring the amended SDA 1975 additionally to outlaw two other wrongs.

The Race Directive defines harassment in Article 2(3) as follows:

Harassment shall be deemed to be discrimination … when an unwanted conduct related to racial or ethnic origin takes place with the purpose or effect of violating the dignity of a person and of creating an intimidating, hostile, degrading, humiliating or offensive environment. In this context the concept of harassment may be defined in accordance with the national laws and practice of the Member States.

Article 2(3) of the Employment Directive is in the same terms, although the unwanted conduct must be 'related to any of the grounds referred to in Article 1', namely 'religion or belief, disability, age and sexual orientation'. The amended Equal Treatment Directive's core concept is in the same terms except it refers to 'unwanted conduct related

---

[107] EERBR 2003 and Employment Equality (Sexual Orientation) Regulations (EESOR) 2003.
[108] EESOR 2005, SI 2005/2467.
[109] EEAR 2006.
[110] [2007] EWHC 483 (Admin), [2007] ICR 1234.
[111] See the Sex Discrimination Act 1975 (Amendment) Regulations 2008, SI 2008 No 656.
[112] EqA 2010, s 26.
[113] Equality Act 2010 (Commencement No 4, Savings, Consequential, Transitional, Transitory and Incidental Provisions and Revocation) Order 2010, SI 2010/2317.

to the sex of a person'.[114] There is also no qualification allowing harassment to be defined in accordance with the national laws and practice of the Member States.

In respect of each ground the main UK version of harassment included the following components:

(1) unwanted conduct;

(2) for which *either* the purpose *or* the effect was:

either to violate the dignity of another person,

or to create an intimidating, hostile, degrading, humiliating, or offensive environment for them;

(3) where the alleged harasser acted, respectively, for a reason related to a disabled person's disability, on the ground of the target's sex, on the ground that the target intended to undergo, was undergoing or had undergone gender reassignment or, finally, on one of the other prohibited grounds.

The more general wording in respect of age, race, religion or belief, and sexual orientation seemed to signify that the conduct in question need not have been on ground of the target's age etc, but only on the impugned ground *at large*. In other words, unwanted conduct with one of the requisite purposes or effects could, for example, be on grounds of a third party's race and still count as racial harassment of the person (or people) to whom it was directed.

Finally, the legislation provided that conduct was to be viewed as having either violated a victim's dignity or created an intimidating etc environment for them if it was reasonable so to view it in all the circumstances. It was specifically stated that the circumstances to be taken into account included the victim's perception. This made it necessary for judges sometimes to take into account the target's point of view in deciding whether conduct had a sufficiently negative effect to count as harassment.[115]

Only a brief word is necessary about the two additional forms of sexual harassment legislated in 2005. These were not much litigated, neither figuring in any of the cases on behavioural conflict in my sample. Be that as it may, the first was called sexual harassment in Article 2(2) of the amended ETD and defined as:

where any form of unwanted verbal, non-verbal or physical conduct of a sexual nature occurs, with the purpose or effect of violating the dignity of a person, in particular when creating an intimidating, hostile, degrading, humiliating or offensive environment.

Here there is no requirement that the conduct be 'related to' sex. Rather, the focus is on the sexual nature of the behaviour. The UK enactment of this version mirrored that for the core concept with the dignity and environment purposes and effects being listed as alternative bases for liability, and the presence of an effect being judged in the same way. No legislative definition was given of 'conduct of a sexual nature'.

The final form of harassment in the amended ETD was translated into the SDA 1975 as a kind of victimization provision. A prohibition was included on treating a person less favourably than they would otherwise have been treated, on the ground either of their

---

[114] Art 2(2).

[115] See *Grant v HM Land Registry* [2011] EWCA Civ 769, [2011] ICR 1390 in which the CA applied this provision to a gay employee who was 'out' in one location and moved to another, where he alleged he was harassed including by his sexuality being made known to his new colleagues. Mr Grant succeeded in some harassment allegations but not in respect of that one.

rejection of, or submission to, unwanted conduct that fell into either the core or sexual conduct definitions of harassment.

There followed case law developments regarding the new core concept of discriminatory harassment. The first dealt with the UK implementation of the main sexual harassment provision, and specifically the contrast between the Directive's reference to unwanted conduct *related to* the sex of a person and UK law requiring such behaviour to have been *on the ground of* the target's sex. This element in the 2005 gender changes, amongst others, was successfully challenged in *R (EOC) v SS for Trade and Industry*.[116] The legal objection to the UK transposition was that the 'on the ground of' wording was narrower than 'related to' in the Directive. As a result Burton J ruled that the core concept of sexual harassment should be recast 'to eliminate the issue of causation'.[117]

The Secretary of State for Trade and Industry in fact argued that the phrase 'on the ground of' should be construed in light of EU law to mean 'related to',[118] but the court did not see it as either appropriate or possible so to reinterpret the SDA 1975.[119] A strikingly wide interpretation of the underlying wrong seems accordingly to have been agreed by all parties, to the effect that unwanted conduct of the relevant kind need only have a 'connection or association' with sex to come within the prohibition.[120]

The second sense in which the transposition was found to have been too limited was that it referred only to conduct on the ground of the *target's* sex. It was regarded as clear that the Amended ETD meant that 'there could be harassment of a woman if the effect of denigratory conduct, directed towards another party—perhaps a man—related to sex, but not of a sexual nature, had the effect of creating a humiliating or offensive environment for her'.[121] This reflected the wide linguistic formulation in the EU Directives of the other forms of discriminatory harassment (except regarding disability) and the broad approach to direct race discrimination in UK law.[122] Finally, UK law was found to have been inadequate in the provision made for vicarious liability for the acts of third parties,[123] revisiting that aspect of the decision in *Pearce*.

An odd legal hiatus followed this decision. First, until the SDA was altered in 2008, only employees in public employment were able directly to rely on the judgment. Second, it was not known if the ruling had knock-on implications for other UK definitions of discriminatory harassment. For example, the government initially only conceded that the SDA 1975 would have to be amended.[124]

Later rulings, however, indicated that an analogously broad interpretation of the connection to identity was required across the board. In July 2008, the European Court of Justice decision in *Coleman v Attridge Law* clarified that disability harassment occurs where 'the unwanted conduct amounting to harassment which is suffered by an employee who is not himself disabled is related to the disability of his child, whose care is provided primarily by that employee'.[125] In October 2008, the EAT in *Saini v All Saints Haque Centre*[126] found that the 2003 provision on religion or belief harassment was breached, not only where an employee was harassed because *he* held certain religious or other relevant beliefs, but also where this happened because another person had such beliefs. Aside from considering

---

[116] *R (EOC)* (n 110).   [117] ibid, [63].   [118] ibid, [19].   [119] ibid, [61]–[62].
[120] ibid, [6].   [121] ibid, [29] and [63].
[122] See *Showboat Entertainment Centre v Owens* [1984] 1 WLR 384 (EAT) and *Weathersfield Ltd v Sargent* [1999] ICR 425 (CA) and the limits to this logic discussed in *Serco Ltd v Redfearn* [2006] EWCA Civ 659, [2006] ICR 1367. See the text to n 144 and n 145 below.
[123] *R (EOC)*, [63].
[124] DCLG, *Discrimination Law Review, A Framework for Fairness: Proposals for a Single Equality Bill for Great Britain* (2007), 162.
[125] [2008] ICR 1128 (ECJ), [63].   [126] [2009] IRLR 74 (EAT).

the UK authorities regarding direct race discrimination, Lady Smith observed that this interpretation was consistent 'with the aims and intention of the Framework Directive', and she cited the Advocate General's comment in *Coleman v Attridge Law* that '[a]s soon as we have ascertained that the basis for the employer's conduct is one of the prohibited grounds then we enter the realm of unlawful discrimination'.[127]

Finally, in December 2008 the CA by a majority (Laws LJ dissenting) went still further in *English v Thomas Sanderson Blinds Ltd*.[128] It was found on assumed facts that there could be sexual orientation harassment where a person, who was neither gay nor thought to be so, was tormented with homophobic taunting. Sedley LJ said of the alleged situation that:

[t]he incessant mockery ... created a degrading and hostile working environment, and it did so on grounds of sexual orientation. That is the way I would prefer to put it. Alternatively, however, it can be properly said that the fact that the claimant is not gay, and that his tormentors know it, has just as much to do with sexual orientation—his own, as it happens—as if he were gay.[129]

Lawrence Collins LJ reached the same conclusion, reasoning that all the elements in the wrong of sexual orientation harassment in the 2003 Regulations were present and that no case law stood in the way of the legislation being interpreted to this effect.[130]

(b) 2008 changes to the law on sexual harassment

The Sex Discrimination Act 1975 (Amendment) Regulations 2008 made several changes to the law on sex discrimination from April 2008, all in response to *R (EOC) v SS for Trade and Industry*. First, regarding the core concept of sexual harassment, it was provided that unwanted conduct towards a claimant need only be 'related to her sex or that of another person' (with appropriate adjustments if the claim was by a man).[131]

Second, the law on employer liability for sexual harassment by third parties was adjusted. The Explanatory Notes to the Regulations indicated that this was required by the judicial review decision.[132] The change was a precursor to the provision for employers to have some third party liability for all types of discriminatory harassment in section 40 of the EqA 2010. This aspect of the EqA 2010 was, however, repealed with effect from October 2013.[133] *Sheffield CC v Norouzi* nonetheless confirmed that EU law to some extent imposes liability on employers for third party harassment.[134]

(c) The EqA 2010 on discriminatory harassment

Finally, the EqA 2010 harmonized the core concept of discriminatory harassment on the version enacted in 2008 in respect of sex. There is, therefore, now discriminatory

---

[127] *Coleman* (n 125), [AG17]. [128] [2008] EWCA Civ 1421, [2009] ICR 543.
[129] ibid, [37].
[130] ibid, [44]–[70]. The other two judges also considered the direct race discrimination case law on the analogous issue. Unlike Lawrence Collins LJ, however, Laws (at [21]) and Sedley LJJ (at [41]) were troubled by the issues raised in *Serco*. See the text to n 144 and n 145 below.
[131] Sex Discrimination Act 1975 (Amendment) Regulations 2008, SI 2008/656, reg 3.
[132] I have some difficulty following this conclusion, comparing paras 4.2–4.3 and 7.10 of the Explanatory Notes & *R (EOC)* (n 110), [40]. Still some employer liability for harassment by third parties followed anyway from the provision that unlawful harassing conduct need only be 'related to' sex. See further J Hand, 'Employer's liability for third-party harassment: an "unworkable" and superfluous provision?' (2013) 42 ILJ 75.
[133] Enterprise and Regulatory Reform Act 2013, s 65.
[134] [2011] IRLR 897 (EAT) and Hand (n 132).

harassment where a person engages in unwanted conduct related to age, disability, gender reassignment, race, religion or belief, sex or sexual orientation which has either of the purposes or effects provided for by the pre-EqA 2010 law. It is also stated that whether conduct had the specified effect is to be decided, taking account of the perception of the claimant, the other circumstances of the case, and whether it was reasonable for the conduct to have that effect. At the same time, while not making any substantive change, the Act simplified the language for the sexual conduct and victimization concepts of harassment.[135]

(3) Liability III: Direct discrimination and victimization in behavioural conflict cases

Other aspects of anti-discrimination law were deployed in behavioural conflict cases from 1995 to 2010. In particular, there were allegations of direct discrimination that did not focus on harassing behaviour and also victimization claims. In what follows I explain the key features of the general law on direct discrimination, sketch the law on victimization, and briefly describe how the EqA 2010 defines these wrongs.

(a) Non-harassing conduct as direct discrimination

The basic legislative definition of direct discrimination, the need to establish that discrimination was prohibited in respect of challenged actions, and the rules on primary and vicarious liability were the same as for harassment claims, but in more general cases there tended to be less controversy about, first, whether allegations were covered by the anti-discrimination statutes and, second, whether the employer was legally responsible for what had been done. This followed from these claims focusing on typical employer actions such as dealing with complaints and dismissing people.

More importantly, the two lines of direct discrimination case law diverged in their substantive approach to the wrong. From the mid-1980s until *Pearce* was decided in 2003, many lawyers, as explained earlier, took the view that harassing conduct that was overtly related to sex or race straightforwardly counted as direct discrimination; they saw no need to worry about the treatment of a real or hypothetical comparator nor separately to consider the ground of such conduct. Putting the law on pregnancy and maternity discrimination aside, there was no hint of so relaxed an approach in non-harassment cases. From the perspective of those decisions, the position taken by the HL in *Pearce* was entirely predictable.

Important background to note is that the law on pregnancy and maternity discrimination developed separately under the influence of EU law. The effect was that in such situations there was frequently no requirement to show that a comparator would have been better treated.[136] Extensive case law then interpreted the meaning in other situations[137] of 'on the ground of' in the SDA 1975 definition of direct discrimination, and the equivalent, 'on grounds of' in the RRA 1976 definition. These decisions became

---

[135] EqA 2010, s 26.

[136] See especially the seminal decisions in *Webb v Emo Air Cargo* by the ECJ, reported at [1994] QB 718 and by the HL applying the ECJ's reasoning, reported at [1995] 1 WLR 1454. An important corollary is that employers are protected from direct discrimination claims by men in respect of benefits for women connected with pregnancy and childbirth.

[137] Note in this connection that the RRA 1976 also prohibited racial segregation as direct race discrimination.

authoritative in respect of most of the new forms of direct discrimination outlawed when anti-discrimination law was extended to protect other groups. The exceptions were the particular legislative approaches taken to direct disability discrimination in 2003,[138] and to pregnancy and maternity discrimination in 2005 and 2008 (the latter reflecting the pre-existing case law position).[139] The impact was also different for direct age discrimination because a justification 'defence' was legislated to apply where less-favourable treatment on grounds of age was a 'proportionate means of pursuing a legitimate aim'.

There were two main strands to the general direct discrimination decisions. The early cases employed an objective causation-based test on a 'but for' model. Later cases moved towards a more subjective enquiry into the alleged discriminator's reasons for their conduct. Finally, the SC in *R (on the application of E) v Governing Body of JFS* reconciled the two approaches.[140] The reasoning of the majority split direct discrimination cases into two types, reflecting the two strands of earlier decisions. In all cases what ultimately mattered was, as Lord Phillips described it, the 'factual criteria' that determined what had been done. In some cases, however, objective, causation-based analysis demonstrated that these included a prohibited ground. In others cases, subjective enquiry was necessary to decide if that had been so.[141] Each judge in the majority in essence analysed the law in this way, albeit in the course of separate speeches.[142]

Case law over the years also explored the significance of slight variations in wording in the direct discrimination provisions in the SDA 1975 and the RRA 1976. The RRA 1976 phrase 'on racial grounds' was held to signify that conduct could be directly racially discriminatory in circumstances where the racial grounds for what was done related to a different identity to the victim's. The cases in which this view of the law was established in particular enabled direct race discrimination to be found where the claimant was penalized for refusing to act in a racist way.[143]

The facts in *Serco Ltd v Redfearn*,[144] however, led the CA to limit the circumstances in which such reasoning would apply. Mr Redfearn was dismissed from his job for the Council driving disabled adults and children, the majority of whom were of Asian origin. The dismissal occurred shortly after Mr Redfearn had been elected as a local councillor for the British National Party and resulted from concerns about the effect of his political affiliation. The ET rejected a direct race discrimination claim, finding the dismissal had been for health and safety reasons and not 'on racial grounds'. The

[138] See DDA 1995, s 3A(5) inserted by the DDAAR 2003 from October 2004.

[139] See SDA 1975, s 3A, inserted by the Employment Equality (Sex Discrimination) Regulations 2005 (SI 2005/2467) from October 2005 and amended by the Sex Discrimination Act 1975 (Amendment) Regulations 2008 SI 2008/656, reg 2 from April 2008, as required by *R (EOC)* (n 110).

[140] [2009] UKSC15, [2010] 2 AC 728. But see now *Hall v Bull* [2013] UKSC 73, [2013] 1 WLR 3741, which the three justices in the majority (Lady Hale, Lord Kerr, and Lord Toulson) saw as a straightforward example of the first category of direct discrimination. Lord Neuberger and Lord Hughes seemed to conflate the two types suggesting that difficulties may recur.

[141] *JFS*, [13]–[23].

[142] ibid, at [55] Baroness Hale agreed with Lord Phillips, Lord Mance, Lord Kerr, and Lord Clarke in the result and with their reasons, and she gave an account of the distinction between different kinds of direct discrimination cases at [62]–[64]. Lord Mance put the point in his own words at [78]. Lord Kerr agreed with Lord Mance on direct and indirect discrimination at [123] and gave his view about the direct discrimination split at [113]–[116]. Finally, Lord Clarke reached the same conclusion as the rest of the majority, 'essentially for the reasons they have given' [125] and gave his version of the two categories at [132], [137], and [141]–[145]. See also Underhill J's very similar earlier analysis in *Amnesty International v Ahmed* [2009] ICR 1450 (EAT).

[143] *Showboat* & *Weathersfield* (n 122).   [144] [2006] EWCA Civ 659, [2006] ICR 1367.

EAT reversed the ET, whose decision was restored by the CA. Mummery LJ observed as follows:

It is a non-sequitur to argue that [Mr Redfearn] was dismissed 'on racial grounds' because the circumstances leading up to his dismissal included a relevant racial consideration, such as the race of fellow employees and customers and the policies of the BNP on racial matters. Mr Redfearn was no more dismissed 'on racial grounds' than an employee who is dismissed for racially abusing his employer, a fellow employee or a valued customer. Any other result would be incompatible with the purpose of the 1976 Act to promote equal treatment of persons irrespective of race by making it unlawful to discriminate against a person on the grounds of race.[145]

Adjudication over time of the direct discrimination provision in the EqA 2010 and of the dedicated harassment wrongs is likely to implicate these decisions given the expansive approach taken there to the requisite link between identity and, respectively, less favourable treatment or harassing conduct.

A further general consideration regarding the concept of direct discrimination is the depth of controversy that can arise about the characteristics of comparators, whether real or hypothetical. This was amply illustrated by *Pearce*, while the HL decision in *Shamoon v CC of the Royal Ulster Constabulary*[146] contained perhaps the most profound discussion of how the comparison exercise should be conceived. It was in that case, however, that Lord Nicholls also made the influential comment that 'employment tribunals may sometimes be able to avoid arid and confusing disputes about the identification of the appropriate comparator by concentrating primarily on why the claimant was treated as she was.'

Finally, there has been much case law discussion of the effect in direct discrimination cases of the partial legislative transfer of the burden of proof resulting from successive EU law directives. The first change was in 2001 to the SDA 1975,[147] implementing the EU Burden of Proof Directive 97/80/EC. The EU inspired changes to disability and race law, and the enactments regarding age, religion or belief, and sexual orientation discrimination in turn extended the same approach to the other protected groups (although not covering colour and nationality discrimination under the RRA 1976). According to the various changes, where a claimant proved facts from which the court was technically permitted, absent an adequate explanation, to find there had been unlawful discrimination, the burden of proof shifted to the employer to disprove discrimination. This was, on the face of it, a minor shift from the existing law.[148] The change seemed to be only from *permitting* to *requiring* courts to make findings of unlawful discrimination where sufficient facts had been proved to found an inference of discrimination and no adequate alternative explanation was proved.

Still, there was much convolution and argument about exactly what was required, substantively and procedurally, for the burden to transfer.[149] The key cases in which guidance was ultimately given were *Igen Ltd v Wong*,[150] *Laing v Manchester CC*,[151] and *Madarassy v Nomura International plc*,[152] the last two included in my sample. In the event, the substantive change ended up being as a plain reading of the legislation had suggested from the start. The eventual effect of the litigation, however, was eye-wateringly

---

[145] ibid, [46].   [146] [2003] ICR 337 (HL).

[147] See the Sex Discrimination (Indirect Discrimination and Burden of Proof) Regulations 2001, SI 2001/2660 in force from October 2001.

[148] See in particular *King v Great Britain-China Centre* [1992] ICR 516 (CA).

[149] See *Madarassy v Nomura International Plc* [2007] EWCA Civ 33, [2007] ICR 867, [1]–[14].

[150] [2005] EWCA Civ142, [2005] ICR 931.   [151] [2006] ICR 1519 (EAT).

[152] *Madarassy* (n 149).

technical guidance and commentary by judges. Ironically, therefore, the changes arguably ended up adding to the difficulty, including for claimants, of navigating this area of law.[153]

(b) Victimization

The wrong of victimization as previously enacted involved treating someone 'less favourably' than others, 'by reason that' first, they had taken steps under the anti-discrimination statutes, second, that they were known to intend such steps, or third, that they were suspected either of having already taken them or of having this intention. The acts covered were enumerated in the victimization provisions. They included bringing anti-discrimination proceedings, making allegations under anti-discrimination legislation, giving evidence or information in connection with proceedings, and, indeed, doing anything else with reference to the relevant statutes. The protection, however, was specified not to apply to false allegations not made in good faith.[154]

There has been particular controversy about the meaning of 'by reason that' in the victimization wrongs, echoing the case law debates about the 'on grounds of' elements in the direct discrimination wrongs. In *CC of West Yorkshire Police v Khan*,[155] however, this phrase was treated by a majority of the HL as meaning the same as the 'on grounds of' formulation in the direct discrimination provisions.[156]

(c) The EqA 2010 on direct discrimination and victimization

We have seen above that the EqA 2010 provisions relevant to discrimination at work, while expressed in simpler language, appear mostly to have the same effect as the pre-existing law. This is true for who is protected, for the actions at work in respect of which discrimination is prohibited, and for most of the rules about primary and vicarious liability, including the potential defence. Further, the significant change regarding third party harassment has now been repealed. All that remains to be outlined is consequently how the EqA 2010 defines direct discrimination and victimization.

(i) The EqA 2010 on direct discrimination

The 'protected characteristics' in respect of which direct discrimination is prohibited by section 13 are age, disability, gender reassignment, marriage and civil partnership, race, religion or belief, sex (not including pregnancy and maternity), and sexual orientation.[157] More detailed definitions of what is meant by these different characteristics are set out in the Act where necessary,[158] with pregnancy and maternity discrimination provided for separately.[159]

The basic definition of direct discrimination is that '[a] person (A) discriminates against another (B) if, because of a protected characteristic, A treats B less favourably

---

[153] See *Amnesty* (n 142), [24(4)].

[154] See SDA 1975, s 4; RRA 1976, s 2; DDA 1995, s 55 (which from the start protected non-disabled people); EERBR 2003, reg 4 (in which the good faith etc requirement was extended also to cover evidence and information); EESOR, reg 4, and EEAR, reg 4.

[155] *Khan* (n 85).

[156] But see M Connolly, 'Racial Groups, Sub-Groups, The Demise of the *But For* test, and the Death of the Benign Motive Defence' (2010) 39 ILJ 183, 189–90 on the difficulty of reconciling *Khan* with the majority view in *JFS*.

[157] EqA 2010, s 13.   [158] ibid, ss 5–12.   [159] ibid, ss 17 and 18.

than A treats or would treat others.' The definition is, however, distinctive between different grounds in some respects, most significantly regarding age and disability.[160]

The question is whether earlier authority about 'on grounds of'/'on the ground of' governs interpretation of 'because of'. This seems inevitable in that the promoters of the legislation made clear that they intended the two phrases to mean the same thing. For example, the Explanatory Notes to the December 2009 print of the bill repeated that '[t]his clause uses the words "because of" where the current legislation contains various definitions using the words "on grounds of". This change in wording does not change the legal meaning of the definition, but rather is designed to make it more accessible to the ordinary user of the Bill.'[161] While such notes are drafted by civil servants, they seem accurately to reflect a settled governmental intention and that is how the case law is currently unfolding.

Another notable aspect of the legislative process was that it evinced the intention to extend protection in respect of conduct due to a protected characteristic that the victim did not share, adopting the earlier race model and that now contained in EU and UK harassment law. This is implicit, first, in the wording of the basic definition of direct discrimination. Second, it is spelled out for actions by non-disabled people that more favourable treatment of a disabled person is not prohibited.[162] Third, there is an exception for workplace marriage and civil partnership cases, according to which protection is limited to where treatment is 'because it is B who is married or a civil partner'.[163] The Explanatory Notes also recorded this purpose, indicating that this would ensure uniform protection for what was termed discrimination based on association and perception.[164] This is a significant change on any view, although in respect of disability it was to some extent required by *Coleman v Attridge Law*.[165] However, the precise ambit of the development may turn out to be unpredictable.

This follows from it being mistaken to assume that the government's proposed model necessarily tracks factual situations that depend on either a claimant's associations or on how they are perceived. The earlier case law, discussed above, rather suggested that a broad interpretation may extend protection to *any* situation where someone was treated less favourably because of a prohibited characteristic, regardless of whether that person either had an association with anyone with that characteristic or was perceived to be from that group. The case of *English v Thomas Sanderson Blinds Ltd*[166] demonstrated in the harassment context how far protection on this analysis might go. *Serco Ltd v Redfearn*,[167] however, illustrated the potential for judges to recast earlier interpretations in the face of factual exigencies.

Aside from these questions about the interpretation of the new direct discrimination law, the EqA 2010 seems to have simplified the previous wording, while for the most part retaining the existing substantive position. On comparison then, the new law states that 'there must be no material difference between the circumstances' of the claimant and those of the person with whom their treatment is compared.[168] The wording of the

---

[160] As in the previous law, there is a justification 'defence' to direct age discrimination, racial segregation is expressly defined as direct race discrimination and there is a savings provision regarding 'special treatment afforded to a woman in connection with pregnancy and childbirth'. An innovation is that direct discrimination is defined also to protect breastfeeding women.

[161] HL Bill 20, Explanatory Notes (TSO, Dec 2009), para 80. See also the initial Explanatory Notes to the Equality Bill as it was presented in April 2009, (TSO, April 2009), para 73.

[162] EqA 2010, s 13(3).   [163] EqA 2010, s 13(4).

[164] See HL Bill 20—EN (n 161), para 24.   [165] *Coleman* (n 125).

[166] [2008] EWCA Civ 1421, [2009] ICR 543.   [167] *Serco* (n 122).

[168] EqA 2010, s 23. But note that there is specific provision in s 23(2) for the comparison in direct disability discrimination claims and in 23(3) to ensure discrimination between married people and civil partners is covered.

burden of proof section is also more straightforward and, unlike the pre-existing law, applies across the board. A court must accordingly find for the claimant where 'there are facts from which the court could decide, in the absence of any other explanation', that a person contravened a (civil liability) provision of the Act, unless that person shows that in fact they did not.[169] It needs to be remembered, however, that whenever the EqA 2010 uses new language, its meaning will only be known for sure once the provision has been authoritatively interpreted by the courts.

(ii) The EqA 2010 on victimization

Finally, the EqA 2010 simplified the wording of the victimization wrong,[170] but this time made a significant substantive change. The provision removed the need for a comparison. Instead of it being necessary to show 'less favourable treatment' than someone who has not done a 'protected act', it will be enough for victimization liability if an employer subjects someone to a detriment on one of the prohibited bases.[171]

(4) Remedies

Anti-discrimination legislation has provided for several options in terms of remedies, yet in practice it is compensation that has been the most significant. It is possible that the EqA 2010 will bring about some change in this respect and its remedial provisions will be considered later in this chapter. For the purposes of filling in the legal background to behavioural conflict judgments and organizational practices, however, it is necessary only to concentrate on the rules about damages.

(a) Pre-EqA 2010 remedies

The main potential individual remedies[172] were declarations of rights, compensation, and recommendations for an employer to take action to obviate or reduce the adverse effects on the claimant of the unlawful discrimination. The ET was also given power either to award or to increase compensation where an employer did not comply with a recommendation. Neither declarations of rights nor recommendations have, however, been much used.

Experience with unfair dismissal suggests that compensation would probably have been the remedy most frequently sought and ordered in discrimination regardless of how the remedial provisions were designed. Still, it remains noteworthy that discrimination rules about compensation are unusually generous. First, there has since the mid-1990s been no cap on awards. Second, the legislation from the start specified that damages were available for injury to feelings. Finally, while it was provided for tortious principles to determine the assessment of damages, the anti-discrimination legislation has been interpreted not to include a common law foreseeability limitation on the recoverability of losses and expenses. The level in practice of awards should however not be exaggerated. The vast majority remain modest.

---

[169] EqA 2010, s 136.

[170] It also rationalizes the definition across the various grounds, such that the more modern formulation is used whereby there is no protection for false allegations, evidence, or information that were, respectively, made or given in bad faith.

[171] EqA 2010, s 27.

[172] There was also the possibility of institutional enforcement by equality bodies and of judicial review proceedings, eg to enforce public sector equality duties.

The most important decision on remedies was another from my sample, *Essa v Laing Ltd*.[173] Building on observations by Stuart-Smith LJ in *Sheriff v Klyne Tugs (Lowestoft) Ltd*,[174] Pill and Clarke LLJ found by a majority that damage flowing directly and naturally from unlawful discrimination was in principle recoverable. They found no requirement for loss or expense to have been reasonably foreseeable,[175] although claimants must show the wrong caused the damage and are under the duty to mitigate. The decision was under the RRA 1976 but the equivalence of the wording elsewhere made it of general application. More recently, *Chagger v Abbey National plc*[176] illustrated how difficult it may be for a claimant to mitigate their losses, including because of the stigma that attaches to jobseekers who have previously sued their employers. It also made the significant ruling that stigma losses are in principle recoverable despite arising from unlawful victimization by others.

Other notable cases were those interpreting the courts' novel power to award damages for injury to feelings. The grant of this power especially mattered in situations where unlawful discrimination caused no separate loss or expense. A case exemplifying this was *Prison Service and Others v Johnson*,[177] another behavioural conflict case analysed later in this book. The decision was of general importance for issuing guidance about the assessment of damages for injury to feelings. Smith J summarized the relevant principles as follows:

(i) Awards for injury to feelings are compensatory. They should be just to both parties. They should compensate fully without punishing the tortfeasor. Feelings of indignation at the tortfeasor's conduct should not be allowed to inflate the award. (ii) Awards should not be too low, as that would diminish respect for the policy of the anti-discrimination legislation. Society has condemned discrimination and awards must ensure that it is seen to be wrong. On the other hand, awards should be restrained, as excessive awards could, to use the phrase of Sir Thomas Bingham MR ... be seen as the way to 'untaxed riches'. (iii) Awards should bear some broad general similarity to the range of awards in personal injury cases. We do not think that this should be done by reference to any particular type of personal injury award, rather to the whole range of such awards. (iv) In exercising that discretion in assessing a sum, tribunals should remind themselves of the value in everyday life of the sum they have in mind. This may be done by reference to purchasing power or by reference to earnings. (v) Finally, tribunals should bear in mind Sir Thomas Bingham's reference to the need for public respect for the level of awards made.[178]

That passage was specifically adopted by the CA in *Vento v CC of West Yorkshire Police*.[179]

Vento also gave guidance about the level of awards for injury to feelings that has recently been uprated:[180]

Employment tribunals and those who practise in them might find it helpful if this court were to identify three broad bands of compensation for injury to feelings, as distinct from compensation for psychiatric or similar personal injury. (i) The top band should normally be between £15,000 and £25,000. Sums in this range should be awarded in the most serious cases, such as where there has been a lengthy campaign of discriminatory harassment on the ground of sex or race ... Only in the most exceptional case should an award of compensation for injury to feelings exceed £25,000. (ii) The middle band of between £5,000 and £15,000 should be used for serious cases, which do not merit an award in the highest band. (iii) Awards of between £500 and £5,000 are appropriate

---

[173] [2004] EWCA Civ 2, [2004] ICR 746.
[174] [1999] EWCA Civ 1663, [1999] ICR 1170, [17] and [22].
[175] See *Essa* (n 173), Pill LJ [37] and [43], and Clarke LJ [53]. Note however Pill LJ's comment, ibid [40], suggesting some doubt as to whether this approach applied across the board.
[176] [2009] EWCA Civ 1202, [2010] ICR 397.   [177] [1997] ICR 275 (EAT).
[178] ibid, 283.   [179] [2002] EWCA Civ 1871, [2003] ICR 318, [53].
[180] *Da'Bell v National Society for the Prevention of Cruelty to Children* [2010] IRLR 19 (EAT).

for less serious cases, such as where the act of discrimination is an isolated or one off occurrence. In general, awards of less than £500 are to be avoided altogether, as they risk being regarded as so low as not to be a proper recognition of injury to feelings.[181]

There was noted to be flexibility within each band, while the additional award of aggravated damages depended on the 'particular circumstances of the discrimination and on the way in which the complaint …has been handled'. This reflected that such damages, available as a separate head only in England and Wales, are meant to compensate for extra harm done, for example in the way proceedings were conducted. Finally regard should be had to the overall magnitude of the award, especially with an eye to avoiding double recovery.[182]

(b) The EqA 2010 on remedies

The EqA 2010 provisions on individual remedies regarding unlawful discrimination at work again largely reproduce the existing law in simpler language. The one major change is that the ETs' power to make recommendations was altered so that these may benefit persons other than the claimant.[183] This also, however, has now been repealed.[184]

3. Protection from Harassment Act 1997

This time it is the ordinary courts which have jurisdiction for determining claims under the Protection from Harassment (PHA) 1997, including where these relate to work. It is in this instance particularly difficult to separate exposition of the general law from the detailed analysis of behavioural conflict judgments that follows because it was in those cases that judges determined the implications of the Act at work. I merely sketch, therefore, the statutory and general background, touching briefly on the employment cases. Most importantly, I leave it to later in this book to consider in full the critical HL decision in *Majrowski v Guy's and St Thomas's NHS Trust*[185] that employers are vicariously liable for breach by their employees of the PHA 1997, and the extensive case law debates about the impact of civil and criminal liability under the Act being intertwined. It appeared for a time that the possibility of criminal liability would significantly limit the scope of civil liability, but the judges have now retreated from this position. Still, the possibility of criminal liability under the PHA 1997 means that a degree of seriousness is required to establish civil unlawfulness on a lesser standard of proof. The essential question in all claims however remains whether there has been harassment as defined in the Act and elucidated by the courts.

(1) Liability

The first point is that nothing in the PHA 1997 explicitly excludes the workplace from its ambit even though it was designed as a response to stalking. It was a few years into the period from which my sample of judgments is drawn that the Act was legislated, however, and several more before decisions about work began to appear.

---

[181] ibid, [65].
[182] ibid, [66]–[68]. See further *MoD v Fletcher* [2010] IRLR 25 (EAT) and *Commissioner of Police of the Metropolis v Shaw* [2012] ICR 464 (EAT) on aggravated damages (including the different approach in Scotland) and the exceptional circumstances in which exemplary damages will be recoverable.
[183] EqA 2010, s 124.   [184] Deregulation Act 2015, s 2.
[185] [2006] UKHL 34, [2007] 1 AC 224.

To outline the legislative scheme in England and Wales, section 1 prohibits a person from pursuing a course of conduct that amounts to harassment if they know or ought to know that it is harassment. To do so is made a civil wrong by section 3 and a criminal offence by section 2.[186] This means that case law about the section 2 crime tells us when harassing behaviour is a civil wrong, and vice versa. The law is very similar in Scotland, except that a criminal offence was not created because existing criminal law was thought sufficiently to provide for this.[187]

The Act largely left it to judges to decide what unlawful harassment, civilly or criminally, comprises. It spells out only that harassing a person includes alarming them or causing them distress,[188] and specifies that speech is covered and a 'course of conduct' involves at least two incidents.[189] The test for the intent component, either of the civil wrong or of the section 2 offence, is whether a reasonable person in possession of the same information as the alleged harasser would think the conduct harassment. There is additionally a 'catch-all' defence if conduct can be shown to have been reasonable. The prevention or detection of crime, together with action to comply with other legal requirements, are also protected from unlawfulness.

In an early non-employment case, *Thomas v News Group Newspapers Limited*,[190] the CA confirmed the broad application of the legislation, finding that a series of newspaper articles was capable of constituting harassment.[191] Regarding the content of the wrong, Lord Phillips, with the agreement of Jonathan Parker LJ and Lord Mustill, explained what was required. He noted that although the Act spelled out *the effect* that conduct must foreseeably have, it did not explain *the form* it needed to take. In this regard he said:

'Harassment' is, however, a word which has a meaning which is generally understood. It describes conduct targeted at an individual which is calculated to produce the consequences described in section 7 [ie alarming or distressing a person] and which is oppressive and unreasonable. The practice of stalking is a prime example of such conduct.[192]

This early formulation has been influential.

In another important passage, May LJ in the CA in *Majrowski*,[193] in an aspect of the decision that was not appealed, cited the passage above and said:

Thus, in my view ... the fact that a person suffers distress is not by itself enough to show that the cause of the distress was harassment. The conduct has also to be calculated, in an objective sense, to cause distress and has to be oppressive and unreasonable. It has to be conduct which the perpetrator knows or ought to know amounts to harassment, and conduct which a reasonable person would think amounted to harassment.[194]

---

[186] S 4 contains the more serious crime of putting a person in fear of violence.

[187] Note that differences between England/Wales and Scotland were critical to the HL interpreting the PHA 1997 to impose vicarious liability. For several judges in *Majrowski* this was the only reason they agreed to the outcome (see pp 135–36 in Ch 5). See also the recent Scottish case of *Dickie v Flexcon Glenrothes Ltd* [2009] GWD 35-602 (Sheriff Court), for a useful, comparative, discussion of the implications of the PHA 1997 at work. See pp 156–58 in Ch 6.

[188] See s 7(2).   [189] See s 7(4) and (3) respectively.   [190] [2001] EWCA Civ 1233.

[191] ibid, para [15]. See also the explanation in paras [17]–[37] why this was the case notwithstanding the right to freedom of expression. Although see Tugendhat J's analysis in a case from my sample, *Crossland v Wilkinson Hardware Stores Ltd* [2005] EWHC 481 (QB) of the impact of freedom of speech in the work context, including to conclude that foreseeably causing distress is not sufficient to liability, as subsequently confirmed in *Majrowski*.

[192] *Thomas* (n 190), [30].   [193] [2005] EWCA Civ 251 [2005] QB 848.

[194] ibid, [82]. Auld LJ gave a separate judgment for the majority, with which May LJ also agreed. Scott Baker LJ dissented regarding vicarious liability (but not on the more general points).

Lord Nicholls observed in the HL judgment that for conduct to be proscribed it must go beyond being unattractive and unreasonable, to being 'oppressive and unacceptable'.[195] He also confirmed that the fact that harassing behaviour is criminalized under the Act is relevant, in that 'to cross the boundary from the regrettable to the unacceptable the gravity of the misconduct must be of an order which would sustain criminal liability under s 2'.[196]

The intent elements elaborated by May LJ had, in fact, been considered by the CA in the early criminal case of *R v Sean Peter*[197] and in the employment case of *Banks v Ablex Ltd*,[198] decided a few weeks before the CA *Majrowski* judgment. In *R v Sean Peter* it was held that an alleged harasser's mental illness was neither to be attributed to the hypothetical reasonable person nor the reasonableness defence assessed from a defendant's standpoint.[199] The court was mindful that the Act was designed to be protective and preventive. The judges referred to the long title being 'An act to make provision for protecting persons from harassment and similar conduct', and concluded that anything but an objective approach would risk thwarting Parliament's purpose.[200] In *Banks*,[201] a unanimous CA applied this view of the law to the work context.

Several criminal appeals additionally dealt with the requirement to show a course of conduct, finding that the root question was whether it was reasonable to see the challenged behaviour in this way.[202] A recent CA decision, *Iqbal v Dean Manson Solicitors*,[203] decided after the period from which my sample was taken, noted that each individual incident need not on its own amount to harassment. As Rix LJ said, with the agreement of Smith and Richards LJJ:

[T]he Act is concerned with courses of conduct which amount to harassment, rather than with individual instances of harassment … The reason why the statute is drafted in this way is not hard to understand. Take the typical case of stalking, or of malicious phone calls. When a defendant, D, walks past a claimant C's door, or calls C's telephone but puts the phone down without speaking, the single act by itself is neutral, or may be. But if that act is repeated on a number of occasions, the course of conduct may well amount to harassment. That conclusion can only be arrived at by

---

[195] *Majrowski* (n 185), [30]. See also the accounts of the law given in the following cases (several in my sample): *Green v DB Group Services* [2006] EWHC 1898, [2006] IRLR 764, [14], *Allen v LB of Southwark* [2008] EWCA Civ 1478, especially [3]–[9] per Longmore LJ and [27] per Arden LJ, *Dowson v CC of Northumbria Police* [2009] EWHC 907 (QB), [52], *Dickie* (n 187), [69] and [78] (and more generally), and finally, *Rayment v MoD* [2010] EWHC 218, [2010] IRLR 768, [10].

[196] *Majrowski*, ibid. See pp 153–56 in Ch 6 for the way this observation has been interpreted in subsequent cases.

[197] [2001] EWCA Crim 1251 (also called *R v Colohan*).

[198] [2005] EWCA Civ 173, [2005] ICR 819.

[199] [2001] EWCA Crim 1251, [20]–[21]. Judgment was given by Hughes J on behalf of the court, which included Kennedy LJ and Curtis J. See further *Hayes v Willoughby* [2013] UKSC 17, [2013] 1 WLR 935 on the subjective–objective intent analysis required by the prevention or detection of crime defence.

[200] *Sean Peter*, [17]–[19].

[201] [2005] EWCA Civ 173, [2005] ICR 819, [19]. See also at [20] that 'calculated to produce' was interpreted to mean 'no more than that the conduct must be such as is liable to produce those consequences'. It also appears that alarm and distress need not in fact have been caused, as pointed out by Arden LJ in *Allen* (n 195), [27], and in *Dickie* (n 187), [67] and [78] (on the equivalent Scottish provision). Consider also *Ferguson v British Gas Trading Ltd* [2009] EWCA Civ 46, [2010] 1 WLR 785, [24]–[46], [47]–[49], and [51] for *obiter* comments on direct liability of corporations by, respectively, Jacob, Lloyd, and Sedley LJJ, and *Iqbal v Dean Manson Solicitors* [2011] EWCA Civ 123, [2011] IRLR 428, [62]–[63] on direct liability of partnerships. The decision in *Kosar v Bank of Scotland plc t/a Halifax* [2011] EWHC 1050 (Admin) that a company can be criminally liable under s 2 is however in tension with *Iqbal* at [55]–[63].

[202] *Lau v Director of Public Prosecutions* [2000] 1 FLR 799, Div Ct, [14]–[15], and *Pratt v DPP* [2001] EWHC Admin 483, [9]–[10].

[203] *Iqbal* (n 201).

looking at the individual acts complained of as a whole. The course of conduct cannot be reduced to or deconstructed into the individual acts, taken solely one by one.[204]

This reflected the emphasis on repetition in *Pratt v DPP*[205] and *Kelly v DPP*.[206] Burton J in the latter saw the plain purpose of the legislation as to make conduct actionable, criminally and civilly, which might not be alarming if committed once, but which became so because it was repeated.[207]

(2) Remedies

Various possibilities are provided for obtaining injunctive relief in respect of the civil and criminal wrongs contained in the 1997 Act.[208] In employment cases, however, this possibility has rarely been acted upon.[209] It is the damages remedy that is more significant, including how it compares to damages entitlements for other causes of action. Most strikingly, the same generous approach is taken as in equality law. First, the legislation specifies that compensation is available for 'injury to feelings', analogously with the position under the EqA 2010 (and predecessor statutes). Second, the case law in Scotland,[210] and recently in the CA,[211] has applied the more generous remoteness test. Accordingly, losses and expenses that are a direct and natural consequence of wrongful harassment are recoverable, with no need to establish reasonable foreseeability. Third, and again as in discrimination claims, there is the possibility of aggravated damages.

4. The Common Law of Contract and Tort

In this section I explain the law relating to common law actions in the ordinary courts beyond the limited ET jurisdiction in contract cases. An employer's liability in a common law action may be primary, where the employer itself either committed a tort or breached an employment contract. The alternative is vicarious liability, where the employer is held responsible for the acts of its employees. There is very little direct authority regarding vicarious liability for breach of contract although this seems in practice not to create problems.[212] There have, however, been major developments on vicarious liability for tortious conduct, resulting in the net of employer responsibility being spread widely.

---

[204] ibid, [45]. See also *Marinello v City of Edinburgh Council* [2011] CSIH 33, [2011] IRLR 669 applying the same approach in Scotland. This is a successful appeal from a judgment in my sample, in which Mr Marinello's action under the PHA 1997 was reinstated having been stopped below.
[205] [2001] EWHC Admin 483, in particular at [12].   [206] [2002] EWHC Admin 1428.
[207] ibid, [23].
[208] The PHA 1997 provides expressly for the issue of injunctions in respect of s 3, while making contravention without reasonable excuse an offence, giving the criminal courts power to issue injunctive relief on conviction under ss 2 and 4 and, finally, making breach of these injunctions another offence. *Hipgrave v Jones* [2004] EWHC 2901 (QB), [2005] 2 FLR 174 clarified that the civil burden of proof applies to the grant of civil injunctions under the Act notwithstanding the potential criminal consequences of breach.
[209] A rare exception was a case qualitatively analysed below, *First Global Locums Ltd v Cosias* [2005] EWHC 1147 (QB), [2005] IRLR 873. See further on this topic L Barmes, 'Remedying Workplace Harassment' in M Freeman (ed.) [2002] 55 *CLP* (OUP, 2003).
[210] *Dickie* (n 187), [163].
[211] *Jones v Ruth* [2011] EWCA (Civ) 804, [2012] 1 WLR 1495, [32]–[33].
[212] See *Maclellan v Co-operative Group (CWS) Ltd* (EAT, 11 May 2006), [17] from my sample for an unusual example. In particular Elias J made the point that 'it is plain that in certain circumstances, an employer will be vicariously liable for the acts of employees, but it does not follow that where an employee acts unreasonably towards a fellow employee that that means that there is going to be a repudiatory breach sufficient to entitle the employee to leave. It may well depend upon the seniority of the manager.'

The legal question in this regard has become whether, looked at in the round, there was a sufficiently close connection between the nature of the employment and the tort for it to be just and reasonable to hold the employer vicariously liable.[213]

(1) Liability

(a) Torts of intention

The first common law option for claimants is to allege one of the torts of intention; for example, the intentional infliction of physical or psychiatric harm. Before the PHA 1997, this sometimes made sense because recovery does not depend on reasonable fore-seeability if there is actual (as opposed to imputed) intention to harm,[214] but this is unlikely now to make a difference.[215]

(b) Negligence in contract and tort

A much more likely common law claim is for negligence, that an employer failed, either primarily or vicariously, to take reasonable care not to injure or otherwise harm an employee. Much as this duty derives from tort, it is also contractual through being implied by law into every contract of employment.

Section 2 of the Unfair Contract Terms Act (UCTA) 1977 on its face precludes exclusion by agreement of an employer's duty to take reasonable care to prevent injury or death. The HL, however, ignored this when it found in the *Johnson/Eastwood* line of cases that express terms impliedly displaced employers' negligence obligations in dismissal situations, discussed further below in this section.[216] This is despite compulsory liability insurance meaning that there is automatic pooling of the cost of employers' liability for personal injury and that insurance companies step into employers' shoes in respect of such claims.[217] Finally, that ETs cannot award common law damages for personal injury and that only pecuniary losses are recoverable in an unfair dismissal claim means claimants who have suffered injury, and who do not have a discrimination claim, may be well advised to sue in the ordinary courts, perhaps combining actions in negligence and under the PHA 1997.

There is only liability in negligence (whether in contract or tort) if harm was reasonably foreseeable and compensation is only payable to that extent. Furthermore, while personal injury is perhaps the compensatable harm most likely to flow from negligent conduct in the context of behavioural conflict at work, compensation is in theory recoverable for other kinds of damage.[218]

---

[213] See *Bernard v Attorney General of Jamaica* [2004] UKPC 47, [2005] IRLR 398, [18], and the useful summary in *Green* (n 195), [15]–[16].

[214] See the useful discussion on this point, including regarding vicarious liability, in the Scottish case, *Robertson v The Scottish Ministers* [2007] CSOH 186, [14]–[19].

[215] See further Barmes (n 209), 347, and *Wong v Parkside Health NHS Trust* [2001] EWCA CIV 1721, [2003] 3 All ER 932.

[216] S 2 provides that '[a] person cannot by reference to any contract term or to a notice given to persons generally or to particular persons exclude or restrict his liability for death or personal injury resulting from negligence.' S 1(1), in turn, defines 'negligence' to include obligations to take reasonable care or skill whether they arise in contract or tort. Sched 1, para 4 seems to put beyond doubt that s 2 applies to benefit employees.

[217] Employers' Liability (Compulsory Insurance) Act 1969 and the regulations made under it. See p 28 in Ch 2 and pp 239–40 in Ch 9.

[218] See, eg, *Spring v Guardian Assurance Plc* [1995] 2 AC 296 (HL) in which an employer was liable in tort and contract for negligently preparing a reference.

In terms of the content of employers' obligation not to act negligently, this is typically broken down into duties to provide competent fellow workers, a proper system of work, and a safe place of work.[219] There are also some important general points of particular relevance to behavioural conflict at work.

First, *Waters v Commissioner of Police of The Metropolis*, another case in my sample, was a landmark decision for recognizing that employers have common law responsibilities to protect their employees from harmful conduct by colleagues, including harassment.[220] Second, the CA gave guidance in *Sutherland v Hatton*[221] about employees seeking compensation for psychiatric illness caused by stress at work. The guidance was largely endorsed by the HL on appeal (the case then being known as *Barber v Somerset CC*),[222] and has been influential in later cases.[223] These developments are perceived as having made it much harder for employees to succeed in tort claims about 'stress at work'. The significance of the *Hatton v Sutherland* guidelines for behavioural conflict cases is, however, in some doubt, given the focus in that case on allegations about workload, pressure, and stress,[224] when conflict about behaviour at work may well be nothing to do with such matters.[225] Correspondingly, my qualitative analysis of judgments traces tensions between Hale LJ's legal analysis in *Hatton* and adjudication in cases about workplace conduct. The CA in *Yapp v FCO* has, however, now suggested that the *Hatton v Sutherland* guidance should be applied beyond stress-type claims, at least to encompass situations 'where the employer has committed a one-off act of unfairness like the imposition of a disciplinary sanction'.[226] It may therefore be that the *Hatton* guidelines influence will become more extensive.

Third, in terms of litigation choices, an employer's negligence obligations are in theory constant across contract and tort.[227] How such a claim is pursued should consequently make no difference.[228] Litigants need, however, to be vigilant about the potential impact of the HL decisions in *Johnson* and *Eastwood*. For some litigants this will be either that they have no common law claim or that their entitlement to damages is reduced. In particular, *Johnson v Unisys Ltd*[229] determined that employers' contractual dismissal powers are unfettered by duties that law implies in contracts of employment, including in negligence and pursuant to the duty of trust and confidence (about which more below, including the unfair dismissal interface). The HL reasoned that restricting dismissal powers via the common law would be unconstitutional for undermining the

---

[219] S Deakin and GS Morris, *Labour Law* (6th edn, Hart, 2012), 351.

[220] [2000] UKHL 50, [2000] 1 WLR 1607. See in particular Lord Hutton's analysis at 1615–16 of earlier case law on negligence about harassing etc behaviour at work.

[221] [2002] EWCA Civ 76, [2002] IRLR 263, [43].

[222] [2004] UKHL 13, [2005] 1 WLR 1089, [63]–[65], per Lord Walker of Gestingthorpe (with whose speech Lord Bingham of Cornhill and Lord Steyn concurred), and [5]–[7] and [10] per Lord Scott of Foscote (dissenting in the result).

[223] See, eg, the discussion in *Hartman v South Essex Mental Health & Community Care NHS Trust* [2005] EWCA Civ 6, [2005] ICR 782 and *Daw v Intel Corp (UK) Ltd* [2007] EWCA Civ 70, [2007] ICR 1318, the latter also in my sample.

[224] As such only one of the four joined cases in *Sutherland v Hatton*, *Sandwell MBC v Jones* [2002] EWCA Civ 76, [2002] ICR 613 qualified for my sample.

[225] This is well illustrated by *Green* (n 195), also in my sample. Unsurprisingly, the challenged behaviour caused Ms Green stress and ultimately psychiatric illness, but this did not bring the case directly within the *Hatton* guidance in that there were no allegations of overwork. See [2]–[10] for this point and generally on the relevant law.

[226] *Yapp* (n 38), [119].   [227] Freedland (n 22), 141–45.

[228] Note however the uncertainty in this regard expressed by Lord Rodger of Earlsferry in *Barber* (n 222), [24]–[26] and [30]–[36].

[229] *Johnson* (n 4).

will of Parliament as expressed in its legislation on unfair dismissal. The particular concern was that judges would thereby be enabling some claimants to challenge the lawfulness of dismissal when the statute excluded them from protection.

Practical difficulties about when employees still had a common law claim led the
HL quickly to revisit the topic in *Eastwood*. Lord Nicholls gave the leading opinion, with which Lord Hoffmann, Lord Rodger of Earlsferry, and Lord Brown of
Eaton-under-Heywood agreed.[230] *Johnson*, and the constitutional reasoning on which
it was based, was unanimously upheld, but it was acknowledged that a common law
claim that had accrued before dismissal would not disappear if dismissal ensued. As Lord
Nicholls said:

If before his dismissal, whether actual or constructive, an employee has acquired a cause of action
at law, for breach of contract or otherwise, that cause of action remains unimpaired by his subsequent unfair dismissal and the statutory rights flowing therefrom. By definition, in law such a
cause of action exists independently of the dismissal.[231]

The effect was that it was only in respect of dismissal itself that common law liability
based on implied obligations was excluded. This means, for example, that a common law
claim is in theory available in a constructive dismissal situation in respect of everything
except acceptance of the repudiation. Lord Nicholls drew this line in explaining that 'in
cases of constructive dismissal a distinction will have to be drawn between loss flowing
from antecedent breaches of the trust and confidence term and loss flowing from the
employee's acceptance of these breaches as a repudiation of the contract'.[232] The former
losses are recoverable at common law and the latter not.

It is an ongoing puzzle that the judges made no distinction between an employer's negligence duty and that of mutual trust and confidence,[233] given the seemingly
plain wording of UCTA 1977. In my view there remains an open legal question as
to whether that statute preserves a common law claim for a dismissal breach of the
implied duty to take reasonable care to avoid injury. It is also noteworthy that the
judges have not considered the impact of Parliament having legislated for compulsory
employers' liability insurance in respect of personal injury, given that the necessary
implication is that Parliament intended (and intends) compensation for such injury
to be recoverable whether caused in the context of dismissal or otherwise. Questions
have, however, recently been raised by the CA about the status of personal injury
claims in the context of dismissal, Underhill LJ speculating that they may escape the
effects of *Johnson* etc because the claim is not for unfair dismissal but for negligently
caused injury.[234]

Even so, the upshot for now is that someone who is negligently injured (or otherwise
harmed) in the course of a behavioural conflict at work may find either that they have
no common law claim because the negligence was bound up with their dismissal or that,
while they still have a common law claim, any losses consequent on dismissal are irre-
coverable. My case law analysis and interview study explore how this has played out in
practice. A predictable aspect, given how very oddly the law has been developed, is that
organizations, insurers, lawyers, and judges do not seem consistently to notice when a
factual situation raises a *Johnson/Eastwood* issue.

It is also important that the law has become even more peculiar following the
Supreme Court (SC) decision in *Edwards v Chesterfield Royal Hospital NHS Foundation*

---

[230] Lord Steyn gave a separate speech that reached the same result.
[231] *Eastwood* (n 5), [27].   [232] ibid, [31].   [233] Ibid, [32].
[234] *Monk v Cann Hall Primary School* [2013] EWCA Civ 826, [2013] IRLR 732, [32].

Trust & Botham v MoD.[235] In both cases an employee sought compensation for breaches of express terms of their contract regarding disciplinary procedures. Each contended that the breaches had harmed their employment prospects and caused them significant recoverable loss. Further legal background necessary to make sense of these judgments is the HL decision in *Addis v Gramophone*,[236] some 100 years ago, prohibiting recovery of compensation for reputational harm caused by wrongful dismissal (ie dismissal in breach of contract). In 1997, however, the HL in *Malik v Bank of Credit and Commerce Intl SA*[237] found that pecuniary losses caused by reputational harm were compensatable where these resulted from breach of contract during the course of the relationship.

Unusually, seven justices sat in *Edwards*, signalling its significance. Regrettably, however, the depth of disagreement between the six justices who found for either one or both of the employers (Lady Hale dissenting) meant that there was no majority of justices who agreed on the legal basis for the decision. In these circumstances it is arguable that the case sets no legal precedent. Whether or not that is eventually found to be the case, the law was left in further disarray.

While four justices, Lord Nicholls, Lord Walker of Gestingthorpe, Lord Mance, and Lord Dyson, agreed that Mr Edwards' and Mr Botham's claims should be disallowed, Lord Phillips did so on a different basis to the other three justices in this group. He reasoned simply, extending *Addis* and distinguishing *Malik*, that the claims must fail because common law compensation for injury to reputation is not recoverable for breach of express disciplinary procedures in a contract of employment.

Still, it is true that five of the justices (the three mentioned above plus Lord Kerr of Tonaghmore and Lord Wilson, the last two at least implicitly) agreed that the impact of *Johnson* and *Eastwood* should be extended sometimes to disallow common law dismissal claims for breach of express terms. The justices in this group disagreed, however, as to how far this should go, exemplified by Lords Kerr and Lord Wilson ruling that Mr Edwards' claim should be allowed to proceed.

The three in favour of the widest extension of *Johnson* and who disallowed both claims (Lord Walker, Lord Mance, and Lord Dyson) held first, that injunctions to restrain breach are still available,[238] and second, that compensation claims are permissible if this was expressly provided for in the contract.[239]

Lords Kerr and Wilson not only doubted the cogency of the analysis that led to these two propositions but also approved a lesser extension of *Johnson/Eastwood*.[240] They founded any additional exclusion of claims only on *Johnson* having decided that 'compensation for loss flowing from the manner in which an employee is dismissed must be sought' in an unfair dismissal claim. Implicitly, given their view that Mr Botham's claim should not be allowed to proceed, they considered this to apply whether the employer was in breach of an express or an implied contractual term. Yet, relying heavily on *Eastwood*, they regarded common law actions about pre-dismissal breaches of express terms as viable in a wider range of situations than Lords Walker, Mance, and Dyson. Indeed, they only agreed that Mr Botham's claim should be disallowed because his reputational loss was so closely bound up with the dismissal itself, rather than with the procedure leading up to it.[241]

---

[235] *Edwards* (n 8).   [236] *Addis v Gramophone Co Ltd* [1909] AC 488.
[237] *Malik* (n 21).
[238] *Edwards* (n 8), [44] per Lord Dyson (with whom Lord Walker and Lord Mance agreed, the latter also giving a separate speech).
[239] ibid, [39] per Lord Dyson and [94] per Lord Mance.
[240] ibid, [135] regarding injunctions and [154] on contractual intentions, both per Lord Kerr (with whom Lord Wilson agreed).
[241] ibid, [156].

The net effect was that there was no consensus amongst a majority of the seven justices on when dismissal claims based on express terms of contracts of employment are impermissible, seeming to indicate that the SC made no new rule of law on this point. Even if one can somehow or other be divined, its precise contents cannot be known until there have been further rulings, probably in the SC.

I do not presently think these developments are likely to matter very much to common law claims about behavioural conflict at work. This is because these are likely to be founded either in negligence or the mutual contractual duty of trust and confidence, regarding which *Johnson* and *Eastwood* had already significantly confused matters. It is important nevertheless to be aware that the law has developed in this way, including because it demonstrates that technical difficulties arising from overlapping causes of action are continuing and, in fact, getting worse.

(c) *The contractual duty of mutual trust and confidence*

I explained earlier that this contractual duty came into being as a result of legal innovation regarding the statutory right not to be unfairly dismissed. Once it was recognized as a part of all contracts of employment (unless expressly excluded),[242] it acquired a common law life of its own. Apart from often being the basis for unfair dismissal claims of the constructive kind, the duty is therefore highly relevant to common law contractual litigation about behavioural conflict. Following the decisions in *GMB v Brown* and *GAB Robins*, a constructive unfair dismissal claimant may now be pushed into bringing a contract action in the ordinary courts to recover their pre-dismissal losses. This is perhaps the most likely situation in which a claim regarding breaches during the currency of employment would be based on the implied duty of mutual trust and confidence rather than that of negligence. That form of claim, however, is also possible in other factual situations, as *Malik* demonstrated.[243]

In other instances, a contract claim will be for termination of the contract in breach, known as wrongful dismissal. A contract claim of this type will very often appropriately be tacked onto a statutory unfair dismissal claim before the ETs. This will make sense wherever the recoverable contract damages are modest, which they often will be. That follows from the reality that the usual contract measure of damages frequently delivers low awards for wrongful dismissal. The starting point is that the employee should be awarded what they would have received had the contract been performed. The assumption is made, however, that, absent the breach, the employer would have fulfilled the contract in the least onerous way possible. The recoverable damages are also subject to the usual limiting factors, like remoteness and the duty to mitigate. Since most contracts of employment contain either express or implied powers for an employer to terminate on notice without cause, the minimum performance principle typically produces the remedial assumption that lawful notice would have been given as soon as possible. Hence recoverable contract compensation often ends up being net pay for the notice period, potentially lessened further by mitigation.

Even still, an employee might have a substantial contract claim on termination in breach if they have a fixed-term contract with no notice clause, a valuable monetary

---

[242] For authority that the implied term of mutual trust and confidence is excludable, see Lord Steyn in *Malik* (n 21), 45. Lord Goff, Lord Mackay of Clashfern, and Lord Mustill all concurred with Lord Steyn's reasoning.

[243] See also *Gogay v Hertfordshire CC* [2000] IRLR 703 (CA) for a successful personal injury claim during the currency of the employment relationship, where liability derived from breach of the implied duty of mutual trust and confidence.

entitlement under the contract (like a bonus or share options), and/or they were physically or psychiatrically injured by the breach. Substantial damages may still be recoverable because, on the one hand, the principle of minimum performance would in these situations require, respectively, the fixed-term contract to be honoured and contractual monetary entitlements to be paid (subject to mitigation), while on the other hand, contractual liability for personal injury is compensated in the same way as in a tort action subject to any restrictive *Johnson/Eastwood* effects. Incidentally, while reputational damage is another substantial potential loss, *Addis* continues to obstruct recovery for this kind of harm from termination breaches.

The liability basis for substantial contract claims, especially in behavioural conflict cases, may well be breach of the duty of mutual trust and confidence. If so, however, after *Johnson* and *Eastwood*, as noted regarding negligence actions, such claims are liable either to be lost entirely (as Mr Johnson's was), or losses flowing from dismissal (rather than pre-dismissal breaches) are at risk of being disallowed. Equally it again seems that the implications of *Johnson* and *Eastwood* are not consistently noticed by litigants, their insurers, their lawyers, or the judicial system.

Interestingly, the decision in *Edwards* may now make it more likely that the implications of *Johnson* and *Eastwood* are noticed in 'big money' contract cases. This is because the SC there gave detailed consideration to the impact of that line of authority in disputes about complex, highly protective contracts of employment. Many high-value claims deal with contracts not unlike those of Mr Edwards and Mr Botham, albeit individually rather than collectively negotiated. The reasoning of Lord Walker, Lord Mance, and Lord Dyson suggested that, unless expressly provided for, not even carefully negotiated procedural protections for employees, let alone implied ones, will be enforceable through a common law dismissal claim for compensation.

The effect of all this is that litigants with potentially valuable contract claims may be well advised to avoid *Johnson/Eastwood* traps (and now those set by *Edwards*) either by finding any other possible way of pursuing their claim or, failing this, to do all they can to keep their contracts alive so as to bring actions for pure breach, as opposed to in relation to termination. The latter would also enable them to seek common law injunctive relief. Neither option is likely to be straightforward, however. The law in this area is not easy even for experts to keep track of and is, anyway, unstable. It is also often very difficult, especially unilaterally, to keep a contract of employment alive in the context of a dispute, and especially difficult where the issue is behavioural.

(2) Remedies

It was necessary in explaining the rules on liability to discuss remedial possibilities to some extent, in particular to clarify when common law claims for compensation in the ordinary courts might be worthwhile to pursue. I therefore will only recap the essential points here. The obvious starting point is that common law claims have typically been for damages. If the loss derives from personal injury this is calculated in the same way in contract and tort subject to the impact of *Eastwood*. The usual tort measure applies, as it would to actions for other tortiously inflicted losses. In this mode, the law seeks through compensation to put someone in the position they would have been in if the tort had not been committed. An attempt is therefore made to value both pecuniary and non-pecuniary losses. Still, there are the usual limiting factors, like the rules on remoteness and the duty to mitigate.

The compensation available for breach of contract (apart from in respect of personal injury) is worked out from the contractual starting point, namely what would have been received if the contract had been performed. The recoverable sums are then limited by the principle of minimum performance and because damages are generally not available for non-pecuniary loss. There is also the difficulty of obtaining compensation for reputational loss consequent on *Addis*, although circumscribed by *Malik*. Finally, the usual limiting factors are in play, with appropriate adjustments to the contractual context.[244]

The other remedial possibility in common law claims is to seek an injunction. This has been growing in practical significance[245] and is likely to become more important post *Edwards*.[246] Injunctions may be granted either at an interim stage, to preserve the status quo until final judgment, or finally at trial to prevent or restrain unlawful conduct. The award of an injunction always remains at the discretion of the courts. The idea of giving injunctive relief at an interim stage is that it would, in effect, be unfair to leave matters to trial and a possible compensation award. It is necessary, therefore, to show that there is a serious issue to be tried, that compensation would be an insufficient remedy, and that the balance of convenience as between the parties favours an injunction. The claimant may additionally have to indemnify the person injuncted against losses resulting from the grant, to cover the eventuality of losing at trial.

Securing injunctions in employment cases is an especially uphill struggle. First, to enforce a contract requires that it is still in existence, which we have seen may be difficult for an employee unilaterally to achieve. In any event, an employee is unlikely to be aware of this legal need, nor of the consequent urgency of obtaining legal assistance and of going to court. Second, there is a common law presumption against a court enforcing a contract of employment directly by specific performance or indirectly by injunction.[247] Thus, an employee must additionally be able to establish exceptional circumstances that courts will recognize as sufficient to displace that presumption. Examples are where trust and confidence is intact, or it is absent but an injunction is workable because the employee is not at work.[248]

In behavioural conflict cases, the option of applying for an injunction in theory exists both to restrain the challenged behaviour itself and to require employers to respond in accordance with their contractual (or other legal) obligations. In practice, applications for injunctions are not made to stop the underlying behaviour. Injunctions are, however, sometimes sought regarding employer responses, particularly by employees with a great deal to lose if a conflict is handled unfairly. The typical example is doctors whose future employability may be at stake. This was in effect what Mr Edwards alleged, much as he appears to have sued only after the event. In other recent cases about doctors, injunctive relief was obtained before the damage was done. *Kircher v Hillingdon PCT*[249] is a

[244] See in this regard *Yapp* (n 38), [119] about the different remoteness rules governing a claim based on the implied negligence duty and that of mutual trust and confidence.

[245] See for recent illustrations: about a doctor, *Mezey v South West London & St George's Mental Health NHS Trust* [2007] EWHC 62 (QB), [2007] IRLR 237, and [2007] EWCA Civ 106, [2007] IRLR 244 (refusing permission to appeal), both at the interim stage, and *Mezey v South West London & St George's Mental Health NHS Trust* [2010] EWCA Civ 293, [2010] IRLR 512 at trial; about a rabbi, *Lew v Board of Trustees on behalf of United Synagogue* [2011] EWHC 1265 (QB), [2011] IRLR 664. There are also rare instances in which an employee will have a claim for judicial review, in which injunctive relief may be sought. For a recent example see *R (Shoesmith) v Ofsted* [2011] EWCA Civ 642, [2011] ICR 1195.

[246] *West London Mental Health NHS Trust v Chhabra* [2013] UKSC 80, [2014] ICR 194.

[247] In respect of employees, the rule has been enshrined in legislation. Section 236 TULR(C)A 1992 provides that no court shall issue an order compelling an employee to do any work or attend at any place for the doing of any work.

[248] Note that the position is arguably different in respect of tortious obligations. But this area is under-explored in practice. See further, Barmes (n 209) on injunctive relief in employment cases, the contrasting approaches in contract and tort and where bullying and harassment cases fit in.

[249] [2006] EWHC 21 (QB), [2006] Lloyd's Rep Med 215.

good example and it is in my sample. Here, interim relief was granted in the context of a behavioural dispute to stop dismissal before the employer's contractual obligations had been ruled upon.

5. Conclusions

What stands out overall from this account, as indicated at the start, is the extraordinary complexity of the law and practice that is relevant to behaviour at work and the sheer number of rules that are implicated. This is also despite my exerting myself to make the law intelligible.

This state of affairs is the result of several factors. There is the ceaseless change, year after year, always seeming to add new layers while ignoring how the framework of rules and processes fits together. The one exception is arguably the EqA 2010, the *raison d'être* for which was in part to simplify discrimination law. There was, however, little attention to how equality law interrelates to other areas even of labour law. In any event the new Act started to be revised practically as soon as the ink was dry on the statutory page.

As concerns the rules on unfair dismissal, discriminatory harassment, direct discrimination, and victimization, in the PHA Act 1997, from the common law of contract and tort or about associated legal processes, especially in the ET system, the story is the same: endless legislative and adjudicative tinkering, and sometimes wholesale shifts. These by turn correspond to domestic political alterations, EU developments, and significant, unforeseen switches of direction by the higher courts. Further, I have not addressed the more *recherché* ways in which claims are put, some of which preoccupy practitioners, notably the PIDA 1998, also recently subject to another 'reform' process.[250]

Change aside, another complicating factor is the separation of rules into so many different sorts and types. There are the overarching common law norms about how people should be treated at work, especially deriving from terms implied as default rules into all contracts of employment. These, especially the mutual duty of trust and confidence and the duty to take reasonable care, have purchase in relation to a great deal of what people do at work. The common law duties are then augmented by statutory rules in the PHA 1997 that make workplace harassment generally unlawful and which judges have interpreted to place great responsibility on employers, albeit with a relatively high level of seriousness before liability attaches. Separately, there is an extensive web of specific protections from discriminatory harassment at work, widely but variably defined, with their own catalogue of limiting factors and rules about employer responsibility, all again subject to distinctive judicial interpretation. Other equality wrongs are quite often additionally relevant and the rules on unfair dismissal are seen as central for some working people. Here we also come full circle in that fundamental breach of the implied common law contractual duties may be what fixes liability for statutory unfair dismissal.

Finally, as if this dizzying set of interacting and overlapping rules were not enough, there are the very curious splits between different courts at the point of enforcement, to the extent that the remedial rules regarding the same wrong sometimes vary depending on where an action is taken. The jurisdictional oddities have now reached epic proportions, with the recent line of top court decisions culminating in the SC judgments in *Edwards v Chesterfield Royal Hospital NHS Foundation Trust* and *Botham v MoD*. The

---

[250] See Enterprise and Regulatory Reform Act 2013, ss 17–20.

troubling specific implications of this case law for how the law works emerge strongly from the data reported in Chapter 5.

Putting this together, it is clear that UK law is anything but silent about behaviour at work. It imposes substantial and far-reaching obligations in a vast range of workplace situations, all in pursuit of fair, reasonable, and equal treatment at work. There is so much to be celebrated in the societal vindication this gives to emancipatory ideals about working life and more broadly. It is, however, in equal measure concerning that the rules make up so inaccessible a whole. Even though many general precepts are perfectly comprehensible—for example, the wide-ranging requirements not discriminatorily to harass and to comply with the mutual trust and confidence duty—the basic justice norms immanent in the legal rules have been nested in extraordinary overall technicality. This has created significant risk of the wood of high labour and equality standards being obscured by the trees of doctrinal abstruseness. The chapters that ensue expose different ways in which this has in practice eventuated.

4

Factual Themes in Case Law about Behavioural Conflict at Work

1. Introduction and Method for the Qualitative Analysis of Judgments

In this aspect of my project, I gathered and qualitatively analysed authoritative decisions about behavioural conflict at work from 1995 to 2010. The phrase 'behavioural conflict'[1] was intended to capture disputes about how colleagues in vertical and horizontal relationships had behaved towards one another, whether or not there was also conflict about a particular workplace practice or decision and irrespective of how what occurred was labelled.

The overall research question examined was *'how does law about behavioural conflict at work operate through authoritative adjudication?'* My hope was to gain insight into what happens when the myriad substantive laws governing behaviour at work are invoked before courts with power to decide what these laws ultimately mean. This excluded Employment Tribunal (ET) and lower court judgments because they only determine the legal implications of the particular fact situation before them. I therefore examined only judgments in cases that either begun in the higher courts or that reached there on appeal, with the aim of exposing how relevant facts and law are handled in the few instances that advance from being problems at work to being the subject of authoritative judicial pronouncements. That meant including judgments from the Employment Appeal Tribunal (EAT) both in England and Wales and in Scotland, the High Court (HC), the Scottish Court of Session, Outer House (CSOH) and Inner House (CSIH), the Court of Appeal (CA), the House of Lords (HL), and its successor, the Supreme Court (SC).[2]

I chose the period from 1995 to 2010 because it covered a wide enough span to enable patterns to be revealed while also being a time in which, as Chapters 2 and 3 demonstrate, there were extensive developments in relevant research and law. This is also when the language of workplace bullying entered into common parlance and filtered

---

[1] See D Lucy and A Broughton, *Understanding the Decision-making of Employees in Disputes and Conflicts at Work* (BIS, ERRS 119, May 2011), 22, on the difficulties surrounding the definition of conflict and particularly the comment that '[c]onflict is sometimes referred to as the existence of a fundamental disagreement between two parties. This may or may not then become manifest in a dispute, ie a conflict is a state rather than a process. When viewed this way, a dispute is one possible outcome from a conflict. Other possible outcomes may include avoiding the conflict, or capitulation.' Consistent with this approach I kept the meaning of conflict loose in conversations with interviewees, such that it encompassed the range of reactions to an initial issue from nothing much happening to a situation escalating. Some interviewees, moreover, directly commented on this definitional complexity, on which see p 187 in Ch 8.

[2] I have allowed myself to keep one Sheriff Court judgment, *Dickie v Flexcon Glenrothes Ltd* [2009] GWD 35-602 (Sheriff Court), although it does not technically fit my design. This is because I initially overlooked that it had crept into the sample and finally judged that an exception was permissible because its comparative analysis of the developing law under the PHA 1997 has de facto persuasive authority. Note also that judgments from the CSOH, although quite high in the judicial hierarchy, are only persuasive authority.

through to courts, conceivably influenced by growing academic interest and concurrently encouraging research. The judgments examined were not confined to situations in which someone alleged bullying, but the increased interest in this phenomenon helped in gathering cases because searches using some form of the word 'bullying' were the most fruitful. I also deliberately avoided searches that mentioned 'harassment' because of its specific legal meanings. My impression, however, was that any case that employed the word bullying somewhere also mentioned harassment. Use was also made of the Negative Acts Questionnaire (NAQ) from the 1999 UMIST study[3] to aid identification of situations in which the facts involved a conflict about behaviour and the language of bullying was not used.

The original collection of judgments that resulted contained 295 decisions. These were successively culled to remove any in which reference to behavioural conflict, as defined, was peripheral. Detailed analysis was conducted on the remaining 142 judgments. It is probably impossible to ascertain how this final sample relates to the overall 'population' of authoritative judgments about behavioural conflict at work in the period. It is certainly minuscule compared to the number of problems of this type in workplaces and remains a small proportion even of situations in which there was recourse to lawyers and litigation.[4]

At least, however, it is unlikely that there were distortions inherent to the identification process because the databases searched include a vast range of decisions and I know that the research uncovered every judgment with even marginal doctrinal significance. That increased confidence that any relevant decisions of less doctrinal importance were revealed. Finally, there was an equal number of judgments which were insufficiently about behavioural conflict to be worth detailed analysis, further reassuring me that the final sample formed a large subset of the potential whole.

More fundamentally, the idea of representativeness transfers in a complex way to higher court adjudication. Aside from being about behavioural conflict, the level at which these decisions were given means that what unifies them is that they deal with conflicts that are outside the ordinary run of problems at work and even of those that are litigated. In particular, all of the underlying claims were likely to have been especially hard fought because they were either started in the higher courts or went on appeal. In general, there were also appeal points that got through procedural filters which seek to weed out weak legal arguments and there was enough funding for expensive litigation.[5] This signifies that, by definition, the detailed story of how each of these behavioural conflicts reached the point of a higher court decision is likely to have been quite distinctive. The consequence is that what matters is that enough judgments were analysed over a long enough period to disclose the recurrent themes within this category of case law. Even if there are other judgments therefore that might have qualified for my sample, I would contend that I analysed a sufficiently critical mass to give a reliable picture of this form of adjudication.

Tables 4.1, 4.2, and 4.3, offer details about the profile of the judgments within the final sample and the courts in which these were heard. Appendix 1 lists case names and citations in the order in which the judgment was handed down. To explain the figures

---

[3] See H Hoel and CL Cooper, *Destructive Conflict and Bullying at Work* (2000) Manchester, UK: School of Management, University of Manchester, Institute of Science and Technology (unpublished report), 27 and App II.

[4] See W Twining, *Karl Llewellyn and the Realist Movement* (2nd edn, CUP, 2012), 248–50 and 422–23 on the importance of contextualizing case law, which Ch 2 sought to enable.

[5] See M Galanter, 'Why the Haves Come Out Ahead' (1974) 9 Law and Society Review 1, 9, and 46, on the innate skewing of the subset of cases that come before courts for hearing.

Table 4.1 Characteristics of the sample of judgments

Time period	Gender of claimants[1]		Employment sector		Outcome for employee		Mention of bullying		No of judgments
	F	M	Private	Public	Failure	Success	No	Yes	
1995–99	8	6	10	3	6	7	6	7	13
2000–04	22	27	24	23	27	20	13	34	47
2005–09	43	30	42	29	32	39	12	59	71
2010	6	6	3	8	6	5	0	11	11
Totals	82	69	79	63	71	71	31	111	142

[1] There were slightly higher numbers of claimants than of judgments because a handful of judgments related to more than one employee.

Table 4.2 Courts that gave the judgments in the sample

Time period	EAT	High Court	Court of Session		Court of Appeal	House of Lords
			CSOH	CSIH		
1995–99	8	1	1		3	0
2000–04	23	9	2		10	3
2005–09	37	14	2 + 1*	1	15	1
2010	7	1	1		2	0
Totals	75	25	7	1	30	4

* This refers to the one Sheriff Court judgment that I included.

Table 4.3 Judgments in the sample in which litigation was started in the ET system and the ordinary courts

Time period	Litigation begun in the ET system	Litigation begun in the ordinary courts
1995–99	10	3
2000–04	30	17
2005–09	46	25
2010	8	3
Totals	94	48

in Table 4.1 for claimant success or failure, I have counted rulings as successes for employees where they won on any aspect. This, however, ignores any failed allegations and the final substantive result may not have success for the employee, either because the issue was an interim one or an order was made for a re-hearing. By the same token, where an employee lost on appeal, they may have won elements below and final results may have depended on the outcome of other hearings. Finally, there was a handful of judgments in respect of which the employer was the initial claimant, but for the sake of comparability I have in these instances still assessed failure or success from the point of view of the employee.

The judgments taken from 1995 to 1999 enabled me to develop my coding system for identifying patterns in the recounting of facts and the application of legal doctrine. I applied this successively to decisions from 2000 to 2004, 2005 to 2009, and the first half of 2010, checking at each stage whether the coding needed revision. These codings were then grouped into categories in order to identify the most powerful strands in the data. In terms of facts, this enabled me to find out if there were recurrent themes in the way 'stories' about behavioural conflict at work were presented to courts and retold by judges. My explanation and analysis of these follows later in this chapter. In terms of law, the analysis disclosed patterns[6] in how authoritative adjudication determines that behaviour between colleagues is unlawful and then either requires or guides organizations to respond both to such conduct and to allegations of it. The next three chapters substantiate my findings in those respects.

Before turning to what I found out about underlying facts and the judicial reporting of them, it is important to note that I have tried to distinguish allegations by the parties and facts as found by courts. In addition, while factual findings are final in legal terms, they are not necessarily accurate depictions of what was alleged, let alone of what actually happened. Irrespective of how careful judges are, they can only respond to what is placed before them, meaning that legal truth cannot be assumed to be actual truth. It follows that any evaluative comment I make about factual matters relates only to what can be found in these judgments, fully recognizing that the world as described by case reports offers only one point of view.

2. Classic Litigation Stories about Behavioural Conflict at Work

The following story typified the behavioural conflicts recounted at the less-serious end of the sample of judgments. *Veakins v Kier Islington Ltd*[7] was described in the introduction as one such instance. Another was *Cleveland Police Authority ('CPA') v Francis*:[8] an unsuccessful appeal to the Employment Appeal Tribunal (EAT) against the finding that the Police Authority had constructively unfairly dismissed Mrs Francis.

On 18 May 2006 Mrs Francis was promoted to be a Police National Computer ('PNC') operator … Two members of the other team at the Central Crime Bureau were also promoted. It was Mrs Francis's case that she was deliberately isolated and excluded by the rest of the team while working in that department … It was [also] her case that [her manager] treated her in an intimidating and unacceptable manner … She says that she was also entitled to time off by reason of the overtime she worked; but when she pursued that claim [her manager] criticized and tore up the sheets on which she presented it. In late February 2007 she presented a grievance concerning his bullying … On 2 April 2007 at a meeting very shortly before she went on 12 days leave CPA placed Mrs Francis on an 'action plan' on the grounds that she had committed inputting errors. Thereafter she went on sickness absence. Initially this was for a cold and viral infection … Thereafter, however, the absence was certified on the grounds of work related stress … CPA operated its 'capability procedure'. On 10 August there was a lengthy meeting at her home described by CPA as a 'welfare visit'. On 3 September a sickness capability hearing lasting more than 3 hours was conducted at her home. As a result of this hearing CPA issued her with a verbal improvement notice and action plan. On 16 September Mrs Francis resigned.

---

[6] This is in some sense analogous to what Llewellyn did in *The Common Law Tradition-Deciding Appeals* (Little, Brown and Company, 1960) leading to his theorizing of contrasting adjudicative 'styles'. See for discussion, Twining (n 4), 210–15.

[7] [2009] EWCA Civ 1288, [2010] IRLR 132.   [8] EAT, 10 March 2010.

The upshot is that arguably somewhat trivial acts resulted in Mrs Francis becoming unwell and losing her job, while it was clear that the initial problem had been exacerbated by the organizational response.

This narrative, and that in *Veakins*, were typical in suggesting that the effects of poor workplace conduct had rippled out to affect more than the original work group.[9] Burdens, financial and other kinds, were reported that fell not only on the immediate 'victims' but also on their employer and others. I also observed this to occur irrespective of whether legal claims ultimately succeeded. These wider costs included those arising from claimant's illnesses and consequent absences from work, their eventual departure from their jobs, as well as the demands and expense of internal processes, protracted litigation, and compensation awards.

3. Complexity in Litigation Stories about Behavioural Conflict at Work

It was a further recurrent theme that the meaning or significance of what had happened was hard to determine. This was a feature of about one-sixth of the judgments I read and was present across the period investigated. *Jones v ICS Cleaning Services Ltd*[10] exemplified the phenomenon. The claimant here failed in his claim for unfair dismissal and sex discrimination, the latter result being unsuccessfully appealed. The EAT reported the ET's comment that:

[t]he overwhelming evidence before us is that hardly a day went by in this workplace without what has been described before us as horseplay. This included men grabbing each others' genitals as a form of greeting; staff being held down, tickled and trousers removed; arm wrestling; mock fighting; writing an 'M' on peoples' foreheads as an indication that they had been 'managed'; spankings with the two foot ruler as a form of punishment 'meant in fun' as well as various kinds of banter. It is difficult to comprehend such behaviour and even more difficult to understand some of it being described only as 'horseplay'.[11]

The reports of Mr Jones' reactions were reminiscent of Fevre and others' qualitative evidence of convoluted, perhaps coping, reactions to difficult situations at work and the complex thought processes behind deciding to keep quiet, speak out, and sue.[12] It was recorded that Mr Jones objected only to some elements of what had been done to him. In fact, there was evidential conflict about whether he was himself the initiator, the ET concluding: 'On balance we find that the Applicant certainly instigated many of the acts complained of …'. There were also various avenues for complaint that Mr Jones did not take, saying that he thought he would not be believed, he feared recrimination and did not trust that his confidence would be kept. So far as Mr Jones raised the matter with more senior management, he was said to have done so in a half-hearted way.[13]

The first instance decision for the claimant in *Horkulak v Cantor FitzGerald International*,[14] from which there was a partially successful quantum appeal, was another example. Newman J said of the workplace generally:

It has been generally agreed that work at Cantor has certain hallmarks … It is a tough market place where quick thinking, firm determination and risk taking are essential attributes for a successful career. Employees are regarded as 'producers', but the only product is money. Performance and

---

[9] See on this from my interview study at pp 188–89 in Ch 8.   [10] EAT, 11 April 2000.
[11] ibid, [6].   [12] See pp 17, 22–23, and 44–46 in Ch 2.
[13] On these findings see *Jones* (n 10), [7]–[8].   [14] [2003] EWHC 1918 (QB), [2004] ICR 697.

pay are assessed by reference to the 'product' generated by individuals and collectively by groups of individuals within the different departments. Managers are assessed by reference to the 'product' of their sections and their ability to control costs and expenses, which, of course, reduce the 'product' available to be shared. The bond which keeps the employees together is money and everyone's eye is on the size of the share which can be acquired for themselves. Where an individual's share of money can be directly affected by another person's conduct, acute personal instincts are at play. All these factors create a low threshold of toleration for a perceived lack of performance.[15]

It was accepted and established that foul and abusive language was general currency in this world and, what is more, that the claimant was given to its use.[16] Directing such language at him was part of the conduct for which Mr Horkulak nonetheless recovered substantial common law damages in an action for breach of contract.

The sex discrimination claim, *Villalba v Merrill Lynch and Co Inc*,[17] which succeeded on some allegations of victimization, illustrated a perhaps less dramatic version of this phenomenon. Complexity here is found in the extent and detail of workplace events and relationships that were the subject of the litigation. In *Villalba* the EAT only 'sketched' the factual background from the 'much fuller' account of the ET, but their narrative still took some 5,000 words. Some overall context was given and more detailed consideration ranged from what was said at specific meetings to the nature of challenges the business faced.[18] Another instance of this kind was *Green v DB Group Services*.[19] The facts on which the court was required to make findings took place over six years, involved numerous people, and comprised all sorts of behaviours.

Allied to this theme, and perhaps a sub-species of it, there were repeated instances in which the perceptions of those involved dramatically diverged. Stark differences in the accounts of participants in the same events added to the challenge for outsiders, including courts, of working out what had happened and what it signified.[20] I observed around one-sixth of the sample to be cases of this kind, some overlapping with those counted earlier in this section. Mr Commissioner Howell QC gave a useful vignette of this kind of dissension in this passage from *Walton v Image Creative Ltd*:

Ms Walton urged on them a picture of continued mistreatment and harassment of an enthusiastic young girl, who instead of the training and career advancement she had been led to expect found herself demeaned, undermined and forced to do nothing but menial tasks. The Respondents on the other hand said that she had been well treated, although as the most junior employee she must have expected to do her share of the running about as is common in this industry; she had been given all the opportunities she could have expected for training and practice on their equipment. The personal relationships in the office had been informal and good, with a lot of sometimes light-hearted talk of the kind normal for creative people, in which she had taken part.[21]

Chan v Barts & the London NHS Trust offers another illustration, not least in that the claimant was the subject of disciplinary proceedings partly regarding his conduct towards colleagues about whose own behaviour he had made internal complaints.[22] Finally, *Lipscombe v The Forestry Commission*[23] demonstrated the degree to which positions could be polarized. The judge found, for example, that the claimant's managers had

---

[15] ibid, [19]. Compare the account from my interviewee, SM8 at p 220 in Ch 9.
[16] ibid, [17]–[19].   [17] [2007] ICR 469 (EAT).   [18] ibid, [29]–[37].
[19] [2006] EWHC 1898 (QB), [2006] IRLR 764.
[20] See on this from my interview study at p 187 in Ch 8.   [21] EAT, 16 August 2002.
[22] [2007] EWHC 2914 (QB), eg at [62]–[65]. There were also several instances of legal action by individuals alleging bullying or other inappropriate workplace behaviour when their own conduct had given rise to similar complaints.
[23] [2008] EWHC 3342 (QB).

addressed performance problems by offering advice and support, rather than the more drastic step of reassigning tasks, but this was strongly resented by Mr Lipscombe who perceived it as interference with his job. Indeed, a monitoring document, described by the judge as having 'intended to assist and support someone finding difficulty in structuring their efforts and meeting targets', was characterized by Mr Lipscombe as inflicting humiliation on the scale felt by prisoners held in detention at Guantanamo Bay.[24]

4. Complexity about the Influence of Group Identity on Behavioural Conflict at Work

A more specific sort of complexity in the factual accounts, both as allegations and as findings by courts, consisted in doubt and ambiguity about whether breaches of behavioural standards had been merely general unpleasantness, had in some way related to a target's group identity (eg their sex and race), or had involved a combination of these two. Complexity of this kind was apparent in around one-fifth of the cases studied and across the entire period investigated.

It is important to note that difficulty in untangling the part played by identity appeared at times to have been felt by the targets themselves, reflecting various qualitative findings discussed in Chapter 2.[25] As suggested by the House of Lords in *Pearce v Governing Body of Mayfield Secondary School* and *Macdonald v MoD*,[26] this showed that identity-based hostility can be the motivation for negative behaviour that makes no reference to a target's background, while hostile actions that have been taken for other reasons can advert negatively to group identity. Indeed, the same course of conduct can mix motivations and types of behaviour.

Such mixing was apparent from Morison J's comment in *Reed & Bull Information Systems Ltd v Stedman* about identity-based harassment that he regarded also as bullying: 'The tribunal found that the incidents with the manager were unacceptable to the applicant, not only because they were sexual, but because they were "personally intrusive and probably of a bullying nature".'[27] *Sheriff v Klyne Tugs (Lowestoft) Ltd*[28] demonstrated analogous ambiguity, including in that Mr Sheriff brought separate proceedings founded in the same allegations, first under the Race Relations Act (RRA) 1976 and then for the tort of negligence. The allegations were of racial harassment, abuse, intimidation, and bullying at the hands of the master of the ship on which Mr Sheriff had been employed. The conduct was said to have included being made to work longer hours than white employees, being forced to eat pork against his religious beliefs, and being refused permission to go ashore to obtain medical treatment. On complaining of his treatment, Mr Sheriff was told the matter would be investigated but he was instead dismissed. The problematic result for Mr Sheriff of presenting his claims both as race discrimination and as more generally wrongful was that the tort action was thrown out.

In *National Probation Service for England and Wales (Cumbria Area) v Kirby & Holland*,[29] the ET described managerial behaviour towards Ms Holland, the only member of an ethnic minority in her work group, as 'hostile, indifferent, critical and dismissive'.[30] Colleagues had also become involved as the situation escalated, yet the

---

[24] ibid, [23]–[24].   [25] See pp 19 and 22–23 and n 262 in Ch 2. See also pp 227–28 in Ch 8.
[26] [2003] UKHL 34, [2003] ICR 937. See text to n 83 in Ch 3.
[27] [1999] IRLR 299 (EAT), [10].   [28] [1999] EWCA Civ 1663, [1999] ICR 1170.
[29] [2006] IRLR 508 (EAT).   [30] ibid, [5].

complexity of unravelling what had gone on was apparent from the case report. In an investigatory interview, for example, Ms Holland was said herself to have expressed the view that 'her race was an underlying, although not the main reason, for the treatment ... which she characterized ... as persistent bullying/victimization'.[31]

Abbey National Plc v Fairbrother[32] was emblematic of the theme related in this section, recounting a tangled story of unpleasant behaviour directed at various targets. In the case of the claimant, this behaviour had referred to her obsessive compulsive disorder, while other colleagues had been 'picked on' in different ways. The ET found there had been conduct that 'in the case of the claimant, included minor taunts about her need for tidiness and order in her work, using her chair or cup and leaving her office or work area untidy, calling her a "tart" or a "slapper" and refusing to talk to her on one day ... In the case of [a colleague], she was subjected to taunting which focused on the fact that she worked at a slow pace.'[33] Similarly *Munchkins Restaurant Ltd v Karmazyn*[34] described a long-running tale of inappropriate conduct, often related to sex but sometimes consisting in general bad temper and aggression towards the claimants.

Finally, *South London Healthcare NHS Trust v Rubeyi*[35] concerned a drawn-out conflict in the hospital's paediatrics department, of which the court said: 'It is common ground that [the department] was dysfunctional and riven by personality clashes over a period of ten years.'[36] A pay claim by Dr Rubeyi, a consultant, succeeded, but those under the RRA 1976 and the Religion and Belief Regulations of 2003 did not, a victimization finding by the ET being overturned in the EAT.

Dr Rubeyi was reported by the EAT to have raised a number of grievances about bullying and harassment over the years, sometimes successfully, but during the time in question not to have suggested that these might have been based on her race or religion. The possibility that these aspects of Dr Rubeyi's identity had played a part in her experiences was said in fact to have been suggested by a personnel officer who 'had a feeling that there might be something in the air.'[37] The claimant subsequently made a discrimination complaint in 2005, from which these proceedings evolved. An independent review, the factual account and opinions of which were accepted by the ET, found a history of 'bullying and harassment', 'a club culture', 'an old-school regime', and that there was substance in aspects of Dr Rubeyi's grievances.[38] The same report, however, decided against a prima facie case of race and religious discrimination. The reviewer's opinion was that Dr Rubeyi's discrimination complaints had been an afterthought, her focus having been on bullying and harassment. The inquiry also took the view that discrimination would been revealed in earlier internal investigations if it had been present.[39]

5. Complexity about the Role of Colleagues and Management in Behavioural Conflict at Work

Another persistent theme was of the actions of colleagues and management being reported to have interacted in destructive ways.[40] This feature was present in about one-quarter of the judgments and throughout the time period considered.

---

[31] ibid.   [32] [2007] IRLR 320 (EAT).   [33] ibid, 321.
[34] EAT, 28 January 2010.   [35] EAT, 2 March 2010.   [36] ibid, [8].
[37] ibid, [9].   [38] ibid, [15].   [39] ibid, [16].
[40] See further on this in my interview study at pp 193–94 in Ch 8.

The judgment in *Prison Service v Johnson*[41] provides a good illustration. It concerned a successful race discrimination claim by an auxiliary prison officer of Caribbean origin in which compensation awards, including one for aggravated damages, were upheld. It was found that Mr Johnson had been subjected to racial harassment and discrimination for a period extending over several years. From his first days in the Prison Service, Mr Johnson recounted that racial remarks were made to him to which he did not react because he observed that 'other officers would not assist and support a black officer in the way that they would support other white officers'.[42] A campaign against Mr Johnson was nonetheless started when he made a critical comment about the treatment of a black prisoner. Unpleasantness from a number of colleagues over a period of more than a year was compounded by management's reaction to Mr Johnson finally voicing his objections. An investigation, which the ET found to have been 'a travesty of what it should have been', concluded that 'the applicant construed every mishap, mistake or failure to communicate with him as a racist act'.[43] Following this, management took disciplinary action against Mr Johnson that was itself held to have been racially discriminatory.

In *Harris v The Post Office (Royal Mail)*[44] the employer admitted liability for unlawful sex discrimination in how they responded to an internal complaint. Mr Harris had alleged bullying, humiliation, and mistreatment by his fellow employees over a substantial period, but when he eventually complained he was given short shrift by those whose duty it was fairly to investigate the situation. The particularly depressing conclusion of the EAT in *Derby Specialist Fabrication v Burton*[45] was that '[a]t all material times racial abuse was widespread throughout the tube shop. No action was taken by the employers to check this.'[46] In fact, it was said that the HR manager 'did not appear to recognize the climate of racial abuse as a problem. He failed to understand that it might be offensive for a black worker to be likened to a monkey and for another to be described as a "black bastard".'[47]

Abbey National Plc v Robinson[48] epitomized managerial reaction exacerbating the ill effects of bad workplace behaviour. A swift and appropriate investigation found Miss Robinson's line manager, Mr Middleton, had bullied and harassed her and disciplinary action was taken against him. The disciplinary measures, however, were not as severe as the claimant had been led to expect because more senior management decided Mr Middleton should not be moved from his job. This made it 'extremely difficult if not impossible'[49] for Miss Robinson to resume work after a period of illness. The EAT recorded that '[t]he tribunal's findings leave no room for doubt that it was the management decision not to move Mr Middleton despite these assurances, coupled with the way that this was put to Miss Robinson in the summer of 1997, which not only prolonged her illness and her inability to return to work but started the breakdown in trust and confidence which eventually led her to resign.'[50] Furthermore, it was found that the applicant was treated in an 'insensitive, unsatisfactory and unreasonable' way for a further nine or ten months, all culminating in her departure and successful claim for unfair constructive dismissal.[51]

In the cases discussed here it was striking that the judgments described colleagues, including senior ones, either colluding in negative treatment or at least condoning it. *Dunnachie v Kingston upon Hull CC*[52] again illustrated this. It concerned an individual

---

[41] [1997] ICR 275 (EAT). See also the text to ns 177–78 in Ch 3 on the general significance of this case to assessment of damages for injury to feelings.
[42] ibid, 277.   [43] ibid, 278.   [44] EAT, 25 February 2000.
[45] [2001] ICR 833 (EAT).   [46] ibid, [1].   [47] ibid.
[48] EAT, 20 November 2000.   [49] ibid, [4].   [50] ibid. [5].   [51] ibid, [7].
[52] [2004] UKHL 36, [2005] 1 AC 226.

who had been employed by Hull City Council for fifteen years. Mr Dunnachie had joined at nineteen years of age, qualified as an environmental health officer, and had risen through several ranks. His later years of employment were found to have been blighted by undermining conduct by a superior, ending in a covert investigation of Mr Dunnachie's work and a threat of disciplinary action being left to hang over him. Lord Steyn recorded the ET's conclusion that senior management had effectively sanctioned what had been done. Not only was Mr Dunnachie not reassured that disciplinary proceedings would not be commenced against him but senior employees were said by the ET to have 'either failed or refused to recognize that the applicant had been a victim of bullying'. Attempts were also found by a senior colleague to stop Mr Dunnachie making a formal complaint.[53]

The factual findings in *Miles v Gilbank*[54] were particularly distressing. The claimant, Ms Gilbank, was employed for over seven years by a hairdressing business of which Ms Miles was a director and major shareholder. Multiple acts of unlawful discrimination were found once the claimant became pregnant. For example, she was refused adjustments to her usual work practice of continuous appointments notwithstanding medical advice that she needed to rest and eat during the day. A request for flexibility was met by her hours being unilaterally cut and the intensity of her working time increased. There was no provision for ante-natal appointments, even when an episode of bleeding made an emergency scan necessary. Ms Gilbank was subjected to derogatory remarks about her physical appearance and to degrading and humiliating abuse, swearing and shouting, sometimes in front of clients and junior colleagues. When she either complained or sought redress, managers laughed audibly as she left the room.

The ET concluded:

[a]ll in all, there was a catalogue of behaviour towards [Ms Gilbank] on the part of [Ms Miles] and the other managers … which goes beyond malicious and amounts to downright vicious. It was an inhumane and sustained campaign of bullying and discrimination which could not, in the circumstances … be reasonably seen to have been accidental or merely insensitive. It was targeted, deliberate, repeated and consciously inflicted. It not only demonstrated … a total lack of concern for the welfare of the claimant herself, but a callous disregard or concern for the life of her unborn child.[55]

Ms Miles was also found, on the balance of probabilities, consciously to have 'fostered and encouraged a discriminatory culture to grow up'.[56]

6. Judicial Scrutiny of Behavioural Conflict at Work

In addition to the themes described above in the underlying factual accounts in the judgments, I found there were common features in the way that claimants' stories were recounted by judges. About one-fifth of the judgments included extraordinarily detailed narratives about the subject matter of the dispute, not always in judgments comprising one of the typically complex elements. Further, while the extent of the factual recounting quite often corresponded to the length of the history, even a single instance could attract long expositions of disputed points and the court's response.[57] Overall, the careful, minutely expressed way in which courts dealt with the presentation by litigants of their rival contentions, even on appeal, was remarkable.

[53] ibid, [6].   [54] [2006] EWCA Civ 543, [2006] ICR 1297.
[55] ibid, [20].   [56] ibid, [35].
[57] See, eg, *Ormsby v CC of Strathclyde Police* [2009] CSOH 143, 2008 SCLR 783.

Yeboah v Crofton[58] is a paradigm example. Claims against both Mr Yeboah's employer, the London Borough of Hackney, and his colleague, Mr Crofton, led to various findings of race discrimination. Mr Crofton alone appealed successfully to the EAT, but the CA reinstated the ET result. Lord Justice Mummery commented of the proceedings:

The hearing of seven applications before the employment tribunal sitting at London North between 7 April 1997 and 17 March 1998 was the longest ever held: all the applications were heard together lasting a total of 104 days, a record which I truly hope will never be broken … There was 'evidence of complex and contested matters covering a period from mid-1990 to early 1996'. Mr Yeboah gave evidence for 25 days, Mr Crofton for 20 days. Fourteen other witnesses gave evidence.[59]

The CA was, of course, the second level of appeal. This would normally mean that facts were sidelined but they were central in this instance because Mr Crofton argued that the decisions against him had been perverse. This meant contending that no reasonable ET, reasonably directing itself on the law and the evidence, could have reached the decisions this tribunal had. There was extraordinary factual scrutiny by the CA to decide whether or not this was the case. Substantive speeches were given by both Mummery and Brooke LJJ, the whole judgment comprising around 20,000 words, almost all directed to a careful recounting and discussion of the factual position.

A similar case was *Bahl v Law Society*[60] in which much of the CA decision dealt with the facts. The CA this time upheld the EAT, overturning findings by the ET that the Law Society and two of its senior employees had unconsciously racially and sexually discriminated against Dr Bahl, the Society's erstwhile vice president. The judgment of the Court, given by Peter Gibson LJ, comprised just under 22,000 words that were largely given over to intense analysis of myriad factual points.

Three more instances of this type are *Crossland v Wilkinson Hardware Stores Ltd*,[61] *Merelie v Newcastle PCT*,[62] and *Cheltenham Borough Council v Laird*.[63] All of these were, however, first instance judgments in the HC and in each the claims were put in unusual ways. In *Crossland* the respondent company sought and obtained summary judgment in an action by Mr Crossland for libel, slander, malicious falsehood, and for common law damages for harassment. The unusual way in which the case was put, libel, slander, and malicious falsehood not being causes of action that are usually alleged in this kind of claim, was most likely explained by the earlier strike out of an ET action that was brought despite acceptance by Mr Crossland of a settlement in return for not going to the ET.[64] The strike out of this HC claim was then based on Tugendhat J's conclusion that the various further actions had no real prospect of success. There were no final determinations of fact since the hearing was at an interlocutory stage.[65] Even in this context, nonetheless, lengthy, anxious consideration was given to the allegations and the documentation.[66]

[58] [2002] EWCA Civ 794, [2002] IRLR 634.
[59] ibid, [3]. Note there was a further, partially successful appeal by Mr Crofton about quantum, reported at *Yeboah v Crofton* (Quantum) (EAT, 15 April 2003).
[60] [2004] EWCA Civ 1070, [2004] IRLR 799. [61] [2005] EWHC 481 (QB).
[62] [2006] EWHC 1433 (Admin). [63] [2009] EWHC 1253 (QB), [2009] IRLR 621.
[64] The ET strike out had also been confirmed on review, taking account, eg, that Mr Crossland had received independent legal advice before agreeing to the settlement. *Crossland* (n 61), [2]–[3].
[65] ibid, [9]–[19], but especially at [13].
[66] ibid, [20]–[47] and more generally. See also the CA decision refusing permission to appeal, the neutral citation for which is [2005] EWCA Civ 1668.

The claims in *Merelie* included one for defamation. Here again there were separate ET proceedings for unfair dismissal which were stayed pending the HC decision.[67] The HC hearing was of two actions, both unsuccessful.[68] The first was at common law for breach of contract and for the tort of negligence. The second was under the PHA 1997 and for defamation. The judgment is impressive for the sheer breadth, depth, and conscientiousness of the investigation. The majority of the ruling, which ran to some 42,000 words, was dedicated to relating and analysing factual issues. The events considered ranged in time from 1975 to the early 2000s, involved a considerable cast of characters and covered many incidents. The following passage gives a flavor of the exhaustiveness of the adjudicative enquiry:

> In June 1998 Ms. Weisser injured her ankle, which was put in plaster, and was unable to come into work. She had with her at home a set of keys and the 'order book' ... The Claimant decided to call at her flat ... and collect them. On the morning of 26th June she drove there with the dental nurse who was replacing Ms. Weisser, Kerry Fawcett: she had tried to ring first but could get no answer. On [the Claimant's] account, there was nothing untoward in the visit: she simply asked for the keys and was given them and then left. But Ms. Weisser saw it differently. She resented being visited at home, with no prior notice. She said that the Claimant, instead of waiting at the door, had followed her into the flat and had, intrusively, looked into her bedroom, where her sister was in bed: her sister confirmed this in evidence before me. She believed that the Claimant's tone was accusatorial: she thought that she did not believe that she was really injured and that she had come round to check up on her. In my view the truth lies somewhere between the two accounts. I do not believe that any of the Claimant's overt acts were objectionable: Ms. Weisser should not have had the keys, and there was nothing wrong in principle in the Claimant calling to collect them. In a contemporary note Mrs. Fawcett, who witnessed the encounter, described the conversation as 'amiable but business-like'; and she told Mr. Ferguson, who recorded it in a contemporary note, that the Claimant had 'behaved perfectly well towards [Ms. Weisser]'. It would have been better if the Claimant had not called unannounced and if she had not gone into the flat itself but waited at the door—I accept the evidence of Ms. Weisser and her sister that she did come sufficiently far into the flat to look into the bedroom—but in another context those would be matters of no significance. However, the visit has to be viewed against the background of the already poor relationship between the Claimant and Ms. Weisser. I have no doubt that Ms. Weisser was right to detect a tone of suspicion and confrontation in the Claimant's conduct. It is significant that Mrs. Fawcett, despite the evidence which I have quoted above, thought the visit unnecessary: she asked the Claimant before they set out whether they really needed to go, but she said that the Claimant was insistent.[69]

This is only one among many examples of factual minutiae to which the judgment gave close attention, building to a nuanced set of findings about what had happened, its meaning, and its legal consequences.

The same kind of scrutiny can be observed in *Cheltenham Borough Council v Laird*, a quite extraordinary action in which the Council sought, unsuccessfully, to reclaim costs incurred during the employment of its managing director, Mrs Laird. The Council claimed damages for the torts of deceit and of negligence, as well as under the Misrepresentation Act 1967, for what it claimed were fraudulent or negligent misstatements in Mrs Laird's medical questionnaire that she submitted as part of her job

[67] *Merelie* (n 62), [14]. But see *Merelie v Newcastle PCT* (EAT, 26 August 2009) in which the later strike out of these proceedings by the ET was upheld.
[68] Note that leave to appeal was refused by the CA in a judgment by Pill LJ, the neutral citation for which is [2007] EWCA Civ 171.
[69] *Merelie* (n 62), [68].

application. Mrs Laird brought a defensive counterclaim, also unsuccessful, seeking compensation for breach of contract and under various statutes, including the PHA 1997 and the DDA 1995. There were also separate proceedings, for example in the ET, in what was another long-running, multifaceted dispute.[70]

Much might be said of this litigation, but for present purposes what is notable is the depth to which the judgment went in unravelling factual questions, great and small, over a considerable period. This time the judge felt the need to append a list of the forty-four people who were involved.[71] While there was more legal discussion than in *Merelie*, a substantial portion of the 59,000 word ruling was devoted to keen dissection of factual issues.

It is important to end this section by highlighting that the longest, most detailed factual accounts were in first-instance decisions in the HC, when most of the judgments in my sample were given on appeal. This suggests that consideration of factual issues in the entire sample of judgments was much less detailed than if the sample had generally comprised first instance decisions.[72] This tends to suggest that this data disclosed only the tip of the iceberg in terms of judges carefully recounting sagas about behavioural conflict at work and is suggestive about their approach to fact-finding more generally.

7. Behavioural Conflict at Work Lost in a Litigation Maze

This is arguably the most contentious of the factual themes I extracted from the sample of cases and it relates to the litigation process rather than to accounts of what had happened and what was alleged. There was a set of judgments that left the reader with the sense of litigation that had escalated in ways that appeared destructive for everyone involved. I observed this in about 10 per cent of judgments and found instances throughout the whole time period.

In noting this, I must state again that I am responding only to the disputes as they appear from the case reports; I recognize that aspects of the underlying situation may not have been covered and that judicial narratives might be contested. What the judgments conveyed, however, was repeated instances of litigation that placed particularly damaging burdens, financial and of other kinds, on everyone involved. This was, furthermore, irrespective of the formal outcome.

I see the three HC cases discussed earlier as examples of this, with *Cheltenham Borough Council v Laird*[73] perhaps the most conspicuous. The Council sought damages of around £1 million representing the extra costs they said they had incurred from employing Mrs Laird rather than another managing director.[74] Mr Justice Hamblen summarized the

---

[70] *Cheltenham* (n 63). [18], [23], and [29]–[32], [355]–[355], [448]–[453], and [484]–[519]. See also *Cheltenham BC v Laird* [2010] EWCA Civ 847 about the costs award at the close of the substantive litigation.

[71] ibid, [33] and Appendix, *dramatis personae*.

[72] See, eg, the routine comment by Wall LJ comparing the factual detail in the ET and appeal courts decisions in *Perkin v St George's Healthcare NHS Trust* [2005] EWCA Civ 1174, [2006] ICR 617, [4]: 'The tribunal's reasons extend to some 66 pages. Of those, pp 4–55 are taken up with the tribunal's findings of fact, which run to some 217 sub-paragraphs. Whilst I will need in due course to identify a number of these findings, I can, for the time being, take the essential facts from a succinct summary contained in the judgment of the appeal tribunal.'

[73] *Cheltenham* (n 63).

[74] See also the comment by Stanley Burnton J in *Chan v Barts & the London NHS Trust* [2007] EWHC 2914 (QB), [164] expressing concern at the costs involved in that case, regarding both internal disciplinary proceedings and litigation.

factual basis for this sum, documenting some of the cost and expense the dispute was alleged to have occasioned:

> As a consequence of differences which arose between Mrs Laird and the leader of the council, Councillor McKinlay, and other members and officers, much time and expense was spent by CBC [Cheltenham Borough Council] in dealing with the resulting disputes which arose rather than the normal running of CBC business. These included Joint Negotiating Committee … disciplinary proceedings brought against Mrs Laird and grievance and court proceedings brought by Mrs Laird, as well as a complaint made by her to the Standards Board of England ('SBE'). Outside support had to be brought in to help CBC staff deal with these disputes and to support them. Mrs Laird was off sick for substantial periods, was then suspended and ultimately retired on an ill-health pension. CBC claim as damages the time and costs of dealing with these various disputes and their consequences as well as the ill-health element of the pension paid.[75]

Whatever originally occurred, it seems clear that this litigation made huge demands of many kinds. Not the least of these fell on the legal system and its personnel, especially the judges with responsibility for dealing with the case.

In *Fernandez v Office of the Parliamentary Commissioner for Administration and Health Service Commissioners* the EAT commented, quoting the ET, on the way the dispute had escalated:

> In what appears to [the EAT] to be a justified sense of disapproval, the Tribunal said this: … 'Out of this simple set of facts, the parties have conjured a very substantial piece of litigation. The Tribunal file is about a foot thick. On the Applicant's side, the case has been bedevilled for the greater part of its history … by pedantry and legalism of a high order. For their part the Respondents have joined in the fray on every point of complaint (however fatuous), generating astonishing volumes of paper in the process. We have been surprised and alarmed by their liberality in expending public resources on the case, and have regretted the cost which must inevitably have resulted not only to the public purse but also to those who rely on their services … At more than one point during the hearing it was suggested by the Tribunal that the parties might not have approached this matter with an appropriate sense of proportion. For the most part, these suggestions were met with polite puzzlement.'[76]

Hammond v International Network Services UK Ltd[77] also dealt with long-running, ultimately unsuccessful litigation in which there appeared to have been considerable expenditure of time, energy, and, no doubt, money by the litigants and others. These proceedings were in the HC and sought damages for breach of the PHA 1997 and for the tort of negligence. There had also been an earlier, unsuccessful (including on appeal) ET action for unfair dismissal and for race discrimination. Judge Peter Coulson QC observed that '[m]any of the underlying facts and matters in these proceedings have already been investigated as part of the claimant's claim for unfair dismissal and race discrimination.'[78] Moreover, he made the comment that, despite the rejection of that earlier claim: 'on numerous occasions during this trial, the claimant demonstrated that he was, in reality, seeking to use these proceedings to re-open that failed claim …'.[79] Before giving a fully reasoned (nearly 20,000 word) judgment rejecting the claims, the judge refused Mr Hammond's request during the trial for an adjournment.[80] In doing

---

[75] *Cheltenham* (n 63), [7]. See also the more detailed consideration of the Council's damages claim at [534]–[559] and of related damages issues thereafter.
[76] EAT, 15 February 2005.   [77] [2007] EWHC 2604 (QB), 1 November 2007.
[78] ibid, [3].   [79] ibid.
[80] ibid, [18]–[27]. Judge Peter Coulson QC had also earlier refused a request that he recuse himself for bias (see [14]–[15]), making the point, amongst others, that 'I would add that in a case such as this, where every tribunal and judge has been accused by the claimant of bias in some way or another, the result of automatic recusal would be that the underlying claim would never be determined.'

so he commented on the time it had taken for the case to get to this point and observed that '[f]inally, I have concluded that the claimant's case is without any merit at all and utterly hopeless … Since I have concluded that the claimant has no case in fact or in law, such a result needs to be confirmed to all parties as soon as possible. No benefit can be derived, least of all to the claimant himself, from giving him yet another adjournment of his patently hopeless case.'[81]

8. Conclusion

My findings here consider the fine detail in cases about behavioural conflict adjudicated by higher courts in the UK. By definition these conflicts were hard fought: they were in the minute proportion of employment problems litigated to the point of a contested hearing and they mostly went to appeal, some more than once. That also means there was generally sufficient funding of legal costs to permit this to happen, although it should be noted that some litigants represented themselves.

I extract two overarching themes from the data, of *complexity* and *adversarialism*. There were the different strands of complexity that emerged, some concerning the facts alleged, some about how these were handled by courts. These came from accounts of workplace behaviour that any outsider must struggle to interpret, disputes that ranged over time and involved large numbers of people, stark divergences in litigants' narratives and analyses of the same events, indications of particular difficulty, sometimes even for targets, in isolating whether group identity had played a role,[82] managerial reactions that appeared to interact with initial conduct in destructive ways, and judges conscientiously grappling with sometimes extraordinarily detailed histories.[83]

Further there were signs of *extreme adversarialism*. These involved instances of deep dispute about what had happened and what it meant, long-running contention in situations where courts came clearly to condemn managerial reactions, immense factual detail that judges were asked to rule on, and claims sometimes being vigorously disputed for reasons that were difficult to fathom. It is important, however, to note that these elements appeared, respectively, in only (approximately) one-sixth, one-quarter, one-fifth, and one-tenth of the judgments I analysed. These are not statistics that can be generalized, given the difficulty of documenting how my sample relates to the population of judgments about behavioural conflict from 1995 to June 2010. It is suggestive, nonetheless, that even if reaching the outer limits of adversarialism is a feature of higher court adjudication about behavioural conflict, it is far from ubiquitous.

That leads to my first extrapolation: *peculiarities in the subset of cases that get to this stage must affect the perceptions of anyone who works close to litigation and legal process*. Tracing exactly how that happens would be impossible, but we can be confident that intimate experience of litigation and legal process influences the beliefs, attitudes, thought processes, and ultimately, common sense of what may be termed 'legal insiders'. This group will especially include barristers, solicitors, 'repeat player' litigants like those from HR departments in large organizations, court personnel, and judges. It may also extend to others, like claimants who pursue either long-running or multiple claims, and journalists who specialize in court proceedings. This data suggests that we should expect 'taken-for-granted' attitudes among those groups to reflect experiences during litigation

---

[81] ibid, [24].
[82] See pp 19 and 22–23 and n 262 in Ch 2 and 227–28 in Ch 8.
[83] This theme reflects Pollert's observations reported at the text to n 197 in Ch 2.

of various types of complexity, and sometimes of extreme adversarialism. The findings of my interview study support and extend this analysis.[84]

My second general point is that *these findings show judges working incredibly hard, carefully sifting what really happened to arrive at some kind of truth.* This begs a whole host of questions about whether that adjudicative effort is being optimally directed and what impacts it ultimately has. We know from the evidence surveyed in Chapter 2 that it does not generally result in working people being able to resolve problems at work, with many left to cope with continuing difficulties. Involvement in litigation also seems to be a mixed experience, with real questions about whether underlying problems are resolved, justice norms are injected into organizational life, or wider benefits accrued. More specifically, there were vignettes of obvious and sometimes serious breaches of legal rights, for example in relation to situations in which unhelpful managerial reactions had made things worse, that are concerning because of how far the litigation process had to go before the law was finally applied. A similar cause for concern was that relatively trivial, legally straightforward claims reached higher court adjudication without resolution, whether through settlement of strong cases or withdrawal of weak ones. While some degree of waste is no doubt inevitable in any litigation system, this evidence begs serious questions about whether all the resource and effort put into this form of adjudication could be harnessed to deliver more.

---

[84] See esp pp 183–84 and 212–13 in Ch 8, 217, 239–40 and 242 in Ch 9, and 256–57 in Ch 10.

5

Legal Themes in Case Law
about Behavioural Conflict at Work I

Overlapping Rights and the Snakes-and-Ladders Effect

This chapter explains how the many overlapping legal rules regulating workplace behaviour have led to arbitrariness in the adjudication of similar factual situations. The result has been a kind of legal 'snakes and ladders' in which the technical framing of claims has led to similar sets of facts sometimes being adjudicated according to rules that were clear and remedially generous (eg in a claim under the Protection from Harassment Act (PHA) 1997), and at other times according to rules that were convoluted and remedially restrictive (eg in a statutory claim for constructive unfair dismissal). Such distinctions in the treatment of analogous situations have often resulted from courts drawing novel jurisdictional boundaries, as outlined in Chapter 3. Indeed, the legal fate of a set of facts could be the consequence of it being adjudicated either before or after a particular line was drawn. In other instances it was litigation choices that led to varying legal treatment of comparable facts situations. Either way, these adjudicative distinctions make little sense as a matter of internal legal coherence and are in many ways unjustifiable when evaluated from an external perspective.

The board game analogy may further be pressed in the sense that it was not always possible for litigants, represented or not, to know in advance whether their legal strategy contained a snake or a ladder. For example, exposition of when and how different causes of action could be asserted or remedies claimed in, for example, *Johnson v Unisys Ltd*,[1] *Essa v Laing Ltd*,[2] *Eastwood v Magnox Electric plc & McCabe v Cornwall CC*,[3] *Majrowski v Guy's and St Thomas's NHS Trust*,[4] *GMB Trade Union v Brown*,[5] and *GAB Robins (UK) Ltd v Triggs*[6] were all significantly unpredictable. That meant dilemmas were posed not only to claimants choosing how to put claims but also to respondents in working out the implications of actions against them. This trend also continued after the period from which my sample of judgments was drawn, with the Supreme Court (SC) decision in *Edwards v Chesterfield Royal Hospital NHS Foundation Trust & Botham v MoD*.[7] Further, future legal development of this kind cannot be ruled out and my analysis suggests that the joins between the PHA 1997 and other relevant legal sources pose a particular risk.

Finally, a related issue was of claims being presented in artificial ways in apparent attempts to fall on the better side of technical distinctions. Litigants and their advisers appeared sometimes consciously to try to shoehorn events either into or out of legal categories. Notably, this was at times associated with legal developments steering claimants to bring several sets of proceedings. It was not, however, always possible to tell the

---

[1] [2001] UKHL, [2003] 1 AC 518. [2] [2004] EWCA Civ 2, [2004] ICR 746.
[3] [2004] UKHL 35, [2005] 1 AC 503. [4] [2006] UKHL 34, [2007] 1 AC 224.
[5] EAT, 16 October 2007. [6] [2008] EWCA Civ 17, [2008] ICR 529.
[7] [2011] UKSC 58, [2012] 2 WLR 55.

extent to which this had occurred from the judgments alone. It may, therefore, have been a more significant factor than the data disclosed.

1. Snakes I: Pre- and Post-Dismissal Compensation

The scene for this 'snake' for claimants is set by the outline in Chapter 3 of first, the *Eastwood* distinction between compensatable harm caused separately from dismissal and that caused by dismissal itself, and second, the remedial findings in *Dunnachie v Kingston upon Hull CC*,[8] both judgments within my sample. The difficulty for litigants has been either to predict or to navigate the rules about which losses related to dismissal are recoverable in a common law action in the ordinary courts and which are recoverable in an ET claim for unfair dismissal, with multiple actions sometimes the only option for claimants to secure their full entitlement. However, this does not necessarily translate into being a 'ladder' for respondents in that they may struggle accurately to evaluate their potential liability and end up incurring extra costs dealing with more than one set of proceedings.

For Mr Eastwood and Mr Williams, legal uncertainty meant they had to go all the way to the House of Lords (HL) on assumed facts to find out that their common law claims in the ordinary courts fell on the right side of the *Johnson* line. They were only then permitted to proceed and subject to recovery of any losses and expenses caused by dismissal itself being disallowed at common law.

In *Dunnachie*[9] what was critical to the decision was the court's interpretation of the statutory provision on compensation,[10] the HL confirming that only damages for financial or pecuniary loss are recoverable in a claim for unfair dismissal, notwithstanding the obiter comment to the contrary by Lord Hoffmann in *Johnson v Unisys*. The impact for Mr Dunnachie and his employers was again that they had to go to the HL to ascertain the law on a pretty elementary point. The HL decision itself then contained a somewhat abstract, formulaic determination of Mr Dunnachie's entitlement. Lord Steyn said that the ET found Mr Dunnachie to have suffered total losses of £123,328.28, including £10,000 for injury to feelings, but application of the statutory cap resulted in a compensatory award of £51,700, together with a basic award of £3,240 and costs of £2,752.[11] Reinforcing how artificial the reasoning was, I cannot tell if the outcome in the HL made any practical difference to Mr Dunnachie, as his total pecuniary losses were far above the compensation cap even after subtraction of the sum originally awarded for injury to feelings. If it made no difference, the litigation story becomes even more difficult to fathom.

Furthermore, these proceedings amply demonstrated the difficulties that technical obscurities in the law create for claimants and respondents, in that these meant that neither Mr Dunnachie nor his employer had much chance of making optimal litigation choices. A negligence claim was, in the circumstances, not a viable option because Mr Dunnachie seems not to have sustained any personal injury. There was also, on the face of it, no relevant identity issue that might have founded a discrimination claim. Still, the case report begged the question why, as was implied, there was no claim under the PHA 1997 given that at least some of the bullying conduct appeared likely to have

---

[8] [2004] UKHL 36, [2005] 1 AC 226. See pp 70–71 and 94–95 in Ch 3.   [9] *Dunnachie* (n 8).
[10] ibid, in particular at Lord Steyn [14]–[29] and Lord Rodger [32]–[33]. Lord Steyn also agreed with Lord Rodger. Lord Nicholls, Lord Hoffmann, Lord Brown, and Lord Rodger all agreed with Lord Steyn.
[11] ibid, [6].

taken place after entry into force of that legislation in June 1997. Compensation for Mr Dunnachie's injury to feelings might quite straightforwardly have been available by this route as well as, incidentally, for his full pecuniary losses. That there was not such a claim was probably in part because it took time for lawyers to notice the workplace implications of the PHA 1997. It was also, however, natural for Mr Dunnachie and his advisers to be influenced by the UK's most senior judges taking the view that damages for non-pecuniary loss were available in an action for unfair dismissal. Whatever the explanation for how the claim was put, the corresponding uncertainty for the employer as to the nature and extent of its legal exposure must have been considerable.

The implications for unfair dismissal law of the *Johnson/Eastwood* line of authority had also not at that stage been determined. That these authorities had an effect on unfair dismissal compensation only emerged some time afterwards in *GMB Trade Union v Brown*[12] and *GAB Robins (UK) Ltd v Triggs*,[13] both of which concerned behavioural conflicts. These two decisions therefore also illustrated adjudicative arbitrariness because of jurisdictional complexity.

It was three years after *Eastwood* that the Employment Appeal Tribunal (EAT) decided *GMB Trade Union v Brown*. The judgment described an ongoing dispute from July 2003 until Ms Brown's resignation in May 2005, after which she established constructive unfair dismissal in the ET. While the original conflict concerned the content of Ms Brown's job, behavioural issues seem to have been present from the initial stages. Ms Brown and her regional secretary, Mr Brennan, were each said to have accused the other 'of being hostile, unco-operative and uncompromising' at an early meeting. Ms Brown subsequently raised two grievances. The first, in August 2003, included allegations of harassment and sex discrimination, linked to the contention that her physical and mental well-being was being adversely affected. Ms Brown was then, aside from a period of maternity leave, on sick leave from September 2003 until the end of her employment. The second grievance was lodged in February 2005 under the GMB's relatively new dignity-at-work procedure.

The significance of the case here is that while the union's appeal against the finding of constructive unfair dismissal was unsuccessful, the compensation of £40,883.63 was reduced on appeal by £4,664.70 on the following reasoning:

> [W]here the damage flows from conduct which preceded the dismissal, it is recoverable for breach of the trust and confidence term rather than falling under the auspices of the unfair dismissal claim ... we are satisfied that the loss flowing from the failure to work immediately following the resignation did not stem from the dismissal itself. It was the consequence of conduct which preceded the dismissal ... Applying the approach set out by Lord Nicholls at para 31 of the *Eastwood* decision, we are satisfied that even if some breach had been identified which caused the sickness, the loss consequential upon that did not flow from the dismissal.[14]

The upshot was that because of her inability to work, some of Ms Brown's losses were only recoverable in a common law action. Although technically this was a 'win' for her employers, it probably led to another claim being made by Ms Brown and to two sets of proceedings becoming probable in similar situations in the future.

The correctness of this outcome was confirmed by the Court of Appeal (CA) in *GAB Robins (UK) Ltd v Triggs*. Again, the factual situation covered some years in which combined complaints of overwork and bullying were made. The claimant's health had been affected, such that she was finally placed on sick leave from September 2004 until

---

12 *GMB v Brown* (n 5).   13 *GAB Robins* (n 6).
14 *GMB v Brown* (n 5), [62]–[63].

February 2005 when her employment ended. Ms Triggs unsuccessfully sought a solution that would enable her to return to work, ultimately resigning in what was found by the ET to have been a constructive unfair dismissal. Ms Triggs' unfair dismissal compensation was limited, however, because the legally wrongful conduct that caused her reduced earning capacity occurred prior to dismissal. As Mummery LJ said, with the agreement of Lawrence Collins and Tuckey LJJ:

> It is correct that the dismissal was a constructive one, that is that it was the result of, and followed upon, [Ms Triggs] acceptance of the employer's antecedent breaches of the implied term of trust and confidence that had caused her illness and, in turn, her reduced earning capacity. But it is fallacious to regard those antecedent breaches as constituting the dismissal. The dismissal was effected purely and simply by her decision in February 2005 that she wished to discontinue her employment. On a claim for unfair dismissal, that entitled her to compensation for whatever loss flowed from that dismissal. But that loss did not include loss (including future loss) flowing from wrongs *already* inflicted upon her by the employer's prior conduct: those losses (including any future lost income) were not caused by the dismissal.[15]

This time the CA recorded that Ms Triggs had started common law proceedings.[16] In a way this is ironic as those would have entitled her also to compensation for her non-pecuniary losses, which it looks like she had originally been prepared to forego.

Earlier, I described *Cleveland Police Authority v Francis*[17] as a somewhat typical example of less serious disputes about conduct in the judgments surveyed. Interestingly, this is a factual situation in which the kind of apportionment decided in *GMB v Brown/GAB Robins* would now appear necessary. The EAT decision that upheld the ET's finding of constructive unfair dismissal did not specify this: it said nothing about the compensation eventually paid nor about whether there was a separate common law action. As far as Ms Francis' ill health was caused by her employer's wrongful conduct, however, the factual findings made clear that this occurred prior to her dismissal. First, the actions that added up to the employer's repudiatory breach of contract had continued over some time, and second, Ms Francis was absent on sick leave for work-related stress for several months before dismissal. If, accordingly, I am right in viewing this case as somewhat typical of its kind, this jurisdictional conundrum is of particular practical significance for behavioural disputes at work.[18]

2. Snakes II: Group Identity and Compensation for Personal Injury

The potential pitfalls for claimants of mistaking the overlaps between different kinds of claims were vividly apparent in the case of *Parchment v The Secretary of State for Defence*.[19] Mr Parchment had brought a claim alleging racial discrimination in the Industrial Tribunal (as it was then). That application was withdrawn, however, because it was out of time. Subsequently, he started proceedings in the tort of negligence for compensation for personal injury. Judge Griffiths Williams QC recorded the allegation that Mr Parchment had been caused psychiatric injury 'by systematic verbal, racial abuse by

---

[15] *GAB Robins* (n 6), [34].   [16] ibid, [20].   [17] EAT, 10 March 2010.
[18] See also *Geary v Amec Logistics & Support Services Ltd* (EAT, 1 November 2007) in which Mr Geary succeeded on liability in a claim for constructive dismissal, affirmed by the EAT two weeks before their decision in *GMB v Brown*. The facts again suggested that an apportionment would now be required.
[19] QB, 23 February 1998.

non-commissioned officers in particular but condoned by officers and imitated by fellow recruits and by ... two particular acts of physical violence'.[20] Apart from finding that the claim was time barred, however, the HC held that it had no jurisdiction. This was on the reasoning that all Mr Parchment's allegations fell within the scope of the Race Relations Act (RRA) 1976 and should have been pursued under that Act according to a special procedure for persons serving in the armed services. Rejecting the argument that the existence of substantial personal injury made a difference, the judge found that Parliament had made clear that remedies under the 1976 Act were exclusive.[21] Moreover, following removal of the upper limit on compensation for unlawful race discrimination in 1994:

damages in respect of an unlawful act of discrimination are not restricted to compensation for injuries to feelings and any compensation for past and future losses of earning, but may include compensation for personal injury by reason of psychiatric illness ... I can find no difference between the remedies available to the plaintiff under the Race Relations Act and those which would be available to him if proceedings could be instituted at common law and so it cannot be argued that this plaintiff, or any other claimant, is disadvantaged in any way by the *exclusive* jurisdiction intended by Parliament.[22]

The claim in *Sheriff v Klyne Tugs (Lowestoft) Ltd*[23] foundered in a similar way. Mr Sheriff's common law action for damages for personal injury was struck out on the basis that he could have pursued the further compensation sought in earlier ET proceedings that had been settled. The bases of Stuart-Smith LJ's judgment, with which Sumner LJ agreed, were first, that the compromise agreement covered the present claim because the ET could have awarded damages for personal injury, and second, that Mr Sheriff should not anyway be permitted to reopen the matter. It is important, however, that the CA explicitly left open, noting the difference of opinion with the judge in *Parchment*, the matter of whether allegations that amounted to allegations of racial discrimination could be the subject of a claim for damages based upon the tort of negligence.[24] In other words, the CA seemed to suggest that Mr Sheriff might have been entitled to pursue a tort claim if that had been made first. These analyses moreover sit uneasily with the HL decision and reasoning, discussed below, in *Waters v Commissioner of Police of the Metropolis*[25] decided only a year later and in which their Lordships did not consider these authorities.[26]

Convolutions produced by this set of jurisdictional issues were apparent in subsequent cases. In *Banks v Ablex Ltd*,[27] proceedings were brought in the county court for breach of contract, in tort and under the PHA 1997, but it emerged that Mrs Banks had also made a sex discrimination claim to an ET, apparently on the same facts, which was stayed pending the outcome of her other claim. Consequently, Ablex Ltd challenged the jurisdiction of the county court, arguing that the claims there amounted to claims for sex discrimination and for wrongful termination within the ET's exclusive jurisdiction. This allegation was not ultimately ruled on because Mrs Banks' county court action failed for other reasons and yet was a lurking complication.[28]

---

[20] ibid, [14].   [21] ibid, [13]–[14].   [22] ibid, [14].
[23] [1999] EWCA Civ 1663, [1999] ICR 1170.   [24] ibid, [19].
[25] [2000] UKHL 50, [2000] 1 WLR 1607. See pp 130–31 below.
[26] See also now *Nayif v High Commission of Brunei Darrusalam* [2014] EWCA Civ 1521, [2015] IRLR 134 allowing a claim to proceed in the ordinary courts where an ET claim had failed only because it was out of time and discretion was not exercised to extend this, again with no reference to this line of authority.
[27] [2005] EWCA Civ 173, [2005] ICR 819.
[28] Note that the outcome in the ET was not revealed in the CA judgment.

Smiths Detection Watford Ltd v Berriman[29] concerned claims for unfair dismissal and under the Disability Discrimination Act (DDA) 1995. The EAT observed that Mr Berriman had been absent from work for many months. Since he planned to bring separate county court proceedings, however, he requested the ET not to investigate the possibility of a causal link between his employers' actions or omissions and his disability.[30] This seems likely to have been part of a strategy to avoid jurisdictional problems. Again, however, what happened to the common law claim, and specifically whether the strategy worked, is not apparent.[31] *Pakenham-Walsh v Connell Residential*[32] was another situation in which it seems likely that care was taken to keep allegations in the county court and the ET separate to avoid jurisdictional problems of the *Parchment/Sheriff* type.[33] It was also necessary in *Daniels v Commissioner of Police for the Metropolis*[34] for the court to chop up the allegations in an unsuccessful negligence and PHA 1997 action for compensation for personal injury. This followed from acceptance that *Sheriff* precluded some allegations being pursued because they had been the subject of three compromised ET discrimination claims.[35]

3. Snakes III: Litigation Strategies

The cases considered in this section were not ones in which there was a particular jurisdictional dilemma. Each of them simply begged the questions first, had there been other claims, and second, if not, why proceedings had been limited in the way they were. As such, these were either instances in which claims were brought only in a jurisdiction to which the facts did not seem ideally to suit them or the cause of action in the judgment I read was in addition to others, offering evidence of a different form of convolution associated with overlapping causes of action.

We have seen the considerable potential since *GMB v Brown* and *GAB Robins* for people alleging unfair dismissal to be caught out by failure to make a separate common law claim, but these were not the only situations that raised questions about whether there had been such an action. The CA in *Royal Bank of Scotland v McAdie*[36] said nothing about whether personal injury proceedings were brought in the ordinary courts, yet this was evidently indicated, to the point that the EAT (upheld by the CA) observed that potential recovery for injury suffered by Ms McAdie lay in such a claim.[37] The situation was that Ms McAdie had been dismissed because of ill health which it was accepted was caused by her employer over an extended period. Her condition meant that, ironically, the EAT and CA held, reversing the ET, that it had been reasonable for Royal Bank of Scotland to dismiss her. *Abbey National Plc v Robinson*,[38] *Yellow Pages Limited v Garton*,[39] and *Johnson v Bank of England*[40] all involved claims for constructive unfair dismissal

---

[29] EAT, 9 August 2005.   [30] ibid, 37.
[31] The ET found that Mr Berriman had been unfairly dismissed and this was not appealed. The employer however successfully appealed the ET's findings of unlawful disability discrimination.
[32] [2006] EWCA Civ 90.
[33] ibid, [17]. The CA judgment related that the ET claim for unfair dismissal was settled. The common law claim was unsuccessful, including on appeal, for lack of reasonable foreseeability of injury.
[34] [2006] EWHC 1622 (QB).   [35] ibid, [4].
[36] [2007] EWCA Civ 806, [2008] ICR 1087.   [37] ibid, [37] and [39].
[38] EAT, 20 November 2000.   [39] EAT, 13 March 2003.
[40] EAT, 10 April 2003. This was also an example of a situation in which there was no constructive dismissal, and hence no statutory unfair dismissal, despite the ET's determination that there had been a repudiatory breach in the form of bullying conduct by Mr Johnson's manager. This was because the claimant did not resign until nineteen months after the breach and was held to have done so for other reasons. See ibid, [18]–[20].

and in the latter two actions also under the DDA 1995. Only Ms Robinson's and Mr Garton's claims for constructive unfair dismissal succeeded. Notably, however, all three judgments suggested that the claimants believed that events over the long-running disputes had made them ill. There were background questions, therefore, as to whether separate personal injury claims were brought and if not, why not.[41]

Behavioural disputes pursued as unlawful discrimination also raised jurisdictional questions of this type. Equality law seemed repeatedly to be relied on when it did not map easily onto the matters in dispute and another cause of action, for example in contract, tort, or pursuant to the PHA 1997, might better have fit the facts. Note, however, that separate claims may sometimes have been made without this being apparent from the judgment. Also, factual accounts in judgments might have constructed the impression that another cause of action was more suitable by making what happened sound clearer than it was in reality. Still, Chapter 4 suggested there was a factual theme in the judgments of complexity about the role of identity, backed up by evidence in Chapter 2, and my interview data also supported how complicated and difficult it is for employees to attribute negative conduct at work to their group membership.[42]

Accordingly, while some litigants may have been determined to assert that conduct was unlawful as a type of discrimination, this feature of the judgments seems to support the notion that technical legal factors have directed the tiny proportion who litigate in the direction of equality claims, a view that my interview data also supports.[43] First, until employment tribunal fees were introduced, and certainly for the period from which my sample of cases was taken, costs rules and the specialism of ET judges made ETs the more obvious place to litigate. Second, success in an equality law claim means uncapped damages and more generous rules about recoverability of loss. Third, there are the *Parchment/Sheriff* jurisdictional risks of failing fully to pursue a possible discrimination claim. Finally, patterns of legal specialism and representation, as also intimated by my interview study,[44] may be important, in that how different kinds of lawyers think about litigation options is likely to influence the way that claims are put.[45]

At the level of particular judgments in my sample, *Leavers v The Victoria University of Manchester*[46] was a classic instance of an equality claim seeming not to fit into that category very well. Rather, it looked like a breach of contract claim, or conceivably one in the tort of negligence, would have mapped more easily onto the conflict described by the court.[47] Dr Leavers' claim for direct sex discrimination failed not because she had not been treated badly but because she had been treated no worse than her male colleagues. Notably also, there appeared to have been a great deal at stake, in that the ill treatment occurred when Dr Leavers was in the formative years of her academic career.

We have seen that the cases of *Pearce v Governing Body of Mayfield Secondary School* and *Macdonald v MoD*[48] were legally important for the way they interpreted the SDA 1975. But they also evidenced this tendency. Both situations arose before there was

---

[41] Note also that *Robinson* & *Garton* may well be instances in which, following *GMB v Brown* & *GAB Robins*, apportionment of loss would now be required and, accordingly, in which the case for a separate common law personal injury claim would be even stronger. As such, they are equally examples of cases where a jurisdictional issue did not arise because of when they happened to be decided.

[42] See, respectively, pp 109–110 in Ch 4, pp 19, 22–23 and n 262 in Ch 2, and pp 227–28 in Ch 8.

[43] See pp 187–88 in Ch 8.   [44] See pp 239–40 in Ch 9.

[45] It is also worth noting that recent changes focusing state-funded legal help regarding employment on equality claims may in the current environment be an additional factor pushing some litigants in this direction. See n 115 and surrounding text in Ch 2.

[46] EAT, 21 February 2000.

[47] The facts pre-dated the coming into force of the PHA 1997 in June 1997.

[48] [2003] UKHL 34, [2003] ICR 937.

the possibility of a claim for sexual orientation discrimination.[49] Taking actions under the Sex Discrimination Act (SDA) 1975 is interesting given that the success of other legal options would not have turned on whether the claimant's treatment was comparatively bad. Yet it may be especially likely—for example, given the prominence of these cases—that jurisdictional choice was explained by the claimants, their supporters, and advisers wanting to do all they could to show that what had been done to them, whatever else it was, was sexually discriminatory. Be that as it may, their SDA 1975 claims failed despite it being clear that they had been treated deplorably.[50]

A different kind of claim would also arguably have been more obvious in *Brumfitt v MoD*.[51] It was accepted that '[A] substantial number of offensive and obscene remarks … were directed at both the male and female personnel attending [a one-day course]'.[52] The indiscriminateness of the conduct, however, prevented liability for direct sex discrimination.[53] The same point[54] might be made of elements of the claim in *Madarassy v Nomura International Plc*.[55] In the course of a decision that is doctrinally significant for what was said about the burden of proof, the CA commented on the ET's rejection, upheld on appeal, of the complaint that Ms Madarassy's line manager had conducted a discriminatory campaign against her. In the CA's words: 'The tribunal held that it was satisfied on the evidence that Mr Boardman shouted at members of staff whether they were male or female: "There was equality of shouting regardless of gender or level within ECM." This was the culture of this workplace. It might be horrible, but it was not sexist.'[56]

There were also many cases in which the claimant crossed the hurdle of showing worse treatment than their real or hypothetical comparator, but there was no unlawful discrimination because the behaviour was held not to have been on one of the prohibited grounds. Again, therefore, a cause of action in which liability did not depend

---

[49] Note, however, that I would not analyse the absence for historic reasons of a particular statutory claim as a jurisdictional oddity of the type considered here. The unavailability to some of a statutory claim that is created later is inherent to democratic legislative process, while the situations examined here resulted from the vagaries of when court decisions happened to be taken. I therefore do not categorize *Harris v The Post Office (Royal Mail)* (EAT, 25 February 2000) as problematic in this way, much as the outcome for Mr Harris looks quite unfair when compared to that for others. This is because he was unable to challenge the bulk of what he alleged had been done because it pre-dated both the PHA 1997 and equality law protection regarding sexual orientation. *Leavers* (n 46) and *Wong v Parkside Health NHS Trust* [2001] EWCA CIV 1721, [2003] 3 All ER 932 are further examples in relation to the PHA 1997.

[50] *Pearce* (n 48), in which the HL recounted that Ms Pearce was subjected to homophobic (and I would argue independently sexist) bullying by pupils at the school where she taught, as well as to a complacent reaction by her employers (Lord Rodger's speech, [127]–[133]), and that Mr Macdonald was intrusively and unpleasantly interrogated about his personal life (Lord Hope, [46]) and subsequently dismissed.

[51] [2005] IRLR 4 (EAT).

[52] ibid, 5. Note that Ms Brumfitt was successful in the victimization element of her claim.

[53] There was also no breach of the SDA 1975 in the employer's inadequate response to Ms Brumfitt's complaints because the ET (and EAT) held they had not acted on the grounds of her sex. Moreover, much as a discriminatory harassment claim regarding the behaviour on the course would now likely succeed, that regarding the response may well still not. See the discussion of a similar issue and the relevant case law, including *Brumfitt*, in *Spencer v Primetime Recruitment Ltd* (EAT, 2 March 2006). Claims for breach of contract and unfair dismissal were also made but did not proceed to a hearing.

[54] *Laing v Manchester CC* [2006] ICR 1519 (EAT) involved an unsuccessful claim, confirmed on appeal, for direct race discrimination and victimization. See in this context the EAT's comment: 'The tribunal found in essence that the claimant was a difficult man, not a team player, that he was not handled with the sensitivity he might have been, but that Ms Taylor's insensitivity was directed to all employees, and that the claimant's subsequent dismissal had nothing to do with race.'

[55] [2007] EWCA Civ 33, [2007] ICR 867.   [56] ibid, [93].

on identity influencing poor treatment would appear to have been more apposite. In *Greater Manchester Passenger Transport Executive v Sands*,[57] for example, a claim was brought in respect of the employer's wholly inadequate response to complaints of sexual harassment and bullying. There were some findings of victimization, but the direct sex discrimination element of the claim failed on the basis that the requisite connection to sex was absent.[58]

Riley v Nick Base t/a Gl1 Heating[59] is worthy of comment in this context although Mr Riley won his appeal against dismissal of his sex discrimination claim (having already recovered £275 in the ET for breach of contract). The reason to include the case is that Mr Riley so nearly lost. The EAT said of the facts:

The Respondent is a sole trader—a plumbing and heating engineer. The Appellant, who was born in September 1986, went to work for the Respondent as an apprentice in June 2003 … The Appellant's case is that he was physically abused on a number of occasions … He alleged that the Respondent had something called an 'apprentice correction stick' and used it to beat the Appellant on a number of occasions and also pushed him against the wall, put his hands around his throat and punched and hit him around the head and the body. There were also allegations of verbal abuse of a kind far more common in working environments than the physical abuse which was alleged in this case … The Employment Tribunal, who heard evidence from both parties, were satisfied on the balance of probabilities that the Applicant's account of what happened … was substantially true.[60]

The controversy in the case was again about whether or not the employer's conduct was influenced by Mr Riley being a man. Even though only a prima facie case of direct sex discrimination was needed for the burden to disprove unlawful discrimination to shift to the employer, the ET did not accept that Mr Riley had done so, reasoning as follows:

Our difficulty here is that we find it difficult to see evidence that the respondent … treated the applicant as he did because the applicant was a man, rather than because the respondent had a short temper and flared up quickly when faced with what he thought was poor performance. We strongly suspect that when he said that he would have clipped a woman round the ear in the circumstances in which he has admitted hitting the applicant, he was actually telling the truth. Considerations of sex simply did not apply. It was all down to bad temper and a lack of self-control … It has also been suggested that the term 'fucking wanker' is discriminatory, in that it is gender-specific abuse. In the industrial experience of the lay members, however, that term of abuse has been applied to both men and women, and we did not therefore accept that argument.[61]

The EAT, however, analysed the evidence differently and reversed the ET on this point, remitting the case for assessment of Mr Riley's damages for both the personal injury to him and the injury to his feelings. In these circumstances, however, it looks like a PHA 1997 claim would have been indicated. Apart from anything else, failure under the SDA 1975 would most likely have ousted any other action on *Sheriff* grounds.[62]

---

[57] EAT, 11 January 2001.
[58] In this case, incidentally, it is not clear why the underlying negative acts were not included in this claim, but it is possible that these were challenged by other means without this being recorded in the judgment of the SDA 1975 claim.
[59] EAT, 19 July 2005.   [60] ibid, [2].   [61] ibid, [5].
[62] *Swift v CC of Wiltshire Constabulary* [2004] ICR 909 (EAT) pointed to a further variant of this syndrome. The underlying complaints were of bullying and harassment by two colleagues and, in turn, that Ms Swift's employers failed appropriately to respond to her request not to be rostered to work with these individuals. Yet a DDA 1995 claim was presented that foundered, including on appeal to the EAT, on a highly technical issue regarding whether Ms Swift continued at the relevant time to be disabled within the meaning of the Act.

Some of the technical difficulties in these cases would not now arise because of the modern definitions of unlawful discriminatory harassment, surveyed in Chapter 3, which take a non-comparative approach to liability and provide for a loose connection to a protected group identity. It remains the case, however, that situations in which there really was no provable link between harassing behaviour and a protected group identity—perhaps because the harasser was uniformly unpleasant without adverting in any way to identity—would still not constitute unlawful discriminatory harassment.

I also found a new oddity in the later years of claims being pursued as direct discrimination when discriminatory harassment appeared more appropriate. An example of a successful claim to which this observation applies is *Islamic Cultural Centre v Mahmoud*.[63] There were claims of direct race and sex discrimination, the latter successful in the ET and upheld by the EAT (whereas an ET finding of direct race discrimination was overturned). In fact the employer here tried, albeit unsuccessfully, to defeat the direct sex discrimination claim on the basis that Ms Mahmoud's comparator would have been treated in the same way.[64] *Cartamundi UK Ltd v Worboyes*[65] is another instance.

Then, in *Johnson v The Governing Body of Coopers Lane Primary School*,[66] Ansell J in the EAT related a troubled and contested history, some of which was argued by the claimant to have involved direct race discrimination. Although aspects of what was done were accepted to have been unreasonable, Ms Johnson's claim foundered because she was unable to establish the requisite link to race. Inclusion of a claim for discriminatory harassment might have made no ultimate difference, but its omission is notable given how Ms Johnson put her objections to her treatment and how hard the case was fought.[67]

4. Ladders I: Common Law

Sometimes, however, all of these potential problems were either avoided or overcome. This was evident in various common law claims, particularly those for personal injury damages. There could be an upward spiral for the claimant and a downward one for the respondent simply because their case fell on a particular side of a jurisdictional line. A variation on this theme occurred when a case happened to be heard before a jurisdictional problem emerged. On other occasions a claimant, perhaps skilfully advised, managed by their choice of jurisdiction to avoid a difficulty that would otherwise have arisen. Finally, there were cases in which, without explanation, courts simply ignored jurisdictional issues.

Moore v Welwyn Components Ltd[68] is a clear example of a factual situation that contained no jurisdictional glitches. In particular, there was no dismissal and so no *Johnson/Eastwood* issue, since Mr Moore had been forced by depressive illness to take early retirement. The illness was found to have been caused by nearly three years of bullying by his superior. This conduct was described by the court as 'appalling' and of a kind that 'would have exposed any employee of reasonable fortitude to the risk of psychiatric illness'.[69] On this basis, the employers were found liable in negligence for Mr Moore's ill health and its effects, damages being assessed at £164,530.[70] The employer was unsuccessful in its attempt to establish on appeal that the award should be reduced because the claimant

---

[63] EAT, 27 June 2007.   [64] ibid, [27] and [37].   [65] EAT, 4 December 2009.
[66] EAT, 1 December 2009.   [67] ibid, [32]–[34].
[68] [2005] EWCA Civ 6, [2005] ICR 782 (one of several conjoined appeals, known as *Hartman v South Essex Mental Health & Community Care NHS Trust*).
[69] ibid, [115].   [70] ibid, 787.

would have suffered either a similar or at least some psychiatric illness irrespective of the negligent conduct. *Clark v CC of Essex*[71] and *Daw v Intel Corp (UK) Ltd*[72] were further cases of this kind pursued uniquely in tort, the latter combining allegations of overwork with some of inappropriate behaviour. Mr Clark was medically retired[73] and Ms Daw was on long-term sickness absence while seemingly remaining in Intel's employment.[74] The full amount of the compensation award is not clear from the judgment in *Clark* and was £134,545 in *Daw*.[75]

In *Green v DB Group Services*[76] the claimant was dismissed, but this was explicitly because of illness which had left her unable to work for some time.[77] As such, the dismissal caused no loss independent to that already resulting from her employers' unlawful conduct prior to dismissal. This meant that no *Eastwood* apportionment was required. Ms Green was notably successful in her tort claim and, in an early case of this type, under the PHA 1997, recovering just over £850,000.

Long v Mercury Communications,[78] mentioned in Chapter 1, is an example of a case that avoided jurisdictional difficulties because of when it happened to be decided. This was a few months after the HL decision in *Johnson* and before the first instance strike-outs in *Eastwood* and *McCabe*.[79] The employer admitted common law liability for having injured Mr Long but only on the second day of the hearing. The judge commented on the effect of this delay that, 'for a man who had his self esteem and self confidence shattered this no doubt was a continuing blow'.[80]

A technical consequence of the defendant's admission is that it is not apparent if the employer ever tried to argue that their duty not negligently to injure Mr Long fell away at some point before dismissal because of *Johnson*. In any event this was a case of ill treatment continuing over some considerable time meaning there was likely to have been liability anyway. The usual tortious assessment of damages resulted in an award of £327,710, reflecting what the judge found to be the compensatable injury, losses, and expenses, whether caused by dismissal or anything else. Following the HL decision in *Eastwood*, however, the judge would have had to apportion the losses and expenses flowing from antecedent breaches and from the dismissal, the latter of which would have been recoverable only in an unfair dismissal claim. Therefore, Mr Long would not only have lost some of his award but he would have had to take a second set of proceedings in a separate court to obtain his full entitlement.

The artificiality and obscurity of such an apportionment exercise is particularly well exhibited by this case. For example, the judge related the following about the final stages of Mr Long's employment:

Eventually in May 1994 he was summoned into the Sales Manager's office and told that, in fact, that appointment would not go ahead. This he said resulted in him suffering both a physical and a mental breakdown and he was left with a feeling of complete exhaustion. He felt that he had been completely humiliated by the way in which he had been treated and then some days later he was told to attend a selection assessment for supervisors. He was at that stage, or had previously been, several rungs more senior to supervisors but he still had to attend. Having undergone the assessment he failed it and consequently he was then made redundant.[81]

---

[71] [2006] EWHC 2290 (QB).   [72] [2007] EWCA Civ 70, [2007] ICR 1318.
[73] *Clark* (n 71), [249].   [74] *Daw* (n 72), [50].   [75] ibid, [1].
[76] [2006] EWHC 1898 (QB), [2006] IRLR 764.   [77] ibid, [45].
[78] [2002] PIQR Q1 (QB).
[79] *Long* was decided by HH Judge Anthony Thompson QC in the QB Division on 4 May 2001, while the first instance decision in *Eastwood* was by Judge Elystan Morgan at Llangefni County Court on 19 June 2001 and that in *McCabe* by Judge Overend in the Queen's Bench Division on 6 June 2002.
[80] [2002] PIQR Q1, [35].   [81] ibid, Q5, [19].

Given the interconnections between the whole series of events and the harm to Mr Long, distinguishing elements in the way *Eastwood* now requires would surely have resulted in absurdity and injustice.

Unwin v West Sussex CC[82] is also relevant despite being difficult to categorize. There were separate ET proceedings under the SDA 1975 that were stayed pending the outcome of a common law claim in the HC for damages for personal injury, perhaps to protect the claimant's position if a jurisdictional point was successfully taken that all or part of the action should have been pursued as unlawful discrimination.[83] There was, however, no allegation that the claimant's eventual resignation from work was a constructive dismissal, perhaps to make sure *Johnson* was irrelevant. As such, the case was dealt with as a somewhat straightforward—at least in legal terms—tort claim. While the claimant was largely unsuccessful, the case was determined according to clear and accessible liability and remedial rules, the legal waters unmuddied by jurisdictional puzzles. What I cannot tell from the judgment, however, was whether this was because the facts naturally fell on one side of the *Johnson* jurisdictional line, or if, rather, the claimant mindfully constructed her claim in a particular way to secure that legal approach. In any event, the stayed ET proceedings meant jurisdictional complications were in the background.

In *Waters v Commissioner of Police of the Metropolis*[84] some technical problems on the facts were simply ignored. The decision was on assumed facts since it dealt only with the question of whether or not Ms Waters' common law claim could proceed. Her allegations concerned the reaction of colleagues and the Commissioner to a complaint of rape by a fellow officer. The causes of action asserted were that 'in breach of contract and of statutory duty and negligently [the Commissioner of Police for the Metropolis] failed to deal properly with her complaint but "caused and/or permitted officers to maliciously criticize, harass, victimize, threaten, and assault and otherwise oppress her".'[85] She contended in the alternative that the defendant was vicariously liable for the acts of officers under his command. The HL overturned the decisions of all the courts below that the claim should be struck out. Lord Slynn reasoned as follows:

If an employer knows that acts being done by employees during their employment may cause physical or mental harm to a particular fellow employee and he does nothing to supervise or prevent such acts, when it is in his power to do so, it is clearly arguable that he may be in breach of his duty to that employee. It seems to me that he may also be in breach of that duty if he can foresee that such acts may happen and, if they do, that physical or mental harm may be caused to an individual.[86]

Lord Jauncey of Tullichettle, Lord Clyde, Lord Hutton, and Lord Millett all concurred in Lord Slynn's speech, Lord Jauncey and Lord Hutton also giving separate opinions.

It was of general significance that the HL here acknowledged that there was a cause of action. What is curious, however, is their Lordships' failure even to comment on the *Parchment/Sheriff*-type issues that arose on the assumed facts. Lord Slynn related that '[a]t the heart of [Ms Waters] claim lies the belief that the other officers reviled her and

[82] QB, 13 July 2001.
[83] ibid, [30]. There had also been earlier unsuccessful EPA 1970 and SDA 1975 tribunal proceedings relating to an earlier time period.
[84] *Waters* (n 25).   [85] ibid, 1609.
[86] ibid, 1611. Applying these ideas to this situation, he went on to say: 'I would accept … that, if this sort of sexual assault is alleged (whether it happened or not) and the officer persists in making complaints about it, it is arguable that it can be foreseen that some retaliatory steps may be taken against the woman and that she may suffer harm as a result. Even if this is not necessarily foreseeable at the beginning it may become foreseeable or indeed obvious to those in charge at various levels who are carrying out the commissioner's responsibilities that there is a risk of harm and that some protective steps should be taken.'

failed to take care of her because she had broken the team rules by complaining of sexual acts by a fellow police officer'.[87] Equally, he specifically acknowledged that Ms Waters had unsuccessfully brought proceedings for unlawful sex discrimination, including victimization, before the (then) IT. That outcome had been confirmed on appeal to the EAT and the CA and not appealed to the HL, yet nothing was said about the possible impact either of those proceedings, or of overlap in discrimination and common law causes of action, on whether a common law claim could proceed.[88]

Horkulak v Cantor FitzGerald International[89] is another case in point. By the time it was heard in the HC, the CA had given its judgment in *Eastwood* and *McCabe* such that *Johnson's* potential effect on common law claims involving dismissal had become clear.[90] Like *Waters*, however, the evident jurisdictional issue on the facts attracted no comment. Perhaps the fact that Mr Horkulak was a high-earning employee with a fixed-term contract and a potentially large bonus claim somehow obscured the rather obvious issues as to, first, *Johnson's* possible impact on liability, and second, whether losses that flowed from Mr Horkulak's dismissal by acceptance of a repudiatory breach were compensatable at common law. That the court ignored these points cannot, however, be justified as a matter of internal legal reasoning, let alone horizontal equity.

5. Ladders II: Statute

Here again claimants sometimes found themselves on a ladder (and their respondents on a snake) simply because, through luck or judgement, they fell on the right side of a jurisdictional line. Some such instances were counterparts of common law situations in which there was a favourable result for the claimant because of when a claim happened to be heard. Also, where claimants won discrimination claims and recovered substantial damages for personal injury, they had by definition skilfully negotiated a jurisdictional minefield, both taking advantage of the more generous remedial rules in discrimination claims and avoiding the kind of problems encountered in *Parchment* and *Sheriff*. Here though, I did not find cases in which jurisdictional problems on the facts were simply ignored. There were, however, striking examples of it taking time for use to be made of new statutory options, with the PHA 1997 the most important example.

Blackburn with Darwen Borough Council v Stanley[91] is a case that avoided the *GMB v Brown/GAB Robins* jurisdictional problem because it happened to be decided before the judges had extrapolated the consequences of *Johnson* and *Eastwood* for unfair dismissal claims. Ms Stanley's successful claim, confirmed on appeal, was that she had been unfairly constructively dismissed in circumstances where her employer had failed over several years adequately to respond to complaints of bullying and harassment. There were indications of various psychiatric consequences and compensation was awarded of £23,032. While this would not have included anything in respect of Ms Stanley's non-pecuniary losses, there was no need to subtract anything for harm caused before the dismissal. As such, the case is another example of the arbitrariness from the point of

---

[87] ibid, 1610.

[88] While *Sheriff* was cited in argument to the HL it was not mentioned in its judgment.

[89] [2003] EWHC 1918, from which there was a partially successful appeal on quantum, [2004] EWCA Civ 1287, [2004] ICR 697.

[90] The judgment in *Horkulak* was given by Newman J on 3 July 2003 and that of the CA (on quantum only) on 14 October 2004. The CA decision in *Eastwood* was on 22 March 2002 and in *McCabe* was on 19 December 2002.

[91] EAT, 20 January 2005.

view of litigants. In 2005 Ms Stanley was able to recover most of her losses in an unfair dismissal case; by 2007 this had become impossible.[92]

Essa v Laing Ltd[93] involved a claimant injured by unlawful race discrimination making optimal use of the discrimination statutes. We have seen the importance of the case remedially. For present purposes what is notable is that Mr Essa established his entitlement to a meaningful assessment of the effects of various harms resulting from an appalling racial insult. *M and L Sheet Metals Ltd v Willis*[94] was to like effect, in that Mr Willis obtained total damages of £68,714.84, including to compensate for personal injury he suffered consequent on sexual orientation harassment and 'plain' bullying.[95]

In terms of innovative uses of new legislative options, *Green* successfully relied on the PHA 1997 although it did not make a difference to her claim because she would anyway have won at common law.[96] That makes *Veakins v Kier Islington Ltd*[97] a better example of a case in which bringing proceedings under the PHA 1997 cut through the thicket of jurisdictional complexity. While the judgment addressed contentious issues about the meaning of the PHA 1997 and the behavioural standards it set, to which I return below, it was not weighed down by jurisdictional concerns. Indeed, it did not even make clear whether Ms Veakins departure from work was alleged to be a constructive dismissal.

Rayment v MoD[98] also demonstrated the potential of a PHA 1997 claim.[99] This was another long-running conflict in which the employers' conduct was alleged wrongfully to have damaged the employee's health. A negligence claim went nowhere, but Ms Rayment successfully established that dismissal, amongst other things, was harassment in breach of the 1997 Act. This entitled her to compensation for consequent losses and expenses according to the more generous PHA 1997 remedial rules. In the event the award was only £6,560 plus interest, owing to the finding that Ms Rayment's employment would have ended anyway for other reasons. The case, however, showed how a PHA 1997 claim might enable employees to obtain full compensation and even for dismissal.

6. Conclusion

Tables 5.1 and 5.2 depict some of the incongruities in the judgments. They leave aside, however, situations first, in which elaborate steps had apparently been taken to avoid jurisdictional problems, and, second, where mistakes might have been made in the framing of the claim.

It is also worth demonstrating the oddities by focusing on some parallel factual situations. One striking pair of cases is *Horkulak v Cantor FitzGerald International*[100] and *Villalba v Merrill Lynch and Co Inc.*[101] The HC judgment for Mr Horkulak on

---

[92] See also *Abbey National* (n 38) and *Yellow Pages* (n 39).
[93] [2004] EWCA Civ 2, [2004] ICR 746.   [94] EAT, 12 March 2010.
[95] ibid, [11]. Although Mr Willis also succeeded in a claim for constructive unfair dismissal, the EAT pointed out, ibid at [16], that there was no need for a *GMB v Brown/GAB Robins* apportionment (and hence a separate common law claim) because the personal injury and consequent loss of earning had been found by the ET to have been caused purely by the unlawful sexual-orientation harassment.
[96] *Green* (n 76), [172].   [97] [2009] EWCA Civ 1288, [2010] IRLR 132.
[98] [2010] EWHC 218 (QB), [2010] IRLR 768.
[99] Note also the unsuccessful attempt in *Crossland v Wilkinson Hardware Stores Ltd* [2005] EWHC 481 (QB), [72]–[74], discussed further below, to pursue allegations under the PHA 1997 which could not be argued as breaches of contract because of a valid compromise agreement (in respect of which separate ET proceedings had accordingly been struck out).
[100] *Horkulak* (n 89).   [101] [2007] ICR 469 (EAT).

Table 5.1 Overlapping causes of action causing arbitrariness in adjudication: liability

Determination of Liability in Comparable Behavioural Conflicts at Work		
	Workplace Behaviour either Adjudicated or Jurisdiction denied according to Convoluted, Abstract Legal Rules	Workplace Behaviour either Adjudicated or Jurisdiction accepted according to clear, accessible Legal Rules
1995–99	*Parchment v The Secretary of State for Defence* February 1998 (discrimination jurisdiction denied) *Sheriff v Klyne Tugs (Lowestoft) Ltd* June 1999 (discrimination jurisdiction denied; earlier ET claim settled)	
2000–04	*Leavers v The Victoria University of Manchester* February 2000 (unsuccessful discrimination claim) *Pearce v Governing Body of Mayfield Secondary School; Macdonald v MoD* June 2003 (ditto) *Brumfitt v MoD* July 2004 (partially successful discrimination claim)	*Waters v Commissioner of Police of the Metropolis* July 2000 (common law tort jurisdiction accepted) *Horkulak v Cantor FitzGerald International* July 2003 (successful common law contract claim)
2005–09	*Villalba v Merrill Lynch and Co Inc* March 2006 (partially successful discrimination claim) *Daniels v Commissioner of Police for the Metropolis*, July 2006 (unsuccessful common law and PHA 1997 claim in which jurisdiction partially denied)	*Moore v Welwyn Components Ltd* January 2005 (successful common law tort claim) *Green v DB Group Services* August 2006 (successful common law tort and PHA 1997 claim) *Clark v CC of Essex* September 2006 (successful common law tort claim) *Daw v Intel Corp (UK) Ltd* February 2007 (ditto) *Veakins v Kier Islington Ltd* December 2009 (successful PHA 1997 claim)
2010	*South London Healthcare NHS Trust v Rubeyi* March 2010 (partially successful discrimination claim)	*Rayment v MoD* February 2010 (ditto) *M and L Sheet Metals Ltd v Willis* March 2010 (successful discriminatory harassment claim)

liability for breach of contract was given in July 2003. In *Villalba* the EAT gave judgment in March 2006 rejecting the claimant's appeal against the denial of several SDA 1975 claims. Both claimants had been high-flying employees in the finance industry and alleged they had been treated badly over a period of time, culminating in the loss of prestigious and highly paid jobs. The factual histories presented different versions of complexity, as explained in Chapter 4.[102] In *Horkulak*, moreover, a potential jurisdictional problem was ignored.

What stands out in considering the cases together is how far the manner in which they were presented resulted in distinct adjudication of comparable underlying problems. Of

---

[102] See pp 107–108 in Ch 4.

Table 5.2 Overlapping causes of action leading to arbitrariness in adjudication: remedies

Determination of Remedy in Comparable Behavioural Conflicts at Work		
	Compensatable Losses etc were Only (Potentially) Recoverable by Multiple Claims	Compensatable Losses etc were Recovered in One Action and Sometimes According to Generous Rules about Causation and Compensatable Losses (in Discrimination and PHA 1997 cases)
1995–99		
2000–04	*Eastwood v Magnox Electric plc* July 2004 (common law contract and tort claim; pre- and post-dismissal compensation issue)	*Long v Mercury Communications* May 2001 (tort compensation but only full because pre-dated *Johnson* & *Eastwood*)
		Horkulak v Cantor FitzGerald International July 2003 (contract compensation but obvious *Johnson* points ignored)
		Essa v Laing Ltd January 2004 (discrimination compensation)
2005–09	*GMB Trade Union v Brown* October 2007 (unfair dismissal claim; pre- and post-dismissal compensation issue)	*Blackburn with Darwen Borough Council v Stanley* January 2005 (unfair dismissal compensation, but only full because pre-dated *GMB v Brown*)
	GAB Robins (UK) Ltd v Triggs January 2008 (unfair dismissal and common law claims; pre- and post-dismissal compensation issue)	*Moore v Welwyn Components Ltd* January 2005 (tort compensation)
		Green v DB Group Services August 2006 (tort and PHA 1997 compensation)
		Clark v CC of Essex September 2006 (tort compensation)
		Daw v Intel Corp (UK) Ltd February 2007 (ditto)
		Veakins v Kier Islington Ltd December 2009 (PHA 1997 compensation)
2010	*Cleveland Police Authority v Francis* March 2010 (unfair dismissal claim; pre- and post-dismissal compensation issue)	*Rayment v MoD* February 2010 (PHA 1997 compensation)
		M and L Sheet Metals Ltd v Willis March 2010 (discrimination compensation)

course, this may have been the result of deliberate choice and other actions may have been instituted without that being apparent from the judgments I read. Equally, it cannot be known if the result would have been different if the claims had been pursued in other ways. Even so, the contrasts beg questions about the overall justice done by this body of law and whether anything is gained from the horizontal distinctions it results in.

In the event, Mr Horkulak succeeded in his common law contract claim on the basis that his colleagues' treatment of him breached his employer's implied contractual duty of trust and confidence so fundamentally as to amount to constructive dismissal. This was found, conceivably erroneously in light of *Johnson*, to entitle him to very substantial damages for the losses and expenses caused by the unlawful premature termination of his fixed-term contract. Ms Villalba, on the other hand, succeeded in her unfair dismissal action but only in some of her SDA 1975 claims. While some ill treatment was held to have been unlawful victimization, no direct sex discrimination was found because the courts determined other negative acts had not been on the ground of her sex. The EAT judgment did not record the compensation Ms Villalba received, but this should have reflected the relatively generous compensation rules in discrimination cases. Still, it seems unlikely that overall she recovered an award approaching that which Mr Horkulak received, given how hard the litigation was contested and that only part of it was successful.

Another interesting pairing of cases is *Daw v Intel Corp (UK) Ltd*[103] and *GAB Robins (UK) Ltd v Triggs*.[104] The CA gave its decision for Ms Daw in February 2007 when it rejected the employer's appeal against the HC finding of negligence. The CA decision that Ms Triggs' unfair dismissal compensation must be reduced was given in January 2008. As we have seen, this was on the basis that the *Johnson/Eastwood* line of cases prevented the recovery in an unfair dismissal action of losses etc caused by pre-dismissal breaches of contract.

Ms Daw was a long-serving employee of Intel, having risen from being a finance assistant when she joined the firm in 1988 to becoming a mergers and acquisitions payroll integration analyst in May 2000.[105] Goldring J found that she was 'an able, committed and very conscientious employee'.[106] Ms Triggs' employers were chartered loss adjusters carrying on their business nationwide. She worked for them as a secretary/personal assistant and was described by the ET judge as 'a conscientious and loyal employee'.[107] Both complained about a mixture of overwork and of poor interpersonal conduct.

Again, it is conspicuous that how Ms Daw and Ms Triggs pursued their somewhat analogous complaints led to very different litigation experiences. Again, it cannot be known if the outcomes would have differed if they had changed the way they put their cases. The contrasts, however, still raise issues about how justly this body of law is working and what goals its distinctions ultimately serve.

Ms Daw was able in one action to recover £134,545 on familiar tortious liability and compensation rules. Ms Triggs' unfair dismissal award was truncated and she was pushed into a second action. To add to the irony, liability in that second action would have depended on the same rules as her unfair dismissal claim while it was potentially more lucrative because of the recoverability at common law of non-pecuniary losses.

All four of these cases can in turn profitably be compared to those pursued under the PHA 1997, for example *Green v DB Group Services*,[108] *Rayment v MoD*,[109] and *Veakins v Kier Islington Ltd*.[110] The point here is that the PHA 1997, at least for now, provides the most straightforward route for scrutinizing the acceptability of workplace conduct in combination with the most generous compensation rules.[111] In this way it has only added to the inscrutability of the rules considered as a whole.

Nonetheless, it is perfectly possible that doctrinal technicality arising from the multiple relevant causes of action in this area will increase. This possibility is especially apparent in relation to the connections between the PHA 1997 and other laws. Oddities at this interface were certainly noticed by some of their Lordships in *Majrowski v Guy's and St Thomas's NHS Trust*,[112] although they saw the legislative wording, and particularly distinctions between Scotland and England and Wales, as forcing the conclusion that employers are vicariously liable. Lord Nicholls in particular commented on the problematic relationship between the modern wrongs of discriminatory harassment and those under the PHA 1997, observing that the harassment changes to the discrimination legislation had created 'a discordant and unsatisfactory overlap with the 1997 Act.'[113]

[103] *Daw* (n 72).   [104] *GAB Robins* (n 6).   [105] *Daw* (n 72). [2].
[106] ibid, [5].   [107] *GAB Robins* (n 6), [5].   [108] *Green* (n 76).
[109] *Rayment* (n 98).   [110] *Veakins* (n 97).   [111] See pp 89–92 in Ch 3.
[112] [2006] UKHL 34, [2007] 1 AC 224.   [113] ibid. [38]–[39].

Baroness Hale also doubted the wisdom of extending the reach of the PHA 1997, given employers' existing obligations. She put her concerns as follows, incidentally making questionable assumptions about how working people use law:

The promoters [of the PHA 1997] might have thought that employers already owe a duty of care towards their employees, to take reasonable steps to protect them from foreseeable harm to their physical or mental health … Liability turns on the foreseeability of such injury to the particular employee and what the employer might reasonably have been expected to do to avoid it. If employers can be vicariously liable for anxiety and distress caused without any breach of duty on their part, such claims will not only be routinely added to stress at work claims, they will also found a quite separate stream of, admittedly probably small, claims for harassment at work. The promoters might have thought that there were better ways than a myriad of new small claims to encourage better practice in the workplace if such were needed.[114]

Baroness Hale also questioned damages for injury to feelings being available under the PHA 1997, citing arguments for the more limited common law rule that compensation is only available for recognized psychiatric illness.[115]

There had in fact already been an attempt in *Crossland v Wilkinson Hardware Stores Ltd*[116] to pursue allegations under the PHA 1997 which a valid compromise agreement prevented being litigated in contract, the claimant having turned to the HC after ET proceedings were struck out. His strategy was unsuccessful as the respondent obtained summary judgment. Tugendhat J however thought proceedings under the PHA 1997 were in principle open, observing:

There is nothing unusual in English law in having a variety of different causes of action available to a claimant to rely on cumulatively or alternatively. Claims in contract and tort are a common example. So in principle a claim in harassment is available at the suit of a person against a former employer.

In *Veakins v Kier Islington Ltd*,[117] further, the CA noted certain common law developments that they thought might be 'causing more employees to seek redress by reference to harassment and the statutory tort'. Somewhat optimistically perhaps, they indicated that such cases would normally be better pursued in the ET:

It should not be thought from this unusually one-sided case that stress at work will often give rise to liability for harassment. I have found the conduct in this case to be 'oppressive and unacceptable' but I have done so in circumstances where I have also described it as 'extraordinary'. I do not expect that many workplace cases will give rise to this liability. It is far more likely that, in the great majority of cases, the remedy for high-handed or discriminatory misconduct by or on behalf of an employer will be more fittingly in the employment tribunal.[118]

This observation did not reflect the factual themes in the cases surveyed, nor specifically the impression that the facts in *Veakins* were somewhat typical of the milder end of behavioural conflicts at work.[119] This perception was also supported by Rubenstein commenting that 'the conduct does not really appear "extraordinary" at all. On the contrary, it appears to be an all-too-typical case of unpleasant workplace bullying.'[120]

---

[114] ibid, [70].
[115] ibid, [69]. See also and more generally [64]–[72] for Baroness Hale's analysis of the range of considerations that might have persuaded the legislators not to provide for vicarious liability for breaches of the PHA 1997, as well as the speeches of Lord Hope of Craighead (at [44]) and Lord Brown of Eaton-under-Heywood (at [81]–[82]).
[116] *Crossland* (n 99).   [117] *Veakins* (n 97).
[118] ibid, [17], in the judgment of Maurice Kay LJ, with which Rimer and Waller LJJ agreed.
[119] See p 7 in Ch 1.   [120] [2010] IRLR 93.

I take from these case law debates that there are lurking jurisdictional dilemmas for the courts, somewhat akin to those about the relationship between the statutory claim for unfair dismissal and various common law causes of action. This time they concern the proper relationship between the PHA 1997 and overlapping statutory discrimination and common law wrongs. Viewed in this light, the worries expressed in their Lordships speeches in *Majrowski* perhaps hint at developments to come.

It is also perfectly possible that other jurisdictional puzzles will arise as further litigation possibilities are explored. In *Cumbria CC v Carlisle-Morgan*,[121] for example, a claim about conduct at work was successfully pursued under the Public Interest Disclosure Act (PIDA) 1998, together with a separate action for constructive unfair dismissal. The claim does not seem to have been taken in this form to avoid jurisdictional trouble, but it points to the scope for imaginative claimants to think up new litigation strategies and, in turn, for courts to have more interactions between jurisdictions of which they will be required to make sense.

It is hard, however, to see any point to the various distinctions that have been made. For example, where similar behaviour is wrongful as unfair dismissal, as breaches of the common law and as unlawful harassment under the PHA 1997, it is unclear what normative implications employers and employees could logically extrapolate from the various limits that now attach to common law and unfair dismissal claims. In any event there is an inherent futility to these contrasts because the law anyway steers its subjects to guard against all these kinds of liability.

If, however, these distinctions are substantively pointless, the different litigation experiences and outcomes surveyed in this chapter are wholly unjustifiable. There is also the question whether all the jurisdictional technicalities which takes the general complexity in this area of law to yet greater heights, actually obstructs the infiltration of legal standards into working life. My interview study makes challenging findings in this regard, suggesting a lack of organizational awareness of the splits between different causes of action and of concern amongst practitioners, amidst generally patchiness of legal influence.[122] If anything, this reinforces the urgency of an external analysis of all this anxious drawing of legal distinctions, the curious individual outcomes to which it can lead and about how legal efforts in this area could more fruitfully be directed.

[121] [2007] IRLR 314 (EAT).
[122] See pp 183, 197–204 and 209–13 in Ch 8 and pp 217 and 239–40 Ch 9.

6

Legal Themes in Case Law about Behavioural Conflict at Work II

Consistency in Applying Behaviour Rules

The very different theme illustrated here and in Chapter 7 is of a remarkably consistent approach by courts to working out the implications of substantive behavioural rules in specific situations, assuming of course that jurisdictional problems enabled them to get to that point. This starkly contrasted with the adjudicative variety reported in Chapter 5 and undercut the legal convolution that orthodox doctrinal exposition in Chapter 3 conveyed. Rather, I observed judges in this aspect of the judgments to take a congruent approach across courts, causes of action, and time periods. Irrespective of the legal rule being applied, they treated their essential task as being to locate two sets of boundary lines and employed similar methods for doing so. The first line drawn was between conduct at work which law required working people to accept and that which it deemed 'beyond the pale'. The second line was between acceptable and unacceptable employer responses either to complaints about or actual occurrences of bad workplace behaviour.

Again and again, I saw the same basic questions being asked and answered. Had either workplace behaviour, or employers' responses, fallen within the bounds of acceptability? Had what was done been sufficiently 'OK' to avoid legal sanction? The courts' consistency in their approach was further instantiated by recurrent decision-making tropes. As regards workplace conduct itself:

(1) There was profound immersion in the precise situation. Great attention was given to untangling the exact meaning of what had happened in the milieu in which it occurred.

(2) The significance of events having happened in a sequence was emphasized.

(3) There was a recurrent seam in which the seriousness of what had been done, whether on one occasion or over time, was readily acknowledged.

In terms of employers' responses, either to bad behaviour or to allegations against colleagues:

(1) There was the same thorough contextualization to determine the meaning of what had happened and, hence, on which side of the legal line an employer's conduct fell.

(2) Judges' musings frequently led them explicitly or implicitly to guide employers about the law's requirements. In this mode judges seemed to balance a wide range of interests to decide on the precise standards that governed a situation. The interests considered included those of claimants, of the rest of the workforce, of management, and of society more broadly.

Locating these two sets of boundaries was critical to liability decisions for all the causes of action. The impossibility of constructing counterfactuals to 'real-life' cases means I cannot say that the specific rules never made a difference to the analysis and outcome, just as I could not tell in Chapter 5 if cases would have turned out differently if they had been pleaded another way. The point is that beyond the jurisdictional puzzles and inconsistencies, judicial decision-making employed a consistent approach to adjudicating substantive behavioural issues. What is more, case law debates about the acceptability of conduct at work, and of employer responses to disputes about this, were conducted in highly accessible, non-technical language. One could imagine the same discussions taking place in many different contexts and amongst many different kinds of people.

In contract and constructive unfair dismissal cases, this judicial line-drawing was primarily directed to deciding whether conduct had been unlawful for breaching employers' and employees' implied mutual duties of trust and confidence. In tort claims, including when pursued via the implied contractual negligence term, it typically enabled judges to rule on whether conduct by colleagues and employers had taken reasonable care to avoid foreseeable harm to co-workers and to employees. Under the Protection from Harassment Act (PHA) 1997 it was used to decide whether or not conduct fell within the concept of harassment prohibited under the Act.

The same approach was present in claims of direct discrimination and victimization but tied more indirectly to doctrine, since the unacceptability in itself of conduct was only tangentially in issue, as illustrated in Chapter 5.[1] Even so, courts used the same methodology to illuminate first, whether or not someone was in fact being less favourably treated than their comparator, and second, whether this was either on grounds of a protected identity or by reason of the claimant having done a 'protected act'. Evaluations of conduct accordingly helped courts to work out if a claimant was being singled out and what lay behind behaviour. Equally, it could be a relatively easy step from conduct being condemned to finding that it was in some sense related to a protected identity or act.

Under the modern discriminatory harassment provisions there is a paramount need for courts to distinguish conduct that law requires employees to put up with and that which it proscribes. This goes especially to deciding whether first, either the purpose or effect of conduct was to violate the dignity of another person or to create an intimidating, hostile, degrading, humiliating, or offensive environment for them. Second, it enables determination of whether it was reasonable in all the circumstances, including the victim's perception, to view conduct in this way. In addition, as in direct discrimination and victimization cases, working out whether or not negative behaviour was sufficiently related to a protected characteristic sometimes required nuanced evaluation of whether, and how far, a behavioural line had been crossed. Finally, it is noteworthy that there was analogous line-drawing at the remedial stage in discrimination actions generally, but there it was to determine where conduct fell on the scale of wrongfulness, especially in order to settle the appropriate amount of damages.

I document this consistency of decision-making in relation to behavioural standards themselves in what follows, both in terms of general boundary setting and in the use of more specific reasoning methodologies, while Chapter 7 focuses on the data about employer responses. I have divided the analysis in this way to help the reader. The two aspects were, however, at times so closely intertwined that it is difficult to separate them. This was especially so for decision-making about the PHA 1997, such that the consistency theme in those judgments is only reported in this chapter. This made sense given that the primary judicial focus was on identifying unacceptable behaviour. I point out,

---

[1] See pp 125–28 and 132 in Ch 5.

however, where explicit guidance was given to employers and where there was implicit guidance from specific determinations of unlawfulness. It is also important to note that counterexamples to the repeated features of decision-making I found were virtually non-existent and the odd trace of a different approach is noted in what follows.

Finally, there is an important preliminary point on the exposition in this chapter. It deliberately goes through relevant data in some descriptive detail, albeit not recording all instances that supported my overall findings. To some extent this is to show where the judicial line-drawing and recurrent decision-making tropes that I found fit into legal doctrine. In most cases, however, the detail is to show the provenance of my findings about how law about behavioural conflict at work operates through authoritative adjudication.[2] The use of description accordingly in no way evinces a generally uncritical approach and my hope is that readers will recall the criticisms, internal and external, of law and legal process in earlier chapters.

1. Statutory Unfair Dismissal

There was more engagement with employers' responses in this kind of case given the structure of many unfair dismissal analyses outlined in Chapter 3. Where, however, behavioural standards were addressed, adjudication showed the analytical features outlined earlier.

Cumulation was vital to judges in finding the line between legally acceptable and unacceptable behaviour in cases about constructive unfair dismissal. In *Abbey National Plc v Robinson*,[3] for example, the issue in legal terms was whether the employee had affirmed her contract by delaying her departure in circumstances where it took time for her predicament to become clear. If so, Ms Robinson would have lost the chance to sue for constructive unfair dismissal and been left to a possible common law claim for breach of contract. Judicial sensitivity to the effects of events unfolding over time made all the difference, leading the Employment Appeal Tribunal (EAT) to treat a series of actions by the employers as creating a sufficient breach of the implied term of mutual trust and confidence.[4]

Aberdeen CC v McNeill[5] is a straightforward instance of behavioural standards being applied, albeit in a judgment that has since been reversed in the Inner House of the Court of Session (CSIH).[6] Be that as it may, close attention was given to exactly what had happened over time in the particular context in which it occurred, with attention to organizational position and the employer's stated behavioural standards. Equally, the judgment illustrated the recurrent theme of some behaviour being readily categorized as 'beyond the pale'. These familiar decision-making styles were adopted in the course of the EAT overturning the Employment Tribunal's ruling that Mr McNeill had been

---

[2] See W Twining, *Karl Llewellyn and the Realist Movement* (2nd edn, CUP, 2012), 250–51 for criticisms of Llewellyn's approach in this regard in *The Common Law Tradition-Deciding Appeals* (Little, Brown and Company, 1960).

[3] EAT, 20 November 2000.

[4] This was so even though some of the incidents in response to which Ms Robinson had not previously reacted had been sufficiently bad on their own to have entitled her to leave, ibid, generally, [12]–[17].

[5] EAT 9 February 2010. Consider also *Perkin v St George's Healthcare NHS Trust* [2005] EWCA Civ 1174, [2006] ICR 617, in which there was judicial consideration of what the ERA 1996 permitted employers, in effect, to require of senior employees in the conduct of their work relationships.

[6] *McNeill v Aberdeen CC (No 2)* [2013] CSIH, [2015] ICR 27.

constructively unfairly dismissed and should be awarded £26,028.92 in respect of his resignation before the end of an investigation into his conduct. The justification for the ET's decision had been their view that the investigation had been conducted oppressively. The successful challenge to the ET decision, in turn, was on the ground that Mr McNeill's own conduct put him in repudiatory breach of contract, precluding the assertion that he had been constructively dismissed by a corresponding breach by his employers. The technical effect of the EAT decision (now reversed) was therefore that Mr McNeill had not, in law, been dismissed and had no statutory claim for unfair dismissal.

A series of findings were made by the ET about the conduct of Mr McNeill, a long-serving and senior employee with responsibility for about 500 members of staff. The EAT commented as follows:

[T]he evidence accepted by the Tribunal demonstrated that LK, a young woman in relation to whom the claimant was in a dominant position was subjected to wholly improper and inappropriate verbal sexual harassment over a significant period ... Shortly put, the claimant abused his dominant position in relation to her and in so doing, set a bad example to other employees. The culture that subsisted right up until the time of the claimant's suspension was, similarly, wholly improper and inappropriate. He should have taken the lead and stopped it but he did not do so. He did not see to it that a high standard of professional conduct was maintained by him and by others, as, in terms of the respondents' [Bullying and Harassment at Work P]olicy, he should have done.[7]

The EAT were critical of the Employment Tribunal (ET) appearing to play down the sexual harassment. Even if friendship might involve sexual banter, that would not render verbal sexual harassment in the workplace any less serious. Neither would it do so if a victim did not complain at the time,[8] nor if they used similar language 'where the employee perpetrating it was a senior manager'.[9] As regards the 'laddish culture', the EAT could not see why the ET treated it as relevant to mitigation that training had not been given. Mr McNeill knew from the respondent's behavioural policies that he was responsible for the maintenance of a high standard of professional conduct amongst all employees under his authority. In the EAT's words: 'On no view can it have been thought acceptable, even in the 1990's, to allow a laddish culture such as existed in Aberdeen Leisure to persist unchecked.'[10]

2. Statutory Wrongs of Discrimination I: Discriminatory Harassment

'Old-style' harassment cases used the same methods for locating the boundaries of acceptability regarding allegedly negative behaviour at work. There were detailed analyses of all sorts of interactions between colleagues; the history of dealings loomed large and some instances of behaviour were readily condemned.

There have not yet been that many 'new-style' discriminatory harassment cases on appeal, such that there were not many judgments of this type in my sample. Nonetheless, the earlier approach to decision-making seemed to be continuing. There was a hint, in fact, of courts engaging in keener, more layered scrutiny to be able coherently to judge

---

[7] See *Aberdeen CC* (n 5), [106].

[8] This is welcome counter-evidence to the suggestion from research into sexual harassment litigation that a passive reaction might lead to failure discussed at pp 43–45 in Ch 2. See further such evidence at pp 147–48 below.

[9] ibid, [74]–[75].   [10] ibid, [77].

the reasonableness in all the circumstances of either regarding a person's dignity as having been violated or of concluding that an intimidating, hostile, degrading, humiliating, or offensive environment had been created for them. In particular, the specification in the legislation that the claimant's subjective point of view is relevant to this issue at times required courts to go into what conduct signified to different participants and to assess what each should have realized about the potential impact of their behaviour. This was graphically illustrated by *Stafford and Rural Homes Ltd v Hughes*,[11] in which material factors in the finding of disability harassment were that the claimant's perceptions were affected by his illness and that the employer should have taken this into account in responding to grievances by him.

(1) Drawing behavioural lines in 'old-style' harassment cases

We have seen that the CA decision in *Jones v Tower Boot Co Ltd*[12] was critical for the development of anti-discrimination law and arguably beyond, because the ambit of vicarious liability was drawn widely. At the same time, it was a case in which the courts were emphatic in their condemnation of the egregious treatment of Mr Jones, described in Chapter 1. Recognition of the awfulness of what was done to Mr Jones was part of what persuaded the CA to take an expansive approach to interpretation of the vicarious liability provisions in the Race Relations Act (RRA) 1976. The point could not, with respect, be better put than in Waite LJ's speech, with which McCowan and Potter LJJ both agreed:

It would be particularly wrong to allow racial harassment on the scale that was suffered by the employee in this case at the hands of his workmates—treatment that was wounding both emotionally and physically—to slip through the net of employer responsibility ... To do so would seriously undermine the statutory scheme of the discrimination Acts and flout the purposes which they were passed to achieve.[13]

In *Reed & Bull Information Systems Ltd v Stedman*,[14] touched on earlier, the question was whether the employer was liable to Ms Stedman under the Sex Discrimination Act (SDA) 1975 for several incidents of unwanted sexual behaviour by her manager that involved, for example, flippant remarks about sex and 'dirty' jokes being told close by her. Ms Stedman put deterioration to her health down to her manager's conduct and consequently left work. While no single incident was thought by the ET to be serious enough in itself to constitute sexual harassment, the Tribunal concluded that the behaviour overall crossed the line because 'there had been a series of sexual inferences with a pervading sexual innuendo and sexist stance'.[15]

In deciding the case, the ET struggled with several of the facts.[16] It was found that Ms Stedman did not always complain about what had been done and that her manager desisted when either she did complain or the negative impact on her was obvious. Ultimately the ET found for Ms Stedman, in respect both of a course of conduct and of her employer's failure appropriately to respond. They reasoned that Ms Stedman's employer knew enough that it should have investigated both why she became ill and what was behind her complaints to colleagues. The behaviour and the employer's failure adequately to respond therefore put the employer in repudiatory breach of contract, making Ms Stedman's departure a constructive dismissal that breached the SDA 1975.

---

[11] (2009) 107 BMLR 155 (EAT).   [12] [1997] ICR 254 (CA).   [13] ibid, 265.
[14] [1999] IRLR 299 (EAT).   [15] ibid.   [16] ibid, [11].

The decision was upheld by the EAT on the employers' appeal. At the same time, general guidance was issued. There are elements in the decision and the guidance that were legally controversial even at the time but that *Pearce*[17] made clear were wrong. In particular, consideration was apparently not given to whether the employer's reaction and the original conduct constituted less favourable treatment than an appropriate comparator received or would have received.[18] The account of the relevant law in the guidance in fact made no mention of the 'less favourable treatment' element of the wrong of direct sex discrimination, subsuming this into the need for a claimant to show they had suffered a detriment.[19] The necessity for conduct to have been on the ground of sex was, however, noted, although the EAT observed that 'in a sexual harassment case, the answer will usually be quite clear without resort to a comparator, actual or hypothetical'. Still, the judgment was forward-looking in that the EAT described the idea of sexual harassment in a way that echoed the formulation in modern EU and domestic legislation.[20]

Beyond these legalities, the guidance about how tribunals (and hence employers and working people) should work out if conduct at work had edged into unlawfulness, was emblematic of the recurrent decision-making methodologies I found. First, examining what had happened in context was held up as the solution to various knotty factual dilemmas. These included the difficulties caused by the fact that it is for a person to decide for themselves if they object to behaviour. Rejecting the notion that ETs faced with this problem should impose their substantive opinion of the conduct, the EAT said:

It is particularly important in cases of alleged sexual harassment that the fact-finding tribunal should not carve up the case into a series of specific incidents and try and measure the harm or detriment in relation to each. As it has been put in a USA Federal Appeal Court decision (eighth circuit) (*USA v Gail Knapp* [1992] 955 Federal Reporter, 2nd series at p 564): 'Under the totality of the circumstances analysis, the district court [the fact-finding tribunal] should not carve the work environment into a series of incidents and then measure the harm occurring in each episode. Instead, the trier of fact must keep in mind that "each successive episode has its predecessors, that the impact of the separate incidents may accumulate, and that the work environment created may exceed the sum of the individual episodes."'[21]

Contextualizing the facts also provided the answer when determining whether or not conduct was properly characterized as unwelcome, considering that people may justifiably, especially at the lower end of the scale of seriousness, not realize that others, also justifiably, object to conduct. On this the EAT observed that:

[a] woman may appear, objectively, to be unduly sensitive to what might otherwise be regarded as unexceptional behaviour. But because it is for each person to define their own levels of acceptance, the question would then be whether by words or conduct she had made it clear that she found such conduct unwelcome. It is not necessary for a woman to make a public fuss to indicate her disapproval; walking out of the room might be sufficient. Tribunals will be sensitive to the problems that victims may face in dealing with a man, perhaps in a senior position to herself, who will be likely to deny that he was doing anything untoward and whose defence may often be that the victim was being over-sensitive. Provided that any reasonable person would understand her to be rejecting the conduct of which she was complaining, continuation of the conduct would, generally, be regarded as harassment.[22]

---

[17] [2003] UKHL 34, [2003] ICR 937. See further on the technicalities involved at pp 173–74 in Ch 3.
[18] The EAT judgment was notably difficult to decode on these issues. See the appellant's arguments at *Reed & Bull* (n 14), [15]–[16] which contended that some of the behaviour found to have been direct sex discrimination was not capable on the ET's factual findings of being 'less favourable treatment' in the required sense. The EAT's reasoning by which these arguments were rejected at [21] did not clearly address the points made.
[19] ibid, [25].   [20] ibid, [27].   [21] ibid, [28].   [22] ibid, [30].

Second, the first quotation cited above demonstrated that there was recognition of the potential significance of an action forming part of a course of conduct, for example because this could alter the meaning of otherwise innocuous acts. The EAT observed in this regard:

Thus, for example, as here, a blatant act of a sexual nature, such as the deliberate looking up of the victim's skirt whilst she was sitting down, may well make other incidents, such as asking to be shown personal photographs which the victim was looking at … take on a different colour and significance. Once unwelcome sexual interest has been shown by a man in a female employee, she may well feel bothered about his attentions which, in a different context, would appear quite unobjectionable.[23]

Third, despite the importance sometimes of contextualization and of repetition, it was made clear that some incidents should readily be condemned. So '[S]ome conduct, if not expressly invited, could properly be described as unwelcome. A woman does not, for example, have to make it clear in advance that she does not want to be touched in a sexual manner'.[24] Equally: 'A one-off act may be sufficient to damage [a woman's] working environment and constitute a barrier to sexual equality in the workplace ….'[25]

In *Jones v ICS Cleaning Services Ltd*,[26] considered in Chapter 4, the EAT approved the ET's rejection of Mr Jones' claims under the SDA 1975. They summarized the underlying reasons as follows, focusing on the meaning of interactions in this particular workplace:

The Tribunal held that this was an extraordinary métier, with Mr Jones having himself given the impression of being a willing participant, willingly having instigated much of the behaviour of which he later complained. They held also that Mr Trigg was a man incapable of managing people or of grasping the full import of the culture which he had allowed to develop and indeed, had encouraged. Mr Trigg, was a man who needed things to be pointed out to him. In this particular case it was necessary for the Applicant to spell out what was unwelcome.

Contextualizing here permitted layered, perhaps unexpected, analyses of what had occurred. The somewhat controversial result was that the line drawn excused, at least in the sense of there being no breach of the individual legal rights invoked, quite extreme sexualized misbehaviour at work.[27]

It was explained in Chapter 3 that *Essa v Laing Ltd*[28] was important to the development of the law on compensation for unlawful discrimination. It was further a paradigm of judicial line-drawing regarding behaviour that acknowledged the seriousness of certain transgressions even where they occurred only once. Here, a 'grotesquely offensive'[29] racist comment by a superior had dramatic negative consequences for the claimant. He was treated for depression and stopped looking for work, believing that other managers

---

[23] ibid, [29].   [24] ibid, [30].
[25] ibid. See the text to n 2 in Ch 7 for another eg and n 14 and accompanying text in Ch 2 on the different approach in the organizational psychology literature, whereby a single act is not categorized as bullying.
[26] 11 April 2000, EAT.
[27] Note that the action here concerned only the conduct itself, not the employer's reaction. It might be speculated that the management reaction once they knew what was happening played a part in the ET's thinking. The facts, at ibid, [10], related that more senior management took strong action when Mr Jones left work and made a complaint. Disciplinary proceedings were brought against Mr Trigg that resulted in summary dismissal. In addition it was recorded that: 'Senior members of the company … were held by the Tribunal … to have spoken to all the managers, who, following the meeting were left in no doubt that the culture of this workplace had to change. Behaviour of the sort described was to cease forthwith'.
[28] [2004] EWCA Civ 2, [2004] ICR 746.   [29] ibid, [3] and [34].

were thinking of him in similar terms. Most poignantly, the ET related the effect on Mr Essa's career as an elite sportsman:

> He was picked to carry the Welsh flag before boxing for Wales against Scotland but became upset whilst carrying it, asking himself what right he had to be representing Wales. He was overcome with similar feeling[s] during the fight. He says why cannot people see him for what he is and not for the colour of his skin. He says it was 'the way he spoke to me, it was the way he treated me, I'll take it to my grave ... The only thing I'd done was to be black and to go to work ... I am Welsh and no one can take that away from me'. His sense of rejection as a Welshman has so distressed him that he intends to leave Wales and to take up professional boxing in England.[30]

While the ET at first limited the remedial consequences, it is noteworthy that this was the incident in relation to which it was established that compensation for unlawful discrimination should be awarded on an unusually generous basis.

(2) Drawing behavioural lines in 'new-style' harassment cases

The enactment of dedicated definitions of discriminatory harassment from 2003 onwards reduced the need for judicial exposition of what such conduct comprised. Yet the value of contextualization for understanding complex factual situations, the significance sometimes of repetition and awareness that there are clear-cut instances of legal wrongfulness, including in the form of single events, all underlay the new legislative definitions. The greater legislative precision may have made it harder to see judges' distinctive contribution to drawing behavioural lines at work, yet there are signs of the old approach continuing.

In *Cumbria Probation Board v Collingwood*,[31] a disability case, an effect of the new law seemed to be that the ET, upheld in this regard by the EAT, was expansive about what could constitute discriminatory harassment. Combined with the customary dissection of what had happened, this resulted in fine distinctions being drawn between elements in the employer's conduct that were found to be unacceptable and others that were not. The management of Mr Collingwood's sickness absence, for example, was split into actions that did and did not count as disability harassment. On the wrong side of the line fell the HR manager refusing to have discussions in confidence, her suggestion that she was unaware of staffing issues that concerned Mr Collingwood and, finally, a more general refusal to discuss matters that Mr Collingwood said were making him ill.[32] On the right side of the line was lack of discussion of occupational health service reports, evasiveness in a particular letter from the relevant HR manager, and the way certain meetings were minuted.[33]

Stafford and Rural Homes Ltd v Hughes,[34] mentioned at the start of this chapter, again involved more intricate dissection of workplace interactions. In relating and upholding various findings of unlawfulness, the EAT described the ET's conclusion that the 'tone and content' of management's response to the claimant's grievances constituted disability harassment. The employer had not accepted that Mr Hughes was disabled and had consequently made no allowance for the effect of his illness on his perceptions. The

---

[30] ibid, [5].   [31] EAT, 7 August 2008.

[32] ibid, 25. Note also that, while these actions were found to have been taken for a reason related to Mr Collingwood's disability, the ET accepted this was not with one of the *purposes* in the statutory definition of harassment, but the conduct came within the definition because it had these *effects* and it was reasonable in all the circumstances, including the particular perception of the claimant, for it to be regarded in this way.

[33] ibid.   [34] (2009) 107 BMLR 155 (EAT).

judges found it reasonable in these circumstances to conclude that management's failure to adjust their response created an intimidating working environment for Mr Hughes for a reason related to his disability. The upshot was that even if the employer did not accept that Mr Hughes had the claimed disability, the law required it to adjust their behaviour as if he did.

In *Richmond Pharmacology v Dhaliwal* the EAT re-emphasized the importance of context. Liability was again found for a single incident[35] after a subtle line was drawn between conduct that was acceptable and that was not. The Tribunal further observed that the facts may have been 'close to the borderline',[36] stating that 'not every racially slanted adverse comment or conduct may constitute the violation of a person's dignity. Dignity is not necessarily violated by things said or done which are trivial or transitory, particularly if it should have been clear that no offence was intended.'[37]

Subtle evaluation of the detail of a working situation was at the heart of the line-drawing in *Munchkins Restaurant Ltd v Karmazyn*,[38] in which the EAT upheld the ET's findings of unlawful sexual harassment and its substantial awards of £15,000 for injury to feelings to each of the four claimants. A group of waitresses had worked at a restaurant in central London for variable periods. The controlling shareholder in the restaurant, who also worked there, was found to have subjected them, for example, to 'persistent attempts to have conversations ... and to question them about sex; and to show them photographs and catalogues of sex toys and gadgets'.[39] In this and other ways the ET found the claimants had been unlawfully sexually harassed (with an additional finding of sexual orientation harassment).

It was argued, however, that the employer's conduct had not been unwelcome. The ET rejected this contention, finding the relevant facts to have demonstrated that the waitresses were trying to manage the situation as best they could, in ways that are reminiscent of the qualitative evidence surveyed earlier of employees' reactions to harassing behaviour. In a poignant instance of informal collectivism, this included senior waitresses initiating conversations in order to contain unwanted behaviour and to deflect it from more junior colleagues.[40] In the end, however, the claimants were held to have left when the situation became intolerable. In rejecting the respondents' perversity appeal the EAT said:

We do not find it at all extraordinary that these waitresses should have soldiered on as they did for the years that they did, in the circumstances they did ... In particular [the Employment Tribunal] made the point that in its view the waitresses were migrant workers with no certainty of continued employment, save at Munchkins, that there were considerations of convenience for one, that they were constrained by financial and in some cases parental pressure; that they had the fear that they might not obtain other work; that they had the comfort of Miss Guillery acting as a cushion until she left; and that they managed, therefore, to find a balance between conduct which was unwelcome and unlawful, as the Tribunal went on to find, and the advantages which their job gave them.[41]

---

[35] [2009] ICR 724 (EAT).

[36] ibid, [22]. Moreover, the award of compensation was relatively modest, being £1,000 to compensate for injury to the claimant's feelings.

[37] ibid, [22]. [38] EAT, 28 January 2010. [39] ibid, [6].

[40] This points to possible explanations for instances in which claimants have been seen even to initiate conduct of which they complained, to do again with attempting to cope with the work environment and culture in which they find themselves. See pp 107–108 in Ch 4 for discussion of this form of complexity in the sampled judgments and pp 22–23 and n 262 in Ch 2 for relevant qualitative evidence.

[41] ibid, [23].

This interestingly depicts a court analysing failure to complain in a sophisticated way, contradicting the suggestion from qualitative analysis of harassment judgments that there may be a more general failure in this regard. The EAT in fact related one of its lay members' observing that there are many situations in which people will put up with unwanted or even criminal violations of their dignity because of social constraints, for example, in the case of some battered women.[42]

3. Statutory Wrongs of Discrimination II: General Discrimination Cases

As we have seen, claimants sought redress in these claims by alleging a range of wrongs under the anti-discrimination legislation. There was a particular tendency to challenge negative conduct and employers' responses as direct discrimination and victimization. But even then allegations were put in various ways.[43]

Line-drawing according to the usual model, while very much in evidence, worked more indirectly in respect of this form of liability than for the other causes of action. The structure of direct discrimination and victimization wrongs meant that adjudication was constrained by the need to test first, if there had been less favourable treatment than a complainant's real or hypothetical comparator, and second, if this had been on a proscribed ground. Drawing behavioural lines did not, therefore, directly determine whether there was liability. Rather, as seen in Chapter 5, it enabled courts to construct answers to the technical questions that the legislation poses. At the same time, it had a direct impact on decisions regarding remedies.

Even where line-drawing worked differently, however, the decision-making methodologies found elsewhere were very much in evidence. There was the usual intense scrutiny of what had happened and employers' responses, with events carefully evaluated in relation to the particular working environment. There was also, especially in the assessment of compensation, marked appreciation of the importance of events being sequential and a readiness to condemn some actions strenuously. There was also pragmatic balancing of interests to determine the precise content and limits of employers' obligations, as explored in Chapter 7.

Zaiwalla & Co v Walia[44] was an example of the successful deployment of general anti-discrimination law to challenge negative conduct at work, with clear demarcation of boundaries about the unacceptability of certain workplace behaviours. The ET, upheld by the EAT, found the decision not to transfer Ms Walia from a paralegal position to a training contract was direct sex discrimination contrary to the SDA 1975. Other directly sexually discriminatory acts were the employer's failures to prevent the office manager from bullying and intimidating Ms Walia and to take reasonable steps to prevent male employees from treating her in a demeaning and discriminatory manner. There was also primary and vicarious liability for the office manager's direct sex discrimination in first, treating Ms Walia differently to her male counterpart, and second, subjecting her to intimidating, hectoring, and bullying behaviour. In addition to various remedial

---

[42] ibid. The CA refused Munchkins permission to appeal on the papers and at a hearing (reported at [2010] EWCA Civ 1163) and see p 142 above on another eg and pp 43-45 in Ch 2 on the related evidence.

[43] Some of the cases discussed here might conceivably have been categorized as 'old-style' discriminatory harassment cases. I did not do so because that potential way of putting the case seemed not to be emphasized.

[44] [2002] IRLR 697 (EAT).

recommendations, the compensation award to Ms Walia (following a partially success-ful quantum appeal) was £37,646. This included sums in respect of lost future earnings, injury to feelings (with £500 to be paid personally by the office manager), aggravated damages, and interest. The aggravated damages award, upheld on appeal, was made because the defence was found to have been deliberately conducted in such a way as to intimidate Ms Walia and to cause her 'the maximum unease and distress'.

The outcome in *Villalba v Merrill Lynch and Co Inc*[45] was, as we have seen, more mixed. Only some victimization claims succeeded and all the allegations of direct sex discrimination and under the Equal Pay Act (EPA) 1970 failed. In reaching its decisions, some of which were unsuccessfully appealed, the ET engaged in considerable behav-ioural line-drawing to build to its liability conclusions.

As the judgments related, Ms Villalba had a long and successful career with Merrill Lynch before she was dismissed in June 2003.[46] In May 2002 a senior manager, Mr Yu, promoted her to a new and challenging post, but the ET and EAT found that he quickly raised issues regarding her performance. Only a few months later, Mr Yu went on to transfer another individual, Mr Abbas, to a position senior to Ms Villalba in the hierarchy. This was in circumstances in which, as the ET found: '[t]he job which [Mr Yu] described to Mr Abbas was very similar to that which Ms Villalba had been per-forming. The tribunal found that in fact Mr Abbas was taking over some of Ms Villalba's functions. However, Mr Yu told Ms Villalba that the appointment of Mr Abbas did not involve her demotion.'[47]

Perhaps unsurprisingly, matters deteriorated from there. The ET related that Ms Villalba complained in December 2002 that Mr Abbas was bullying and 'micro-managing' her. The ET, in familiar line-drawing guise, did not agree that Mr Abbas was then bullying Ms Villalba, characterizing his communications as 'terse and frank' but not unreasonable.[48] In this assessment account was taken, for example, of the pressure on Mr Abbas and of the grave view taken internally of the financial position in that part of the business.[49] The situation was found to have deteriorated in succeeding weeks such that the working relationship between Mr Abbas and Ms Villalba broke down completely. Still the ET found that, much as there had been 'a very frank exchange' at a meeting on 23 January 2003, Mr Abbas did not bully Ms Villalba.[50] Other behavioural findings included that Mr Abbas belittled Ms Villalba behind her back and 'did not speak warmly of her'.[51] These factual findings together built to the ET's conclusion that it was not Ms Villalba's sex that accounted for the treatment of which she complained.[52]

The rejection of Ms Villalba's direct sex discrimination allegations was also supported by several comments approving Mr Yu's conduct. For example, it was noted that he worked hard to find a new post for Ms Villalba and that he was genuine in dealings with her.[53] A script which Mr Yu read in a phone call with Ms Villalba was characterized by the ET as a 'gracious and dignified attempt to move forward', and as having been respect-ful of her.[54] There was also some commendation of the behaviour of a human resources (HR) colleague called Mr Woodroffe.[55] It was, however, recognized that legal considera-tions may simultaneously have influenced Mr Woodroffe's behaviour.[56] Moreover, there came a point, said by the ET to have occurred by June 2003 after Ms Villalba was put

[45] [2007] ICR 469 (EAT).
[46] ibid, [3] and see generally for the EAT's outline of the facts, [3]–[37].   [47] ibid, [12].
[48] ibid, [21].   [49] ibid.   [50] ibid, in particular, [28]–[29].   [51] ibid, [54].
[52] ibid, [40] and [52]–[54]. See also the comment in the EAT at [76]–[77] in relation to Ms Villalba's appeal against the dismissal of part of her victimization claim.
[53] ibid, [31]–[32].   [54] ibid, [33].   [55] ibid, [31]–[33].   [56] ibid, [33].

on leave in March 2003, when Mr Woodroffe was only 'going through the motions' in trying to identify suitable alternative posts for her.[57]

In terms of victimization the ET's behavioural conclusions, however, painted a different legal picture. At some point the ET found HR staff to be guiding Mr Abbas' dealings with Ms Villalba to reduce the risk of victimization claims.[58] Matters were held to have reached a pitch at which HR was no longer looking for a solution but solely trying to prevent Mr Abbas from victimizing Ms Villalba.[59] In this context, the ET found the tone of e-mails changed:

However when we come to see the e-mail traffic between Mr Abbas and the human resources department (in particular Mr Woodroffe and Pauline Cahill) from mid-January 2003 onwards, and, importantly, the e-mail to Mr Gorman of 3 February 2003 … a different picture emerges and we accept … that they displayed a degree of hostility, personal attack and denigration disproportionate to Ms Villalba's perceived shortcomings. They border on the vindictive. She was being isolated and disrespected in a quite unpleasant and personal way behind her back and no cogent explanation has been given. In fact the only plausible explanation for such treatment was her allegations of sex discrimination. There is a stark contrast to the e-mails about Mr San Salvador when his performance was perceived as wanting, when he is discussed in a matter of fact way. They were looking for things to criticize her for, and not seeking to assist her and support her in performing her role.[60]

This supported findings of victimization, the ET making the additional point that '[w]e wish to emphasize our disappointment at the behaviour of the human resources department in Ms Villalba's victimization and their unprofessional behaviour.' The ruling in this way moved away from line-drawing about behavioural standards to doing the same about employer responses, giving implicit guidance about the stance that human resources ought to take in conflictual situations.[61]

Some of the claims in *Derby Specialist Fabrication v Burton*[62] were out of time, but the court's familiar approach to cumulation meant that this did not make much difference. A climate of racial abuse at Mr Derby's workplace was held to form the backdrop to racial abuse by his managers. Once redundancies were mooted, Mr Derby was held reasonably to have concluded that he would be treated less favourably than colleagues and to have resigned in consequence. This gave rise to a constructive dismissal on the basis that the employers had over time committed a repudiatory breach of the implied mutual trust and confidence term. The dismissal was in turn direct race discrimination. The EAT upheld the ET, commenting that it would be wrong to isolate individual incidents where the repudiation consisted of an accumulation of events over a period of time.[63] Rather, ETs 'should have regard to the totality of successive incidents because there may well be a cumulative effect'.[64] If the breach of contract so found could be seen, or inferred, to be on racial grounds, such that the complainant would have been treated differently but for his race, the repudiation would then rightly be categorized as racially discriminatory contrary to the RRA 1976.[65]

---

[57] ibid, [35].   [58] ibid, [29].   [59] ibid.
[60] ibid, [55]. This is a clear account of the phenomenon found in qualitative evidence (see pp 17 and 44–45 in Ch 2) and supported by my interview study (see pp 191, 193–94, and 209 in Ch 8 and pp 231–33 in Ch 9) of employers and colleagues turning on individuals who make a complaint. And see further n 65 below and n 51 in Ch 7.
[61] See *Laing v Manchester CC* [2006] ICR 1519 (EAT) for another example, especially for the careful attention to the personalities involved and how these affected the status and meaning of workplace conduct.
[62] [2001] ICR 833 (EAT).   [63] ibid, [20].   [64] ibid, [27].
[65] Despite these findings the employers pursued an appeal against part of the interest element in the compensation award. The total award was £19,551.02 of which £1,267.95 represented interest. The employers unsuccessfully contended on appeal that the interest should have been calculated to run from a later date than that taken by the ET. See ibid, [34]–[41]. This is suggestive of the lengths to which

4. Breach of the Protection from Harassment Act 1997

The individual focus of the wrongs in PHA 1997 makes it difficult to disentangle the two forms of line-drawing, namely regarding behavioural standards on the one hand, and employers' obligations on the other. I report on all the relevant data in this chapter because the cases generally dealt with negative conduct at work, with employer responsibility and guidance often an implicit consequence of vicarious liability being imposed. Even so, the decisions at times gave general direction to employers, for example about the limits either of acceptable management conduct or techniques, as explained below.

In terms of decision-making style, judges' entry into the minutiae of what had happened was, in several of these cases, quite remarkable. There was also repeatedly sensitivity to the relationship between acts in a series. While some behaviours might be especially legally condemned, however, liability could not be found for a single incident given specification in the Act that harassment is a course of conduct comprising at least two events.

A further distinctive feature of this case law was that it grappled with the definitional effect of the conduct prohibited by the PHA 1997 having been made both a civil and a criminal wrong. Arguably this could be seen as another problem rooted in the multiplicity of means by which a claim regarding behavioural conflict can be brought, but I think the issue here was of a different order to those described in Chapter 5.

First, it would be unusual for criminal proceedings to be brought by anyone other than the state prosecuting authority. Second, the problem was not the overlap or interface between different causes of action. Rather, the question was whether wrongs should be interpreted differently because of having criminal as well as civil consequences.

Turning to the drawing of boundaries in these cases and how it was done, the conduct in *Banks v Ablex Ltd*[66] alleged to have breached the PHA 1997 was 'loud and aggressive swearing and abuse accompanied by gesticulating and finger pointing' by Mrs Banks' colleague, Mr Briggs. This culminated in an incident on 14 October 1998 after which Mrs Banks left work and never returned, the court finding that she was suffering from a depressive disorder that precluded work. The PHA 1997 issue on appeal became, by an odd procedural route, whether the judge had sufficiently examined evidence about Briggs' earlier conduct to reject that aspect of the claim for, in effect, not disclosing a course of conduct.[67] The Judge had observed on this that '[w]hilst it is true that there had been past exchanges between Briggs and the claimant … there is no evidence that Briggs's outbursts were targeted at the claimant as opposed to anyone else or, indeed, to inanimate tools and equipment.'[68] He also did not find the requisite mental element, noting that Mr Briggs 'concerns on these occasions were to give vent to his own frustrations, not to cause alarm or distress to others'.[69]

---

adversarialism can take litigants even when workplace conduct is found obviously and seriously wrongful. See pp 110–12 and 117 in Ch 4 on this, and p 207 in Ch 8 for some senior lawyers' view that obvious cases are likely to be resolved. The latter seems likely to reflect the kind of employers those interviewees' had worked with, such that this vignette is a good illustration of quite how hard some workplaces make it to assert and enforce individual employment rights, in keeping with the accounts of some other lawyers and my analysis at p 254 in Ch 10.

[66] [2005] EWCA Civ 173, [2005] ICR 819.

[67] ibid, [17]. There was an appeal also against rejection by the judge of Mrs Banks' negligence claim (although not regarding rejection of the rest of her tort claim). That appeal was also unsuccessful on the ground that the reasonable foreseeability requirement was not met (see ibid, [38]).

[68] ibid, [14].   [69] ibid.

The Court of Appeal (CA) supported and approved the mode of analysis which entailed familiar, careful uncovering of the meaning over time of interactions between work colleagues to ascertain whether behavioural lines had sufficiently been crossed to attract legal sanction. First, the CA praised the judge's concentration on the personalities of Mrs Banks and Mr Briggs, observing that he had rightly considered these to be at the heart of the matter. Hence the judge recorded what other people said about them, namely that Mrs Briggs was 'tough, a woman of strong character, not likely to be upset by comments or offensive language, a woman who was known to give as good as she got', and that Briggs was 'a capable engineer, a volatile character, someone who could often be frustrated with his work, but who had calmed down as the years went by ...'.[70] Second, the evolution of the relationship between the two over the critical period had been examined. As a result of this, the CA found the judge's reasoning to have been sufficient to support his conclusion that unlawful harassment had not occurred.[71]

The HL decision in *Majrowski v Guy's and St Thomas's NHS Trust*[72] that employers are vicariously liable for breaches of the PHA 1997 by their employees was highly significant for this area of law. For present purposes, however, the importance of the case lay in explicit recognition by their Lordships of the crucial role of judges in locating the boundary between acceptable and unacceptable behaviour at work.

The decision was at an interlocutory stage, the HL reversing, in agreement with the CA, the county court's summary strike out of the claim. Mr Majrowski, formerly employed as a clinical auditor coordinator for Guy's and St Thomas' NHS Trust, had objected to what he regarded as bullying and intimidation by his departmental manager. The allegations included that his manager had been rude and abusive in front of other staff, was excessively critical of Mr Majrowski's work and time-keeping, imposed unrealistic performance targets, threatened disciplinary action if these were not met, and had isolated him at work. Lord Nicholls recorded also that Mr Majrowski, a gay man, saw this treatment as fuelled by homophobia. A formal internal complaint of harassment was upheld and the manager resigned as a result. Mr Majrowski was later dismissed for unconnected reasons and the action under the PHA 1997 was brought nearly four years after his departure. Only vicarious liability was asserted, there being neither common law claims nor an individual action against the manager.[73]

Lord Nicholls saw the main concern of employers in general as being 'the prospect of a multiplicity of unfounded, speculative claims'. He characterized this as 'real and understandable' despite the evidence surveyed in Chapter 2 that shows how unlikely this actually is.[74] Even so, Lord Nicholls did not see this concern as providing sufficient

[70] ibid, [26]. See also ibid [13] in which findings regarding Mr Briggs' knowledge of Mrs Banks' personality were important to rejection of her tort claim for the intentional infliction of injury, since it led to the conclusion that an intention to harm should not be imputed to Mr Briggs. In a classic instance of judicial line-drawing, the judge had said: 'There having been no assault ... all that is left is a catalogue of rudeness and unfriendliness, behaviour not to be expected from grown-up colleagues in the workplace, but not behaviour so "calculated to infringe her legal right to personal safety" that an intention to do so should be imputed to Briggs.' This element in the first instance decision was not appealed.
[71] See ibid at [27]–[32] generally and at [27] specifically for a vignette of the detail entered into, in this instance about different subjective perceptions of a working relationship, including as these altered between interactions.
[72] [2006] UKHL 34, [2007] 1 AC 224.
[73] [2006] UKHL 34, [2007] 1 AC 224, [2]–[4] for the factual account in Lord Nicholls' speech, and [68] in Lady Hale's speech regarding the departure of the manager after the internal grievance.
[74] See ibid, [29] where Lord Nicholls elaborated on the risk as he perceived it, making the familiar, mistaken assumption that: '[d]isgruntled employees or ex-employees, perhaps suffering from stress at work unrelated to harassment, perhaps bitter at being dismissed, will all too readily advance unmeritorious claims for compensation for harassment.'

grounds to justify denying of the usual right to pursue an employer to victims of serious harassment. In particular he noted that harassment by employees may be of third parties. Lord Carswell also saw that possibility as significant at the same time as he viewed the arguments as 'very evenly balanced' and was persuaded by the specific construction point that convinced all of their Lordships.[75] It was in this context that Lord Nicholls recognized and elaborated the courts' line-drawing function:

> Courts are well able to separate the wheat from the chaff at an early stage of the proceedings. They should be astute to do so … Where the claim meets [the close connection test for vicarious liability] … and the quality of the conduct said to constitute harassment is being examined, courts will have in mind that irritations, annoyances, even a measure of upset, arise at times in everybody's day-to-day dealings with other people. Courts are well able to recognize the boundary between conduct which is unattractive, even unreasonable, and conduct which is oppressive and unacceptable. To cross the boundary from the regrettable to the unacceptable the gravity of the misconduct must be of an order which would sustain criminal liability under s 2.[76]

Neither Lord Hope, Lady Hale, nor Lord Brown supported Lord Nicholls' substantive reasoning. Each only agreed that the 1997 Act provided for vicarious liability as a matter of statutory construction and expressed doubts about the wisdom of Parliament having legislated to this effect.[77] In doing so, nonetheless, Lady Hale, with the agreement of Lord Brown, recognized the courts' role in defining the limits of acceptable workplace conduct. Commenting that conduct might be harassment even if it in fact caused no alarm or distress, she said: 'A great deal is left to the wisdom of the courts to draw sensible lines between the ordinary banter and badinage of life and genuinely offensive and unacceptable behaviour.'[78]

In *Sunderland CC v Conn*[79] the claimant failed in his county court negligence action for damages for psychiatric injury, but was at first awarded £2,100 under the PHA 1997. This went on to be overturned by the CA on the basis that no course of harassing conduct had been established, the first of two incidents complained about being held not to have been sufficiently serious. The CA took the opportunity to give general guidance, building on Lord Nicholls' comment quoted earlier, about how the line should be drawn between conduct that did and did not breach the 1997 Act. In so doing the judgment started a technical controversy about the significance of the 1997 Act providing in England and Wales for unlawful harassment to be both a civil and criminal wrong. In the event, the approach the CA took has since substantially been departed from, initially in the Scottish jurisdiction and then in England and Wales. The case remains significant for the present analysis, however, because the nub of the judicial discussion in both courts was how judges should acquit the boundary-setting aspect of their role. There was also, along the way, the usual detailed factual consideration and repeated acknowledgments of the significance of context.

Mr Conn was a longstanding employee of the council and had known his site foreman, Mr Dryden, for many years. Only two of five alleged incidents were found by the county court Recorder to have crossed the threshold of unlawful harassment. The

[75] ibid, [78]–[79]. [76] ibid, [29]–[30].
[77] ibid, [43] per Lord Hope, [64]–[74] per Lady Hale, and [81] per Lord Brown. See further at pp 135–36 in Ch 5.
[78] ibid, [66]. Note also at [71] her comment in relation to the six-year limitation period on the value of consideration being given to the whole course of harassing conduct: 'The promoters did address their minds to the appropriate limitation period and deliberately disapplied the ordinary three-year period for personal injury claims: s 6. Harassment can take place over very long periods and they would not have wanted the earlier conduct to be left out of account.'
[79] [2007] EWCA Civ 1492, [2008] IRLR 324.

first consisted in Mr Dryden asking Mr Conn and two colleagues, Mr Harrison and Mr Welsh, to name people who had been leaving the site early. When Mr Conn refused, his evidence and that of the others was that 'Mr Dryden became angry and threatened to punch out the windows of the cabin and have them up before the personnel department.'[80] The judge accepted that Mr Dryden had made this demand to the three men, but said of the other two that '[n]either of them were particularly bothered about the threat to punch through the windows. Mr Welsh said that he was not intimidated, nor indeed did it make him feel uncomfortable. Mr Harrison said that he had not been afraid of Mr Dryden and had not been affected by his conduct upon that occasion.'[81]

The second incident was more serious, the judge having found that Mr Dryden had been angry and aggressive with Mr Conn, threatened him with violence, told him that the two of them were finished, and called him 'a little shit'.[82] Of the two events the Recorder concluded, in typical line-drawing style, that:

[t]he language and actions used went well beyond those which would normally be regarded as acceptable, even in that environment. They were potentially intimidating, and on the second occasion, very personal toward Mr Conn … I find that this type of behaviour went well beyond the normal pressures of the job and well beyond what could and should be expected from a manager.[83]

In evaluating the county court judgment, Gage LJ observed that the location of Lord Nicholls' boundary may well depend on the context in which conduct occurred: 'What might not be harassment on the factory floor or in the barrack room might well be harassment in the hospital ward and vice versa.'[84] He saw the touchstone for recognizing what was not harassment, however, as being whether conduct was of such gravity as to justify the sanctions of the criminal law.[85] Buxton LJ also drew on Lord Nicholls' remarks to say that for conduct to cross the line that demarcated unlawful harassment it must have been of an order that would sustain criminal liability, 'not merely civil liability on some other register'.[86] Ward LJ agreed with both judgments.

Noting that the Recorder had not referred to Lord Nicholls' guidance, the CA went on to re-decide the case against Mr Conn. While regarding the point as not free from doubt, Gage LJ was prepared to accept that the second incident had gone far enough, observing that it had caused the claimant a great deal of distress. The first, however, had not. There was no physical threat, Mr Conn was not singled out, and the others present had not been troubled. The Recorder had in fact reported the claimant's evidence that he had not felt threatened until the final incident. It followed for Gage LJ that this was: 'the sort of bad-tempered conduct which, although unpleasant, comes well below the line of that which justifies a criminal sanction'.[87]

Both Buxton and Ward LJJ were more trenchant in their condemnation of the lower court findings. Not only did Buxton LJ expressly reserve his position on the second incident, he concluded that if the Recorder had properly taken account of Lord Nicholls' guidance it would have been 'completely impossible' for him to categorize the first act as unlawful harassment.[88] What had occurred, he found, was 'a very long way away from anything that, in a sensible criminal regime, would lead to a prosecution, much less to a conviction'.[89] In particular, he could not see how Mr Dryden ought reasonably to have

---

80 ibid, [5].   81 ibid.   82 ibid, [7].   83 ibid, [4].   84 ibid, [12].
85 ibid.   86 ibid, [18].   87 ibid, [15].
88 ibid. See also Buxton LJ's observation at [17] that the fact that Mr Conn had at the time been on the verge of a mental breakdown should not affect the assessment under the 1997 Act of what the alleged harasser ought to have known of the implications of his conduct seeing as this was to be assessed objectively.
89 ibid, [18].

known that what he was doing amounted to a criminal course of conduct when two of those to whom it was directed had not been upset by it.[90] Ward LJ gave his view more pithily:

I am tempted only to add: what on earth is the world coming to if conduct of the kind that occurred in the third incident [the first above] can be thought to be an act of harassment, potentially liable to giving rise to criminal proceedings punishable with imprisonment for a term not exceeding six months, and to a claim for damages for anxiety and financial loss? ... The conduct here does not come close to harassment.[91]

There was a different, and, respectfully, more faithful reading of Lord Nicholls' comment by the Outer House of the Court of Session (CSOH) only three weeks later in *Robertson v The Scottish Ministers*.[92] Ms Robertson's common law claim for compensation for damages for psychiatric illness was struck out on foreseeability and causation grounds. Lord Emslie, however, rejected the employer's argument that Lord Nicholls' speech in *Majrowski* meant that only criminal conduct was capable of constituting harassment under the 1997 Act. As we have seen, the legislation in any event made no provision for criminal liability in Scotland since the criminal law there was thought already to cover the conduct the new Act prohibited. Lord Emslie made the points that:

[c]riminality is ... explicitly a consequence, rather than a prerequisite, of civil harassment under section 1(1) ... As it respectfully seems to me, the observations by Lord Nicholls on which reliance was placed were truly directed to a different point altogether, namely the obvious need for caution in branding everyday conduct "harassment" where criminal consequences would (in England and Wales at least) automatically follow.[93]

He noted that similar caution had recently been urged in other actions in pursuit of damages for non-physical harm[94] and extrapolated that 'everyday upsets and incidents—even extending to rude, boorish, abusive or offensive behaviour—should not too readily be held actionable, either at common law or under the 1997 Act'.[95] Ms Robertson's allegations of 'a persistent course of victimization, intimidation and harassment', however, were in a different, more serious category altogether and she was allowed to proceed with this aspect of her case (as well as that regarding intentional infliction of harm).[96]

The issue raised by overlapping civil and criminal liability under the PHA 1997 was put beyond doubt for England and Wales in *Veakins v Kier Islington Ltd*.[97] Maurice Kay LJ gave the only substantive speech, with which Waller and Rimer LJJ agreed. The facts

---

[90] ibid.   [91] Ibid, [19].   [92] [2007] CSOH 186.   [93] ibid, [10].

[94] ibid. Reference was made to the comments by Hale LJ (as she then was) in *Hatton*, subsequently approved by the House of Lords in *Barber* and elsewhere.

[95] ibid, [27].

[96] ibid, [13] and [18]–[19]. Compare, however, *Dowson v CC of Northumbria Police* [2009] EWHC 907 in which three of a series of joined PHA 1997 actions by a group of police officers were struck out, including because the underlying allegations were not sufficiently grave. It was, eg, said of one of the struck out actions at [89] that: 'this was a simple case of people not getting on in the working environment, where at most, a junior officer disagreed with instructions and methodologies adopted by his superior officer. I believe that the courts should be reluctant to conclude that such common circumstances can give rise to harassment claims under the 1997 Act, whether criminal or civil; in my judgment, the circumstances of the present case fall far short of the oppressive behaviour identified by Lord Nicholls in *Majrowski*.'

[97] [2009] EWCA Civ 1288, [2010] IRLR 132. Sheriff Peter J Braid in *Dickie v Flexcon Glenrothes Ltd* [2009] GWD 35–602 (Sheriff Court), summarized the position for both jurisdictions at [77]: '[I] ... proceed on the basis that caution must be exercised in branding conduct as harassment, and to that extent I accept the defenders' submission that the potential criminal consequences of conduct amounting to harassment, in Scotland as in England, should merely colour one's appreciation of the sort of conduct which is required in order to amount to harassment.'

were earlier described as a somewhat typical example of the less serious forms of behavioural conflict at work. The case was also factually straightforward because Ms Veakins' evidence was not challenged and the employer called no evidence. The Recorder in the county court, following the line taken in *Conn*, found it clear that the conduct in question had not constituted harassment under the PHA 1997.[98]

Maurice Kay LJ referred to the key passages from Lord Nicholls' and Lady Hale's speech quoted earlier, as well as to relevant findings of Jacobs LJ's in the non-employment case of *Ferguson v British Gas Trading Ltd*.[99] Since *Majrowski*, Maurice Kay LJ observed, the primary focus for courts had been on whether conduct was 'oppressive and unacceptable' as opposed to merely unattractive, unreasonable, or regrettable. In addition, it had to be borne in mind that conduct must be of an order which 'would sustain criminal liability'. The Recorder had been led into error by not setting out Lord Nicholls' comment, instead relying on the judgment of Buxton LJ in *Conn*. The problem was that his primary focus had consequently been on whether a prosecuting authority would have pursued a criminal case and, if there had been a prosecution, whether it would have had any prospect of success. This meant the Recorder had not evaluated the evidence against the primary requirement that conduct was 'oppressive and unacceptable'.[100]

The CA was able to re-decide the matter because it had all the evidence. Applying this different legal approach, it concluded that the Recorder had come to the wrong decision:

It seems to me that the recorder undervalued the evidence. The account of victimization, demoralization and the reduction of a substantially reasonable and usually robust woman to a state of clinical depression is not simply an account of 'unattractive' and 'unreasonable' conduct (in Lord Nicholls' words) or 'the ordinary banter and badinage of life' (in Baroness Hale's words). It self-evidently crosses the line into conduct which is 'oppressive and unreasonable'. It may be that, if asked, a prosecutor would be reluctant to prosecute but that is not the consideration, which is whether the conduct is 'of an order which would sustain criminal liability'. I consider that, in the event of a prosecution, the proven conduct would be sufficient to establish criminal liability. I do not accept that, in a criminal court, the proceedings would properly be stayed as an abuse of process.[101]

There was no need therefore to deal with the alternative submission that the Recorder had erred in failing to consider if there had been malice. Still, Maurice Kay LJ took the opportunity to say that while malice is not necessary to liability, its presence would make it easier to meet the 'oppressive and unacceptable' test. Moreover the evidence was susceptible to a finding that there had been malice since: 'Mrs Lavy's extraordinary conduct must have been motivated by a desire to do whatever she could to force out an employee for whom she had a profound personal dislike.'[102]

Dickie v Flexcon Glenrothes Ltd,[103] another Scottish case and the one judgment I have included from the Sheriff Court, both contained a useful recap of the law and

[98] See ibid, [5].
[99] [2009] EWCA Civ 46, [2010] 1 WLR 785. See [17]–[18] in which, while Jacobs LJ accepted that 'a course of conduct must be grave before the offence or tort of harassment is proved', he observed that: 'the only real difference between the crime of section 2 and the tort of section 3 is standard of proof ... In so accepting I would just add this word of caution: the fact of parallel criminal and civil liability is not generally, outside the particular context of harassment, of significance in considering civil liability. It has never been suggested generally that the scope of a civil wrong is restricted because it is also a crime. What makes the wrong of harassment different and special is because, as Lord Nicholls and Lady Hale recognized, in life one has to put up with a certain amount of annoyance: things have got to be fairly severe before the law, civil or criminal, will intervene.' See also Sedley LJ (who gave a concurring judgment, as did Lloyd LJ) at [52].
[100] [2009] EWCA Civ 1288, [2010] IRLR 132, [11]–[12].   [101] ibid, [15].
[102] ibid, [16].   [103] [2009] GWD 35–602 (Sheriff Court).

first found (but as a matter of persuasive authority only) that losses arising naturally and directly from harassment are recoverable whether or not they were foreseeable.[104] The recurrent features of judicial decision-making in this field were also present to a quite stunning degree, perhaps again reflecting that this was a first instance decision. The facts were entered into in extraordinary detail, with a large number of events subjected to exhaustive analysis to work out if the boundary had been crossed into unlawfulness. There was deep contextualization, including that was directed to understanding the personalities involved, and careful consideration of the interconnectedness of events. All of this led to general observations about the limits to what can appropriately be expected of employers, with clear-sightedness also about how workplace conduct might go too far.[105]

To illustrate, the personality of the claimant and his antagonist, Mr Harwood, were dissected as follows:

I have found as a fact, based on the medical evidence, that the pursuer has a sensitive personality, needs other people to approve of him and holds unrealistic expectations of how other people should behave towards him. These personality traits undoubtedly colour how he perceives the behaviour of others (and indeed, how he reacts to criticism) and, as will be seen, his interpretation of incidents and of the motivation of others, cannot always be relied upon.[106]

The judge also found that Mr Harwood was not 'a wholly satisfactory witness'.[107] Aside from downplaying his obvious dislike of Mr Dickie, his evidence had sometimes been internally inconsistent. The judge, however, characterized as critical, in a way that was reminiscent of analyses of behaviour in discrimination cases, that Mr Harwood's dislike of the claimant 'was borne of his genuinely held belief that the pursuer did not perform aspects of his job satisfactorily'.[108] The fact that Mr Harwood's dislike was found to be genuinely rooted in negative views about Mr Dickie's work was important to the Sheriff's later findings that the challenged conduct, even if sometimes worthy of criticism, did not amount to harassment.

On cumulation, the Sheriff acknowledged the truth of the rival positions put to him, first that the quality of the whole course of conduct must be capable of being deemed oppressive and unreasonable, and second that it was necessary to evaluate whether each incident had contributed to a course of conduct amounting to harassment.[109] At the same time, the judgment captured how events could change character through forming part of a sequence, as follows:

[The] argument that it is the repetitive nature of certain conduct which makes it harassment is, I think, answered by pointing out that after the conduct has been repeated a stage will be reached when the individual incidents do become distressing and can in themselves be categorized as harassment.[110]

He also regarded it as important to consider incidents chronologically since the view taken of any particular incident might be affected by what had gone before.

There followed a meticulous examination of each incident complained of, leading to findings that although aspects of Mr Harwood's behaviour could be criticized, none had entailed unlawful harassment. The Sheriff further synthesized his thinking into an

---

[104] See now *Jones v Ruth* [2011] EWCA (Civ) 804, [2012] 1 WLR 1495, [32]–[33], authoritatively establishing this proposition.

[105] See ibid, [115] where the Sheriff gave a specific indication of behaviour that would have crossed the line.

[106] ibid, [10]. [107] ibid, [19]. [108] ibid. [109] ibid, [80]. [110] ibid.

overall assessment of what occurred between the two men, notably drawing on his earlier estimations of them to understand their mutual dislike:

So, the pursuer was genuinely helpful to others, sometimes at the expense of properly prioritizing his own duties. Harwood's main concern, by contrast, was to ensure that the stock ran smoothly and that the Madisun system was kept up to date, something which the pursuer on his own admission did not always manage to achieve, although which he sought to justify. Having regard to the incidents as a whole, this difference in approach and antipathy towards each other did bring the men into conflict on a number of occasions and almost inevitably led to justifiable criticism being levelled at the pursuer from time to time. Given his dislike of criticism, it would not be surprising if such criticism was not well received.[111]

The Sheriff's interpretation of events pointed to an overall categorization of the various events.[112] First, there were incidents in respect of which Mr Dickie had 'formed an irrational and unjustified view that Mr Harwood's conduct was targeted at him'.[113] These were to be disregarded in considering the overall situation. Second, there were incidents involving conduct by Mr Harwood that was 'either justified, or at any rate [that] disclosed a view which one could not say [Mr Harwood] was not entitled to hold'.[114] In effect these arose out of a difference of opinion as to how the two men should be doing their jobs, Despite Mr Harwood swearing on occasion and flaws in his management style, it was not possible to view his conduct on these occasions, even taken as a whole, as oppressive. This in turn led the Sheriff to enunciate a general limit on what was capable of breaching the Act, saying that '[o]n no view of the 1997 Act can it strike at mere bad management technique, or at the mere use of swear words in the work place.'[115] In so doing, he gave general guidance to employers that the 1997 Act did not prohibit genuine management even if poorly executed.

Third, there were incidents for which there was no justification for what Mr Harwood had done. In this mode he had twice acted boorishly for no defensible reason, yet neither occasion involved unlawful harassment, in part because the evidence tended to show that the conduct had been 'relatively insignificant and of the type to be expected to occur from time to time in a work environment'.[116] One of the incidents in question had in fact not seemed to affect Mr Dickie at the time. The other did have an impact but, again drawing on the Sheriff's estimation of Mr Dickie's personality, did not result in liability because the reaction had been rooted in an unjustifiable perception of what had occurred. Finally, there was the last incident following which Mr Dickie definitively left work. The Sheriff held that on this occasion Mr Harwood had not even acted unattractively, nor in fact directed any specific behaviour towards Mr Dickie.[117] In a finding of some subtlety, the Sheriff said of this incident that it 'was caused more by the pursuer's perception of Harwood's behaviour towards him than anything else'.[118]

Rayment v MoD,[119] remarked on earlier, was another long-running dispute. Ms Rayment brought claims in negligence and under the PHA 1997. She alleged that she had suffered an adjustment disorder as a result of 'persistent, offensive, abusive, intimidating, bullying, humiliating and insulting behaviour'.[120] The negligence action was unsuccessful before Mrs Justice Davies in the HC but elements of what had been done were held to have breached the PHA 1997.

---

[111] ibid, [118].   [112] See generally ibid, [119]–[126].   [113] ibid, [119].
[114] ibid, [120].   [115] ibid.   [116] ibid, [121].   [117] ibid, [122].
[118] ibid, [26], in which he also went on to say that: '[v]iewed objectively, it illustrates too that the pursuer felt angry towards Harwood, and that the feelings of antipathy felt by Harwood towards him were reciprocated.'
[119] [2010] EWHC 218 (QB), [2010] IRLR 768.   [120] ibid, [1].

Davies J took the usual approach of closely scrutinizing the factual situation to unpick and categorize what had occurred. This gave rise to a nuanced evaluation of the behaviour of different actors. There was, for example, criticism of Mrs Rayment's own conduct.[121] The judgment also recorded the Commanding Officer's response to one of two formal grievances, including comments that Mrs Rayment's absence record had caused 'considerable disruption', and that she should be 'sensitive to the feelings of colleagues' affected by her being away.[122] The absences in question had been on account of Mrs Rayment's ill health and care obligations as a single parent to a disabled daughter.[123] All of this reflected the complexity of the situation, the judge's analysis of which led to findings in favour of both sides.

The communication by Mrs Rayment's line manager of his opinion that she was unsuitable for a new job, for example, was held not to breach the 1997 Act. Davies J saw no substance to the harassment allegation in circumstances where this opinion was honestly held and was one the line manager was entitled to express.[124] Davies J's rejection of other allegations drew on her appreciation of the complexity of the situation:

> I do not seek to minimize the other incidents but having read or listened to the relevant evidence, I am satisfied that none would satisfy the test enunciated by Maurice Kay LJ in *Veakins*, namely that the conduct was 'oppressive and unacceptable'. There were faults on both sides. The claimant was a challenging employee, those who worked with her were increasingly frustrated by her attitude and conduct and on occasions, this showed. In 2003 to 2004, the claimant presented as a woman well able to challenge that which she did not accept and accustomed to military establishments where robust language could be used.[125]

Still, the judge's perception of fault on both sides did not prevent her from also making findings in Ms Rayment's favour, including that a formal warning during sickness absence and her subsequent dismissal had breached the 1997 Act.[126] The kernel of the wrong in these particular instances was that she had been penalized for the effects of 'certified medical unfitness for normal duties' and for complaints she was entitled to make. Irrespective of Ms Rayment's failings as an employee, the employer's conduct was condemned as 'unacceptable and oppressive', Davies J observing that it 'had one purpose and that was to rid the Regiment of the claimant'. Recognition of the intricacies of the situation however reduced the compensation payable to the somewhat modest sum of £6,500.

Finally, in *First Global Locums Ltd v Cosias*[127] the courts took the unusual step of restraining an employee by injunction because of breaches of the PHA 1997, including from going to his past place of work and from contacting named ex-colleagues.[128] The facts demonstrated how troubling misconduct at work can be. Fine distinctions were nonetheless again made in evaluating Mr Cosias' conduct. When continuing the injunction, but for a fixed period of twenty-four months rather than indefinitely, Judge Bernard Livesey QC said:

> [A]lthough Mr Cosias does lack control of his temper and has intimidated those with whom he has worked closely, he has not ever inflicted violence on any occasion and, even though he has expressed the threat, there does not appear to me to be a real risk that he might put it into action. Secondly, although he has shown a tendency to retaliate in the heat of the moment ... he can return to control by himself ... His retaliation is impulsive and not, it seems to me, the product of long-term grudge. Thirdly, it should be remembered that the claimants were once people who shared [Mr Cosias'] life and were colleagues working together, at times in harmony and in some cases in friendship for at least a part of the time.[129]

---

[121] ibid, [49].   [122] ibid.   [123] ibid, [13] and [20].   [124] ibid, [63](iv).
[125] ibid, [70].   [126] ibid, [61]–[62], [69], and [71].
[127] [2005] EWHC 1147 (QB), [2005] IRLR 873.   [128] ibid, [30].   [129] ibid, [36].

There is something sad, almost poignant, about that last comment, evoking how very difficult it can be to make sense of the ebb and flow of workplace encounters. Equally, the passage is further testimony to judges' unflinching stance in the face of this often difficult task.

5. Unlawful Conduct in Contract and Tort

The same recurrent themes were strongly in evidence in the common law decisions. The depth and extent of the factual analysis that several of the judgments entered into was astonishing, as presaged in Chapter 4.[130] This was perhaps influenced by there being more first instance judgments in this category and that the judgments in which factual scrutiny was most detailed were from the HC, the most senior first instance court. Too much should not be made of the latter point, however, given the strong impression from the sample of a congruent approach to fact-finding whatever the forum.

Again in this context I found it more difficult to separate the elements in the judgments which focused on behavioural standards in themselves from those which concentrated on employer responses. This was sometimes because it was very senior employees whose behaviour was challenged such that there was little distinction between them as people and the employer as an entity. At other times it was because the issues seemed to merge into one another, for example in relation to what should and could have been done to prevent injury, and what the contractual duty of mutual trust and confidence required once a behavioural conflict had started. Even so, this time I was able to make the separation while accepting that there is some overlap with the findings reported in Chapter 7.

There also seemed to be notably prominent discussion of the impact on negligence liability (in contract and tort) of the limiting factor that there is no duty to take reasonable care if injury was not reasonably foreseeable.[131] This seemed to be a means by which judicial worries about keeping liability within proper bounds were brought to the surface, when these might appear elsewhere in respect of other wrongs. This feature of common law cases was especially relevant to the balancing analyses I observed about employer responses, discussed in Chapter 7, while not being wholly absent from line-drawing about the acceptability of behaviour itself.

The style of decision-making in *Rorrison v West Lothian College*[132] in which the CSOH threw out a tort claim, was of the kind I repeatedly found. Lord Reed carefully reviewed Ms Rorrison's complaints, encapsulated in her claim as 'constant harassment, criticism and humiliation'.[133] The judge categorized her various allegations as concerning first, what Ms Rorrison perceived to be unjustified criticism, second, the imposition of time pressure, and third, conflicting understandings of Ms Rorrison's role.[134] It was claimed that Ms Rorrison had suffered psychological damage to the extent that she was said still 'to become visibly distressed and tearful when thinking about her experiences with the defenders'.[135]

For Lord Reed, however, even if true, the allegations were not such that her managers should have foreseen risk of a psychiatric disorder:

They might have foreseen that [Ms Rorrison] would at times be unsatisfied, frustrated, embarrassed and upset, but that is a far cry from suffering a psychiatric disorder. Many, if not all, employees are

---

[130] See pp 112–15 in Ch 4.   [131] See the doctrinal explanation at p 93 in Ch 3.
[132] [2000] SCLR 245.   [133] ibid, 249.   [134] ibid.   [135] ibid.

liable to suffer those emotions, and others mentioned in the present case such as stress, anxiety, loss of confidence and low mood. To suffer such emotions from time to time, not least because of problems at work, is a normal part of human existence. It is only if they are liable to be suffered to such a pathological degree as to constitute a psychiatric disorder that a duty of care to protect against them can arise.[136]

Lord Reed seems here to have differed from other judges in where he drew the line between unpleasant behaviour that tort law requires employees to put up with and that which gives rise to a duty on employers to take reasonable care to prevent injury. It is striking however, that despite an arguably divergent substantive view, the mode of reasoning remained familiar.

Deep contextualization was apparent in *Long v Mercury Communications*[137] regarding the effect of a vendetta that was found to have been pursued against Mr Long by a manager and then compounded by the reaction of others. As noted earlier,[138] the analysis in this case would now be complicated by jurisdictional problems, yet entry into the factual detail would still be required in evaluating the compensatable damage.

According to this method, it mattered that Mr Long was found prior to this experience to have been 'a man of very high caliber', 'obviously very hard working', 'ambitious', and 'extremely successful'.[139] This demonstrated the serious impact of what had been done to him. In a graphic illustration of how badly a person can be affected by nastiness at work, the court now found Mr Long 'a broken man'.[140] In arriving at a figure for damages for non-pecuniary loss of £20,000, the judge treated as significant that there had been 'a sustained attack … which ran over quite a considerable period'.[141] Mr Long's humiliation had then continued after the departure of the manager who initially targeted him. Finally, instead of Mr Long being completely vindicated, the unacceptability of how he had been treated was acknowledged only 'in a very roundabout fashion and qualified by the way in which he was spoken to by the Personnel Manager'.[142] All of these elements influenced the award of a relatively large sum for pain and suffering and a considerable total award.

The background to the proceedings in *Unwin v West Sussex CC*, decided by Crane J in the HC on 13 July 2001, was another long-running, factually complex dispute. This had, as set out earlier, given rise to multiple actions, this one being in tort for damages for personal injury. The action was partially successful in that taking and renewing disciplinary action were found to have breached the employer's duty of care, foreseeably aggravating the stress from which Ms Unwin was suffering. The breach, however, was not determined to have caused an early cessation of work. The effect was relatively modest compensation of £2,500 for aggravation of Ms Unwin's depression for about six to nine months.

This result was reached after truly painstaking analysis of the extensive facts. Account was taken of the difference cumulation could make[143] and the judge went into exhaustive detail in trying to understand the various work relationships.[144] His factual analysis led Crane J at times to criticize the employer,[145] but at the same time ultimately to hold that the challenged behaviour was on the right side of the line because it fell short of bullying.[146] On this basis liability was not found for this aspect of Ms Unwin's treatment.

---

[136] ibid, 254.   [137] [2002] PIQR Q1 (QB).   [138] See pp 129–30 in Ch 5.
[139] ibid, [21].   [140] ibid.   [141] ibid, [41].   [142] ibid.
[143] See *Unwin v West Sussex CC* (QB, 13 July 2001), [11]: '[I] have borne in mind that seemingly trivial incidents may have importance if they form part of a course of conduct.'
[144] See, eg, ibid, [43], [51], [61], and [86].   [145] See, eg, [28], [43], [48], [51], and [63].
[146] See [56], [79], and [111].

Reliance on the language of bullying and harassment to distinguish acceptable and unacceptable conduct at work, however, was disapproved by Hale LJ, as she then was, in a speech for the CA in *Sandwell MBC v Jones*,[147] one of the conjoined appeals in the proceedings known as *Sutherland v Hatton*. *Sandwell* was a case which combined allegations of overwork and inappropriate conduct. The judge found Ms Sandwell to have been 'harassed' by her manager, but whether or not shortcomings as a manager amounted to 'harassment' was, in Hale LJ's view, not the point. Rather, the legal issue was whether behaviour towards Ms Jones had been reasonable in all the circumstances. This made characterizing what had been done as 'harassment' inappropriate, much as the judge's finding of liability was upheld, owing both to unreasonable work demands and an unreasonable reaction to complaints.

Yet only a few months later the language of bullying and harassment was again used as a touchstone for working out if conduct had crossed the line into unlawfulness either as negligence or breach of contract. This was in *Ellis v Eagle Place Services Ltd*,[148] ostensibly relying on *Sutherland v Hatton*. The claim was by a 'comparatively junior employed solicitor'[149] for damages for psychiatric injury. Henriques J saw liability as depending on whether or not Ms Ellis had been bullied and harassed by the partner for whom she worked, Mr McPherson. If so, this had occurred at a time when Mr McPherson must have known that she was 'at least vulnerable and fragile ... by reason of persisting grief consequent upon her mother's illness and death'.[150] The doctors for both sides were in agreement that Ms Ellis had become depressed, leading the judge to reason: 'If bullying is established then it is likely to follow that the pre existing mental illness will have been exacerbated.'[151] The judge also remarked on the need to look at the whole picture, commenting that the impact of an act may be artificially and unfairly trivialized by being considered in isolation.[152]

Another precise analysis of the considerable factual background led Henriques J to find against Ms Ellis. In arriving at this conclusion the court did not flinch from adjudicating on the fine detail of the challenged workplace conduct. The effect here was to find that Mr McPherson's behaviour had been acceptable, albeit that it had at times been difficult for the employee to experience. In this way, the court gave a highly specific illustration to employers and employees of tough management that stayed within the bounds of the legally acceptable.

This was exemplified by Henriques J's ruling about difficult feedback to Ms Ellis after she had challenged a 'nil pay review'. The judge related that Ms Ellis had in essence been told that 'she was seen as a 9–5 person, that she was a disappointment, that she had not had her best year and that her achievements as described in her memo would be treated by the [pay review] committee as laughable.'[153] This was a key event in the history that, on the judge's analysis, would have founded liability if held to have entailed bullying. In analysing whether it had, the judge noted that Mr McPherson's comments had been made in answer to steps taken by Ms Ellis. Henriques J found Mr McPherson was, in the circumstances, obliged to make unwelcome comments and hence that the incident was not bullying.[154]

---

[147] [2002] EWCA Civ 76, [2002] ICR 613.   [148] [2002] EWHC 1201 (QB).

[149] ibid, 'Introduction'.

[150] ibid, 'The Claimant', 'The psychiatric findings pre Nabarro Nathanson'.

[151] ibid. He also evaluated Ms Ellis and Mr McPherson as witnesses and more generally. See, eg ibid at 'Conclusions, Sentinel Event No 1—(Compassionate Leave Saga)', (xi) and (xii).

[152] ibid, 'The Law'.   [153] ibid, 'Conclusions, Sentinel Event No 2—(Nil Pay Review)'.

[154] ibid. There were similarities of approach in the ET (whose judgment was upheld) in *Smith v Martin & Co (Marine) Ltd* (EAT, 4 June 2003) when determining that robust performance management had not given rise to a constructive unfair dismissal.

A similar approach was taken in *Barlow v Broxbourne BC*,[155] partly in reliance on *Ellis*. Gray J accepted that if there had been bullying and harassment within the ordinary meaning of those words, liability in negligence would follow provided injury had been both reasonably foreseeable and preventable by reasonable steps.[156] The correctness in law of this approach was this time implicitly defended through an analytical split being made between claims, on the one hand, of 'bullying and intimidation' and, on the other hand, of the negligent failure to prevent stress-related illness.[157] It was in relation to the latter only that reliance was placed on *Sutherland v Hatton*.

It seemed almost routine here to comment on the need to consider the cumulative effect of what had been done.[158] There then followed the usual conscientious analysis of the factual background, assiduously contextualized. This led the judge to exonerate workplace conduct even of quite an extreme type. This followed from Gray J's evaluation of the meaning of what had been done in that particular workplace, and for those particular colleagues.

Mr Barlow was a senior employee of the council,[159] a fact that turned out to be significant. In the bullying aspect of the claim[160] he alleged that three more senior colleagues had 'created or permitted a "culture of abuse".' Some of the alleged instances were described as 'blunt and obvious', while others were argued to have been more subtle and 'designed to exert pressure on a man already clearly bending under the strain'. It was the claimant's case that this group of hierarchically superior colleagues was at a certain point 'gearing up' to get rid of him.

Gray J in fact accepted that one of these individuals was given 'on occasion to shout and swear at members of staff and to do so ... in the presence of other more junior employees'.[161] He related various incidents in which highly offensive language and insults were directed at Mr Barlow.[162] The judge commented that it was obviously undesirable for senior managers to use foul language and especially within earshot of junior employees. He went on, however, to remark:

> But the incidents which I have described must be seen in context. In so far as they involved the claimant, they are not numerous. He did not suggest that he had been sworn at by anyone other than Mr Robertson. They took place because (as Mr Robertson testified) he became exasperated at what he described as 'a catalogue of errors' in the section for which the claimant was responsible. Mr Robertson was not gratuitously picking on a vulnerable junior employee; the claimant was himself [someone] in a relatively senior position who did not strike me as particularly sensitive. Both Mr Robertson and Dr Leadbeater testified that the claimant did not appear to be upset.[163]

Overall, Gray J's conclusion was that the incidents relied on by the claimant, whether considered individually or cumulatively, did not amount to bullying or victimization such as to entitle Mr Barlow to compensation.[164] In any event, the judge did not regard injury to have been reasonably foreseeable. Mr Barlow had appeared to his senior colleagues, as he did to the judge, as 'a phlegmatic and laid-back individual and not as someone who would be likely to crumple under pressure'.[165]

---

155 [2003] EWHC 50 (QB).
156 ibid, [17]. There was also in this case, as in many others, the requirement to establish vicarious liability, but this was conceded.
157 ibid, [15] and generally.   158 ibid, [16](i).   159 See, eg, ibid, [6]–[7].
160 ibid, [18].   161 ibid, [19].
162 ibid, [20]. Eg Gray J said: 'I further accept that on a later occasion ... Mr Robertson in the presence of Mr Ferrari called the claimant "a useless cunt" and told him to "fuck off out of this office ... or I will do something that both of you fucking bastards will not like".'
163 ibid, [21].   164 ibid, [25].   165 ibid, [26].

There was the same conclusion regarding the 'stress' claim. This related to pressure put on Mr Barlow, as the judge found, to improve his performance.[166] The steps taken culminated in Mr Barlow departing in tears, described by the judge as an appalling way for his career with the borough to end.[167] Gray J was critical of management's conduct in that he doubted a barrage of documents was the best way to improve performance even by a senior employee.[168] This aspect of the claim still failed, however, because the claimant had always appeared to key senior colleagues to be 'a stolid and unflappable individual'. This precluded liability because it meant the negative effects of the employer's behaviour had not been reasonably foreseeable.[169] It is perhaps an irony that it was senior colleagues' lack of insight that relieved them and their employer from legal responsibility for harm caused by unappealing managerial conduct. Still, this provided evidence of the usual contextualized judicial line-drawing about behaviour, here leading again to tough management being categorized as acceptable.

Horkulak v Cantor FitzGerald International[170] is in some ways comparable in factual terms, while the familiar decision-making style led to a different outcome. The claim here was for constructive dismissal based only on breach of the implied duty of mutual trust and confidence. As noted earlier, enormous sums were at stake because Mr Horkulak was a senior employee with a fixed-term contract that had some time left to run and which contained no unconditional power to dismiss on notice. A liability decision for Mr Horkulak in the HC was upheld by the CA. The initial damages award, however, was overturned and the case returned to the trial court for that aspect to be re-decided. Even so, important points of legal principle in Newman J's reasoning about compensation were affirmed.

Mr Horkulak's contention was that he had been treated so badly by the president of the company, Mr Amaitis, that his employment contract had been repudiated. Mr Amaitis was alleged over some months to have conducted 'a vicious and premeditated campaign of bullying, harassment and intimidation', with the effect that Cantor FitzGerald had fundamentally breached its implied obligation of mutual trust and confidence. Cantor FitzGerald, however, argued that Mr Amaitis' behaviour had been contractually permissible in light of Mr Horkulak's shortcomings as an employee. Working out where the behavioural line fell and whether it had been crossed drew Newman J into familiar, multifaceted analysis of what had occurred.

In terms first of standards of conduct at this workplace, Newman J related that it was accepted and established that 'foul and abusive expressions and swear words' were general currency.[171] The judge argued that even in this environment, and despite the work allowing little time for thought, the words used conveyed: 'some meaning, a viewpoint ... or emphasis and an attitude going well beyond the barren coarseness of the language itself'.[172] It was against this background that the behaviour of Mr Horkulak and Mr Amaitis fell to be assessed.

Regarding personalities, Newman J extrapolated a need to exercise some caution with the claimant's evidence. He summarized his view as follows:

He has an anxious personality, but he could not have survived in the industry without a strain of tenacity and determination, which has been demonstrated by his conduct of this litigation. Unlike Mr Amaitis he has a discernible sensitivity. He would rather be liked than feared. It is likely that his use of cocaine accentuated an inclination to sensitivity to criticism and did overlay his perceptions of Mr Amaitis with elements of paranoia. I have no doubt that he felt vulnerable to the disclosure

---

[166] ibid, [39].   [167] ibid, [36].   [168] ibid, [38].   [169] ibid, [40].
[170] [2003] EWHC 1918, [2004] ICR 697.   [171] ibid, [17].   [172] ibid, [18].

of his alcohol and drug addiction and that he had the intention of concealing the evidence. But the evidence has been disclosed, the truth is out and subject to my expressed reservations I am satisfied he gave his evidence in court honestly.[173]

Note also that Newman J had already accepted that Mr Horkulak was given to foul language. While the judge treated this as a factor to be considered he did not think the claimant should for that reason be deprived of objecting to its use towards him.[174]

With regard to Mr Amaitis, there had been shifts in his evidence that Newman J said might in certain circumstances have led a court to doubt it, but he saw the situation as more complex. He observed that Mr Amaitis rarely criticized people in a way that communicated the *reason* for his negative opinion. Instead his manner conveyed the *level* of his disapproval, at the same time reinforcing his authority. Once Mr Amaitis had 'lost faith' in Mr Horkulak, therefore, the detail of any particular issue was unimportant to him. Mr Amaitis had sought at trial to answer precise points, but the judge perceived this as rationalization after the event. It may nonetheless have been possible for Mr Amaitis at the time rationally to have registered a ground for complaint. That Mr Amaitis had not done so was explained, on the judge's analysis, by his view of discussion as a sign of weakness.[175]

Overall Newman J concluded of Mr Amaitis that he was 'a dictatorial manager and executive'.[176] He had brought the habits of the trading floor to the executive and managerial level. In relation specifically to bad language Newman J concluded that:

rather than being occasional, the use of swear words, expletives, and foul and obscene language is an everyday and frequent aspect of the communications uttered by Mr Amaitis ... I do not accept that its use can be regarded as incidental or meaningless. It is commonly the language of dictatorial leadership and for Mr Amaitis it exemplifies his attitude as an employer. He does not set out to accommodate employees but to dictate to them, to require them to perform and to be available to explain themselves at any moment he requires.[177]

The effect in practice was that an employee would be outside the direct range of Mr Amaitis' outbursts only so long as he had faith in them.

These findings led to the overall conclusion that Mr Horkulak had been constructively dismissed. As the judge stated:

Even when full allowance is made for Cantor's right, acting through Mr Amaitis, to set and maintain a very strict, demanding regime of performance for its employees, I am unable to conclude that such criticisms as it had in connection with the claimant's conduct were properly raised and handled. Threats of dismissal should not be used to intimidate. Nor should they be issued in intemperate language. The level of the rebuke must be proportionate to the alleged failing on the part of the employee.[178]

Mr Amaitis was specifically criticized for doing nothing to address the problems that had led him to lose faith in Mr Horkulak. In particular it was noted that he had neither given advice nor initiated disciplinary proceedings after forming the belief that Mr Horkulak's failings at work were related to addiction to alcohol and cocaine. In any event, the judge concluded from the evidence that Mr Horkulak had not failed in 'grave or serious respects, as opposed to fault being found with his judgment and availability whenever an opportunity arose'.[179]

It had not been legally permissible for Mr Amaitis to 'assert his authority by the use of foul and abusive language which gave no chance for the claimant to respond to any

[173] ibid, [47].   [174] ibid, [18].   [175] ibid, [59].   [176] ibid, [39].
[177] ibid, [40].   [178] ibid, [70].   [179] ibid, [75].

criticism'. Neither should Mr Amaitis have continued to insist on 'his levels and stand-ards of performance where he had grounds to believe that the claimant could not attain them'.[180] Instead the contractual requirement was that problems 'should be addressed, in an appropriate manner'.[181] In the circumstances, the frequency of bad language had not sanitized its effect and Mr Horkulak had remained entitled to proper treatment irrespective of his own behavioural shortcomings.[182] Overall the judge observed, argu-ably in guidance mode, legitimate work demands must be balanced by a fair system of enforcement reflecting the particular conditions affecting the employment.[183]

We have seen that *Green v DB Group Services*[184] was another case in which very large damages were recovered, at common law and under the PHA 1997. The award was so large because Ms Green had been a high earner and was forced by the consequences of her employer's wrongs to retrain for a less lucrative career. Owen J, in familiar vein, went into considerable detail in uncovering what had happened in different time periods and with various configurations of colleagues. In determining the issues, moreover, he again used the bullying label to draw the line between lawful and unlawful conduct at work, treating it as the touchstone of tortious liability.

To begin with, Owen J ruled on conduct by a group of four female colleagues over a period of some months in which: '[Ms Green] was subjected to a relentless campaign of mean and spiteful behaviour designed to cause her distress.'[185] This was 'a deliberate and concerted campaign of bullying within the ordinary meaning of that term'.[186] In determining that what had been done caused reasonably foreseeable injury Owen J also observed that:

[s]uch behaviour when pursued relentlessly on a daily basis has a cumulative effect. It is designed to make the working environment intolerable for the victim. The stress that it creates goes far beyond that normally to be expected in the work place.[187]

It followed that there was vicarious liability in tort and under the PHA 1997.[188]

Tortious liability extended also to the employer in its own right because of manage-ment's inadequate response. According to Owen J:

[a] reasonable and responsible employer would have intervened as soon as he became aware of the problem. The claimant's managers ... simply failed to take any or any adequate steps ... In short the management was weak and ineffectual. The managers collectively closed their eyes to what was going on, no doubt in the hope that the problem would go away.[189]

There had, however, been obvious steps that would have stopped the bullying. The judge made clear that 'by whatever means the bullying could and should have been stopped',[190] also noting 'a culpable want of care' on the part of the defendant's HR department.[191]

In the next period of about eighteen months, following which Ms Green suffered the first of two breakdowns, it was the conduct of a close peer, Mr Preston, and of his boss, Mr Cummins, that came under scrutiny. Owen J was satisfied that Mr Preston undertook a concerted campaign to advance himself at the expense of Ms Green. He was disrespectful and aggressively competitive. This particularly took the form of interfering with Ms Green's work, including on occasions giving the impression that he was her

---

[180] ibid, [78].   [181] ibid.   [182] ibid, [80].
[183] ibid, [81]. See also, for a somewhat comparable example some two years earlier, *Mullins v Laughton* [2002] EWHC 2761, [2003] Ch 250.
[184] [2006] EWHC 1898 (QB), [2006] IRLR 764.   [185] ibid, [99].   [186] ibid.
[187] ibid, [105]. See also regarding the cumulative effect of Mr Preston's behaviour, [151].
[188] ibid, [99]–[101] and [105].   [189] ibid, [102].   [190] ibid, [103].
[191] ibid, [103].

manager.[192] Owen J judged Mr Preston's behaviour to fall within the bullying description, being 'domineering, disrespectful, dismissive, confrontatory, and designed to undermine and belittle'.[193] Accordingly it attracted tortious liability and was in breach of the PHA 1997.[194]

The more senior colleague, Mr Cummins, was described by the judge as a role model to Mr Preston, and 'a forceful, highly competitive and arrogant personality, dismissive of those whose work he did not respect or who did not share his overtly competitive attitude to his fellow employees'.[195] He was only found, however, probably to have influenced Mr Preston through signalling the acceptability of negative behaviour towards Ms Green.[196] Further, another event involving a senior colleague did not found liability despite the judge considering his conduct 'unjustified and deeply discourteous'.[197]

Owen J also placed other conduct towards the claimant in the months between when she returned to work and her second breakdown on the other side of the liability line. The judge was satisfied, for example, that her employers had taken reasonable steps to avoid her coming into contact with Mr Preston. Her negative reaction to seeing him and to hearing his name was in fact a continuing effect of his earlier conduct towards her rather than the consequence of a further breach of duty.[198]

Clark v CC of Essex[199] related another convoluted tale, this time of worrying treatment of a police officer by various senior colleagues. The exposition and application of the law came across as somewhat routine, in that Mr Clark was successful on a relatively straightforward analysis of tort liability for personal injury.[200] It is notable that the language of bullying again enabled the line to be drawn between workplace behaviour that was legally acceptable and which was not. In comparison, the facts were extraordinarily complicated, making it something of a feat that Tugendhat J unravelled them. Having done so, the judge found behaviour by several of Mr Clark's superior officers to have been either bullying or otherwise worthy of criticism, including for failing appropriately to respond to complaints of mistreatment.[201]

6. Conclusion

The painstaking care that goes into adjudication in British courts is evident in this strain of data, reinforcing this aspect of my findings in Chapter 4. Contrasting with the findings reported in Chapter 5 and the impression gained from exposition of the doctrine in Chapter 3, there was remarkable congruence across causes of action in judicial approaches to applying substantive behavioural rules to specific workplace situations where jurisdictional convolution allowed this to happen. Adjudicative debates and reasoning on workplace standards were also highly accessible and intelligible. The

---

[192] ibid, [149]–[150].   [193] ibid, [151].   [194] ibid, [151]–[154].
[195] ibid, [148].   [196] ibid, [155].   [197] ibid, [156].   [198] ibid, [168]–[169].
[199] [2006] EWHC 2290 (QB).
[200] Contrast the difficult legal questions raised by *Connor v Surrey CC* [2010] EWCA Civ 286, [2011] QB 429. The CA upheld the HC's finding that Surrey was liable at common law for psychiatric injury to Ms Connor, the erstwhile head-teacher of a primary school. The injury to Ms Connor was held to have been negligently caused by the LEA's response to external pressure on the school, its staff and particularly Ms Connor, including in the form of negative conduct. The legal dilemma, resolved in Ms Connor's favour by the CA on slightly divergent reasoning by the three judges, was whether there could be private law liability in circumstances where the LEA's breaches of duty had involved the exercise of public law powers.
[201] [2006] EWHC 2290 (QB), [218]–[232] and also at [199] (although the latter criticism, while it makes disturbing reading, was not relevant to Mr Clark's claim).

contextual detail into which courts entered may have been extraordinary, yet regardless of the particular behavioural rule being applied, it led to the kind of discussion that anyone might have, in any working environment, to reason whether or not behaviour at work had been acceptable. Indeed, this adjudicative approach was mirrored in what senior managers said about how, irrespective of legal influence, they think through the rights and wrongs of workplace conduct (although the similarity of reasoning approach did not extend to judicial and organizational reflections about employer responses).[202]

Even so, it is not permissible to conclude that the differences between the various legal rules about workplace conduct made no difference to judicial assessments of wrongfulness in specific situations, just as I could not tell in Chapter 5 if different litigation strategies would have delivered different outcomes. These data nevertheless raise the distinct possibility, assuming that jurisdictional problems do not block substantive decision-making, that similar adjudicative approaches between causes of action and courts lead to similar assessments of blameworthiness and, hence, to the same conclusions about liability. Note, however, that this would still produce divergent remedial decisions because of differences between regimes and courts in that regard even when adjudicating the same cause of action. Also, there are perhaps more likely to be different outcomes when equality rules are applied, because the need to show a link between negative conduct and either identity or the commission of a protected act is apt to result in similar reasoning arriving at different liability conclusions.

Be those uncertainties as they may, the differentiations between legal requirements, jurisdictions, and remedial rules regarding individual labour and equality rights are rendered even more questionable by the findings reported in this chapter. Chapters 3 and 5 showed the harms of complexity and adjudicative arbitrariness jurisdictional variety causes, while my interview study suggests that the consequent fine-grained legal distinctions do not get through to organizations.[203] The futility of all this convolution is accentuated by de-emphasis on differences between the rules once judges engage in substantive adjudication. Instead, at this adjudicative point distinctions were minimized with common, accessible reasoning processes across jurisdictions, all geared to working out whether specific instances of conduct at work were acceptable or had crossed a behavioural line to such an extent as to attract legal censure.

What one is again left with are quite general legal norms of reasonableness, fairness, and egalitarianism at work, this time operating through the medium of higher court adjudication. Beyond the regrettable intricacy in which Chapters 3 and 5 showed the law in this area to be mired, this depicts legal process presenting a challenging, context-sensitive, and thoughtful account of lawful workplace conduct. It shows, in other words, judges acquitting what is arguably their core function, of evaluating knotty factual situations against general justice norms, with insight and integrity. This aspect of how courts handle individual labour and equality rights appears therefore to have wide-ranging emancipatory potential. The most the vital question however remains, especially taking account of the high and probably increasing proportion of unsolved problems at work, what all this endeavour is ultimately delivering for individuals, organizations, and society at large.

---

[202] See pp 203–205 and 210 in Ch 8 below.
[203] See pp 197–204 and 209–210 in Ch 8 and p 250 in Ch 10.

7

Legal Themes in Case Law about Behavioural Conflict at Work III

Consistency in Analysing Employer Responses

In this chapter, I offer further support for my overall finding of a remarkably consistent adjudicative approach by courts when decision-making moved beyond jurisdictional issues to applying behavioural rules to specific workplace situations. The chapter goes through examples that illustrate the second set of boundaries that judges, irrespective of the court, cause of action, or timing, treated as essential to this aspect of their decision-making. These examples all show courts determining the line between acceptable and unacceptable employer responses either to the fact of, or to complaints about, workplace behaviour and the use of recurrent decision-making tropes to do so:

(1) There was the same thorough contextualization to determine the meaning of what had happened and, hence, on which side of the line an employer's conduct fell.

(2) Judges' musings frequently led them explicitly or implicitly to guide employers about the law's requirements. In this mode judges seemed to balance a wide range of interests to decide on the precise standards that governed a situation. The interests considered included those of claimants, of the rest of the workforce, of management, and of society more broadly.

Claims under the PHA 1997, however, are not separately considered because, as explained earlier, decision-making regarding the two sets of boundary lines was so intertwined. Guidance to employers was often implicit simply on vicarious liability being attributed, in the signal this gave that conduct is within employers' responsibility to prevent and address. Some explicit guidance, however, came from later decisions on the limits to what was required of employers. A good example is *Dickie v Flexcon Glenrothes Ltd*[1] which made clear that poorly executed but genuine management is not unlawful harassment under the PHA 1997.

It is important also to reiterate that the degree of description in this chapter is to give readers a sense of the material on which I base my findings. It seeks fully to back these up while not exhaustively recounting every supportive feature in the judgments. In addition, any hint of a counter-example that I found is included. This mode of exposition is therefore not in any sense meant to imply a generally uncritical approach to relevant law and legal process, but merely to justify this strand of my findings and argument.

---

[1] [2009] GWD 35-602 (Sheriff Court).

1. Statutory Unfair Dismissal

Boundary setting about the acceptability of employers' responses as opposed to about particular instances of allegedly poor conduct figured prominently in adjudication about unfair dismissal. As ever, minute factual analysis was central and I found a marked strain of situation-specific balancing by judges to determine, and to guide employers about, the content of their obligations and the limits to what the law requires. This built on the aspect of the judgments, more common in analyses of behaviour itself, that emphasized the significance of events occurring in a sequence.

It mattered here that a series of acts, potentially including some trivial ones, might combine to constitute a repudiation of an employment contract and hence, most probably, a constructive unfair dismissal. It has been established elsewhere that the 'last straw' provoking an employee's departure need not itself be a breach of contract.[2] *Omilaju v Waltham Forest LBC*[3] took the doctrine even further, holding that a 'last straw' need not even be unreasonable or blameworthy. The CA explained this finding as follows:

The quality that the final straw must have is that it should be an act in a series whose cumulative effect is to amount to a breach of the implied term. I do not use the phrase 'an act in a series' in a precise or technical sense. The act does not have to be of the same character as the earlier acts. Its essential quality is that, when taken in conjunction with the earlier acts on which the employee relies, it amounts to a breach of the implied term of trust and confidence. It must contribute something to that breach, although what it adds may be relatively insignificant.[4]

It is true that the CA reiterated that whether there had been a breach must be judged objectively and noted an employee's subjective sense of hurt could not turn an innocuous act into a 'last straw'.[5] It would also be unlikely in practice for behaviour that was 'perfectly reasonable and justifiable' to constitute a 'last straw'.[6] Even so, aside from the judges ascribing importance to the relationships between events in a sequence, this guided employers to expect highly contextualized scrutiny of their responses to a problem against the multifaceted trust and confidence norm.

In *Blackburn with Darwen Borough Council v Stanley*[7] the Employment Appeal Tribunal (EAT) went into typical guidance mode, filling in the content of contractual obligations[8]

---

[2] This is another instance in law of a single event being seen as sufficiently serious to be characterized as wrongful, unlike in organizational psychological investigations of bullying. Here, the concept of constructive dismissal allows for one incident to precipitate the lawful departure of an employee and consequent liability on the part of the employer. See n 14 and accompanying text in Ch 2 and pp 145–46 in Ch 6.

[3] [2004] EWCA Civ 1493, [2005] ICR 481.   [4] ibid, [19].

[5] Reasoning from this proposition was in fact the basis on which it was found by the CA that Mr Omilaju had not been constructively dismissed, in agreement with the ET (ibid, [26]–[30]).

[6] ibid, [26].   [7] EAT, 20 January 2005.

[8] See also *Fernandez v Office of the Parliamentary Commissioner for Administration and Health Service Commissioners* (EAT, 15 February 2005), *Thornett v Scope* [2006] EWCA Civ 1600, [2007] ICR 236, and *Birmingham CC v Samuels* (EAT, 24 October 2007) for successful unfair dismissal claims by employees who had been dismissed after internal investigations had found their interpersonal conduct to have been wanting. Each provided contextualized illustrations of the law on unfair dismissal evaluating employers' responses in such circumstances. In *Fernandez* dismissal was seen by a majority of the ET (upheld on the unfair dismissal aspect of the appeal) to have been too strong a sanction. In *Thornett* liability resided in the failure to do more to resolve the interpersonal difficulties, much as it was accepted that the employer faced a very difficult managerial situation and that Dr Thornett had made a 25 per cent contribution to her dismissal. Finally, aside from findings also of race discrimination and victimization in *Samuels*, there were criticisms of the disciplinary steps taken against him as being, eg, 'totally harsh and inflexible' [47], unreasonable [49], and pursued with 'undue haste' [52]. This was despite the EAT reporting at [54] that the ET had noted Mr Samuels to be 'literally the author of a lot of his misfortune', with the effect that contributory fault would be a serious issue in relation to remedy.

where employers have a 'bespoke' policy to deal with workplace bullying. The council, against whom we have seen that Ms Stanley was successful in a claim for constructive unfair dismissal, appealed the ruling that it should have done more about her complaints after it introduced this kind of policy. The employer argued that it could not be criticized because the claimant had not activated the bullying procedure. While the employer accepted that implied contractual obligations to support employees and reasonably to investigate complaints were not entirely displaced, they argued that law should treat the policy as shaping what could reasonably be required of them.[9]

The EAT saw the policy as representing: 'a highly commendable approach by a responsible local authority in conjunction with its recognised trade unions to very real problems faced by people at work ... and ... a sensitive and important development in the way in which these issues are handled'.[10] More than this, a dedicated policy should normally be used, all the more so when agreed by trade unions.[11] Striking a different balance between employer, collective, and individual workplace perspectives than the policy embodied, however, the Tribunal did not see its existence as removing 'the fundamental obligation to take reasonable steps to ensure that an employee is supported in times of difficulty'.[12] The upshot was that the employer's ongoing failure to remedy Ms Stanley's complaints of bullying and harassment gave rise to a constructive dismissal.

GMB Trade Union v Brown, the first unfair dismissal action to be caught in the dismissal/post-dismissal remedies trap,[13] also vividly demonstrated the startling potential consequences of judges' intensity of focus on specific situations. This led the ET and EAT to conclude, notwithstanding the rich irony, that an employer's adherence to the letter of their dignity at work procedure was so fundamental a breach of their implicit obligations as to repudiate Ms Brown's employment contract.

The employee had objected to going through the first stage of the procedure because this involved raising her complaints with the person to whom they related. The ET rejected the union's argument that there could not be a constructive dismissal where there was a dedicated policy and the employee had not used it.[14] It drew on its status as an 'industrial jury', at the same time guiding other employers and employees against rigidly sticking to written procedures:

It is widespread and good industrial practice to adopt a flexible approach to grievance and disciplinary procedures in circumstances where the rigid application would result in hardship or potential unfairness ... We do not criticize the respondent's procedures as such ... Our conclusion is that the respondent did in the particular circumstances of this case, by its unreasonable unwillingness to assess the effect of its procedures on the Claimant and its unwillingness to relax those procedures

---

[9] ibid, [16].   [10] ibid, [6].   [11] ibid, [20].

[12] ibid. It is interesting to compare the approach in *Walton v Image Creative Ltd* (EAT, 16 August 2002) in which it will be recalled there were stark evidential disputes about the treatment of a junior employee at a tiny company. Ms Walton's claims for constructive unfair dismissal and under the Sex Discrimination Act (SDA) 1975 were unsuccessful. The Employment Tribunal (ET), affirmed by the EAT, carefully contextualized events to determine that there had been no repudiatory breach and rejected the sex discrimination claim. Here it was the small size of the employer that especially influenced the ET's view of what could reasonably be expected of both employer and employee, eg as follows: '[20] ... This was a small organization with four employees which muddled its way through each day ... We therefore found as a matter of fact that the circumstances in which the Applicant worked, finding that she had to do some cleaning, some washing up, some errand running and not having her own work station, were not in any way connected to her sex, nor could they be said to be intolerable working conditions. They were the working conditions in which everybody worked because it was a small company with key tasks in the form of editing.'

[13] EAT, 16 October 2007.   [14] ibid, [29]–[30].

so as to allow her to progress them beyond Stage 1, in effect prevent … the Claimant from airing her grievance effectively and promptly.[15]

The EAT refused to overturn the ET, commenting that the key issue was that the manager knew any further meetings with him would be likely to damage the claimant's health further.[16]

There was a long history in *Geary v Amec Logistics & Support Services Ltd.*[17] Mr Geary complained over some years about conduct towards him before his absence on sick leave for about two months and then his resignation on receipt of the investigation report regarding his grievance. Mr Geary's subsequent constructive unfair dismissal claim was successful although others were not.

The investigation had taken some time and 'considerable resources', some forty people having been interviewed.[18] It uncovered evidence that Mr Geary had been bullied and harassed although the investigators made no explicit findings in this regard.[19] What caused Mr Geary's departure was not the rejection of his grievance but that evidence supporting his claims appeared to have been ignored. Before he saw the report the employer's HR manager told him verbally and then in writing that there was no evidence of bullying and harassment. The relevant sentence in the letter was that 'there is no evidence that would constitute bullying and harassment'.[20] When Mr Geary himself saw the report he realized that it did in fact recount such evidence. The ET recorded that he felt devastated by this discovery, concluding that the investigators had ignored evidence in his favour. The ET agreed and found there to have been a constructive dismissal,[21] reasoning as follows:

Mr Geary had made very serious allegations that he had been bullied and harassed … He had made those allegations sincerely and trusted that his employer would investigate them fairly. Although the respondent commendably poured much time and effort into the investigation the final report concluded that there was no evidence of bullying and harassment: although in fact there had been … We consider that it must seriously undermine the relationship of trust and confidence when—in a matter so emotive, stressful and important to the employee as an allegation of bullying—the employer asserts that there is no evidence to support the allegation when there is … There was no reasonable or proper cause for the respondent to deny the existence of such evidence and accordingly the respondent is in breach of the implied term of trust and confidence.[22]

The EAT refused to overturn the ET decision, commenting that it was for the Tribunal to 'weigh up [what it found to have happened] in the context of the history … and of the case as a whole'.[23] In any event it considered that in the circumstances, Mr Geary could only conclude that his complaints were not being taken seriously.[24]

There is considerable subtlety in the way the judges here drew the line between what was and was not acceptable for the employer to do. Both tribunals acknowledged the effort and time put into dealing with Mr Geary's grievance, but this did not stop them concluding that the employer had repudiated the employment relationship by failing in its overarching obligation, inherent in the implied duty of trust and confidence, to take the claimant seriously. A clear signal was also again thereby given to employers that the

---

[15] ibid, [32].   [16] ibid, [39].   [17] EAT, 1 November 2007.   [18] ibid, [13].
[19] See the comment by the EAT at ibid, [17]: '[F]indings in relation to all of the allegations were made except in relation to the allegation of bullying … The report … surprisingly makes no findings at all beyond setting out the evidence that had been collected, but evidence there undoubtedly was of bullying or harassment.'
[20] ibid, [14].   [21] ibid, [15].   [22] ibid, [34].   [23] ibid, [47].
[24] ibid, [49].

mutual trust and confidence duty imports significant substantive obligations irrespective of the procedural position.[25]

2. Statutory Wrongs of Discrimination I: Discriminatory Harassment

Assessment of employers' responses either to the fact of, or to allegations about, discriminatory harassment occurred in a variety of legal contexts, not always related to equality law claims. Irrespective of the technical legal terms in which courts were required to determine where the boundaries lay, the judgments bore the usual hallmarks of profound contextualization and the pragmatic balancing of points of view to find the limits of what was required and to guide employers as to their obligations. This came across mostly from 'old-style' discriminatory harassment cases since there were so few new-style ones. Still, the analysis in Chapter 6 showed line-drawing about managerial conduct under the new law to overlap with this form of decision-making.

In *Driskel v Peninsula Business Services Ltd*[26] the EAT used the typical methodologies to overturn the ET's rejection of a direct sex discrimination claim[27] and to assess the employer's response to complaints. Even so, contextualization led the judges to limit what the law required. The effect was that dismissing the claimant rather than her harasser was found not to be statutorily unfair, nor unlawful victimization, since her refusal to work with him had put the employer in an 'impasse'. This conclusion resulted from balancing Ms Driskel's situation with the facts as found that the employer's 'genuine' internal investigation had exonerated the manager, he would not move voluntarily, the employer had tried to find the claimant acceptable employment, and finally, it had sought to persuade the two employees to find a compromise.[28]

Smith v Zeneca (Agrochemicals) Ltd[29] exhibited similar features in dealing with vicarious liability for sexually harassing conduct. A claim was settled against the individual employee, a Mr L.[30] An action against the employer, however, was unsuccessful because the ET, upheld by the EAT, found the statutory defence was made out. This time an ET judgment, excerpted by the EAT, illustrated judicial line-drawing regarding how an employer should conduct itself, with contextualized assessment and pragmatic balancing again leading to the conclusion that the employer's actions had been sufficient.

The precise circumstances were that Ms Smith had worked for Zeneca as a telephonist/receptionist, initially temporarily and then on a one-year fixed-term contract. The ET found she was the victim of 'numerous incidents of unwarranted sexual harassment' over six months.[31] The employer was not, however, aware of this until Ms Smith

---

[25] See the EAT also in (implicit) guidance mode in: first, *Smiths Detection Watford Ltd v Berriman* (EAT, 9 August 2005), in which it stressed, particularly relying on the lay members' industrial relations experience, that the appointment of a highly regarded independent mediator 'reflected well on the Respondent and the way in which it approached the Claimant's complaints'; second, *West Coast Trains Ltd v Tombling* (EAT, 3 April 2009), where the manner in which an investigation was carried out (eg questioning of the claimant that 'read like an interrogation') was held to have contributed to the unfairness of the dismissal.

[26] [2000] IRLR 151 (EAT).

[27] See on contextualizing the allegations (including in the sense of considering the totality of what had happened), ibid, [3]–[4], [12](a), (d), (3), and (4); on repetition, [12](d)(3); and on 'obvious' incidents, [12](d)(3).

[28] ibid, [16]–[17].   [29] [2000] ICR 800 (EAT).   [30] ibid, [2] and [7].

[31] ibid.

made a formal complaint. An investigation and disciplinary proceedings followed which determined summary dismissal to be warranted, but Mr L was given, and took, the option of immediate early retirement without the privileges that usually accompanied this.[32]

The ET observed that the employer operated an equal opportunities policy to which there was detailed reference in various publications to employees. These referred 'in some detail to sexual harassment and [to] how staff who feel they are being harassed should respond'.[33] These were said by the ET not to be only reference documents, but rather:

> their widespread circulation amongst all employees, including managers, were instrumental in creating a culture which made all employees aware of what was expected of them in all aspects of their employment and in particular the culture of equal opportunity which was free from discrimination of any kind.[34]

Knowledge of the culture did not come so much from formal courses but instead from discussions in workplace meetings. Mr L himself agreed that he understood the company's philosophy of non-harassment and anti-discrimination. There had been only two complaints of sexual harassment in the three years prior, despite the total workforce numbering 2,005 with only slightly more men than women.[35] More specifically, while an earlier allegation against Mr L had not been proved, he had been warned about his management style, his conduct monitored and a later similar recruit assigned to a different manager with the reason explained.[36] There had further been no additional complaints and no others emerged in the investigation leading to Mr L's departure.

In deciding that the employer had established the section 41(3) SDA 1975 defence, the ET observed that it had 'a clear and unambiguous policy on equal opportunities'.[37] The ET was 'satisfied that the employers took steps to ensure that management had the responsibility for implementation of the company policies' and that they provided specific, relevant training.[38] In the ET's view, short of ensuring that Mr L 'was shadowed by senior management at all times, which would not be practical or reasonable, it is difficult to see what else they could do' to prevent the unlawful conduct.[39]

3. Statutory Wrongs of Discrimination II: General Discrimination Cases

Despite the range of ways that claims in this category were put, evaluation of employer responses showed the usual hallmarks both of contextualization and balancing analyses to determine and explain the content and limits of employer obligations. The ET in *Vento v CC of West Yorkshire Police*[40] used reasoning about remedies to give full vent to its disapproval of the employer. Having related the serious effects of the unlawful behaviour, it noted that the Chief Constable had apologized late in the day and individuals to whom recommendations had been directed never had. Overall, the ET characterized the attitudes of the Chief Constable and his officers as one of 'institutional

---

[32] ibid, [4].   [33] ibid.   [34] ibid.

[35] But see p 51 in Ch 2, p 189 in Ch 8 and p 229 in Ch 9 that low levels of complaint are not necessarily a good guide to the absence of problems.

[36] See on this particular point ibid, [9]. Otherwise see ibid, [4].   [37] ibid, [9].

[38] ibid.   [39] ibid.   [40] [2002] EWCA Civ 1871, [2003] ICR 318.

denial', refusing to see what was wrong with their treatment of Ms Vento.[41] Unusually, aggravated damages were found payable and, while the overall award for non-pecuniary loss was reduced by the CA to £32,000, this still included £5,000 under that head. The CA also made clear that it took no less dim a view of the 'persistent unlawful discrimination'.[42]

The troubling factual findings in *Miles v Gilbank*[43] were related earlier. Two aspects of the decision are notable here. First, it contained important general lessons about individual and collective responsibility for discriminatory conduct, especially amongst senior employees. Second, the remedial findings had features that are familiar from liability decision-making in this area.

The points on individual and collective responsibility arose in regrettably technical form owing to the practical issues in the case. The problem was that Ms Gilbank's corporate employer, Quality Hairdressing Ltd (trading as Hollywood), had been struck off the register of companies and could not pay compensation. The sole director of the company and manager of the hair salon, Ms Miles, did not dispute on appeal that she was personally liable for her own discriminatory acts, but she objected to the ET and EAT finding that she was jointly and severally liable with the company. She argued that this in effect made her personally liable, not only for her own unlawfully discriminatory conduct, but also for that of other employees.[44]

It was earlier explained that UK anti-discrimination legislation casts the vicarious liability net wide and provides for the personal liability of employees through deeming them to have aided and abetted unlawful acts for which their employers are vicariously liable, including those in respect of which the employer would have a statutory defence.[45] Arden LJ extrapolated from the case law that 'in order to "aid" an act of unlawful discrimination a person must have done more than merely create an environment in which discrimination can occur'.[46] In this case the threshold was crossed because the ET found not only that a culture been allowed to develop, but that this was the result of Ms Miles' behaviour. As Arden LJ observed:

> By implication, she had assisted the other managers to act as they did because she was dismissive of Ms Gilbank's complaints against the other managers in their presence and in addition committed acts of discrimination herself, and thus made it clear that such acts were also acceptable for the other managers … Ms Miles could have stopped the discriminatory conduct of both herself and other managers by giving appropriate instructions and acting appropriately herself. Her acts were not ambiguous so that Ms Miles could assert that the managers must have misconstrued what she meant.[47]

Arden LJ did not think the EAT analogy with a senior manager observing and participating in bullying was strictly accurate in that Ms Miles did not, on the Tribunal's findings, actually participate in the discriminatory conduct of her other managers. Still, it was sufficient that she must have known this was happening and that she encouraged it.[48]

---

[41] ibid, [17]–[19].
[42] ibid, [64].   [43] [2006] EWCA Civ 543, [2006] ICR 1297.
[44] See in particular ibid, in the judgment of Sedley LJ, at [49].
[45] The relevant provisions in this case were ss 41 and 42 in the SDA 1975. See further pp 75 and 85 in Ch 3.
[46] [2006] EWCA Civ 543, [2006] ICR 1297, [33] commenting on the HL decision on equivalent RRA 1976 provisions in *Anyanwu v South Bank Student Union (Commission for Racial Equality intervening)* [2001] ICR 391.
[47] ibid, [36].
[48] Sedley LJ reached the same conclusion on slightly different grounds. Chadwick LJ agreed with both Arden and Sedley LJJ, while also giving a separate speech in which he commented, ibid, [65],

The CA thereby gave strong direction to employers and managers that they are responsible for behaviour at their workplaces. This was further reinforced by the compensation analysis. There was a total award of £29,050.60 which included £25,000 for injury to feelings at the top of the bracket for the most serious cases.[49] Ms Miles argued that this was manifestly excessive because the discrimination was relatively short-lived and had no long-term effects. The award was nonetheless upheld.

Only Arden LJ gave detailed reasons for doing so.[50] She placed importance on closely contextualized analysis and on wrongdoing having been repeated, as was common in assessing the acceptability of conduct itself.[51] She noted that the CA had previously contemplated that an award could exceed the guidelines, with the effect that the law as it had developed catered for even more serious cases. She commented that there had been multiple acts of discrimination and that the conduct of Ms Miles was found to have been deliberate, very hurtful, and very distressing. There was also added seriousness because the well-being of her unborn child was implicated, imposing an extra layer of stress on an expectant mother.

In *South London Healthcare NHS Trust v Rubeyi*[52] there was no liability for termination of the complainant's employment under either the RRA 1976 or the 2003 Religion and Belief Regulations. The judgment especially put pragmatic limits, balancing the varied interests in play, on what was required of the employer in dealing with a long-standing behavioural conflict.[53] An independent investigation was praised by the ET and the report's factual account and opinions accepted. These included the recommendation, in all the circumstances and despite there being substance in elements of Dr Rubeyi's grievance, that it should be she who left the department either by internal transfer or by her departure being 'facilitated'.[54] In turn, the EAT overturned the ET's conclusion that there had been victimization, asserting that there was no basis for the finding that the employer had been influenced by Dr Rubeyi's discrimination complaints in taking the independent investigator's advice.[55]

---

that his reasons 'do not, I think, differ in substance from the reasons which have led each of the other members of the court to the same conclusion.' My own reading of the speeches is that Sedley LJ's legal analysis was different to that of Arden and Chadwick LJJ, such that it is Arden LJ's speech that contained the ratio.

[49] *Vento* (n 40) and pp 87–89 in Ch 3.   [50] *Miles* (n 43), [42].

[51] See also the reasoning in *Prison Service and Others v Johnson* [1997] ICR 275 (EAT) by which the EAT upheld awards of £21,000 for injury to feelings and £7,500 in aggravated damages. The compensation for injury to feelings included awards of £500 each against individual colleagues who the ET had judged should bear personal responsibility for their unlawful actions. On the question of aggravation, the EAT said, at [287], of the employer's response to Mr Johnson's complaints that '[i]nstead of providing the applicant with a remedy for the wrongs which he had suffered, they added to his injury by attributing all his problems to his own defects of personality. We think that this was a true case of aggravation; a case where the employer's actions rubbed salt in the applicant's wounds.' This is another graphic example, in keeping with other evidence including in my interview study (see pp 17 and 44–45 in Ch 2, pp 191, 193-94 and 209 in Ch 8 and pp 231–33 in Ch 9), of an employer turning on someone for making a complaint, on which see further at p 111 in Ch 4, and also ns 60 and 65 in Ch 6 for other examples. In *D Watt (Shetland) Ltd v Reid Appeal* (EAT, 25 September 2001) analogous reasoning was used to uphold compensation of £7,500 for injury to feelings but an award of £2,500 aggravated damages was overturned because these are not available in Scotland.

[52] EAT, 2 March 2010.

[53] *Lambeth LBC v Owolade* (EAT, 30 November 2004) arguably contained a counterpoint. Despite scrutiny and criticism by the ET of the claimant's conduct (in the course of recounting a tangled history), Lambeth LBC was found liable for automatically unfairly dismissing Mr Owolade for taking part in the activities of a trade union and for victimizing him contrary to the RRA 1976.

[54] ibid, [15]–[17].   [55] ibid, [26]–[34].

4. Unlawful Conduct in Contract and Tort

The common law judgments considered in this section are those where the emphasis was more on employer responses than alleged poor behaviour. Still, it was sometimes difficult to separate the strands of reasoning and there is some overlap with material covered in Chapter 6. It was notably even clearer in this context that the limiting factor of there being no duty to take reasonable care if injury was not reasonable foreseeable, was an important means by which judges engaged in balancing analyses to determine and explain the content and limits of employers' obligations.

Waters v Commissioner of Police of The Metropolis,[56] as explained earlier, was important for recognizing that there may be common law liability if an employer knew or could foresee that the conduct of some employees might harm others. The behaviour towards Ms Waters was said to have included ostracism, 'advice' to leave the police force, harassment, and victimization. Lord Slynn of Hadley, with the agreement of the other four Law Lords, disagreed with the courts below that the claim should be struck out because what was alleged to have been done could not have injured Ms Waters. While he accepted that many of the individual acts were most unlikely on their own to have been harmful, he noted that it was the effect of cumulation that the claimant emphasized.[57] Still, aside from helpfully reviewing the case law, Lord Hutton specifically referred to the boundary between unpleasantness that employees should accept and that which required their employers to some extent to protect them. In this way he evoked courts' balancing interests in the way I repeatedly observed, such that not every course of victimization or bullying by fellow employees would, on his analysis, give rise to a claim.[58]

The idea of work as a place in which a measure of interpersonal difficulty may have to be tolerated was again expressed in *Garrett v London Borough of Camden*.[59] Simon Brown LJ, concurring with the main speech by Tuckey LJ (with whom Mance LJ also agreed), noted the difficulty of a claim in negligence based on work-related stress. He attributed this to the requirements that injury be both reasonable foreseeable and preventable by reasonable steps, saying that:

[m]any, alas, suffer breakdowns and depressive illnesses and a significant proportion could doubtless ascribe some at least of their problems to the strains and stresses of their work situation: be it simple overworking, the tensions of difficult relationships, career prospect worries, fears or feelings of discrimination or harassment, to take just some examples. Unless, however, there was a real risk of breakdown which the claimant's employers ought reasonably to have foreseen and which they ought properly to have averted, there can be no liability.[60]

It is significant in this excerpt that he was clearly including much more than workload issues.

This claim was in fact another drawn out, wide-ranging dispute. Tuckey LJ exhaustively related the history, criticized some of the conditions in which Mr Garrett had to work and yet did not find liability. Rather, he concluded that responsibility for problems was shared:

Standing back from the detail, it is quite clear that the conditions in which the appellant was working during the relevant time between 1992 and 1994 were chaotic and counterproductive, but this was partly of the appellant's own making. With the benefit of hindsight, more effective management was required to bring the situation under control, but that may have been easier said

---

[56] [2000] UKHL 50, [2000] 1 WLR 1607.   [57] ibid, 1611.   [58] ibid, 1616.
[59] [2001] EWCA Civ 395.   [60] ibid, [63].

than done given the catalogue of complaints and counter complaints which those involved were entitled to have investigated through grievance procedures, which the applicant and others refused to co-operate with until the end of 1994.[61]

Despite negative comment about management, therefore, no tort liability was found on the court reasoning that injury to Mr Garrett was not reasonably foreseeable.

Merelie v Newcastle PCT,[62] mentioned earlier, contained a quite remarkable analysis of a long-running and exceptionally tortuous behavioural dispute. Underhill J painstakingly analysed a considerable number of events stretching over a period of years and involving many people. The evaluation of what the employers and others did in turn provided implicit guidance about how people should, at least in terms of the law of contract and tort, deal with intricate behavioural disputes.

In a classic example of the contextualizing I consistently observed, great care was taken to grasp and analyse the various strands in the history and there was prominent analysis of the main personalities.[63] For example, Underhill J's consideration of character led him to find against the claimant on the background factual question whether she had been either sexually or generally harassed by her line manager, Mr Ferguson. Of this relationship the judge observed:

It is impossible now [either] to reconstruct how the deterioration in the relationship between the Claimant and Mr. Ferguson started or to apportion blame. It may perhaps be that Mr. Ferguson was at times rather insensitive in dealing with the Claimant … but I am satisfied that there was no conduct on his part which could fairly be described as harassment. I base that conclusion partly on my assessment of the Claimant and Mr. Ferguson as people and as witnesses but partly also on the views of Mr. Ferguson's colleagues, several of whom both at the time and in their evidence to me paid tribute to him as a fair and conscientious manager.[64]

This conclusion was despite the judge's acceptance that Mr Ferguson had taken 'a closer interest in what [the claimant] was doing' as problems accumulated, as well as taking 'fairly full notes of most of his conversations with her'.[65] The judge regarded these actions as entirely natural in the context of this problematic relationship. Equally, he accepted that Mr Ferguson may at times have shown impatience or exasperation with what he perceived to be unreasonable conduct and over time had developed a fairly strong antipathy towards Ms Merelie.[66]

The key substantive issues in the common law element of the claim[67] were whether the employer had either breached Ms Merelie's contract or had acted negligently towards her first, in its response in 2000 to a set of complaints by a group of hierarchically subordinate colleagues, second, in failing to deal with Ms Merelie's formal grievance about the employer's reaction to the complaints, and third, in the way the employer handled those complaints in disciplinary action against Ms Merelie regarding her conduct after the employer's decision not to investigate them.[68] These issues, however, fell to be decided in light of the extensive background, of which the poor relationship with Mr Ferguson was an important part.[69] Decisions on these points were marked by pragmatic consideration of the range of interests in play, not least giving a strong indication to other employers that sight of the wood of reasonable workplace procedures and substantive decision-making should never be obscured by the trees of escalating conflict.

---

[61] ibid, [53].   [62] [2006] EWHC 1433 (Admin).   [63] ibid, [27].
[64] ibid, [54].   [65] ibid, [55].   [66] ibid.
[67] See pp 113–14 in Ch 4 regarding the other aspects of the litigation.   [68] ibid, [6]–[9].
[69] ibid, eg, [10] and [25].

Underhill J found the initial decision by Ms Prendergast, another manager, not to investigate the year 2000 complaints to have been 'entirely reasonable'.[70] There had been progress in dealing with the dispute between Ms Merelie and Mr Ferguson that created a strong case for not 'rocking the boat'.[71] The judge commented that with hindsight, it might have been preferable for aspects of Ms Merelie's treatment to have been different. Still, he found that Ms Prendergast had made reasonable decisions 'in good faith in a delicate situation'.[72] There was no express contractual right to have the matter addressed in another way and no breach of the implied duty of mutual trust and confidence.[73] The reasonableness findings regarding Ms Prendergast's conduct were also fatal to the negligence claim.[74]

Regarding the failure to respond to the formal grievance by Ms Merelie about the handling of the complaints made in 2000, Underhill J again found no breach of the implied duty of mutual trust and confidence. He observed that the implied duty could not create 'a general obligation to investigate or make findings on any factual dispute relating to the employment which the employee wishes to have investigated'.[75] While there could be such an obligation in the circumstances of a particular case, this was not so here because it was not clear that the relationship would continue and the outstanding matters might need to be addressed only if it was to be ongoing.[76] At the same time there was no breach of an express contractual term. Even if the grievance procedure were part of the contract, there was no liability because the procedure could not 'reasonably be understood as imposing an absolute obligation on the Trust to investigate and reach a conclusion on any and every complaint that an employee might choose to make'.[77] The judge reasoned that there was no obligation to operate the grievance procedure if an issue was frivolous, trivial, or otherwise did not call for investigation, as in this situation.[78] As before, the reasonableness of what had been done additionally disposed of the negligence claim.[79] Finally, the disciplinary proceedings had neither breached the employment contract nor been negligent in failing to deal in full with the earlier complaints. In essence again this was because the approach taken was held to have been reasonable.[80]

In *Sayers v Cambridgeshire CC*[81] there was another long history, this time intermingling workload issues with interpersonal difficulties between the claimant and her line manager, Mr Wrycroft. The claim was ultimately unsuccessful, implicit guidance being given both about what constitutes acceptable behaviour at work and regarding appropriate managerial responses to conflict. Ramsay J observed that the council's handling of a formal grievance by Ms Sayers in 2000 had overcome concerns she then had about 'Mr Wrycroft's manner and the fact that he was undermining and belittling her efforts'.[82] The judge found that the problems had 'to all intents and purposes, disappeared' several months before the situation again flared up at a 2002 supervision session.[83] The judge analysed the dealings between these two individuals, placing importance on Ms Sayers' senior position and on differing management styles:

I do not consider that Mr Wrycroft's attitude after the grievance [in] 2000 can be described as bullying or otherwise criticized. Mrs Sayers was in a senior post as an operations manager and Mr Wrycroft, as Assistant director, was her line manager. Having observed them when they gave evidence, they clearly have different approaches to management ... As the development of their relationship after the 2000 grievance shows, they both learnt from each other.[84]

---

[70] ibid, [134].   [71] ibid.   [72] ibid.   [73] ibid, [172].   [74] ibid, [181].
[75] ibid, [177].   [76] ibid.   [77] ibid, [178](2).   [78] ibid.   [79] ibid, [181].
[80] ibid, [179]–[181].   [81] [2006] EWHC 2029, [2007] IRLR 29.   [82] ibid, [117].
[83] ibid.   [84] ibid, [216].

Mr Wrycroft did, however, behave 'inaptly' at the later supervision session, commenting that Ms Sayers was 'unmanageable',[85] the meeting in turn contributing to Ms Sayers' ill health.[86] Mr Wrycroft's conduct had not engaged liability in the council, however. Nothing had alerted it to the imminent breakdown in the relationship between these two colleagues and, in any event, the supervision session was a single unsatisfactory incident for which, in the judge's view, the two participants shared the blame.

Chan v Barts & the London NHS Trust[87] was a medical case and a further instance of an involved history carefully entered into by the court.[88] The legal issue boiled down to whether Dr Chan had by his behaviour repudiated his contract of employment. In deciding that he had, Stanley Burnton J made interesting observations that balanced managerial and individual responsibility for unacceptable workplace conduct. The central idea was that some employees at least, and irrespective of what management might have allowed them to 'get away with', would necessarily have internalized the capacity to tell acceptable from unacceptable behaviour at work.

An internal inquiry panel found that Dr Chan had been seriously at fault on specific occasions and that there was a repetitive pattern of behaviour.[89] The consequences of his conduct were said by the panel to have 'almost invariably been unnecessary upset and humiliation to his professional colleagues', yet Dr Chan seemed to have 'no insight into the effect of his behaviour'.[90] The panel, however, regarded the employer as bearing some responsibility for what had occurred. Dr Chan's behavioural traits were well known and his negative behaviour had to some extent been tolerated, 'with some of those with the difficult task of managing him choosing to have as little to do with him as possible'.[91]

In deciding that there had nonetheless been a repudiatory breach, Stanley Burnton J did not ignore the role of inadequate management. Aside from doubting whether it could be other than a background factor in such a case, however, he did not see that context as exonerating Dr Chan. The judge pointed out that he was 'an intelligent professional, who should not require effective management in order to appreciate what is destructive of his relationships with his colleagues in management and the boundaries of acceptable conduct'.[92]

5. Conclusion

Evaluation of employer responses and consequent judicial guidance was consistently as contextualized and accessible as consideration of the acceptability or not of conduct, while there were here indications of a shift towards balancing different workplace interests to decide what standards to impose. It followed that the specific implications of the rules deviated case by case: no detailed, 'one-size-fits-all' account of how employers should respond to behavioural problems could be extracted from the judgments. That

---

[85] ibid.   [86] ibid, [114], [41], and [121].   [87] [2007] EWHC 2914 (QB).
[88] See also *Kircher v Hillingdon PCT* [2006] EWHC 21 (QB), [2006] Lloyd's Rep. Med. 215 in which the judge, David Foskett QC, confined himself to relating the essential factual background since he was dealing only with an interim application for an injunction to restrain dismissal. But, as he said at [6]: 'Regrettably, even the shortened version of the story is quite lengthy and complex, but the full story is probably even more complex'.
[89] ibid, [93].   [90] ibid.
[91] ibid, [93]. This is a good example of an account of managerial avoidance of problems, reflecting qualitative evidence surveyed in Ch 2 (at pp 17 and 44–45) and my interview study (see pp 193–95, 198, and 209 in Ch 8 and pp 228–29 and 231 in Ch 9).
[92] ibid, [147].

said, again, general overarching norms of fairness, reasonableness, and equality were treated as immanent in the written law: it was these that were consistently refracted through contextualized judicial analyses, including by balancing interests, to deliver specific outcomes. Those ideals came across therefore as the best guides to what law asks of employers, with little again appearing to turn on which cause of action might be implicated.

A good illustration can be found in rulings and guidance about employers' responses, including procedurally, to problems and grievances that had escalated.[93] Consider, for example, the obligations held to be on employers in *Horkulak v Cantor FitzGerald International*,[94] *Blackburn with Darwen BC v Stanley*,[95] and *Merelie v Newcastle PCT*.[96] All were about whether the employer had breached its implied contractual obligations (although *Blackburn* was an unfair dismissal case). In *Horkulak* liability was rooted in the general precept that work demands should be leavened by a fair system for addressing perceived problems that was adapted to the particular employment situation.[97] In *Blackburn*, while the judges commended the employers' bespoke dignity at work policy, they found liability even though the employee had not used this, reasoning that employers have fundamental obligations 'to take reasonable steps to ensure that an employee is supported in times of difficulty'.[98] In *Merelie*, liability was not found, but again this proceeded from specific, contextual extrapolations from overarching reasonableness requirements on employers in handling delicate situations.[99]

I further observed two adjudicative seams that most obviously grappled with balancing the reality that work is almost always a collective endeavour and working people have individual interests in work. This was highly reminiscent of the evidence in Chapter 2 of working people, managers, and litigants struggling with this issue.[100] The first occurred also in relation to standards of conduct, particularly under the PHA 1997. It consisted in recurrent musings about how far negative interpersonal behaviour ought to be legally tolerated as an inherent, unavoidable feature of working life. Second, evaluation of employer responses was frequently as concerned with finding limits on the law's requirements as with articulating the obligations it imposed. In practice, therefore, the elaboration of legal requirements in respect both of ill treatment at work and allegations about this, especially although not exclusively as regards employer responses, drew judges into articulating their sense of the point at which individual rights should give way to collective interests.

These findings complicate those discussed in Chapter 6. Adjudicative processes still emerged as presenting a serious challenge to managerial power, with legal requirements imposed that consistently reflected general notions of fairness, reasonableness and equality. There were indications, however, of judges wrestling with the uneasy balance between vindicating individual interests at work and recognizing the essentially collective, communal nature of working life. Vitally, however, the notions of collectivity imported were, by definition, adjudicatively constructed, reflecting judges' ideas about reasonable employer conduct in the face of competing workplace perspectives. This highlighted that the growth in individual rights in the UK seems in practice to have handed judges an important role in balancing collective and individual interests at

---

[93] See pp 197–200 and 209 in Ch 8 and pp 245–46 and the text to ns 44–45 in Ch 10 about the tension between this aspect of my case law findings and those about procedural legal influence within organizations.
[94] [2003] EWHC 1918 (QB), [2004] ICR 697.   [95] *Blackburn with Darwen BC* (n 7).
[96] *Merelie* (n 62).   [97] See p 166 in Ch 6.   [98] See pp 170–71 above.
[99] See pp 178–79 above.   [100] See pp 22–23 and 55–58 in Ch 2.

work. This raises arguments for explicit legislative steering of such judicial analyses and for wider, lay involvement, including as judges, in this decision-making.

Again, however, the fundamental empirical question remains: what from law actually becomes embedded in organizations? Irrespective of what judgments actually say or imply, at the end of the day we can only understand what this form of legal process is doing in society, what it means, and whether amelioration is possible, if we can trace how it is received by workplaces. I now turn my attention to this.

8

Senior Managers and Lawyers on Behavioural Conflict at Work and Legal Influence

In this chapter I report on my interview study with senior managers and lawyers. The first feature to mention is that there were strange patterns of legal influence and its absence, overlaid with organizational and judicial thinking sometimes being consonant and sometimes dissonant. Senior managers and lawyers reported that organizations were being influenced by law to adopt formal procedures and there was widespread recognition that equality law has an effect. By contrast, a majority of senior managers denied that substantive legal rules about workplace behaviour outside the equality sphere have any influence. There were at the same time striking overlaps between senior managers' reports about how they think about behavioural problems and my qualitative findings in Chapter 6 about how judges do the same. There was no similarity, however, with what Chapter 7 reported about judicial evaluations of employer responses. These complex patterns of legal influence and parallel reasoning processes raised yet further questions about the point of the distinctions by legislatures and judges that were explored in Chapters 3 and 5. The implication of the data reported in this chapter is that even if it were somehow possible to make sense internally of the effects in practice of jurisdictional variety (which in my view it is not), that aspect of the legal framework would remain futile because the differences between causes of action do not appear to map onto what organizations take from law. More positively, the findings about where legal influence does operate suggested there are real possibilities that law for law to have an impact, perhaps augmented by the similarities that I found between adjudicative and organizational reasoning.

The second aspect of the interview data was that they revealed various means by which law and legal process appear to deflect employers from effectively responding to problems and specifically from doing so by applying general fairness, reasonableness, and equality norms that underlie both the framework of individual rights as written and their detailed application to behavioural issues in authoritative adjudication. In terms of workplace influence that produces these effects, legally induced proceduralization and formality within organizations were seen to take the focus away from solving problems, let alone using justice norms to do so, and particularly to deter early, informal attempts at resolution. In terms of legal process, this tendency was apparent in the remarkable detachment of settlement practice from the underlying law and its normative underpinnings, as well as in interviewees seeing it as obvious that court rulings have little purchase within organizations. Mechanisms of this kind, by which the emancipatory point of legal rules seemed to be lost, resonate with the overall inscrutability of the judicial distinctions discussed in Chapter 5. Taken together, they pointed to a propensity for law to lose its normative integrity in the course of implementation and enforcement.

Distinctions between accounts given by senior managers and senior lawyers supported the notion that the reality of working life is distorted by a purely insider legal gaze. This effect was freely acknowledged by some lawyers and the interview data reinforced the analysis in

Chapter 4 to similar effect.[1] Such dislocation may in turn be expected to influence organizations, judges, legislatures, and society more widely, altering the impact law has and its development over time. The consequent insight is that an external account of law and legal process, which this work seeks to develop, is essential if we are to understand all that is being done with legal tools and to find means to improve their functioning.

Before moving to a detailed exposition of the interview study findings, the next section explains the sample, methodology, and mode of analysis. Sections 2 and 3 contain my interpretations of the data as regards behavioural conflict as an organizational phenomenon and the influence within workplaces of law and legal process. Section 4 summarizes and analyses these findings, extracting some arguably generic features of how law functions. In the next chapter I explain my overarching hypotheses about the impact of individual labour and equality rights within organizations. This explores how the mechanisms identified play out within workplaces, leading to the conclusion that the crucial missing factor is provision for broader involvement in implementation and enforcement, particularly by employees and their representatives.

1. Introduction and Interview Study Method

My interviewees were gathered through a snowball methodology, supplemented with specific invitations to ensure my sample included senior managers from different sectors and varied sizes of organization, barristers and solicitors, and was divided equally between genders. I chose a snowball approach as best suited to gathering a sample of individuals with wide-ranging experience of organizational life, particularly in regard to how problems and conflict unfold. My own background as a litigator, civil servant, and legal academic enabled me to find some interviewees to start the process, but tapping into other people's networks was vital to extending the pool from which the ultimate sample was drawn and to ensuring the final groups of interviewees came from a range of backgrounds. Where gaps or gender imbalance appeared in the emerging sample, I issued additional invitations to address this.

I conducted thirty-six interviews in the period from May 2011 to June 2012, with twenty-two senior managers and fourteen senior lawyers. One of the lawyers was prevented at the very final stage from confirming participation, so my final sample consisted of twenty-two senior managers and thirteen senior lawyers. This included sixteen men and nineteen women. The senior managers comprised nine men and thirteen women and there were seven male and six female lawyers. Interviews were conducted on an anonymous basis and interviewees spoke in a purely personal capacity.

The final sample of senior managers came from a wide range of professional backgrounds and between them had around 550 years of experience. Eleven (or 50 per cent) currently worked for large employers with more than 250 employees. In fact, several were from organizations employing thousands or even tens of thousands of staff. The other half of my sample either worked in small and medium-sized organizations or now had dealings with a range of organizations. Fifteen senior manager interviewees (or 68 per cent) had experience of a different working environment to the one where they currently worked. I also used the description 'manager' even though the current work of some interviewees no longer easily fit into that category. The label seemed appropriate nonetheless because everyone had significant experience of 'hands-on' management

---

[1] See pp 117–18 in Ch 4.

and their organizational position, now and previously, meant their perspective was a managerial one.

The senior manager interviewees were spread fairly evenly between the public, private, and third sectors. There were six individuals (or 27 per cent) in the public sector, eight (or 36 per cent) in the private sector, five (or 23 per cent) from the third (or civil society) sector, plus three (or 14 per cent) whose work took them into a range of settings. While all had substantial management experience, some was either as a consultant or in roles that primarily called on different specialist professional expertise.

It is notable that a disproportionate number of the managers were lawyers who had moved to managerial or other senior positions. To some extent, this reflected my background but also emerged naturally from the snowball process. Just under one-third in the group of managers were lawyers, a similar proportion were neither lawyers nor from human resources (HR), and about two-fifths were from HR backgrounds. A background specifically in employment law unsurprisingly revealed itself in the individuals possessing sophisticated relevant legal knowledge. Some HR specialists were similarly well informed, while lawyer managers from other specialisms were broadly akin to their non-lawyer counterparts in terms of their knowledge of employment and equality law. Overall about three-quarters of the senior managers commented on the technicality and complexity of the law and about half described their own and other people's uncertainty and mistakes regarding the interaction of legal requirements and HR practices.

There was a further disproportion in the sample in the number of senior manager interviewees (twelve individuals or 55 per cent) who came from unionized workplaces. This was unexceptional for the public sector but unusual regarding the private. This feature of the sample reflected the size and history of private organizations for which certain interviewees worked. This is a specific respect in which senior lawyer interviews provided a useful counterpoint in that several acted mostly for employers in the non-unionized part of the economy.

The senior lawyers were all specialists in employment and equality law (broadly conceived), some combining this with knowledge of personal injury law. Six had mixed practices, four acted mostly for employers and four mostly for employees. Two of the group that predominantly represented one group or the other had at some point 'switched sides'. The senior lawyers had around 375 years of experience between them.

The interviews for both samples were semi-structured and the interview guides are included at Appendix 2. They were adapted to the different categories of interviewee but both investigated first, *how people in organizations are affected by law and legal process when either they are involved in, or required to respond to, behavioural conflict at work*, and second, *what causes such conflict to become litigious at all and to different degrees*. It also became clear after the first couple of interviews that the usefulness of my data would be enhanced if I asked about situations where escalation does not occur.

The relevant interview guide was sent to interviewees in advance. There were two procedural matters which I adapted in response to experience. I excluded analysis of organizational paperwork as interviewees were not consistently able to provide this. I also came to perceive too much risk of interviewees' anonymity being compromised if I approached more than one person from the same organization. I did not therefore do so even when this was suggested.

Interviews mostly lasted between one and one-and-a-half hours. I adopted a non-interventionist stance, leaving interviewees to respond to my questions in their own way. I referred back, however, to the interview guides to make sure the central issues were covered. The conversations were recorded and transcribed by me personally. This meant the records that went to interviewees for final annotation and approval were not exactly verbatim in that I rearranged the order of what was said, corrected grammar, and inserted obviously missing words. The final data on which I relied were those records as approved by my interviewees (with specific permission for direct citations). It was at this stage that one senior lawyer was prevented by external forces from continuing to participate.

I undertook the analysis of what was said by senior managers and senior lawyers separately, given the different interview guides used. Coding and categorization of the data that answered my research questions were first undertaken when I transcribed the interviews, then checked and refined once I had the final, approved records from the interviewees (which in fact changed little). At that point I grouped and related codings to identify the higher-order messages that emerged. In the analyses which follow I link what emerged from the two groups of interviewees. This shows where the data converged and diverged and thereby provides a degree of 'triangulation'.

Before turning to my findings, it is important to acknowledge that perceptions of behavioural conflict may themselves be influenced by law, consciously or unconsciously, as the research about complaining and litigating behaviour sometimes documented.[2] My analysis is therefore attentive to when legal sources and categories appeared to be affecting how interviewees understood what they saw and experienced.

The final, central, preliminary point is that the non-representativeness of the sample, as well as the qualitative nature of the data, mean that the themes that emerged cannot straightforwardly be generalized. They are, rather, indicative of first, attitudes to behavioural conflict within organizations, particularly from a management perspective, second, organizational experience of this kind of conflict, and third, the impact of relevant law and legal process on both. I have also given the percentages of interviewees who referred to certain things to enable readers to see for themselves how prevalent a particular code or category was within the sample.

Still, interviewees' breadth of experience of different kinds of organizations, the many years over which this was gained, and their particular interest in problems and conflicts at work mean the data substantially illuminate how individual legal rights and organizational life interact in the UK. This means that interpretation of the data, in combination with the other elements in the study, allows me to construct theories about the role in the UK of labour and equality law in the form of individual rights. My findings also to some extent support wider theorization of how this and other forms of law work.

2. Organizational Perceptions of Behavioural Conflict at Work

In this section I extract the themes that I found in what senior managers said about the phenomenon of behavioural conflict at work. This separated into coding about the nature of this conflict, how much there is of it, its impact on those involved and on the workplace, and the experience of proceduralization and formality in organizational responses. Senior managers' comments were also juxtaposed with those of senior lawyers, uncovering important differences of emphasis. This is most likely because lawyers are almost invariably involved only when conflicts escalate, and reflects the contention in Chapter 4 that they have a distinctive experience as legal insiders. An important related point, explored further below, is that senior lawyer interviewees significantly varied in the extent to which they perceived the innately partial nature of their professional

---

[2] See pp 28–29 in Ch 2.

experience, whereas senior managers more consistently appreciated that their beliefs about working life were influenced by their particular career history.

(1) Contents

Interviewees had advance sight of my definition of a behavioural conflict as 'a dispute about how colleagues have behaved towards one another (whether or not the dispute is also about a particular workplace practice or decision, for example, allocation of work or disciplinary action)'. I explained at the start of the interviews that classic examples are conflicts about whether or not someone had been bullied or harassed, which might either be about free-standing behaviour or about conduct connected with another organizational process or decision, for example about disciplinary proceedings.

There were two ideas about the content of these disputes that were expressed by almost all the senior managers. The first was that it relates to much more than bullying, with one interviewee seeing individual problems as being on a continuum at the other end of which were organizational ways of being:

When I think about a behavioural issue I think of very specific examples of inappropriate behaviour at one end of the scale, and at the other end I think of management style, culture, how we do things, how people generally behave, what sort of behaviours we want from our employees as opposed to those that they may display. SM17 (private, large, HR)[3]

The second, almost unanimous, observation, mirroring one of the factual themes from the case law,[4] was that subjective views often diverged about the subject matter of disputes, for example as follows:

I also think it's very difficult to say when ... a potential conflict becomes a dispute. The views of those involved may well differ about this. If cross words are spoken at work, at what point does that become a conflict and at what point is that just part of everyday life? I think for the two people involved it won't be the same point in time, or in fact they might never agree that there has been a conflict. SM3 (public, large, lawyer)

A smaller proportion of senior manager interviewees, although still about two-thirds of the total, depicted this kind of problem as intrinsically challenging for organizations, sometimes because of disagreement about appropriate behaviour and especially about what constitutes harassment. The final point was that roughly half of the managers saw group identity as significant. This was related by some to legal influence, while several perceived organizations having highly developed diversity strategies as positive for containing and addressing behavioural conflict.

It was more common for legal rules to emerge as important to what senior lawyers recognized as behavioural conflict. There was considerable variety in what was said on this topic, but some lawyer interviewees appeared to conceive of workplace interactions entirely according to their legal status. Further, nearly the whole of this group automatically related the subject matter of the interviews to anti-discrimination law.[5] Some did so in comments about underlying conflicts; for example, characterizing discrimination cases as often involving allegations about subtle, deeply felt behaviours or observing that litigants and their lawyers can find it hard to disentangle discriminatory conduct from

---

[3] This comment further illustrated a general feature of the senior manager interviews to which I return later, of individual and organizational perspectives being intertwined. See pp 224–27, 228–31, 234–36, and 241–43 in Ch 9.

[4] See pp 108–109 in Ch 4.

[5] Another such mechanism was perhaps at work in two-thirds of all senior lawyers commenting on the connections between behavioural conflict and personal injury litigation.

general nastiness.[6] Others made this connection in remarks about how equality law is being used, one saying that:

[t]his is going to sound a dreadful thing to say. But the truth of it is that any general allegation of bad behaviour is invariably accompanied by an allegation of discrimination. Maybe that's because people are being pushed into it by the law if you like. That is so because even where the victim is a white male, they will say: 'I am being discriminated against because I'm a white male.' Oh yeah I've had that experience. Frequently. Frequently. There is not a group in society that cannot allege gender, age or race discrimination. An allegation of general bad behaviour is *invariably* linked to a protected characteristic, however credible or incredible that is. SL4 (solicitor, employer side)

Overall, it emerged that the lawyer interviewees saw themselves and their colleagues as channelling clients towards discrimination claims,[7] albeit with varying degrees of force and without necessarily being successful in persuading them to take this course.

(2) Quantification and impact

About two-thirds of senior managers commented on behavioural conflict being inherent to working life. While a handful did not see problems of this kind as particularly concerning, nearly everyone referred to the harmfulness of such conflict. One interviewee articulated this by noting the value of prevention:

It's *always* worth over-investing in these issues … People who are stressed, anxious, worried, not having *fun*, just don't make long term, happy employees … They're not effective … Relationship issues are the biggest things that get in the way of that. The service/profit chain is a big business theory base: the happiness of your staff means the happiness of your customers … It goes through all the team: the guys who are dealing with the customers day to day reflect the culture of their managers. That has absolutely been my experience. SM4 (private, medium, non-HR)

Several manager interviewees explained the ill effects of behavioural conflict by describing their own experiences, in one case of being bullied and unable to do anything about it:

It still has negative consequences in that I'm not as motivated as I used to be and I probably don't see a long term career in the status quo, or even within my organization. It's made me a toxic employee. And I don't think I'm the only one. I know there are a few other individuals although I haven't talked to anyone. SM3 (public, large, lawyer)

For another, personal harm resulted from managing this kind of problem:

I would say that I'm forever fire-fighting personnel issues, as they used to call it, about behavioural conflict. I would say about 65–70% of my working time is spent dealing with this sort of thing. It's worn me down. It's a war of attrition and they won. I feel totally bullied by all this. SM2 (public, large, lawyer)

Distress was reported to encompass both complainants and those complained about:

It's heart-breaking sometimes the state that people are in by the time they get to me. It's *heart-breaking* and yet the person who is doing it is not 'bastard of the year'. I don't believe he gets up in the morning and thinks: 'How can I make someone's life completely intolerable?' … I know there are psychopaths out there but I've had men cry in an interview saying: 'I don't know why I'm here'. How can that be? These are senior people. SM19 (public and private, various sizes, HR)

---

[6] See in this connection K Perren, S Roberts, B Stafford, D Hirsch, and M Padley, *Report 3—Disputes and Challenges* (GEO, 2012), 11 that the most common ground for complaints regarding protected characteristics, accounting for 43 per cent, was that staff had been bullied or offensive remarks made.

[7] See pp 125–28 in Ch 5 supporting the existence of this tendency, sometimes to suboptimal ends.

These vignettes are indicative of the range of harms reported, often serious and extending well beyond those directly involved.[8]

Various observations that behavioural conflict is intrinsic to working life were implicit that whether or not problems are acknowledged is important, with around one-third of senior manager interviewees explicitly raising this. This was seen as relevant to measurement:

It's really difficult to quantify behavioural conflict because in my experience there is always something bubbling around ... [T]here's always an element of this ... The difference is whether people feel confident enough to name it. SM10 (public and private, various sizes, HR)

In addition, there was discussion of behavioural problems having differential effects according to whether individuals and organizations confront them:

There are things she's said and you think 'Blimey, that's really strong' and you can see people not being happy about it ... Sometimes things are escalated and have resulted in a grievance against her. The atmosphere has got really difficult and poisoned and usually the person who brought the grievance has left or, as they're all on temporary contracts, they haven't had their contract renewed. She will be the victor. Other times the person learns to live with it and they will have a reasonably harmonious working relationship. They'll stand up to her and things will just be fine. At least they'll be fine enough that people don't want to leave, don't actually leave, don't lodge a formal grievance and don't allow the thing to escalate .... SM3 (large, public, lawyer)

This raises the issue of varying subjectivities again, this time not in whether there is a perception of inappropriate behaviour but instead in how people react. It further gives insight into harm, including organizational harm, that the evidence surveyed in Chapter 2 supports, even if problems are suppressed and silenced.[9] Interviewees' accounts of feeling personally harmed also provided evidence of the latter phenomenon.

Turning to senior lawyers, over one-half saw behavioural conflict as occupying a large proportion of their workload and more than two-thirds were clear that it affects a wide range of people and all levels of organizational hierarchies. In an uncanny echo of Fevre and colleagues' conclusions in *Trouble at Work*, one lawyer observed that:

[w]henever you're faced with the practical problem of either a dismissal or a discrimination case, when you unpick what's gone on, often what you have is some kind of conflict or mismatch either about workplace culture issues or about understandings of rules and regulations. So I think this kind of conflict is fairly common. SL3 (solicitor, employee side)[10]

The omnipresence of these issues, particularly in the guise of equality cases, was also emphasized in this account:

Broad brush I would say that eighty per cent of the cases we deal with are discrimination cases about behaviour. They are a massive proportion of the cases I deal with ... The sort of sectors that we're talking about range from health, local government, central government, defence, private companies, FTSE 100 companies, small local companies, independent schools, charities, colleges, manufacturing industry, professional services industries and architects. It's the whole lot, the whole lot. It's the whole gamut from refuse workers to nuclear scientists. Broadly I would say that this kind of conflict is *even more* prevalent in the public sector than the private sector. But can I think of a *single* one of our clients who hasn't had to address this sort of issue? No. SL4 (solicitor, employer side)

As another senior lawyer commented, they saw bad behaviour everywhere.

---

[8] This corresponds to another of the factual themes in the judgments, on which see pp 106–107 in Ch 4.
[9] See pp 17, 22–25, and 51 in Ch 2. [10] See p 24 in Ch 2.

(3) Emergence and escalation

Senior manager interviewees perceived both individual and organizational influences on behavioural conflict emerging and then worsening, analysed separately in the following.

(a) Individual influences

There was great variety in what manager interviewees saw as affecting individuals either in becoming involved in a conflict or in whether it escalated. About one-third saw work pressure as significant, but there was no consensus around issues like awareness of legal rights, the increase in legal rights, greater willingness to challenge, unrealistic expectations of compensation, and having nothing left to lose, although each was mentioned by a few interviewees.

The only relatively consistent theme was that about two-thirds saw personality as playing an important role. This was partly expressed through recognition that most people have straightforward needs when a work problem arises, expressed by one interviewee in language reminiscent of Genn's observations in *Paths to Justice* and of the findings of the Fair Treatment at Work Survey (FTWS) 2008:

[t]he vast majority of people have got an issue which needs to be resolved, and they need some help resolving it. That's absolutely still the vast majority of people. I think it's exactly right also that there must be a lot of situations that never get into our forty to fifty formal processes a year, where something is sorted out before it gets to us. SM5 (private, large, HR)[11]

At the same time over one-third saw very difficult employees as the root cause of really bad conflicts, a few relating this to mental health issues. Interestingly, an additional handful commented that it might be the experience of raising a problem that caused an employee to become 'difficult'. For example:

people become 'pathological'. You can start with a legitimate problem. If you feel that isn't being resolved properly, it's very easy to get into the mindset that everything is conspiring against you. Things are so nuanced in the workplace … Once you get into the mindset of 'The bastards are out to get me' almost anything that happens can be twisted to suit that interpretation. And then it becomes impossible to assess the extent to which that is so, to unravel it. SM3 (public, large, lawyer)

What these interviewees sometimes saw in the worst conflicts, therefore, was problems spiralling out of control due to employees' personalities interacting with their organization's reactions to what had happened.

Turning to senior lawyers, and again probably reflecting the fact that they tend to see the worst situations, personality was mentioned by almost everyone as a factor that determines whether behavioural conflict emerges and escalates.[12] There were rich depictions of what lawyers saw in different types of legal practice. One was reminiscent of the qualitative evidence from discrimination claimants surveyed earlier:[13]

Probably this is slightly stereotyping but often claimants I see have a sense—pride would be the wrong word—but a sense of feeling *very* hurt, *very* hurt, when they are undermined, perhaps because they are insecure, perhaps because they feel they've worked very hard to get where they are, perhaps because they are a bit chippy. I would probably be somebody who would be very hurt in that situation because I'm just that sort of person. I probably feel slightly marginalized anyway because I'm not a typical senior lawyer. If someone else is, for example, black, they might in a

---

[11] See pp 31, 36, and 57 in Ch 2.   [12] See pp 117–18 in Ch 4.   [13] See pp 44–47 in Ch 2.

similar way feel slightly marginalized anyway and so the hurt becomes really damaging to their sense of dignity and worth. And some people feel worn down anyway so the treatment is just something else in their life which they feel they have to put up with. SL14 (barrister, employee side)

Reflecting on experience as an adviser to organizations with commitment styles of management,[14] the following gave another perspective:

It's a good way of putting it to say that in the flatter, more consensual organizations that we come across in the modern world, there are a group of people who won't play by the implicit rules. There is a certain kind of person who, because they don't see the rules, don't choose to see them or don't think the rules apply to them, aren't easily manageable in a consensual workplace. A high proportion of the cases that come across my desk involve those kinds of people. Just thinking about my caseload at the moment, it's a very significant proportion. SL2 (solicitor, employer side)[15]

These narratives notably often stated, where senior managers only implied, that personality was important not only to conflicts escalating but also to people either doing nothing or giving up on action they had started. Disturbingly, abandoning action was sometimes said to result from an employer's reactions to complaints having damaged the employee's health, sometimes poor to start with, to such an extent that the individual could not continue with proceedings. In addition, a larger proportion of senior lawyers (over 50 per cent) referred to the experience of formally raising an issue as itself undermining complainants' capacity to secure a good resolution to the underlying problem.

(b) Organizational influences

The interviews with senior managers were characterized by finely grained and differentiated accounts of the organizational influences they perceived on behavioural conflict. The devil was depicted as being in the detail of how different workplaces operated. While sectoral tendencies were noted, these were complicated by, for example, contrasting accounts of employers within the same sector. Where interviewees' positions seemed to coalesce nonetheless was, first, regarding the paramount importance of organizational culture, in relation to which certain distinctions recurred, and second, in extensive agreement about what was needed organizationally, irrespective of environmental variables, to prevent and address problems.

In terms of culture there was near unanimity about the significance this has to behavioural conflict. This was sometimes revealed by drawing comparisons, as in this instance:

That reflects that you have different expectations of behaviours that are learned because you've been in a culture. When I came into the private sector I very quickly had to shift my expectations of the organization and of behaviours in terms of what I thought was appropriate. There were things that I wouldn't have found acceptable when I worked in the public sector which I quickly had to find acceptable here. SM17 (private, large, HR)

Interviewees also contrasted management styles, associating directive, autocratic, non-communicative management styles with behavioural conflict, albeit perhaps

---

[14] See p 52 in Ch 2 for what is meant by this.
[15] See in the next section, pp 216–17, 222–24, 227–36, and 240–43 in Ch 9 and pp 253–56 in Ch 10 on the possibility that some, perhaps more well-meaning organizations, have a particular vulnerability to damaging individualized conflict, including that escalates to litigation.

suppressed, while more commitment-oriented management approaches were linked to conflict being minimized. The latter was summed up in the following, again relating experience in the public sector:

There's also a culture that we promote where we don't turn a blind eye to offensive behaviour. We lead by example. Generally I suppose it's partly public sector. People tease us about being very political correct and all that, but it's kind of in the DNA about fairness and treating people in the right way. That's how you treat other people ... Maybe I'm being naïve. Sometimes I think that because I'm relatively high up in the organization. But I do think that there is a shared sense that people could describe of what is acceptable and what is not acceptable. There are always a few blurry situations around the edges, but in most situations they'd be able to draw a line between what is ok here and what's not. SM20 (public, large, lawyer)

It was, however, not only public sector workplaces which were described as having positive cultures, nor that every public sector workplace was characterized in this way. This is one of the respects in which what was said about individual workplaces was both varied and specific.[16]

Nonetheless, two sectoral divides were commented on by about half the senior managers. The first compared the public and civil society/third sectors with the private sector. The tendency was to view organizations in the former sectors as likely to have cultures which were less tolerant of negative conduct, albeit not immune, and in some senses, and somewhat paradoxically, vulnerable to individual conflicts escalating. The second contrast was between unionized and non-unionized workplaces, with the tendency to view unionized workplaces as less tolerant of bad behaviour. The variability in descriptions and analyses of the union/non-union distinction, however, was particularly marked. As such, half of all senior manager interviewees made some comment about trade unionism changing, about variety in how it operates, and about trade union collectivism being in a process of decline. The following extract is illustrative and described contemporary experience of even recognized unions being marginalized:

For many years I worked for a labour [local] authority. The union were part and parcel of the management of that authority. They were very close to the Councillors. They were very close to the senior officers. As staff members we daren't do anything that would offend the unions. I then moved to work for a conservative local authority, partly because I wanted to know if HR was different. *Boy was it different.* The unions didn't figure on the agenda at all. The institution did what it wanted to do, and if unions so much as squeaked they were rapidly slapped down. I hardly ever saw a union rep. Almost, in a way, if feels a bit like that [where I work] now to some extent. It feels like we are concerned about what the unions think of us, but that doesn't translate into feeling we must therefore engage with and involve them. It's a bit of a disjointed way of approaching unions. SM1 (public, large, HR)

At the same time, strong views were expressed about the value of trade union collectivism, explored further in the next chapter. There were also some indications of the UK tradition of trade unionism being indirectly influential in non-unionized workplaces;

---

[16] See this nuanced comparison of a public and private sector workplace: 'I also feel this coming from the public sector, where you get all of that protection and support, but it doesn't amount to much. I've come to an organization where, if you're in the right position, it is quite liberating because it's growing, it's entrepreneurial and it's fast-moving ... [Y]ou can put up with a little bit of poor behavior ... [I] end up thinking there's a balance that can be struck between a more directive style, on the one hand, and a more collaborative, coaching approach, on the other, and regarding all the other things associated with the two different approaches that I've mentioned, like whether or not there are unions. Of course, in an environment where you don't have unions and all those other things, managers who do behave inappropriately are more likely to get away with it.' SM17 (private, large, HR)

for example, regarding how far managerial dominance was seen as acceptable and in the possibility of worker-protective measures being adopted in order to prevent staff becoming union members.

The other area of near unanimity, aside from the importance of organizational culture, consisted in almost all interviewees identifying four organizational features which they saw as critical to preventing behavioural conflict and to managing it. The first of these features was the identification of early opportunities to solve problems and these being acted upon; the second was strong, consistent leadership regarding standards of conduct; the third was the existence of good communication up and down the internal hierarchy; and the fourth was management and HR being equipped to deal with behavioural issues. Another three-quarters of the manager interviewees saw employee representation, or at least involvement, as important. It was arresting that, unprompted, senior managers from such a range of workplaces and with so much accumulated experience, almost unanimously identified the same factors as necessary for organizations to deal effectively with the potential or fact of behavioural conflict.

The senior lawyer interviewees gave more varied answers about the organizational causes of behavioural conflict. There was also a marked contrast with the consistency with which managers seemed to grasp that the particularity of their experience limited the conclusions they could validly draw about working life. At one end of the spectrum, lawyer interviewees also realized that what they had seen did not give them a reliable picture of organizational life as a whole. Any general points they made were subject to this caveat, with some displaying quite remarkable dispassion and a rigorously distanced approach. At the other pole, several lawyers were equally surprising in seeing their bounded experience as sufficient to support very general conclusions about how organizations, individuals, and law function. Contrasts of this kind were interesting in themselves and are important to the analysis that follows.

The substantive contrast in reported organizational influences was that senior lawyers emphasized the impact of employers' reactions when specific things went wrong, whereas senior managers tended to talk about higher-level organizational factors, such as formulating strategies about workplace culture and employment relations. This evidently reflected different ways that these two groups become involved in conflicts.[17]

The first strain in lawyers' accounts involved about two-thirds pointing to particular public sector problems. A trenchant example seemed, however, quite obviously to reflect distortion in senior lawyers' experiences:

In the public sector these sorts of conflicts get very aggressive. Things seem to escalate very, very quickly. I think it's partly the expectations of the people involved. They seem to spend a large part of their time *defending* their rights. Heavily unionized, big support, very weak employers, if you're unhappy you push it and you make a fuss and you know you can get what you want. The complainant effectively forces the organization into becoming aggressive. The local union official can also be pretty aggressive. He wants to support the member's perceptions however those perceptions might sensibly be viewed. It's escalated very fast. SL9 (barrister, mixed practice)

The other strand in this data, mentioned by nearly all the senior lawyers, was that poor management, sometimes in response to pressure, was the root of the problem. The view that management is often the underlying cause of behavioural conflict was also in a sense reinforced by around half commenting on the innate difficulty for organizations of articulating meaningful, workable standards in this area. Equally, a similar proportion

---

[17] See pp 22–25 in Ch 2, suggesting that what matters most is the general workplace environment, while also demonstrating the centrality of management.

referred to wider recognition of this, explaining that some organizations are making significant investments in addressing behavioural issues.

An example among many accounts of poor management was the following:

> It comes back to the point about there being a shadow of things that never get addressed. If someone is sitting there for a long period of time putting up with a colleague's behaviour in the workplace, but not particularly liking it, when will that blow up? … I've seen situations where there's been inappropriate, on any analysis, banter between two individuals that has gone one step too far, at which point the recipient of the offensive comment goes off sick and claims race discrimination. You can see that it just went too far and nobody was managing the situation, nobody was seeing what was going on and nobody was giving guidance as to what was acceptable. SL8 (solicitor, employer side)

A particular incarnation, which just under one-half of senior lawyers mentioned, was of management finding ways to avoid a problem, including by turning on the complainant and despite this creating a different problem for the organization.[18] This was illustrated as follows in relation to equal pay complaints in the private sector, offering another perspective on when an employee is labelled as being 'difficult':

> In the private sector a complaint about equal pay isn't seen as a complaint about either process or systems. It's seen as quite a personal thing. So then it becomes about the difficult person, usually a woman, who is making a complaint, who is upsetting things. It's seen as a behavioural matter rather than an issue about pay. She's rocking the boat. It's almost as if by raising the pay issue, she's suggesting that her male comparators *aren't* worth it. That's how it's *perceived* in some of these cases. It probably isn't what she's doing at all. She'd quite like to have the same pay as them. She doesn't want them to have reduced pay. But that's how it's perceived. She's seen as being difficult by raising the issue. So very often it turns into a general discrimination case because of the bullying that goes on in response to someone saying there is a problem. SL12 (barrister, mixed practice)

This is an important passage for explaining how it might be routine within organizations to convert a perfectly valid legal issue into a personal confrontation. Instead of an equal pay complainant being seen as pursuing a straightforward pay query, the extract describes her being seen as personally flawed for raising the issue. It even suggests that the individual will, in this process, be attributed the bizarre desire to punish colleagues rather than the simple, perfectly ordinary wish to be paid appropriately.

(c) Proceduralization and formality

A major set of themes in what senior managers said about the emergence and escalation of behavioural conflict related to proceduralization and the formality that goes with it. Interviewees did not speak with one voice on this but everyone raised and emphasized the topic. The main contrast in views was that one-third of manager interviewees commented on the positive value of formal policies and procedures, while two-thirds saw them as problematic. A nuance to be noted, however, was that about three-quarters related formalizing policies and procedures to organizational size, seeing this positively as necessary to run large enterprises and negatively as an insufficiently questioned feature of how things are done in large workplaces. I will now explore the different strands on this that emerged in the data, turning in the next section to how this interacted with views about legal influence.

---

[18] See further in this chapter ns 19 and 29, accompanying text and pp 191 and 209, pp 17 and 44–45 in Ch 2, ns 60 and 65 in Ch 6, ns 51 and 91 and accompanying text in Ch 7, and pp 228–29 and 231–33 in Ch 9 supporting this aspect of my data. This also reflects another factual theme in the case law sample at pp 110–12 in Ch 4.

I was told about many different defects in the workings of internal procedures. A vociferous handful of senior managers depicted these as being entirely futile:

In two hundred days of working this year I've never heard one person in a senior management role refer to a written policy. Never once. I think they get written and they get forgotten. SM8 (private, various sizes, non-HR)

Two-fifths of senior managers also made critical comments about the use of formal procedures: that managers used them defensively, rigidly, or to avoid a problem.[19] A similar proportion commented on employees misusing procedures.

Over 50 per cent indicated that following internal procedures could be either ineffective or make problems worse. This was expressed in a variety of ways. One senior manager described procedures as preventing early resolution and encouraging escalation:

I'm not allowed to make a decision at an early stage. I have to go all through these procedures and allow the thing in a way to accelerate into something bigger, like a snowball. I think the existence of these procedures gives tacit encouragement to escalate. SM2 (public, large, non-HR)

Others spoke of their organization's collective experience of there *never* being a good outcome to formal grievance procedures and said that employees contemplating this step were told as much. The following was eloquent about this kind of negative view:

By the time a formal complaint has been made, in a sense you've lost it organizationally. You can go through the formal grievance process, the disciplinary process, whichever procedure is deemed appropriate, go through the formal investigation, come up with some form of 'truth', if there is such a thing, But actually what you're left with quite often is a situation where you've got a bunch of individuals who can't work together because the personal relationships that underpin their work have been broken. So the procedure achieves *its* end or *its* goal. But how that team works together is often quite irretrievably damaged. SM10 (public and private, various sizes, HR)

An especially passionate account of the immediate harm procedures can do was the following: 'You've got the emotional impact on everybody. Nobody escapes unscathed. For me this is one of the over-arching things that I wish we could write in very large letters on walls. This affects *everybody* that it touches … I think of it as human wreckage. *Nobody* wins.' SM19 (public and private, various sizes, HR). This point of view was further supported by just under half the senior managers specifically commenting on the negative effects on non-complainants of formal procedures.[20] Perhaps surprisingly, however, there were different perspectives on the alternative of mediation, around two-fifths regarding this positively while a handful were either doubtful or critical.

A point of detail that was raised by several interviewees presents a legal conundrum. This was that legal obligations of confidentiality which organizations impose (eg contractually) can obstruct the resolution of problems. It was observed that complete confidentiality often cannot be maintained and patchy knowledge has all sorts of damaging internal effects. Equally, obligations to keep quiet prevent issues being systematically addressed because they cannot be openly acknowledged. Interviewees also described people against whom a grievance had been brought using confidentiality obligations to intimidate complainants into silence. These concerns arguably encapsulate how difficult it can be for organizations to deal constructively with workplace problems on an individualized basis. There is something curious about hiving off work-related issues with wider implications into confidential, individually oriented processes. That seems, however, to

---

[19] See ibid on other data about managerial avoidance of problems.
[20] This was another type of harm that behavioural conflict was said to cause, on which see pp 198–99 more generally above.

be how organizations routinely approach the individualization of employee relations in general, and the internalization of individual legal rights in particular. Organizational paperwork certainly seems to go much further than legally required in imposing confidentiality duties. Once such obligations are in place, moreover, breach would most likely create a different set of organizational and legal problems.

Negative depictions of organizational procedures from some senior managers were also strongly reflected in the data from senior lawyers. There was near unanimity that proceduralization and formality contribute to problems escalating. Lawyer interviewees were vocal and compelling on this, for example as follows:

Yet the minute you go formal positions become very entrenched and then there's a kind of 'He said, she said' argument, rather than a more mediated solution. I think going formal runs the risk of things becoming very difficult to resolve to everybody's satisfaction. If you've got an employment problem that goes into a formal process, there is the risk of a conflict in the evidence of what happened and then a decision has to be made as to who's right and who's wrong. Therefore the risk is increased I suppose that somebody is found to have been either lying or misconstruing what went on. The general atmosphere in the workplace between colleagues, or between individuals and managers, can then make people very defensive I think, on both sides of the fence, the managers who are being accused of misbehaviour and the employees bringing a grievance. The situation is conflictual but also defensive in the sense that people have to carry on their day to day interactions while the grievance is going on. I think it makes things much more complicated and difficult. And I suppose there is this sense in which lodging a grievance is a sign that an employee actually wants out or is lining up a claim. I think that's the reaction a lot of employers have, right or wrong. SL8 (solicitor, employer side)

Another interviewee illuminated the mechanisms by which an employee can become increasingly disenchanted as a formal process unfolds, picking up on earlier observations about the process itself altering how a complainant feels and is perceived:

I'd say that eighty per cent or more of the discrimination or whistle blowing claims I've dealt with had an element of: 'Here was my initial issue and it became *larger* as soon as I took it through this process.' Then the individual feels they have just the *whole* organization against them, rather than just the individual manager against whom the issue arose. It actually becomes tiers or layers of managers who have just rubber stamped the original decision without looking at it properly … Employees just feel they are being victimized by going through the procedure. *That is a constant complaint that I've had to run. They feel so strongly. They feel as strongly about the failure of the process as they do about the original situation that led to it.* In fact sometimes *the original situation pales into insignificance compared to what happens then afterwards.* SL13 (solicitor, employee side)

Some lawyer interviewees gave specific overarching explanations for the phenomenon of problems being made worse by internal procedures, for example that top management expect HR to achieve results with policy and procedures alone, and linked to this, that the opportunity for resolution diminishes the further the attempt gets from the protagonists. Half the senior lawyers perceived a key problem as the associated absence of early, common-sense resolution based on basic fairness norms.

Interestingly, despite the negative nature of these views, they are perfectly reconcilable with the description by one lawyer interviewee of sincere, conscientious efforts by senior people operating formal processes:

Something that does strike me is that when you have a disciplinary or a grievance, quite often the person who is deciding it will be very senior. There's nothing really in it for them and yet they do treat it very seriously indeed. Over the years I've been struck by how you can get a relatively junior individual bringing a grievance, or being the subject of disciplinary proceedings, and you'll have main board directors or other very senior people, spending a day or two really getting to grips with the rights and wrongs of the issues. I don't get the feeling that this is all done with a sigh and a moan. 'Oh this bloody law making us have to do this.' It's just a given. That is what is done. If you've got to do it, you ought to do it properly. SL10 (barrister, mixed practice)

Around half of my lawyer interviewees, furthermore, commented on organizational procedures sometimes going 'over the top', to the point of grievances being upheld internally and then overturned in the ET. Finally, problematic proceduralization was linked with the public sector by around half the senior lawyers. The following encapsulated this perspective:

One thing I do think often is that formal procedures are unhelpful to the resolution of issues. In a way the better procedures you have I think, bizarrely and madly it actually serves to increase rather than decrease the problem. The moment things go formal you get ten more people involved and everybody takes adversarial positions. So I kind of think that's partly why there's a worse problem with these kinds of cases in the public sector. I think the public sector at a senior level realizes that about its culture and is doing an enormous amount to try to encourage internal mediation processes ... They're having different levels of success. But everybody is trying to do it because I think there is a recognition that, you know, formality actually doesn't help. SL4 (solicitor, employer side)

Interestingly, this observation came after the general point was made that procedures and formality create common problems for organizations, public and private, which have developed systems of this kind. The idea was that this translates into greater difficulties for the public sector given the increased likelihood overall that these employers will take a strongly procedural approach.

3. The Influence of Law and Legal Process

There were clear strands in the data about the influence of law and legal process on, first, behavioural standards at work (or, to put it negatively, what is regarded as unacceptable conduct) and, second, organizational responses to this kind of conflict. Again, I relate what senior managers and senior lawyers said, which demonstrated considerable agreement. The coincidence of perspectives in this context, contrasting to some dissonance on the issues considered earlier, seems likely to be explained by both groups now concentrating on what they perceived the law to be doing, whereas in talking about organizations, senior managers (naturally, I would say) were less focused than lawyers on the background legal framework.

(1) Procedural influences

We have seen that a good proportion of senior manager interviewees and more of the senior lawyers saw proceduralization and associated formality as problematic for dealing with behavioural conflict. These aspects of organizational life were, however, ascribed to legal influence by about two-thirds of senior managers. The picture was again complicated though by interviewees also acknowledging non-legal influences, especially the size of organizations and their internal culture. In addition, many described law's impact being mediated by HR, lawyers, or both, several referring to the effects of cautious and mistaken legal analyses by such intermediaries.

Characterizing law as requiring proceduralization was succinctly captured by the following comment, which also suggests that this has changed over recent decades:

Twenty years ago it was just less complex. The law has changed. The law's now focussed around process. Follow your process. Get your process right. Historically it was *if the facts of what you're doing are right*, then that's the right thing to do. That's not the case any more. You could be *completely okay* with what you did. SM5 (private, large, HR)

The following addressed the day-to-day impact of the law on HR functions:

Any paperwork involved must be absolutely impeccable. You are always thinking, this could end up in an ET. An ET will want to see what we have done every step of the way. Every e-mail I write is very carefully written. I don't write e-mails that I would *cringe* if read out in an ET. Everything has to be considered. I consider my responses to everything ... Arranging hearings, attending hearings. It's huge. SM1 (public, large, HR)

Accounts were also given of how this regime is experienced by front-line managers, with resentment expressed at the attendant constraints. One person contrasted HR commendation of their approach with what had been said of other managers, speculating that being a lawyer helped them adhere to the organization's procedures. Another saw the problem as being that 'the steps you have to take in response to legal advice are so burdensome. You have to record everything and ever little incident.' SM13 (civil society/third sector, small, non-HR).

At the same time, a few interviewees analysed the influence of law in comparison to other factors. The consistent point was that the size, and to some extent culture, of certain organizations dictates that they formalize policies and procedures. These interviewees accordingly saw legal influence at the level of content only. As one stated:

To try to summarize what I think, we would have grievance and disciplinary procedures irrespective because we have so many cases and we need to manage them consistently. Law's always been there all my life, so it's second nature that we write a policy to reflect the law and that we review it in that way too. But we like to keep our policies etc as simple and straightforward as possible. So I don't discuss them with managers as being legal documents. I tell them that this is just how you handle things. SM17 (private, large, HR)

Others mentioned the law's influence being mediated by third parties, either HR or lawyers, sometimes mistakenly, for example as follows:

My own personal bugbear is: 'Why do you have a grievance procedure and a bullying and harassment one?', because then you get into arguments before you even start about which one you go down. *I don't know* why organizations do that. Some say to me that they do it because they're legally required to, which I know they're not. SM10 (public and private, various sizes, HR)

The same interviewee saw mistakes of this kind as exemplifying managerial avoidance of certain issues. 'Things like the proliferation of policies and all that sort of stuff, that's not the law per se, that's around a sort of mistaken response to how we can deal with things that we'd perhaps prefer not to deal with.' SM10 (public and private, various sizes, HR).

There was clear support amongst senior lawyers for the view that legal influence leads to proceduralization and formality, with over three-quarters reporting a connection in one way or another. This overall perception was illustrated by the comment that '[a]s soon as something becomes in the least bit in the arena of formal procedure, clients perceive themselves as having to do all sorts of things because the law requires it'. SL2 (solicitor, employer side). Some senior lawyers, however, focused on particular causes of action, like unfair dismissal, while others distinguished between organizations of different sizes and cultures in the procedural legal influences they perceived.

Subtle analyses resulted. The following is a good example, drawing out the role of lawyers and HR professionals in encouraging organizations to adopt policies and procedures:

HR professionals and employment lawyers will run around saying, implicitly or explicitly: 'You've got to have an equal opportunities policy or it will be taken against you' or 'You've got to have a disciplinary procedure because of the ACAS Code'. Then on whistle-blowing, the legislation comes in, you've got to try to control and channel complaints to make sure they're dealt with properly, so you need a whistle-blowing policy. I suppose that if you really delve into it you have to say that for a lot of those policies, yes they are driven by law in the sense that they are trying to address the legal framework to catch, spot and minimize risks.... SL8 (solicitor, employer side)

There were also interesting meditations on procedural legal influence not having consistent effects. One lawyer made this point regarding poor conduct sometimes being tolerated because of an individual's perceived value to the organization:

The law has created work for HR teams and training teams ... Has it really affected the way people behave? They tend to go through more process when they try to resolve problems. With the kind of formalization I'm talking about, people who behave badly because they know they can get away with it, are still behaving badly because they know they can get away with it. SL5 (solicitor, employee side)

Another, while perceiving formal structures as a feature of large employers under legal and HR influence, was similarly tentative about the impact on people who actually operate them:

[W]hether or not the law informs what is in the mind of the person going through the process in a particular case, as opposed to when the structures are created, I'm not sure. The procedures will be there as a reaction to law, but it's a much more vexed question whether the law filters through to decision-making in an individual case. It probably does at the extremes but the position is much less clear in cases about not fitting in, being a bit marginalized, not going down to the pub, not being tolerant. SL14 (barrister, employee side)

From another perspective, therefore, this comment from a lawyer highlighted significant disconnection between those deciding on policy at a general organizational level and the people at the managerial coalface.

In terms of the damage many senior managers perceived in the operation of formal policies and procedures, it is relevant that several saw legal influence as pivotal. One senior manager, in fact an ex-lawyer, expressed this as follows:

The notion that structures can enflame definitely includes legal structures. Law enflames in that it can give a sense of entitlement on both sides ... Sometimes I think the law purports to put a rather sort of simplistic structure on what's a very complex situation and I think that can encourage people to be rather simplistic and rigid in their responses ... As I say, this is not an anti-employee thing. It's absolutely on both sides ... You either win a case or you lose it and I think that permeates through the whole of this discourse because ultimately if I go to litigation either I win or I lose, ergo there's a very sort of simplistic approach to me being right and you being wrong, or the other way round, and that's really all there is to it and it doesn't allow for the inevitable *fudge* that is probably the most sensible outcome in these situations. SM7 (civil society/third sector, medium, lawyer)

Another captured the day-to-day challenge of operating internal procedures when caught up in a difficult, protracted behavioural conflict:

This was a member of staff whose behaviour and work standard I felt deteriorated over a period of time. We did in the end go down a disciplinary route and involve employment lawyers, and I have to say it was the worst experience of my working life ... She was after all a fairly senior member of staff who you shouldn't expect to have to micro-manage, as I saw it, in this way ... [I] do remember that I felt *so* constrained by what the lawyers were saying that I felt I couldn't speak my mind ... I was having to deal with it on a day to day basis and I was *terrified* really of the organization being sued, so that I found it very hard to know exactly what to say. You don't have a lawyer that you can phone up every five minutes to say: 'She said this and what shall I say?' You still have to try to deal with it. SM13 (civil society/third sector, small, non-HR)

This depiction of trying to abide by internal policies and procedures, in this instance directly influenced by legal advice, illustrated with some precision how a manager might come to feel that legal influence had removed their capacity to address a problem.

Some senior lawyers also depicted the harms of proceduralization being located in legal influence. It is a useful corrective, however, to read this more positive comment contrasting earlier eras:

I've undoubtedly observed legal influences. There is no doubt at all that the introduction of grievance and disciplinary procedures that are premised on an attempt to listen and to be reflective … have been *enormously* beneficial. You don't even have to go into any great depth in reading the Donovan Report to see how awful things were then and comparing the situation now, to see how enormously beneficial they have been. You may say that is a legalization of the process. I think it is. SL11 (barrister, mixed practice)

How much of a paradoxical position lawyers, reflecting their clients, perceived organizations to be in was nevertheless also articulated:

If we walked into an ET on say a discrimination claim where we'd not gone formal at all, we'd tried to have a chat, we'd tried to keep things low level, we'd tried to do it all informally, there were no minuted meetings, then *get your chequebook out*. That's even if all those chats had been done with good heart, with a desire to reasonably, thoughtfully sort things out, with the best, purest intentions, even so, get your chequebook out. If you manage to sort it out, fine. If you don't you will be *absolutely crucified* in the ET, *absolutely crucified*.

That's why people go that route, and that's even though going that formal route often makes things worse, often takes away any chance of sorting out the underlying problem. Even believing as firmly as I do that going the formal route is much more likely to make the problem worse, and that it's much more likely to have you end up in ET, the legal pressures would affect how I'd respond if I was approached today by someone saying: 'This allegation of discrimination, or whatever it is, has been made. What shall I do? Shall I investigate? The person isn't saying they want to raise a complaint. They're not saying they want to raise a grievance. But they've made a very serious allegation. Shall I get A and B in a room and bang their heads together and say: 'Come on. Sort it out' … Or shall I investigate?' I'm afraid my cautious advice would be to investigate, even knowing that that's going to make the problem worse. The reason is that from an organizational risk perspective, if you try to do the right thing you'll be screwed. Or you'll have a big risk of being screwed if it doesn't work. SL4 (solicitor, employer side)

(2) Substantive complexities

The impact that substantive legal rules were reported to have was much more patchy, with a distinct bifurcation in what senior managers reported about anti-discrimination law and about other kinds of rules. As such, a large majority commented in one way or another on the organizational impact of equality law and about one-half seemed somewhat baffled by me asking about other sorts of laws that regulate workplace behaviour. This went so far as some interviewees questioning if there were any such rules, while knowledge and understanding of laws about behaviour outside the equality field appeared generally very weak. This was also supported by about two-thirds of senior lawyers commenting on the significance of equality law within organizations and expressing variable impressions of the impact of other substantive legal rules.

The other noticeable features were that, first, despite the patchiness of substantive legal influence, the way senior managers reasoned about the wrongfulness of conduct bore important similarities to the reasoning approaches of judges in my sample of cases. Second, the influence of senior lawyers in mediating legal rules emerged as important, with settlement practice said to play an especially significant role. Overall, the latter seemed further to distance organizational responses from the values immanent in the legislation, on top of the similar effects coming from legally inspired proceduralization and the patchy influence of substantive law.

(a) Prioritizing equality law rules about behaviour

Over 80 per cent of senior managers commented in some way on the influence organizationally of equality law. While several highlighted only a particular aspect, many reported a general effect. The following instance of a generalized impact explicitly contrasted this with the effect of other relevant rules:

I'm not sure, except for discrimination law, that law affects what people think is acceptable or unacceptable behaviour at work. I don't think most people are cognizant of what the law says about these matters. I'm constantly amazed about how little people know about law that affects them about employment. That's true for senior management also. Other than again that there are certain obligations around race, disability and sex, I don't think they are aware of the law in this area. SM1 (public, large, HR)

There were also sophisticated meditations about how the law had come to have this influence, commenting on the interaction with social change and on whether law causes underlying attitudes to alter:

Certainly twenty years ago I experienced sexist behaviour and racist behaviour on a regular basis and hardly *ever*, ever experience it today. So there is a huge comparison for me. I think it's partly to do with the fact that it's so out there. People quote it to each other ... I think at a certain point the person who makes serially sexist comments probably stops making them when they realize there's a legal implication to doing so. I don't think he suddenly wakes up one morning, reads *The Guardian* and thinks 'I've had the wrong attitude all my life' .... SM8 (private, various sizes, non-HR)

There was some noting also of the difference the public sector equality duty (PSED) in section 149 of the Equality Act 2010 has made in terms of embedding equality norms, at least in the hands of certain employers with 'a thirst to know what to do' (SM22, public, various, non-HR). Still, one senior lawyer emphasized that they had only witnessed this 'in few situations and far between', while often 'compliance with the PSED has been a bit of a sort of tick box exercise' (SL12, barrister, mixed practice).

The perception of equality law as influential was echoed among senior lawyers in a more muted way, both in the sense that only two-thirds observed an effect and that some characterized this in quite narrow terms. The following encapsulated this kind of response, again seeing mistakes about the legal requirements on employers as relevant:

Anti-discrimination law having the effect that organizations assume they have obligations to treat individuals in a particular way, even where sometimes they don't, is the biggest legal influence that I see. There's also the harassment effect, according to which organizations are clear that some things are just beyond the pale. SL1 (solicitor, employer side)

Another saw an impact in extreme instances but linked this to questioning law's capacity to affect less clear-cut situations:

I think law probably helps with finding very clear behavioural boundaries. You cannot touch a woman's breasts at work. You cannot call the black worker who reports to you an explicit racist name. Then at the other end of the spectrum is conduct that is entirely acceptable in managing your workforce in an appropriate way. Then there is the grey area in which the law probably doesn't have an effect ... We all have our own prejudices, they are just different and if manifested they are either unlawful or not. There is a lot of just not fitting in: 'He's just not one of the guys. She's just a bit too stroppy or a bit full of herself.' It's either gender or racially informed but it's not thought about in those terms. So law can't particularly get at that I don't think. Maybe if you've got a really great employer or trainer, and some of it is lack of awareness, there may be room for making the culture of the workplace one in which people are more aware of the impact of their own prejudices. But that's quite a difficult thing to do isn't it? SL14 (barrister, employee side)

Arguably bearing out the difficulty evoked here of adapting equality norms to the complexity of working life, there were also reports of people responding by deploying formality earlier in the process. A senior lawyer, echoing a number of senior managers, thought that situations were more likely to 'go formal' where there was a difference of ethnicity between manager and managed. As this interviewee stated: 'My theory, and it is only a theory, is that managers are fearful of allegations of discrimination and believe that their best protection where they feel they have genuine cause for complaint about someone of a different racial group, is to go the formal route. I think they feel that their actions are more likely to be misinterpreted if they try to have an informal chat. I think that is entirely driven by fear of complaint.' (SL4, solicitor, employer side).

Perhaps most interesting among the comments made by senior lawyers about the role of equality law in working life was the claim by one, not only that this had made a significant cultural difference, but that general behavioural norms were inherent to the rules:

Obviously it's a huge question how far attitudes have changed over my working life and what the causes of that are. But I think employment legislation has had a very beneficial effect in creating a culture ... It's not just that there's the fear that you might be sued, however remote that fear might be, but it's also the perception of what's right and wrong that has been affected by what's lawful and unlawful ... I don't think you can really divorce general behaviour from the law of discrimination actually ... [I] think that what really underpins the law of sex and race discrimination, sexual orientation and everything else, is treating people with respect and fairly ... I think that the very simple headline message is 'Treat people with respect and don't insult them' and that's not compartmentalized as 'Don't insult women or don't insult black and Asian people'. The message is to treat your employees with respect. SL10 (barrister, mixed practice)

(b) Marginalizing behavioural rules of other types

There were some outliers who perceived law in general to have no substantive influence either on behavioural standards at work or on how people respond to conflicts regarding these. Once interviewees who took this position are added to the more than half who reported that, equality law aside, substantive legal influence is either entirely or practically non-existent, nearly three-quarters of all the senior managers conveyed their belief that non-equality legal rules regulating behaviour at work have no impact.

It was in fact a senior lawyer who offered the best insight into this phenomenon:

I think one of the most surprising things when behavioural standards are set, is how little the law is thought about and how poor the grasp of many workers and their managers of legal standards. I find it extraordinary ... The common experience of setting up a Dignity at Work kind of policy is either that it is completely overblown, impenetrable and has so many things that might amount to misbehaviour at work that it's just confusing, or there doesn't seem to be any attention at all to what behaviour is unacceptable because there is legal protection ... You see a lot about light switches, and increasingly recycling, but not about standards of behaviour. SL3 (solicitor, employee side)

When we recall the number of legal rules outside equality law that set standards of workplace conduct, outlined in Chapter 3 and discussed in Chapters 4 to 7, this feature of the data is as remarkable as the fact that so many respondents attributed significance to anti-discrimination rules. Certainly lawyers view the regulation of ongoing employment relationships through common law obligations in contract and tort as being of paramount importance, which is unsurprising given the range of relevant legal rules and litigation developments of this type.[21] I was, therefore, careful to test that interviewees really meant what they were saying. It was particularly in this part of the interviews that I had the impression that manager respondents were somewhat baffled by my probing, suggesting that what they were saying was obvious and uncontroversial in their eyes. Equally, this point of view was sometimes combined with senior manager interviewees explicitly doubting that there are in fact any substantive legal standards that address workplace behaviour outside equality law.

Another way I tested my understanding was by asking what senior manager interviewees thought influenced behavioural standards in organizations either instead of or in addition to law. I asked everyone about this and in doing so examined what those who denied substantive legal influences regarded as instead determining organizational attitudes and experiences.

Practically everyone, whether they perceived law having substantive influence outside the equality sphere or not, said that views on acceptable workplace behaviour derived from personal values and the contextualized judgments these enabled people to make. This attitude was encapsulated in the following, interestingly linked to the premise that equality law contains absolutes and other types of law do not:

I think it is right that law doesn't influence people's ideas of what is fair or unfair, acceptable or unacceptable, in terms of workplace behaviour. It comes from people's internal morality. Context is all in law. And there aren't in fact many absolutes in this area in the way that there are more often in discrimination law. So I think people are more reliant on their own value system. SM3 (public, large, lawyer)

The point was also made by some interviewees that personal and organizational values are mutually influential:

It's interesting this isn't it? I think the people who are dealing with these cases all the time set their benchmarks of how the organization behaves. They set their norms. I think they have those in their heads. I try to get them to have some kind of shared understanding of what's acceptable and what isn't. I think if you ask them, they'll have a gut feel for what goes in the organization and what doesn't go. And I think that's kind of organizationally set ... My responses come from a combination of my personal views, which have been shaped by my experience, and an assessment of what's normal in the organization. What I try to do through the policies and through consistent treatment, is to push up the standards of behaviour. I do that also from an organizational development perspective by teaching managers to coach and talk, to do those things that we'd prefer them to do as an alternative to shouting, which is often what happens. In terms of the way individuals behave, behaviour, conduct, all of those things that as we say merge, it's *just a judgment*. Other than, if I'm honest, in respect of protected characteristics, standards of behaviour are just learned norms. It's absolutely about a contextualized judgment which may alter from one work setting to another. SM17 (private, large, HR)[22]

---

[21] See p 54 in Ch 2 and pp 61 and 92–101 in Ch 3.

[22] See also: 'I don't ... see law really playing any part in making fine, tricky judgments about whether someone has crossed the line to behaving unacceptably. With my law head I suppose you'd say: "What would an ET think?" But I don't think your average manager walking around would ask, or that the feel of the place is about, either that's legal or that's not legal. It's just a matter of: "That's not on and that is, and that situation really depends on the circumstances in which it happened, and the context and everything, which might make it alright or not alright, and that other thing just never would be ok".' SM20 (public, large, lawyer).

One particularly sophisticated analysis questioned the boundaries between the personal, societal, organizational, and legal, illustrating how a person's internal morality might in part be constructed by law. This valuably pointed to the impossibility of isolating different influences on what happens within organizations, but it remains significant that so many disclaimed substantive legal impacts on behavioural standards at work beyond those from equality law, instead perceiving personal and organizational value systems to be what matter.

Underlying several of these musings is that the application of any norms, legal or otherwise, to real-life workplace interactions involves an interpretive process in which a range of people necessarily participate and a variety of influences interact. A corollary is that making sense of events is often complicated and difficult, especially where behaviour is at stake, as my analysis of substantive higher court adjudication bore out. One front-line manager's account of involvement in this process culminated in the view that it is impossible for law meaningfully to set behavioural standards:

I think what was acceptable and unacceptable behaviour at work probably simply wasn't clear. Although it looks clear when it's written down in a policy, and the lawyers would say: 'There are certain standards and you can expect your staff to adhere to them', when it comes to the day to day of what is acceptable in an office and what isn't, it's *very, very* hard. How do you actually define that someone has just been rude to you? Often it's in a tone of voice or it's the way that something has been said, rather than actually what's been said ... How do you write that down so that everybody understands? It's all very well writing down: 'You must respect your colleagues' and some things are easy, like: 'You mustn't make racist or sexist remarks'. That is relatively straightforward. But when it's just insolence and things like that, it's almost impossible to write down exactly what that is. I think the law can't tell you what that is ... [T]o give an example, in a job description it often says: 'Must work as part of a team'. Trying to say that someone doesn't work as part of a team, and then having to explain exactly what that means, when it is things like ignoring somebody or not helping when you should have, that's really hard. SM13 (civil society/third sector, small, non-HR)

This observation was uncannily echoed by a senior lawyer looking back at long experience of difficult behavioural disputes in large workplaces with commitment-style employee relations and often deep-seated trade unionism:

I thought about whether more might be done in these kinds of environments either about articulating the behavioural standards that apply more formally, or about ensuring that they are communicated and shared. I think the difficulty is how hard it is to articulate standards that say: 'We don't expect you to put yourself at the centre of everything. We don't expect you not to notice how your behaviour impacts on other people.' SL2 (solicitor, employer side)

Another who dealt with very different, more managerial environments, made an analogous point, but locating law's limitations in the legal risks that people always take: 'Has law ever made a difference in the area of bad behaviour? I doubt it can. People take risks all the time with legal liabilities. I'm terribly cynical.' (SL5, solicitor, employee side).

(c) Juxtaposing organizational and legal reasoning

(i) Senior managers and judges

This leads naturally to what I find perhaps the most intriguing aspect of my data. This is that there was considerable similarity in modes of substantive reasoning about behavioural conflicts as between senior managers and my sample of judgments. Almost every senior manager conceived the central organizational task as being to find the line between acceptable and unacceptable conduct, believed this ought to be done in a highly contextualized, fact-specific way, and regarded some conduct as simply beyond the pale.

There was, however, not the same discussion about locating boundaries in relation to organizations' procedural responses, with managers' responses instead exhibiting a degree of worry about how internal procedures were working and a tendency to attribute this part of organizational practice to the influence of law. Indeed, the reasoning approach that I extracted from the sample of judgments that only a handful of interviewees described was multifaceted balancing analyses of employers' obligations animated by overarching ideas of fairness and reasonableness.

One senior lawyer seemed to hit the nail of this interaction between legal and organizational decision-making on the head with the following observation:

I suppose the law doesn't do a bad job these days at identifying that there is potentially an invisible line between acceptable and unacceptable behaviour, which is always difficult to identify because it's invisible and when have you crossed it? … The trouble is that in a way the law is just reflecting the difficult issues that come up and the difficult dividing line you've got between what is acceptable and not. So does that provide guidance, as distinct from just saying: 'Oh there's a tricky issue, you've got to look at the situation in the round and the particular circumstances are relevant to whether it was reasonable for the victim to feel harassed in the particular circumstances'? … I suppose the statute and the case law is saying these are the difficult dividing lines. Is the law then giving any positive guidance as to what people should and shouldn't do? Answer probably not because it ends up being so case specific. *But what does the client do with that? What does the client do?* SL8 (solicitor, employer side)

(ii) The mediating effects of legal advice and process
In truth, what senior lawyers said about general legal influences on organizations was highly variable, ranging from extreme skepticism that there had been any, through to deep-seated convictions that the enactment of individual rights has civilized working life. This is perhaps where the difference of epistemic approach between managerial respondents and lawyers was most apparent. This feature of my data therefore suggested various hypotheses about the effects of professional legal experience (eg whether one was a barrister or solicitor). What is more significant for this project, however, is what senior lawyers said about their own influence on clients and the effects specifically of litigation.

We have already seen that some interviewees perceived a tendency for lawyers to steer claimants towards equality law, which hints at one reason this area of law might be perceived as having an organizational impact when other types of law are not so regarded. More generally, almost every senior lawyer described processes by which they mediated legal influence. Several referred to the depth of their relationships with clients having the effect that even negative advice was readily accepted when an adverse court ruling would not be. The following encapsulated this from a solicitor's point of view:

I have a very special relationship with most of my clients. I've known the organizations for a long time. All the ones I deal with tend to take my advice … If I think something has gone really wrong I'll strongly advise my clients to settle and they do learn from those. That's much easier. They do absolutely learn in all sorts of ways from my advice earlier on … They will take a lot of stuff from a trusted adviser that they won't take from a court. It's an extremely interesting point. I hadn't thought of it like that before. SL2 (solicitor, employer side)

A barrister stated the same idea succinctly: 'They'll accept bad news from me but not from the judge.' (SL10, barrister, mixed practice).

What was said about the dynamics of settlement further emerged as central to the organizational impact of legal process as opposed to that of underlying legal rules. Three-quarters of the lawyer interviewees discussed settlement and their role in relation to it. About two-thirds described the decision as to whether employers settle or 'fight' as a balance between the risks and costs versus the benefits of each alternative. A background factor that a similar proportion raised was that cases about behaviour are seen as difficult for employees to win. One explained how this shaped advice to claimants about proceeding to a full hearing: 'I fight a lot of cases ... But I think people have to be *sure*, and I say to them ... "You have to be sure that you will be happy reflecting back and thinking: I did the right thing. I might have lost but I did the right thing."' (SL14, employee, barrister).

What senior lawyers identified as important to settlement discussions conspicuously strayed from either the rights or wrongs of what had happened or whether legal rules had been followed. Various cynical calculations were described, the most worrying involving employers playing on claimants' ill health to secure low settlements.[23] How internal politics work more generally was described in the following:

It's how the claim will play in the public arena that will have the biggest effect. If you get a bad case of sexual harassment that will get in all the newspapers and the organization knows that is what is likely to happen, they will run out of sympathy. Still, the high earner will get away with it for longer than the person lower down the line. It's a cost–benefit analysis. That's exactly what it is. That's *exactly* what it is. It's as cold blooded as that. That is the assessment that goes through the mind of management. Can we afford this? SL5 (solicitor, employee side)

One senior lawyer described a misbehaving senior employee internalizing this approach to the extent that they did not accept personal responsibility for changing their behaviour, considering instead that it was management's responsibility to step in if their conduct created an unacceptable organizational risk. This interviewee logically extrapolated that law merely changes the cost–benefit analysis, and only after the event:

The high performer can ultimately become too great a risk and the downside to the business can be much more significant than the benefit they bring. It's like a nuclear threat. In many organizations that means the legal influence is completely after the event ... [I]n many of the businesses that I deal with I don't see law playing a role until the cost-benefit analysis means they *have to* intervene. But by then it has become very difficult to solve the underlying problem. SL7 (solicitor, mixed practice)

Other considerations affecting settlement that were less blatantly unrelated to substantive norms reflected in legal rules were potential reputational harm, referred to in the citation from SL5 above, and the scale of irretrievable costs in time and money.

There was some comment, nonetheless, about issues of principle influencing settlement practice. About one-third of the senior lawyers made a distinction between the public and private sectors, saying that cost–benefit analysis was more likely to be undertaken in the private sector and that some public sector employers refuse on principle to settle unmeritorious claims. Some noted this especially in respect of discrimination actions. Indeed, around one-half of the senior lawyers referred to discrimination cases being generally more charged (eg emotionally), and therefore more likely to get to a hearing:

Otherwise cases that tend to fight are discrimination cases ... People get more angry about those cases I think. That's on both sides. My impression these days is that nobody minds admitting or accepting that dismissal might have been unfair, because they can always say it was for technical reasons. But nobody wants to hold their hand up and say they discriminated on the grounds of race or sex, and very few people want to be labelled as homophobic. SL5 (solicitor, employee side)

---

[23] See text to p 191 above for the corresponding description of individuals sometimes abandoning claims because they felt their health had been so damaged by their employer's response (and the text to n 270 in Ch 2 for other supportive evidence).

Another version of this point of view was expressed by about one-third of senior lawyers who saw that sometimes the personal element in cases about behaviour, particularly about equality law, can impede settlement. To some extent this intersected with the notion that how far a case goes can depend on the personalities involved.

How far the litigation process shifts litigants' focus from underlying rights and wrongs was further demonstrated by comments about employer responses to judgments. About one-half of the senior lawyers observed that employers simply do not accept adverse findings by tribunals and courts, while a sizeable number saw any impact as constrained and as ignoring the wider implications of particular cases. The following attributed this to the combativeness of litigation:

I don't get a sense that people feel the judgment resolves anything. I think that by the time you get there positions are so polarized that I don't think you can see the judgment like that anymore. I don't think litigants can. Litigation is an adversarial process. It doesn't assist you in how you might learn from things and move on. It puts you at one extreme side. SL12 (barrister, mixed practice)

Litigation 'insiders' also seemed to view the fact that judgments against organizations have little impact as entirely natural and predictable:

[C]lients just don't accept the court's reasoning as being correct. That doesn't happen. Think about the realities. An allegation comes completely out of left field. The organization hasn't taken a view about it. They immediately start taking a view about it. If they think it's got legs they will do their best to resolve it. Why wouldn't they, generally speaking? If they think it hasn't got legs they've already made up their minds as to what they think about it. The fact that some random external person tells them something different is really not going to impact them. It will impact on them only if it's purely instrumental. 'What lesson do we learn from this? We will make this shorter. We'll put an extra layer of thing here. In future we will do x, y and z.' But not: 'Oh God. We were institutionally racist'. SL2 (solicitor, employer side)

I find something intensely depressing about juxtaposing the hard work that Chapters 4, 6, and 7 suggested judges put into their rulings with reports of this kind of dismissive reaction.

4. Summary and Discussion

In terms of the content of behavioural conflict, the main themes that emerged from senior manager interviewees were that it relates to behaviour beyond what people describe as bullying; that subjective views often differ about the subject matter of the dispute; less pervasively, that problems of this kind are intrinsically difficult for organizations to deal with, including due to divergent subjectivities; and (although only for about one-half of my senior managers) that there are links between behavioural conflict and group identity issues, sometimes related to legal influence. In turn, the understanding senior lawyers had of behavioural conflict, although variable, was more influenced by legal categories, sometimes remarkably so. The impact of equality law on what lawyers said was especially noticeable and allied to perceptions that legal advisors channel claimants towards discrimination actions.[24]

Many senior managers saw behavioural conflict as intrinsic to working life and almost invariably referred to the damage it causes. A wide range of negative individual and organizational consequences were alluded to, including where problems were

---

[24] See pp 125–28 in Ch 5 for evidence about the litigation effects that supports this.

silenced or suppressed.[25] In terms of quantification, while a few senior managers downplayed the significance of behavioural conflict, senior lawyers often described matters involving this as a major part of their workload, raising the possibility that this kind of conflict looms large among disputes that escalate beyond workplaces.[26]

There was no consensus from senior manager interviewees about the individual causes of conflict emerging and escalating. Noticeably, potential spurs from the legal framework, like increases in individual rights or the lure of compensation, attracted only occasional comment. The one reasonably prevalent theme was that personality plays an important role in whether behavioural issues become conflictual to different degrees. The figure of the 'difficult' employee was raised by some and characterized as causing the worst conflicts. At times this was ascribed to mental illness, while there was recognition too that the initial problem and the organization's reaction could contribute to a complainant becoming unreasonable.[27] Senior lawyers saw personality as an even greater issue. They were more explicit, however, in pointing out that individual propensity accounts for problems being minimized as well as escalated. Lawyers as well sometimes referred to the deleterious impact that organizational responses can have on individuals, in a sense pushing them to become adversarial.

Amidst varied accounts of different workplace environments, senior managers were practically unanimous about the impact of organizational culture on behavioural issues. Particular salience was given by about one-half of senior manager interviewees to whether a workplace was, first, within either the public and civil society sectors or the private and, second, either unionized or not. The former category was in each instance typically associated with more stringent behavioural standards. Still, there was the perception of some vulnerability to conflict in public sector and civil society workplaces, explored further in Chapter 9.[28] Some senior manager interviewees also described trade unionism as changing and declining amidst acknowledgement of its value. Finally, there was a startling level of agreement about what was needed within an organization to prevent and address behavioural conflict. This was listed by almost every manager as tackling problems early, strong leadership about behavioural standards, good communication, and, finally, management and HR being skilled in handling behavioural issues. In addition, a substantial majority added either employee representation or at least involvement as vital to dealing effectively with this kind of workplace problem.

Senior lawyers, on the other hand, offered a quite different picture of the organizational causes of behavioural conflict. They focused on what happens when things go wrong, no doubt reflecting the different stage at which they tend to become involved and the subset of problems that come to lawyers. There was variation, however, in senior lawyers' responses, both as to what they saw as organizational causes and, perhaps leading on from this, in the extent to which they were cognizant that their perceptions derived from partial experience. Some took exceptional care in drawing conclusions from what they had seen in their practices while others were prone to generalizing on the basis of the limited evidence base that provided.

[25] See further at p 187 above.
[26] See further at p 189 above. See also Ch 3 on the wide reach of UK laws regulating workplace conduct and Ch 4 on themes that come through from higher court adjudication about behavioural conflict, both of which illuminate how this might come about.
[27] See pp 190–92 above and further at pp 227–36 in Ch 9 and pp 253–56 in Ch 10 on the structuring of who complains and litigates about workplace problems.
[28] See pp 216–17, 222–24, 227–36, and 240–43 in Ch 9.

Bearing in mind the fact that senior lawyer views must to some extent reflect the nature of their particular work, the only organizational causes many identified were an employer being in the public sector and deficient management. The latter was also indirectly supported by lawyers reporting employer clients to be taking steps to ameliorate the position. The forms of management failure that were especially commented on were avoiding problems and turning on the complainant.[29]

The final organizational factor in the emergence and escalation of behavioural conflict that both senior managers and lawyers emphasized was proceduralization and formality within workplaces. All senior manager interviewees commented on the importance of this,[30] while there was a split between a substantial minority who viewed these phenomena as positive and a majority who deplored them. A complicating factor was that many related proceduralization and formality to the demands of managing large-scale workforces.[31] A notably challenging aspect in technical legal terms was that several interviewees depicted confidentiality requirements within such processes as impeding the internal resolution of problems.

Senior lawyers were again more damning of the formal aspect of organizational life, relating different ways in which they had seen internal procedures worsen problems. This included mention again of employees being marginalized and becoming more disaffected because of employers' procedural reactions, as well as suggestions that the opportunities for early resolution and compromise were thereby restricted. There were accounts also from about one-half of the lawyer interviewees of employers overreacting to difficulties. Sometimes this was connected to the perceived tendency for conflicts to be more serious in the public sector, albeit perhaps owing to organizational commitment to high labour standards.

A majority of senior manager interviewees, backed up by a larger proportion of senior lawyers, in turn attributed proceduralization and attendant formality within organizations to legal influence, confirming evidence to this effect since enactment of the right not to be unfairly dismissed in 1971.[32] This was allied, however, to recognition that other factors, especially size and culture, were significant and that HR and lawyers mediate the law's organizational effects, sometimes mistakenly[33] and overcautiously. Several interviewees, especially senior lawyers, gave useful illustrations of how policies and procedures, influenced by law, can work to obstruct the resolution of problems. Examples included standards penetrating organizations only to the extent of being included in formal documentation, frontline managers feeling constrained by proceduralization from tackling situations and legal influence pushing towards adversarialism, even internally. A remarkable point of view expressed by one senior lawyer was that, even so, clients ought to be encouraged to 'go formal' early because of the legal risks of trying and failing to sort a problem out informally.[34] In some ways this comment summed up that law and legal process seem truly to push organizations and their lawyers to respond to difficulties in ways they know are likely to hinder resolution. The legal basis for this comment was contradicted, however, by the evaluation of organizational responses to behavioural problems in the sample of judgments.[35]

---

[29] See further in ns 18 and 19 and accompanying text and p 198 above.

[30] See pp 23–24 in Ch 2 for supportive evidence about the perceived significance of process and that this can be problematic.

[31] See pp 40, 49–50, and 53 in Ch 2 on evidence that supports this perception.

[32] See further at pp 48–49 in Ch 2 and p 247 in Ch 10.

[33] See the text to n 338 in Ch 2 about evidence that procedures were viewed as mandatory when they were not.

[34] See p 200 above.   [35] See Ch 7, esp pp 180–82 and pp 245–46 in Ch 10.

In terms of substantive legal influence, interviewees described variable effects. A signifi-cant majority of senior managers commented in one way or another on the impact of equal-ity law,[36] but about half were apparently nonplussed by me asking about the impact of other sorts of legal rules about workplace behaviour. Overall, the net effect (adding those who perceived no substantive legal effects whatsoever) was that nearly three-quarters of senior manager interviewees saw legal rules that regulate workplace behaviour outside of equality law as having no organizational impact. Reinforcing this theme, nearly all the senior manag-ers intimated that personal values and contextualized judgments based on these are the most influential within workplaces on standards of conduct and on responses to behavioural conflict, albeit that some interviewees recognized law can affect people's 'internal morality'. This pattern was further backed up by a lesser, though still substantial, majority of senior lawyers commenting on some version of equality law influencing organizational practice, while they gave more divergent accounts of other non-procedural legal effects.

The arguably related idea emerged via several interviewees, both managers and law-yers, that legal and other norms are necessarily poorly adapted to making sense of com-plex, subtle, and diverse interactions about workplace conduct. This was reminiscent of factual themes regarding complexity that emerged from the sample of judgments. What might sometimes help to explain the tendency to distinguish substantive legal influ-ences between equality law and other kinds was laypersons' descriptions of the former as being so hard-edged that it cuts through the muddle of working life. I would contend that this understanding of equality law is seriously misguided, not least in light of my findings later about senior lawyers' perceptions of litigating discrimination cases, and earlier about how authoritative adjudication in this area works. Instead, my analysis of judgments suggested jurisdictional complexities have effects across the board and that beyond them adjudication, even if it bears out how challenging it is to apply legal rules to workplace interactions, is surprisingly congruent whether the claims are based on equality rights or any other rules that regulate workplace behaviour.

In some ways the insight that it is difficult meaningfully to apply norms, legal and oth-erwise, to actual work problems was both confounded and confirmed by comparing the data on organizational and adjudicative modes of reasoning about behavioural conflicts. When categorizing conduct itself, almost every senior manager conceived their task as being to find the line between what is acceptable and unacceptable, believed this ought to be done in a highly contextualized, fact-specific way, and regarded some conduct as simply beyond the pale. This was uncannily reminiscent of the reasoning approach in the sample of judgments about the lawfulness or not of conduct itself. When, however, it came to assessing organizational responses to problems, instead of replicating judges' contextualized, multifaceted balancing analyses of what employers ought to do, sub-stantively and procedurally, the organizational focus as told by senior managers was on procedure and formality, with associated worry about the problems this could cause and a tendency to attribute this aspect of workplace practice to legal influence.

A final piece in the jigsaw was the mediating effects of legal advice and the impact of litigation. Some advisers reported a relationship with their clients that was close enough to influence what organizations do in a way that official, court-based adjudication does not. At the same time, descriptions of how settlement works pointed to multiple ways in which litigation outcomes are disconnected from the application of the law, let alone from working out the rights and wrongs of an underlying dispute. Balancing risks and costs against benefits was what senior lawyers often saw to be driving employers' deci-sions about settlement. Various extraneous influences were said to figure: how far an

[36] See for other supportive evidence at pp 48–50 in Ch 2 and further at p 247 in Ch 10.

employer could afford a high performer's negative conduct; whether a claimant could be worn down in the course of litigation, including because of poor health;[37] how any reputational risks played out, and the comparative cost in time and money of alternative courses. Overall, the implication was that litigation often changes risk/benefit analyses but rarely, if ever, alters the taken for granted way of doing things within an organization. Nonetheless, principle was sometimes said to play a part, with comment especially about public sector employers refusing to settle unmeritorious claims.

Marginalizing the impact of emancipatory norms that underlie laws was apparent also from judgments being reported to have only narrow effects.[38] Just as senior managers often seemed confused by questions about the effect of substantive behavioural rules outside equality law, senior lawyers appeared puzzled by me expecting court judgments to influence those to whom they are addressed. The impression again was that these senior lawyers, as insiders, saw it as self-evident that judgments have little purchase in terms of influencing organizational life.

I extract several features of how law and legal process is working from these findings, all somewhat generic and hence potentially transferable to other areas of legal endeavour. *First, there were the strange patterns of legal influence and its absence, overlaid with organizational and judicial thinking sometimes overlapping and sometimes not.* These did not, however, fit the legislative or judicial distinctions explained in Chapters 3 and 5, raising further questions as to the point of the doctrinal splits. Law was nonetheless shown to have some capacity to affect organizational practice in the widespread recognition that equality law is influential, even if not always well understood or correctly implemented. The same can be said of law affecting organizational procedures, however problematically some of this was put into practice. In contrast, there was the peculiar ignorance, at least from an internal legal perspective, of substantive legal standards about workplace behaviour outside equality law.

There is a positive conclusion to be drawn from the legal effects that were felt, since their presence points to potential for regulation to fill in the gaps. Moreover, the possibilities seem to me greater given the similarities there were between the decision-making methods demonstrated in Chapter 6 and how organizational actors reported they naturally think about behavioural problems, at least in terms of guiding standards and making judgments about concrete situations.

Overall, the data suggested that there are important legal influences on organizational life but that the basic normative messages animating legal intervention are not getting through. As one senior lawyer said: 'I think that the very simple headline message is 'Treat people with respect and don't insult them' ... The message is to treat your employees with respect.' SL10 (barrister, mixed practice). My exposition of legal rules in Chapter 3, and the findings reported in Chapters 4 to 7 about their application in higher court judgments, support the contention that the basic message of law in this field is to treat employees fairly, reasonably, and in line with equality norms, both procedurally and substantively, and taking account of the difference the particular context and set of circumstances make to what that requires. It feels quite ironic that this comes quite close to ascribing to law the kind of overarching personal and institutional morality from which many of my interviewees thought organizational decision-makers derived their workplace standards and, even more ironic that many saw this sort of reasoning as what organizational actors revert to when they (erroneously) perceive themselves to be in a

---

[37] See p 206 above on this, and p 191 correspondingly on complainants settling because of the impact of continuing on their health.
[38] This is supported by the slight effects suggested by evidence reviewed at pp 35, 41, and 50–53 in Ch 2.

'law-free zone'. Even so, irony aside, such parallels must create opportunities to enhance law's contribution to the construction of more just workplace environments.

Second, however, a major challenge to effecting change comes from the ways that law and its associated processes appear to deflect organizations from effectively responding to problems, and specifically from doing so by applying basic fairness, reasonableness, and equality norms contained in legal rules. An important contributor to this emerged as legally induced proceduralization and formality. This kind of legal impact in fact was reported in a more pronounced way by lawyers than by managers, no doubt related to them seeing situations in which things have gone the most wrong.

The dynamic of organizations being deflected from solving problems and from concentrating on basic norms was even more present in the accounts of litigation. This was evident from the detachment of decision-making about settlement from underlying legal rules, let alone the standards they instantiated. That senior lawyers tended to perceive the minimal impact of judgments as something obvious spoke volumes about the distance between legal process and the dispute resolution ideals court systems are meant to model. Indeed, far from judgments being seen as authoritative pronouncements by those entrusted with justly resolving conflict, one interviewee called them merely the opinion of 'some random external person'.

Third and finally, these disconnections reflected the indications that an insider perspective on law and legal process provides only partial insight into how law interacts with working life. This was most apparent from differences between what senior managers and senior lawyers said, reflecting the fact that lawyers based their views on more particular samples of organizational situations than managers come across. As such, senior lawyers' comments on the antecedents to disputes emphasized convolution and adversarialism. It is not that these features were absent from senior managers' comments; they also spoke of them as mattering to how law and work interact. The point is that the view from legal practitioners was disproportionately based on this kind of experience, missing out the vast number of situations where conflict does not emerge, is abandoned, or sometimes, is satisfactorily resolved. Resonating also with the factual data in judgments discussed in Chapter 4,[39] this dimension of what senior lawyers reported highlighted the distance between the 'population' of behavioural problems in workplaces, as illuminated by the evidence surveyed in Chapter 2,[40] and the subset that turns into conflicts adjudicated by senior judges.

Senior lawyers' views about the public sector provided a specific startling example of those who work close to legal process having a distinctive perspective. Comments about public sector employers being seen to experience more problems with behavioural conflict contradicted the quantitative empirical evidence that suggests the preponderance of ET claims is in the private sector.[41] Equally, evidence about underlying conflict is nuanced as to where this is more likely to occur and does not point to a public sector bias for problems between colleagues because 'trouble at work' so often comes from dealing with the public.[42]

---

[39] See Ch 4, esp pp 117–18.   [40] See pp 28–32 and 53–54 in Ch 2.

[41] See pp 39–40 and 51 in Ch 2. See also IFF Research, *Payment of Employment Tribunal Awards* (BIS, Nov 2013), 6 and 20 for additional, recent supportive evidence from a qualitative survey with a large representative sample, that the majority of successful ET claims after a hearing or on default judgment were against small employers in the private sector and that 'The vast majority of employers (93%) were operating in the private sector.'

[42] See pp 21–25 in Ch 2. See also the specific recent finding at K Perren, S Roberts, B Stafford, D Hirsch, and M Padley, *Report 3—Disputes and Challenges* (GEO, 2012), 6 and 11 that the likelihood of reporting a dispute about unequal treatment or discrimination in the three years before the research increased with size but was not associated with sector.

The explanation for this perception amongst a sizeable proportion of lawyer interviewees is therefore almost certainly that there is more chance in the public sector of concerns being voiced, that cases will get to senior lawyers, and that claims will be litigated to the bitter end. The factors behind this are explored in the next chapter, but include organizational culture, settlement practice when claims are made, and the greater availability of external legal support for claimants because trade union membership remains widespread. We can conclude from what was said in my interview study that there probably are different sectoral experiences of law and legal process, but not that this can be mapped directly on to the underlying incidence of problems. In other words, the lesson, as some senior lawyers acknowledged, is to expect the same events and conflicts in different kinds of workplaces to have different legal trajectories. This chimes with the way that about one-half of my senior managers saw behavioural standards as generally being higher in the public sector but associated with some perception of vulnerability to individual conflict.

Intriguingly, this gives some specificity to how the perceptions of the working life of lawyers, judges, and anyone else close to legal process, are likely to be affected by the unusual sample of situations they witness. The salience of partial experience was also confirmed by other senior lawyers perceiving the problem area for poor conduct and associated conflict not being the public sector, but rather the City and professional services firms.

There are, in turn, multiple routes by which this limited experience may be expected to influence different people. Most importantly, it must to some extent condition how law, legal process, and the problems they interact with are debated, discussed, and perceived in society more widely. The critical conclusion is that the distortions of an internal legal viewpoint only become visible from an outside perspective. This makes external accounts, like the one I seek to build in Chapter 9, vital to improving understanding of how legal intervention in this area functions and, in turn, to finding ways to make it work better.

9

Senior Managers and Lawyers on Behavioural Conflict at Work and the Missing Collective Dimension

Chapter 8 revealed generic features of how individual labour and equality rights are functioning in the UK that may be relevant to other legal topics. In this chapter I draw on the interview data to hypothesize about the effects of this regime in different types of workplaces and on the individuals within them, taking further the discussion in Chapter 8 of varied organizational experiences of law and legal process.

I use the concepts of employer dominance, unitarism, and pluralism to categorize the reported approaches to employment relations.[1] By employer dominance I mean that the organizational view, as defined by management, is prioritized and employee concerns are subordinated. This might take the form of classic command-and-control employee relations, but could also have more subtle incarnations. The core concept is of the working environment being dominated by managerial perspectives in the setting of goals, in determining the means by which these are pursued, and in constructing 'taken for granted' way of doing things. By unitarist I mean managerial philosophies that emphasize the commonality of interests at work and that downplay imbalances of power and resources. It is important to note, however, that when disputes arise, unitarist conceptions default into prioritizing managerial points of view. The net effect is that such approaches are often, explicitly or implicitly, predicated on the idea that employee claims are legitimate only so far as they support or advance organizational interests as defined by management. There might therefore be expansiveness about when it is worthwhile to treat employees well, but only on the premise that the managerial vision of the collective good is pre-eminent.

Finally, pluralism treats conflicts of interests between employers and employees as an inevitable fact of working life. Legitimate balancing of these interests, as well as good management, are seen to require governance that takes the range of organizational perspectives into account. This approach is particularly associated with embedded trade unionism and collective bargaining, although it can be institutionalized in other ways. There is also no suggestion that pluralism is inimical to organizational hierarchy, since many workplace decisions are seen as inappropriate for collective participation in organizations with pluralist employee relations. More fundamentally, there are various mechanisms, not least legal, by which management may ultimately impose its will. Even so, there is less of a theoretical tendency to regard managerial ideas of the good as necessarily trumping those from elsewhere, as well as more commitment to plural involvement in defining employers' goals and strategies.

---

[1] See for a recent discussion JW Budd and AJS Colvin, 'The Goals and Assumptions of Conflict Management in Organizations' in WK Roche, P Teague, and AJS Colvin (eds), *The Oxford Handbook of Conflict Management in Organizations* (OUP, 2014), 20–23.

My central hypothesis is that the patterns identified in Chapter 8 mean that the impact of individual labour and equality rights in the UK depends on how far organizational cultures are characterized by, on the one hand, employer dominance, and on the other, engrained collectivism. The overall message from the data is that the more management dominates the working environment, the more meaningless in practice individual legal protections are for working people. This follows from the efficiency with which overt claims, complaints, and dissent are silenced. As such, even though the organizational culture might espouse the ideology of individualism and see the value of individualizing employee relations, this does not mean challenges presented in those terms will be any less unwelcome than if presented as group claims. In other words, the individualism validated is only that which furthers managerial dominance. This aspect of the study reinforces the point I made in Chapter 2, building on Fevre and colleagues' observations that employers have only partially adjusted to individualization. The idea is that the nature of work means that dealing with employees one by one most naturally translates into (collective) employer dominance and (individual) employee subordination.[2]

This extrapolation from the data is supported by the different organizational forms that interviewees referred to. Moving away from more trenchant forms of employer dominance, management approaches were described that appeared unitarist and, to greater and lesser degrees, espoused either commitment-style or at least engagement approaches to employment relations.[3] While not wholly hostile to legal intervention at work, interviewees from this kind of organization tended to speak about individual legal rights getting in the way of what good employers choose to do for their employees. At the same time, they pointed to conflicts about legal entitlements disrupting the orderly internal resolution of problems, and sometimes to an exceptional extent.

In more collectivist workplaces, often with embedded trade unionism and certainly employee participation, interviewees seemed to perceive more potential for accommodating individual labour and equality rights, and even for building on them. There remained, however, the perception that associated conflict and litigation were liable to cause major disruption, further evidencing the misalignment identified in Chapter 2 between the collectivity of working life and the presentation of individual claims. This impression was given most strongly by senior lawyers, both reporting on their experience of problematic litigation and commenting on unprincipled settlement practices. One gave the following analysis of why some well-meaning employers are particularly susceptible to difficult conflicts, in this instance across both the public and private sectors:

A lot of the cases I see are about really assertive individuals working in non-hierarchical, consensual environments who refuse to accept boundaries … I don't locate that phenomenon in any particular sector. The one thing that seems to characterize the varied organizations I've seen it in, partly I suppose because they end up with people like me, is that they have systems, procedures and a kind of code, of expectations at least, of workplace behaviour. I don't make a public-private divide in these remarks … I think this type of experience is significant in terms of numbers though. SL2 (solicitor, employer side)

Another interviewee focused on discrimination and the organizational acceptability of speaking up:

My strong perception over the years has been that ironically the most common respondents in particularly race and sex discrimination cases are bodies that are trying their hardest not to discriminate. Those are the ones that create an environment in which you are welcome to bring a complaint. That's in contrast to other less enlightened organizations where the infrastructure isn't there to bring a complaint. Also the expectation isn't there on the part of the workforce to

---

[2] See pp 55–58 in Ch 2.   [3] See pp 51–52 in Ch 2 where these terms are explained.

do anything other than leave and try out somewhere else if they feel they are subject to bullying, harassment or some form of discrimination. SL10 (barrister, mixed practice)

It is interesting that this extract explicitly referred to employer-dominated workplaces, pointing out how effective they can be at silencing dissent.

Descriptions of different organizational environments were further allied to repeated intimations of increasing pressure on front-line managers, rather than those further up the organizational hierarchy, to reconcile conflicts between collective understandings of working life, whether employer-dominated or more pluralistic, and the assertion of individual entitlements. There were further indications of strain on human resources (HR) staff, although this was combined with the expression of ambivalence about HR practice in general and how far it helps or hinders front-line managers in particular.

Other elements in the data illuminated the variety of ways that employees engage with their legal entitlements, which in some sense corresponds to the variety of experiences at the organizational level. Between general reluctance amongst working people to complain, the subtle and not so subtle ways that organizations silence dissent, and the harm people report from raising uncomfortable issues, let alone from litigating, it started to appear surprising that even a small proportion come forward, reinforcing my conclusion to this effect in Chapter 2.[4] Even after claims have been made, there are so many ways they can come to an end, some reflecting the strength of the case but others for completely disconnected reasons. It emerged, therefore, that the current model of individual enforcement in a sense steers parties who carry on with a claim to be, or to become, combative and confrontational to a significant degree, and, crucially, within a distinctly individualist frame. This reflects what emerged in Chapter 4 about factual situations that proceeded to higher court judgment despite either liability seeming obvious or that an earlier resolution should have been possible.[5] In doing so it makes clearer how the perspective of those who are close to law and legal process gives a distorted picture of how working life and law interact, given all the situations that legal process misses and the highly particular construction of those that it captures. It also helps to explain the perception of vulnerability to damaging individual legal conflict in more collectivist workplaces, given the mismatch between participatory and individualist approaches to dealing with problems.

Finally, this analysis was supported by indications that senior managers struggle to make sense of the gap between what they perceive enlightened management to involve and their experience of law's influence, particularly where matters escalate to litigation. The positive element in their attitudes to law most likely reflected the nature of the sample of senior managers, including that this was disproportionately drawn from workplaces that were unionized and had commitment-styles of management. Yet managers repeatedly dichotomized what was required by law and the intelligent conduct of employee relations. They also expressed ambivalence towards legal intervention at work, being simultaneously supportive and doubtful of its value. Lawyer interviewees expressed similar uncertainty, while their relaxed attitudes to the jurisdictional oddities explored in Chapters 3 and 5 are arguably another example of the disconnection between a legal insider's perspective, and how law and legal process appear from the outside.

I argue that we must find ways to adapt legal intervention not only to malfunctions as they appear from an internal viewpoint on law, but also to address the variety of organizational and employee experiences. These data and analysis suggest that the key to this lies in integrating a fuller range of ideas about the communal side of working life into the implementation of individual rights within workplaces and their enforcement externally.

---

[4] See pp 57–58 in Ch 2.   [5] See Ch 4, esp pp 117–18.

Providing for worker perspectives on the collectivity of working life to be influential in these processes seems to me to offer the only hope for ensuring, on the one hand, that the emancipatory challenge of individual labour and equality rights penetrates workplaces in which managerial points of view currently dominate to the exclusion of all others and, on the other hand, that law and legal process are more consistently constructive in workplaces where there is broader based involvement in how the organization is run.

1. Organizational Approaches and the Impact of Individual Rights

My interviews posited that organizations with the most need to be influenced by individual legal rights are, in practice, least susceptible. Paradoxically, however, those most alert to the justice demands contained in labour and equality law may consequently have higher workplace standards and yet be at particular risk of damaging conflict, including litigation, and perhaps more likely to encounter truly destructive versions of this.

I now move to describing how some managers gave an overall analysis of developments in employee relations to explain what they saw as happening with law, before exposing the ideal types of organizational and legal interaction that I extracted from what they said. It is important, however, to be clear that the data were complicated by the difference that interviewees' particular organizational experience made to what they perceived, such that it is especially important here that I did not hear from a broader range of employees. Still, the data enabled development of my hypothesis about the impact of individual labour and equality rights on different kinds of workplaces and facilitated further theorizing from that starting point.

For some interviewees there was an overall change in managerial approach even in traditionally organized workplaces that helped to explain what they perceived about law's influence. One individual described how pluralist collectivism used to work in addressing problems, noting both its strengths and limitations:

Quite often ... the industrial relations person ... and the trade union representative... were very much in the process of making sure they formed a view as to what was happening, almost independent from the two people directly involved ... Both the HR person and the trade unionist were in an honest broker role ... In the 20% minority of situations where the employer/trade union relationship didn't work well there would be other factors ... These included all sorts of things like large and small p politics ... It might also be ability, because some of the trade unionists and some of the HR people weren't that good ... If you had an employee relations officer and a shop steward who were inconsistent, who didn't play that honest broker role, and you put the two together, you'd end up with quite a mess sometimes. SM5 (private, large, HR)

One of the senior lawyers gave a similar account:

Traditionally the workplace was quite well regulated by the trade union lay officials in terms of them providing an interface with management. [They] often acted like another supervisor, sharing out the overtime and making sure it was fairly shared out, sometimes not so fairly ... They would also report to the management and there was quite a nice way of resolving disputes without things blowing up too much. But that approach is pretty well dead from a mixture of technological change, the volatility in the industry and changes in workplace culture. I haven't seen that for a long time. SL3 (solicitor, employee side)

We see here clear-sighted acknowledgement of the weaknesses as well as the strengths of pluralist, trade union-based industrial relations regimes, with SL3 returning later to gender equality concerns. Even so, these narratives suggest that movement away from older versions of collectivism is now interacting with other changes to mean that individual legal rights have paradoxical effects. As non-managerial perspectives on the resolution of problems, collectively and individually, lose purchase and legitimacy, there begins to be, first, more scope for outright employer dominance to reduce the practical value to working people of legal entitlements and, second, less likelihood of pluralistic systems having the capacity to reconcile associated collective and individual interests and to resolve potential conflicts, legal or otherwise.

SM5 further described a corresponding shift amongst employees away from politicized trade unionism and towards individualism, albeit still perceiving employee desires for group affiliation:

We're looking at the concept of affinity. Do our employees associate with trade unionism and socialism? And the answer is, 'Not really'. If I look at the difference with twenty years ago, when there was still an element of socialism within that discussion: *none of that* ... It's got nothing to do with political association any more ... If I look at ... HR or finance, they don't associate with the collective. They sort of say, 'Well I'm an individual and I work here for a period of time. But if it doesn't work out I'll go and do something else. I don't need to be part of a collective' ... The individuals might have external affiliations and be part of a broader network. But they don't have that internal affiliation. They're part of the function but they don't need a third party within that relationship. It's quite interesting to watch. SM5 (private, large, HR)

A senior lawyer offered an analogous description:

So I think that the workplace is not seen ... so much as being either a socialist versus capitalist struggle or as an economic one ... In so far as you can generalize about these things, work is very often about self-validation, about your career. People talk about their career more and there's a lot more kind of self identity that's come through the workplace ... Let's take the *complete opposite* to that which was working for the Port of London Authority in the 60s, when you turned up in the Isle of Dogs and were told 'I'll have you and you for today'. You were just a day labourer. Work today is *so completely* the opposite of that. SL11 (barrister, mixed practice)

It seems to me that underlying both these are attempts to trace how changed background conditions are being reflected in more individually oriented workplace conduct.[6]

SM5 addressed how changes in industrial relations interact with the increasing catalogue of individual labour and equality rights, leading to the view that '[t]he tension in the system wasn't to polarize, whereas the tension in the system now is to polarize. The tension then was to try to resolve issues.' A perspective from the trade union side was that:

I've also had contact with union officers and with reps who have said to me that because of time pressures and a more individualistic culture, they feel like they're just spending all their time dealing with individual issues. Then they're not able to pursue the collective dimension and they feel they're losing sight of the collective role they should have and of the preventive work they should be helping to support. SM16 (public and private, various, non-HR)

There was perception of nervousness about getting involved early in trying to sort problems out because of legal risk, notably for unions as well as management. Consequently, lawyers were seen to be involved much earlier,[7] an effect several mentioned as exacerbated by the failed statutory dispute resolution measures and continuing even after these were repealed.[8]

---

[6] Compare also the findings reported at n 95 and the text to n 199 in Ch 2.

[7] The following gives an interesting twist, in that a senior lawyer commented similarly on the change of HR practice and reported involving outsiders in a bid to return to 'old-fashioned' interventionism: 'It would be right to say that in my experience in the past some HR departments were able to play a kind of honest broker role, whereas I don't see that now ... I don't see a lot of that old-fashioned approach of HR being prepared to intervene. In effect when I advise my clients to bring in outside people I'm sometimes trying to get back to that.' SL7 (solicitor, mixed practice)

[8] See the text to pp 60 and 68 in Ch 3.

I will explore in more detail later how these factors were presented in what interviewees said about different workplaces. A common thread in all environments, however, was of pressure to resolve issues being pushed onto front-line managers and, to some extent, HR staff. As SM5 pithily stated:

It's harder for the people below me. I think further down the organization I'm very concerned about the amount of support we're giving more junior people in terms of making sure they stay safe really. They're genuinely doing what they're doing in good faith. And sometimes that's causing them to be exposed. I see the stress on their face. SM5 (private, large, HR)

This level of stress was identified as exponentially increasing where Employment Tribunal (ET) proceedings eventuated, considered further in what follows regarding litigation process.

(1) Employer dominance

The insight that senior managers provided into this kind of workplace was that the employer's perspective, enacted by senior managers, dominated the environment to such a degree that it was highly unlikely any employee would speak out against it regardless of whether law could be invoked in support. Equally, in the rare instances that challenges were somehow made, they were as unlikely to make any difference as if the person making a complaint had kept silent. This atmosphere was captured by one senior manager explaining that the only circumstances in which they thought bringing a grievance might have an organizational effect was where senior colleagues were in the background encouraging it:

[I]t's possible a grievance won't always be a distraction or a sham. Still, my experience tells me that usually it is ... I was involved in one grievance ... that's an example of a grievance working, because of the things that were unearthed and came to light from the target being brave enough to come forward. Even in that example though, management had failed to act on what they knew was going horribly badly wrong. In a sense they almost really sort of forced the junior employee to bring the grievance so that they could use that as ammunition ... So that in fact still fits into my analysis that grievances are a useful avenue only to the extent that they fit in with what management wants ... I'm afraid I am that cynical. SM3 (public, large, lawyer)

Somewhat disturbingly, this senior manager did not differentiate between types of organization in making this point, evidently perceiving that this form of employer dominance was common. Another variant on this referred to poor conduct that had not been addressed and managerial dominance being intrinsic to organizations with stringent individual performance and reward systems:

The way in which you're managing in a very financial goal-orientated company is going to produce bad behaviour ... If you're going to *pit* people against each other, you can't totally be surprised if they start having *massive* rows. Then it's also about the tension of the environment. Because even if two individuals aren't going to go against each other, there can just be a feeling of a sense of failure, of impending doom, of nervousness about: 'If we all don't make our goals, is the company going to be ok?' Or, there's just that awful straightforward thing where everybody is vying for the positive attention from their boss because they've got a company that's very, very systematic and everything's about what grade you get in your review this year. SM8 (private, various sizes, non-HR)

This in fact illustrated my point that what alters in workplaces and over time is not whether collectivism is present but how far anyone outside management is allowed to influence the idea of the common good that prevails. The suggestion here was that in many modern workplaces the only version of collectivism at work is defined by managerial thinking, with individuals recognized only so far as they contribute to meeting the organizational goals that result.

Senior lawyers went further in describing this kind of dynamic, reflecting their experience of more extreme situations. A repeated theme, akin to some of what was reported in Chapter 8,[9] was of unpleasant behaviour being intrinsic to high workplace attainment. One of my interviewees with considerable experience of this sort of employer offered this pessimistic assessment:

One of the things I'm really intrigued about is how one tries to deal with behavioural conflict, because I've found *no way* of solving these problems. I think that the senior people who behave badly and create the behavioural conflict tend to have to get to a senior level before they have licence to conduct themselves in that way. Once they've got that licence they've usually reached a level of success which gives them a degree of invulnerability and people don't speak out against them. I think I've only had one situation when we managed to tackle that kind of problem ... But it seems to have to come to a tipping point where you have *a crisis*. SL7 (solicitor, mixed practice)

There were also accounts of routine practices in hierarchical workplaces of using settlement to 'buy off' complaints that, against the odds, were made:

My experience of that case, and of other cases in the financial sector, is that there's a big part of private industry, well paid private industry in the City, that just buys their way out of problems. It probably applies to City law firms as well. In those environments, if they have a square peg in a round hole they pay an awful lot of money to get rid of the square peg. They see it as a cost of business. There is absolutely no chance of those employers changing the way they do things. That is the way they are going to do business and payouts are a cost of ensuring that. SL3 (solicitor, employee side)

This might, of course, lead to someone whose individual labour and equality rights were breached receiving money, but the importance of this observation is that it shows how settlement practice, as discussed in Chapter 8,[10] can systematically be designed to allow problematic organizational practices to continue.

(2) Unitarism

(a) Flattened hierarchy

An interesting variant involved workplaces in which the organizational culture, while still dominated by the employer, appeared less hierarchical and was at times explicitly altruistic. This might be because a commercial entity had a particular philosophy about how best to make the business profitable:

I'd certainly say that we are proud of what empowerment has achieved ... We give them a sense of ownership of the business. It's *theirs* ... We see the great benefit of this as being in terms of staff motivation, rather than it actually helping staff behaviour. But perhaps they are interlinked ... We also hope that staff will be motivated by giving them autonomy ... Perhaps the simplest way to say it is that there's certainly no 'us and them' factor, which usually crops up in different behavioural issues. SM21 (private, large, manager)

Another instance was provided by a senior manager who had worked for a charity:

I think, perhaps specifically in a charity, that the *vast* majority of people want to do a good job, they've come to work because they believe in a cause and you've got a really good basis on which to enable people to enjoy their working life ... That means you don't need to have too many

---

[9] See p 206 in Ch 8.   [10] ibid.

rules and regulations but they're jolly good if they're there just to support, so you can fall back on them, rather than using them on a day to day basis. SM13 (civil society/third sector, small, non-HR)

This pointed to legal standards providing a backdrop to the organization's set way of operating. It was not that there was hostility to these standards; rather they tended to be seen as imposters given management's conviction that they knew how best to treat employees. Two corollaries were that first, any standard that challenged the managerial perspective would be incorporated to the letter only, and second, legally inspired conflicts could be extraordinarily difficult for managers, and the organization as a whole, to comprehend and handle.

(b) Commitment-style management

Interviewees' accounts of this kind conveyed that employee interests were legitimate only to the extent that they fit managerially constructed ideas of what constituted the organizational good. This was allied, however, to espousal of commitment-style management practices, emphasizing communication, informed consultation, and personalized attention. One senior manager from a civil society, third sector workplace perfectly expressed the unitarist premise that the organizational vision ought to prevail in the face of conflict:

When I say the employee was way out of line I mean they were doing their own thing that served their own interests and didn't support what we were doing as an organization ... But it's interesting this one, because I'm always aware that ultimately I'm here to serve the purposes of the organization. That is the touchstone that I invoke *a lot* actually. I'm glad you've raised that. That is actually quite a powerful driver in all this. I've personally found some of the structural re-organization we've gone through *really* difficult ... If you spent too much time thinking about this you'd think: 'What am I doing? What a horrible person I am doing this, terminating her employment'. But, you have to stand back and think about the organizational objectives and [this person] was *absolutely* obstructing them. So there I don't think I've got any choice. I do think that's a sort of morality in itself. SM7 (civil society/third sector, medium, lawyer)

It is in this kind of context that legal entitlements tended most trenchantly to be depicted as getting in the way of how enlightened organizations wanted to deal with their employees. The impression given was that legal measures were at best tangential to informed, sophisticated organizational strategies for securing employee involvement, commitment and, in particular, the expenditure of discretionary effort. At the same time, conflicts invoking law were characterized as disruptive to organizational life and sometimes truly disastrous for all concerned.

(3) Modern versions of pluralist collectivism

(a) Deep down

There were some senior manager interviewees who described pluralist collectivism based on trade unionism, albeit in a modern form in which individual entitlements and expectations were integrated. This integration might occur through commitment-style management techniques similar to those encountered in less pluralist organizations. Within this category of organizations such management techniques were, however, only one way in which the employment relationship was managed and collective mechanisms were as important.

One interviewee described how an organization of this kind approached behavioural issues, leading interestingly to the familiar point that law is irrelevant:

We have very firm aims and values. Working here for a lot of us, and I'm one of those, is more than just a job ... I suppose for quite a few of us old timers the values are inculcated in us. I don't know whether we had them before we arrived here or we acquired them while we were here, but there is a certain way of thinking and of behaving which I think is just understood. I'm trying to articulate that. It's certainly treating people with decency, with respect and with courtesy ... *No*, I don't think I see any influence from law in our approach. It's about what people *believe* I think and the reasons people work here. SM6 (civil society/third sector, medium, lawyer)

Legal standards were depicted as being incorporated relatively seamlessly into how things were done given adoption anyway of high employment standards. Even so, there was a possibility for significant disruption where an individual dispute erupted. The same interviewee explained this as follows, illustrating how uneasily determined individualist complaint is likely to sit within an environment of this type:

My theory about the 1 per cent of situations that don't get resolved is, bluntly, that more often than not it's people who are actually extremely unreasonable. It's somebody who has just decided they are going to go down a particular route and that they won't agree and won't negotiate their way through it. I'm thinking of examples now of people who are just bloody-minded and *want a row*. That's all of the situations that escalate beyond their immediate work unit. Bluntly, some people have unreasonable expectations and may have behaved unreasonably themselves. SM6 (civil society/third sector, medium, lawyer)

(b) Large scale

Several interviewees described large organizations, public and private, with embedded collective mechanisms. These were often reported to be long-standing and necessary to cope with the size of the enterprise, analogously to how some interviewees characterized the use of formal policies and procedures in such workplaces. Interviewees from these organizations made particular comments on the importance of managers making things work, including at relatively low levels. The following captured this point and noted attendant challenges:

I'm very much of the school of thought that I want to develop managers who see their people responsibility as a *fundamental* part of their role, not the: 'I'm running a call centre and ... then I manage my people.' That's where I strive to get to with an organization ... My feel would be that good managers, through things like team briefings, individual coaching and counseling, and open door policies, resolve lots of little things on a day to day basis ... I think managers are very focussed on delivering results ... I want them to see that resolving and managing people issues are part of them delivering their results. SM15 (private, large, HR)

There was the most ambivalence among interviewees when describing large, unionized organizations regarding whether the law had an influence, and specifically individual legal rights, procedurally or substantively. Acting lawfully was taken as a given, often with commitment to high labour standards. The suggestion, however, was that other things than the law dictated the ways things were done. As we have also seen, senior lawyers nonetheless described difficult disputes and litigation emerging disproportionately from environments in this category, suggesting particular difficulty in coping with individualized dispute in more collectively oriented environments. As one summed this up, comparing more overtly employer-dominated workplaces and public sector employers: 'There isn't the practice in the public sector of paying for problems to go away and carrying on as before, but the tragedy there is that you see the same issues coming round time and time again.' SL3 (solicitor, employee side)

(c) Non-union solidarity

The final version of collectivism involved non-union mechanisms for enabling and channelling workforce 'voice'. It is important, however, not to exaggerate this feature of the data which was very much in the background. The following account of an organiza- tion with developed equality networks provides an example. This interviewee regarded an organization with non-union representative mechanisms as providing a better envi- ronment behaviourally than another more traditionally collectivized workplace, noting again the value of informality:

I think the employee involvement in diversity initiatives helps that culture, in which people know that bad behaviour, whether related to a protected characteristic or not, won't be tolerated. Employees know that if behaviour of that kind is identified, then it is dealt with. It's not to say there's no bad behaviour going on out there. There may well be situations where somebody is not happy with what's happening and they may just be leaving rather than making a complaint ... But certainly in terms of culture, this is a more relaxed environment, a less formal environment and one in which there are well developed networks. SM18 (private, large, HR)

This was also typical in that mention of non-union forms of collectivism was usually connected to organizational strategies about diversity and equality. This points to the strong possibility that employers taking these initiatives in general fit into some version of the unitarist categories mentioned earlier, with the law tending to be viewed, first, as marginal to positive, employee-facing measures, and second, as a potential catalyst for disruptive conflict.[11] I thought it nonetheless worth including reference to the hints in the data of a new kind of collective involvement and of that being seen to help resolve problems.

(4) Managers at the sharp end

A related message to what was said about organizational divergence, interestingly expressed across the board, was of pressure being on front-line managers to cope with problems, either to contain them or to manage the ensuing conflict. This dovetails with the various comments about the significance of management to whether prob- lems emerge and escalate.[12] It also supports another element in Fevre and colleagues' work mentioned in Chapter 2, that focused on managers reconciling strains between the inherently collective nature of working life and the demands, challenges, or claims of individuals.[13] In a sense, front-line managers are the ones left at the coalface when collective means of sorting out problems lose purchase, and they are confronted with particularly difficult situations if individualized legal battles erupt.[14] While this was per- ceived to implicate HR staff as well, there was a variety of opinions about HR practice

---

[11] See L Barmes and S Ashtiany, *Diversity in the City: Initiatives in Investment Banks in the City* (Nabarro Nathanson, 2003); L Barmes with S Ashtiany, 'The Diversity Approach to Achieving Equality: Potential and Pitfalls' (2003) 32 ILJ 274; and S Williams, E Heery, and B Abbott, 'The emerg- ing regime of civil regulation in work and employment relations' (2011) 64 Human Relations 951, 962, and 965.

[12] See pp 191–95 and 209 in Ch 8.

[13] See p 23 on this point in Ch 2, and p 52 in Ch 2 on the changed position of line managers.

[14] See pp 188, 195, and 204–205 in Ch 8.

in general and specifically about whether it worsened line managers' predicament. This sometimes touched on HR translating legal influence in problematic ways, with also other more general indications of law affecting HR approaches.

I heard several *cris de coeur* about just how difficult managers can find dealing with conflicts about behaviour. The following was from an interviewee who had dealt with a conflict that escalated to lawyers being involved:

It did really feel devastating. I don't think I ever felt quite the same again at work … I just felt that I didn't want to *ever* experience that again … [I] think I always felt slightly less enthusiastic about work after that and I think it's because it made me question my management style and I didn't want to change … to a much more directive approach. That just wouldn't be me. My management style reflects the sort of person I am. I want people to do things because they want to do things. I saw my job as enabling them to do that … SM13 (civil society/third sector, small, non-HR)

Outrage was expressed by another interviewee commenting on the distress of ET litigation for front-line managers: 'It's like respondents *aren't people*. It's an employer. *No it's not.* There's no such thing as an employer. It's just a collection of people who happen to work for the same organization.' SM14 (private, large, HR).[15]

It will be recalled that senior lawyers emphasized bad management as an organizational cause of behavioural conflict and yet they also observed increased pressure on managers, one seeing this as itself causative of behavioural problems:

I sense less readiness in a way for the organization to accept responsibility for their managers. I don't know what it is. They're actually saying: 'Get on with it. This is *your* responsibility. *Make it work*. Make money.' The organization is less tolerant of failure to perform. I think that puts a lot of pressure on the particular work unit to perform to a high level, so the leader of that group has to work harder to push things and I think feels the pressure and then passes that down. SL7 (solicitor, mixed practice)

The idea was also expressed that serious problems emerge because some modern workplaces do not equip managers to cope well with challenging conduct:

In flatter organizations I think that one of the problems is that increasingly managers are trained to be more facilitators … so that it seems to be very difficult for them, particularly in environments which are quite collegiate, quite consultative and quite consensual, to say right at the beginning: 'I'm sorry but I'm not going to accept that kind of behaviour. You may have a problem but you can't express it like that'. They keep accommodating, they keep dithering and the monster grows. SL2 (solicitor, employer side)

Another way this perspective came through from interviews with senior lawyers was that about half commented on the deleterious effects of ET litigation on manager witnesses. In some sense this was the culmination of these individuals being under pressure to reconcile the competing collective and individual perspectives that underlie claims:

I had a case recently in which allegations of race discrimination had been made against a female manager. She was wholly vindicated in the ET. At the end of it our barrister actually went up to her and said: 'Well done. How do you feel?' And [the manager] just burst into uncontrollable sobs because no-one had ever asked her up to that point how she was feeling or coping, or ever given a nano-second's thought to what it was like for her. She was sobbing uncontrollably for about fifteen minutes. I thought: 'Why didn't we ask her that question? Why haven't her senior managers done

---

[15] See the text to n 37 in Ch 2 on somewhat limited evidence about the experience of those complained about.

that?' So I think there is insufficient support for people at the crunch line, who are quite often low paid, ill educated and don't have a lot of personal resources of whatever description to deal with what is happening to them. For those people I think litigation of this kind has a terrible impact. SL4 (solicitor, employer)

This uncannily mirrors comments explored below about the costs of litigating on individual claimants. Equally, it is notable that harm done by litigation in this instance involved the employer being inattentive to individual managers' interests, again subordinating these to the employer-dominated construction of the collective good.

In terms of HR, aside from comment about pressure, there was dissension about how far modern personnel practice helps or hinders managers faced with problems. About half of the senior managers expressed general cynicism and negativity about HR, sometimes despite themselves coming from that background. Irrespective of interviewees' organizational vantage point, moreover, almost everyone indicated that HR approaches were a contributory factor to behavioural conflict being handled ineffectively, with comment again about damaging proceduralization and formality. A good example from an HR 'insider' was the following, which also strikingly resonated with SM5's comments above regarding changes to the HR role:

I think there is a difference particularly in how HR people work. There's a sense that as an individual or a manager working with a couple of people where I can see that all is not well, rather than having conversations and seeking to resolve the issue, I'll usually these days phone my HR colleague. They will then advise me to take a certain formal route. That's what happens instead of having a conversation maybe with said HR colleague, or with anybody else, about my options for dealing with this, which may include going down a formal route, mediation and also actually just taking each of the individuals out for a coffee and asking: 'What is this all about?' Exploring that greater range of potential responses and which might be appropriate is something that people now seem reluctant to do. SM10 (public and private, various sizes, HR)

The following expresses how under pressure and alone a line manager can feel when called upon to deal with a problem:

HR casts a very heavy shadow over the grievance process while making it clear that I'm on my own. The sheer weight of HR policy here, and of HR consultancy … When I have an issue that comes up I talk to the HR consultant. He then bombards me with a series of e-mails giving links into HR policies, rather than sitting down and explaining. So I have to do all that work. That's not their role you see. SM2 (public, large, lawyer)

Another senior manager related inappropriately cautious attitudes held by HR personnel to legal influence, despite this interviewee feeling able to counteract this owing to personal legal expertise:

One of the things I've noticed is that I've really had to lead HR because they are *very* cautious. I think HR people *are* sometimes … They see the problems and therefore that influences their attitude towards change sometimes … The law is a nightmare as you will well know. It's *really complicated* … I'm utterly unsurprised that it's very, very difficult for HR managers just to steer their way through this. I think that induces over-caution in them. It's partly the rigidity in saying: 'No we can't do this because the rules say x, y and z'. That leads to a rather cautious approach, not to resolving things, you don't get out there and just do it. You think 'Oh you can't'. SM7 (civil society/third sector, medium, lawyer)

It is easy to see how someone with less legal or other relevant experience would not even perceive that the law allows another approach, let alone have the confidence to go against HR advice (including SM2 above, also in fact a lawyer). Furthermore, this seems all the more likely given that some senior lawyer interviewees described caution as appropriate even though they were convinced that timidity of this kind would worsen the initial conflict.[16]

2. The Silencing and Constructing of Individual Complaints

In some way the data considered in this section represent the other side of the coin to how employers perceive and handle legal influence, in that interviewees also commented on why employees react to problems in the ways they do. We have already seen that senior lawyer perceptions of organizational life and the influence of law were likely skewed by the subset of situations they see. The data analysed here build on that by exploring distortions in the sample of conflicts that get to court and are hardest fought. Most importantly, these are the situations that may be expected to influence judges, senior lawyers, and those closest to legalized conflict, with probable disproportionate knock-on effects on legal doctrine, policy-making, organizational practice, and public debate.

To give an overall sense of what interviewees said on this topic, about half of the senior managers commented that employees are generally reluctant to speak up. This was linked to a similar proportion noting the importance of organizational culture to whether people feel able to take action and the costs that complaining and litigating are perceived to have. It seems likely that this is part of why many saw personality as so important to whether conflict emerges and escalates.

(1) General reluctance to complain

The reluctance to complain that interviewees perceived reflected quantitative and qualitative findings, discussed in Chapter 2, which show that many facing workplace problems either do nothing or give up on initial action and also provide evidence of how hard it is to cross the Rubicon of pursuing a complaint and, especially, of litigating.[17] This general phenomenon was encapsulated by this description of passivity in the face of poor conduct witnessed by a senior manager at the start of their working life:

[S]he was my mentor. She led me into working for [an *absolutely vile bully* of the most obvious kind] and she never *once, once,* shared with me the fact that he did those things to her as well. She knew they were happening to me. That's just *unbelievable behaviour* … [A]s she grew up with the organization she had more and more power to comment or notice with somebody that he was doing that, and she chose not to. SM8 (private, various sizes, non-HR)

Another senior manager, in turn, gave a nuanced account of factors that might account for reluctance to speak out:

I think there are a much larger number of situations in which people don't complain … I think they put up with it because what happens when you flip over into being a victim is that you feel powerless, you feel the system can't help and support you, that it must only be you, you must have done something wrong, you feel guilty, it's your *fault.* There may be a point at which you're angry. But it's quite hard to sustain anger because after a while anger just wears you out. It uses up a huge amount of emotions. Actually you start going downwards. You start introverting. SM11 (public and private, various sizes, HR)

---

[16] See p 200 in Ch 8.   [17] See pp 31–37 and 44–47 in Ch 2.

There were analogous musings by senior lawyers reflecting on their experience of clients:

[I] will ask the client what they think is behind what is going on. 'Why do you think this is happening?' It's such a nebulous thing that they very often don't want to tell their lawyer what they're feeling. They don't like coming to tell you that they felt someone was getting at them because it sounds a bit feeble. A lot of people don't want to portray themselves as victims. SL5 (solicitor, employee side)

Another version of reluctance lawyers saw involved people turning to law only because they felt they had no other option:

My sense, although it is entirely impressionistic and subjective, of how situations generally get to the point of litigation is that people feel they haven't got a choice. They feel that there is nowhere left to go. Maybe their only alternative is to leave their job with the risk that they won't get a good reference and find another one. Maybe they don't have the option of leaving because they are in work that realistically they're going to find very difficult to find elsewhere. They think: 'What do I do now? I've lost my grievance and appeal. All this is doing is compounding the sense of injustice that I feel and I'm going to go nowhere in this job.' That's my experience. There are exceptions. There are those who feel that this is a matter of principle. 'I need to do this.' ... But for most people it's: 'I don't want to do this. I've been forced into this.' And often they are very, very unhappy. Having depressed clients is very common. SL14 (barrister, employee side)[18]

(2) Constructing reluctance (and complaint): Organizational culture

Other vivid depictions demonstrated organizations framing individual problems in such a way as to convey the opinion that employees ought not speak out. It might, for example, be organizational constructions of success that had this effect:

I think people who get to the top will generally have ignored work conflict or solved it in an informal way to their advantage ... So on the whole I think their attitude will be dismissive ... To someone who is rather high achieving and successful it can look like a loser thing to do to lodge a grievance. Even to have a problem could be perceived as making you a loser ... That's in part because success in organizations is about solving problems, being opportunistic and moving things forward. Complaining is about looking backwards and showing it's not within your own power to sort something out, so therefore it's an expression of powerlessness. SM3 (public, large, lawyer)

Another gave a more prosaic example about the silencing effect of managers hating conflict and seeing it as irrelevant to what they are meant to be doing. As this senior manager explained, commenting too on managerial avoidance: '[Managers want to avoid] everything that involves moaning, complaining, whining and crying'. SM8 (private, various sizes, non-HR).

This kind of silencing was sometimes mentioned in relation to specific problems to which the workplace culture was inhospitable, for example in the following account of becoming a mother:

---

[18] See also in this regard A Brown, A Erskine, and D Littlejohn, *Review of Judgments in Race Discrimination Employment Tribunal Cases* (DTI, ERRS 64, 2006), 44 that '[i]t was striking that a significant proportion of cases involved claimants who appeared to be suffering from mental health problems or were in some way traumatised by their experiences—resulting, for example, in long periods off work due to stress. This aspect was rarely discussed explicitly in judgments.'

I think people won't speak up particularly where they have a feeling that: 'That's just the way this particular organization works and nothing I do will change that'. I think that happens where employees perceive, first, that senior people within the organization really endorse certain behaviours, and ways of doing things, a certain culture and, secondly, that most of their colleagues buy into that ... I can think of examples of women who become mothers who are working in environments that tend to be either really male dominated or particularly young, where very few of their colleagues have children and there's a complete lack of understanding of any of the issues those women face ... So that woman will probably just keep going and going until she reaches a breaking point, and then she'll decide: 'That's not the kind of job or organization I can work in now that I'm a Mum'. SM16 (public and private, various, non-HR)

To some extent, interview data reviewed in this section illustrated the distinctions between the ideal types of workplace described earlier from employees' points of view. The counterpoint to organizations in which dissent is shut down were those where interviewees perceived a cultural norm that complaining is acceptable. This was then the seed both of constructive resolutions and of a greater risk of problems erupting, including to the point of litigation. Embedded trade unionism was particularly credited with making complaint culturally acceptable:

I think that whether people are prepared to speak up depends on how established the trade unions are in an organization ... I think that is one of the benefits that trade unions bring and they don't necessarily recognize how big a benefit it is to their members, giving people a voice and confidence. SM15 (private, large, HR)

There was also comment on the misleading appearance that conflict is worse in unionized workplaces, given that suppressed problems still corrode and are liable to erupt in more damaging ways:

Sometimes it can look like there's more conflict because there's more discussion in the workplace going on day to day about particular issues.... I've also worked in a non-unionized workplace where on the surface it might look like everything's fine. But actually when you've been there a while and you start talking to colleagues, there's a lot that's festering. Then it can be *particularly* conflictual when it does come out. I've seen people leave, exit organizations quicker in that environment as well. Where it comes out and doesn't get resolved, it just leads to conflict and exit. SM16 (public and private, various, non-HR)[19]

An entirely logical point that several senior manager and lawyer interviewees made needs also to be noted: that complaints increase with cultures that enable and empower working people to speak up. Evidently this is one of the mechanisms by which it can come to appear to those close to the ET and court systems that workplaces with more enlightened approaches experience more conflict and litigation, including that is of the most damaging kinds.[20]

I'm sure it's right that better processes etc in the public sector and in large private sector organizations engender more disputes that go further down the line. I think that's a function of several different things. One is that ironically public authorities and large private companies *really do want* to do the right thing. They have equal opportunities policies that they *actually try* to implement. So if somebody makes a complaint say of sex or race discrimination, it's treated very seriously indeed. I think also that the expectations of the individual employees are much greater because they are handed these policies when they join. SL10 (barrister, mixed practice)

---

[19] See p 51 in Ch 2 and p 189 in Ch 8.   [20] See Ch 8, esp pp 193 and 212–13.

Even so, several senior managers supported the notion that trade union involvement can be an effective tool for managing conflict, with representatives intervening to sort things out, steering members to let problems go, giving realistic explanations of the options, and, of course, providing support and representation where complaints went ahead, albeit calibrated to the strength of the individual's arguments. This is the kind of more broadly based involvement that arguably is increasingly missing as managers are left on their own to sort out problems that pit individual and collective interests against one another. One senior manager described good union representatives acting this way, while suggesting there is less scope for this kind of intervention in workplaces where trade union pluralism is less embedded:

I always remember a particular rep from my first employment who said to me: 'If you think I bring you ridiculous/no hope cases, you don't know how many issues I kill before they get to your door'. That's always stuck with me. He told me that: 'For every one I bring to the HR office, I probably kill forty'. I thought that was really powerful. Good reps don't bring everything. They stand up. They'll act like the line manager and sort it on the shop floor. They'll either say: 'Get over it' or they'll go to talk to the other person and sort it out on the shop floor. But it's a very different environment here. That worked where it was highly unionized and everyone was a trade union member. Here you more see full time officials playing that role. SM15 (private, large, HR)[21]

That trade unions, through both representatives and more formal systems, habitually judge the strength of members' requests for representation, including by lawyers, was also mentioned by several senior managers, for example as follows:

The union reps are very good. Speaking for the ones I know, they'll fight their members' cause, absolutely. But they know when it's a cause that's likely to win and when it's not. They would absolutely be advising their members not to go down a litigious route if there is no case ... The unions have their own legal advice system anyway so they can't represent someone all the way to ET without it going through their regional office with clearance around the likelihood of success, because obviously they are not resourced to take every case that comes across their desk. SM20 (public, large, lawyer manager)

An interviewee whose remarks on equality networks I saw as gesturing toward new forms of collectivism also talked about network members' role, making explicit analogies with what union representatives do. 'The employee networks I think help. They almost provide a go-to person about: "How serious is this? What shall I do about it? Who can help with it?"' SM18 (private, large, HR).

Senior lawyers also discussed third party involvement. Around one-half commented on some version of this, referring not only to trade unions but also equality bodies, outside experts, lawyers, and family members. Sometimes this was to reiterate the point that good union representatives can help defuse situations:

How strong the union officers are, and how good they are at looking through a problem and coming up with a solution that some level of management might be prepared to accept, very much depends on the area and the industry you're dealing with, The lay and full-time officers who do it well are problem-solvers ... Mostly I think employers appreciate that side of what trade unions do. SL3 (solicitor, employee side)

Senior lawyers also commented on the availability of union funding for legal representation, although they did not always notice that this is subject to assessment of the strength of the claim. As mentioned earlier, this is a further factor that probably

---

[21] See p 51 in Ch 2 and pp 192–93 and 208 in Ch 8.

accounts for organizations which are less employer-dominated, and specifically public sector workplaces, being more vulnerable to litigation, including that reaches the stage of a full hearing.[22]

(3) Constructing reluctance: The costs of speaking out and litigating

In Chapter 8 I touched on the wide range of harms that senior managers perceived behavioural conflict to cause.[23] Here I turn to what was said about the fact and perception of damage from internal and external complaint at work. For many this was an important factor in why individuals refrain from speaking out and litigating.

Some focused on the damage done simply by going through internal procedures, including hardening individual positions and destroying relationships. This again evoked the negative aspects of organizational procedures and formality. As this senior manager interviewee said: '[t]he personal costs are really high', illustrating this in relation to a sexual harassment complaint:

For example if you're a woman who feels that she is being harassed or inappropriately treated, it's *a really big thing* to lodge a formal complaint, *it's a really big thing. You know* that in the whole power system thing it's going to be painful and it's going to be difficult ... I think people often don't make formal complaints because they're scared, particularly if they see their managers colluding. SM10 (public and private, various sizes, HR)

Another spoke of potential consequences to someone's career, with reluctance to raise issues exacerbated by difficult economic conditions:

Sometimes this person is in a position of power so you are fearful that if you say something that person will take it out on you, your reports will suffer ... I'm under no illusion that in the current climate fear is there all the way down ... [They're] even more likely to keep quiet about it if something is going wrong. SM11 (public and private, various sizes, HR)

Senior lawyers supported the notion that claimants are put off by the harms that are perceived to arise from complaining, also emphasizing that this extends beyond the current workplace.[24] There was recognition of the discomfort that going through internal processes could cause, and further comment on managerial tendencies to avoid problems and to turn on the complainant.[25] This quotation shows how this might happen in response to a complaint of discrimination:

I think discrimination situations *are* different because sometimes what is needed to manage them well is actually to confront the discriminator ... But it often can be easier to marginalize the victim, to see them as a troublemaker ... I think most white men are quite familiar with low level racism I suppose you'd call it, and low level sexism and misogyny. I mean just jokes in the pub about women, jokes about where people come from and stereotyping their origins. That means they don't perceive that kind of behaviour as seriously as you might if you were a victim of it. Consequently the victim *becomes* the problem. 'You know Bloggs is a great manager. He's been here for 25 years. He's popular. Everybody likes him. He's a bit of a joker. We all like a bit of a joke. And actually if you just didn't complain life would be easier.' SL14 (barrister, employee side)

---

[22] See pp 193 and 212–13 in Ch 8.   [23] See pp 188–89 in Ch 8.
[24] The existence of these effects is supported by case law accounts of stigma that attaches to claimants for litigating and the recoverability of compensation for their consequent losses. See particularly the text to n 176 in Ch 3.
[25] See pp 228–29 and further in the rest of this section, as well as pp 17 and 44–45 in Ch 2, pp 110–12 in Ch 4, ns 60, 65 and accompanying text in Ch 6, ns 51, 91 and accompanying text in Ch 7, and ns 18, 19, accompanying text and pp 198 and 209 in Ch 8.

There were also repeated indications that clients would not complain or sue because they were frightened of the impact this might have on their career.

> The other thing you quite often find, and again this is right across the board, is that the individuals are very loathe to make a formal complaint. They'll make an informal complaint but they don't allow the organization to deal with it. They are concerned about how they will be treated, not only when they're in employment but when they leave. Quite often the people behaving badly can be big players in the marketplace or whatever it might be, and the people on the receiving end feel their careers will be harmed by them, for example saying that they couldn't hack it. SL7 (solicitor, mixed practice)

Several mentioned high status and professional environments as particular contexts in which this would be the case, for example as follows:

> It can be that culturally suing is just not something you do. So the City workers who are outrageously bullied, the lawyers who are bullied in law firms, or the accountants who are bullied in accountancy firms—which happens *all the time*, absurd demands being made on people—it's just not something they want to be seen to do. It's actually about the fear that it will have an impact on their ability to get another job, that basically it will damage them in the marketplace. None of my clients really thinks that an ET is a solution to *anything*. SL5 (solicitor, employee side)

Another lawyer said: '[y]ou can always leave your job and find another one, because the thought of raising the complaint feels either career destroying or just too much. Where is it going to get you?' SL13 (solicitor, employee side).

Senior managers and lawyers also described costs imposed by litigating. Here is one blunt overall assessment of the ET system, which chimes closely with the qualitative evidence reviewed in Chapter 2 regarding discrimination and other complainants:[26]

> I don't think that bringing ET claims benefits anyone except lawyers. Seriously I've never seen anybody come out of the process enriched, except possibly financially ... If it's not that a claimant wants money, what I really want to say is to them is: 'Then you're going down the wrong route because an ET can't give you anything except money. And if you want justice, *forget it* because actually the system is not going to make you feel any better. SM14 (private, large, HR)

The depressing effects of adversarialism were referred to here, especially as this affects complainants:

> Once it gets to litigation it is completely combative. By the time you've got to that point the individual is *absolutely determined* that they're right, rightly or wrongly ... I think that's because, particularly when you get to litigation, the respondent will do all they can to unpick the complaint. Therefore it's an incredibly painful process for the claimant. Witness statements are such that the company will be out to rubbish the statements that the individual has made and absolutely to defend their corner. SM18 (private, large, HR)

Another individual described employees who had become involved in big cases as having their lives 'almost destroyed': 'I'd describe them as broken ... [T]hey've become anxious, depressed, marriages have split up, because it's become an all-consuming passion. They *had to* pursue it.' SM15 (private, large, HR).

Observations by senior lawyers supported this perspective, often going even further in the damage they perceived litigation to inflict. Almost every senior lawyer commented on this, with hearings seen as especially harmful. About half of these interviewees described the process either worsening existing health conditions or making claimants

---

[26] See p 47 in Ch 2.

ill. Several reported claims being abandoned for this reason and respondents, as we've seen, sometimes making tactical use of the claimant's poor health.[27]

An especially heartfelt account of harm to claimants involved discrimination cases:

[M]yself and another colleague who does far more [discrimination cases now], got to a stage about three years ago where we felt that bringing an ET claim for discrimination, no matter how strong, was career ending, That's because, particularly with the best cases, relationships become *so* fractured and *so* tense and the litigation process itself of course brings out the worst in everybody. Once witness statements have been exchanged, the most qualified, the best working member of staff who has brought a discrimination case becomes a social pariah ... The litigation process then blames the complainant. I don't know whether that's because of lawyers, or maybe it's the management approach. I don't know, it's quite difficult to unpack that one ... Litigation is *just devastating*. It's just *personally devastating* ... A lot of people end up quite ill through the stress of the process, *not* because of what originally happened. SL3 (solicitor, employee side)

Another observed more generally that litigation could be '*absolutely destroying*' irrespective of whether claimants settled or fought, again referring to the inevitably detrimental impact on careers.

To take the step of litigating I think you've got to have resigned yourself at some point that you've either lost your employment or your career positioning. For so many people their employment is bound up with their identity, who they are, it shapes their relationships, it's such a big part of their lives. That goes and everything goes out of kilter. It just does. And it takes a long time for it to come back. SL13 (solicitor, employee side)

A version of this perspective referred to claimants' work performance routinely being criticized, including in judgments and even when they had won their case.

My approach to settlement takes account of the fact that it is *very hard* to be cross-examined for two days when it is put on the basis that you're useless at your job or whatever. Also that you may win a case but in that process you will have lost certain things. Let's take a common example, somebody who is subject to minor warnings, work allocation is unfair, they are not exposed to important clients or management tasks, they are gradually undermined at work. The employer's response when they present a grievance is: 'You're just not very good at your job. We've been trying to get you to work properly but you're useless and you don't get on with anybody.' You go to the ET and you may win ... But it may also leave some people not feeling very nice about themselves, because they ended up with a decision that formally vindicated them but in the process mandated some view of them that they feel very uncomfortable about. SL14 (barrister, employee side)

The personal harm experienced even by successful claimants was also reported sometimes to take a highly tangible form: having to cope with large legal bills over and above what was recovered. '[W]hen it's all gone then suddenly the cold reality ... hits. They have to pay the mortgage they might have taken out on their property to pay the lawyers' fees. The lawyers ... are now saying: " ...We'd like to be paid please." The [claimant is] isolated and it really wasn't of such great value.' SL12 (barrister, mixed practice).

How much is at stake for individuals beyond purely financial considerations is amply illustrated by this poignant description of a claimant's reaction to winning:

[T]he claimant burst into tears and started hugging his wife even though he recovered only a very modest sum. This was because he felt vindicated. You get a bit cynical about people's motivations if you do too much of this sort of work. *It was not about the money.* Cases can be so personal. SL8 (solicitor, employer side)

---

[27] See n 261 in Ch 2 on evidence of similarly cynical use of mediation.

Still, the preponderance of negative descriptions of litigation was reflected in about two-thirds of all the senior lawyers alluding to litigants' overall dissatisfaction and feelings of being let down by 'the system'. These reports sometimes extended to claimants who had recovered hundreds of thousands of pounds. One lawyer interviewee reported that they always told claimants looking for vindication and 'catharsis': 'It's not going to feel as good as you think it is even if you win.' SL10 (barrister, mixed practice). The following explanation for this phenomenon uncannily echoed qualitative evidence about discrimination claimants:

There are a lot of people who would say looking back that they regret having gone through it ... It's the *whole process*. Ultimately you get a decision and you get money and what the individual was really looking for was some sort of recognition ... The claimant is out, out and broken. It's this kind of: 'I wanted some reparation. I wanted to see these people in some way damaged, like I'm damaged.' But actually all I see is this organization going back with a bad judgment and I've got some money, but nobody is losing their job as far as the individual knows. *What is the actual outcome here in terms of the organization?* SL13 (solicitor, employee side)

The following quotation explains how official confirmation that an individual had been mistreated, maybe for years, could itself be difficult to come to terms with:

I've done cases where ... the ET has found that they were good at their job, had tried to find a way to work with these people, had put up with this for a long time and that they were subjected to lengthy harassment and it was handled very badly etc, etc. That's fantastic. But it doesn't in fact always make people very happy. That's a peculiarity isn't it? Maybe it does in the longer term ... In the shorter term it can be very hurtful to have it proved that you have indeed been harassed for all that time ... Even if it's true and you've been saying it, to see it written can create an immediate trauma. It may be that after ten years you can reflect and say: 'I'm really glad I did that. I'm going to frame it and put it in the living room.' But in the shorter term it can be quite painful, funnily enough. SL14 (barrister, employee side)

I was shocked when I heard this, yet it quickly came to make sense. It is reminiscent of Fevre and colleagues' findings about the strength of commitment that people often feel for their employers, clinging against the odds to positive visions of the organization and to their sense of belonging to it.[28]

(4) Constructing claims: Being 'difficult'

We have seen earlier that some senior managers and many senior lawyers viewed personality as important to whether behavioural conflict emerges and escalates, including to the point of involving lawyers and litigating.[29] The issue explored here is that all the factors that militate against individuals doing much, if anything, about problems at work, and that discourage them from engaging lawyers and suing, will more likely be overcome if an individual is either naturally at peace with being highly adversarial or has the capacity to become so. This raises the possibility that talk of personality or of claimants being 'difficult' may be another indication that the UK approach to enforcement of individual rights in some sense pushes employers and employees to be confrontational and uncompromising about workplace problems and, critically, in an individualist way. So far as there is more scope for this form of complaint in some environments, that is in turn likely more often to lead to damaging litigation, along the way probably unsettling and undermining more plural, collectivist ways of sorting

---

[28] See pp 22–24 in Ch 2.   [29] See pp 190–91 in Ch 8.

things out. By the same token, it is likely that a good proportion of working people who perceive this dynamic see in it yet another prompt to remain silent and withdraw when problems at work cannot be resolved through, for example, their own efforts, trade union assistance, or managerial help.[30]

Consider this perhaps unwitting summary of this dimension of the UK individual labour and equality rights regime:

There are some who are going to want access to justice in every sense of the word. 'No, I want to see you in the ET and I want to see you pay.' Well that's fine. That is you exercising your individual right. Some people might say it's also a bit short-sighted. But you know that is what individual rights are all about. SM22 (public, large, manager)

Another interviewee described self-involvement and intransigence contributing to repeated, unresolved internal grievances:

This manager listened to everything the employee had to say regarding her latest grievance ... [The employee is] a relatively senior individual. She said: 'Have you got any questions for me?' The manager said: 'No I think you've put your case quite clearly and very succinctly. But there is one thing which worries me, which is the complete and utter absence either of any acknowledgment of responsibility on your part or of any taking of accountability'. That is absolutely true but my colleague who is the [HR] procedural adviser was shocked by the manager saying it, because I think we tend not to push back. The employee said: 'Well I see what you mean' but proceeded to tell him why it was indeed everybody else's fault. There are some who are just not going to take any feedback at all. They won't recognize it. Yet my experience suggests that in situations that get sorted out people are prepared to listen to other people. SM14 (private, large, HR)

There were further evocations of this expressed in the discomfort and frustration interviewees felt about the experience of defending hopeless cases:

Funnily enough when I was a practising lawyer it felt absolutely right and proper that there should be free access [to ETs]. But as an employer I've been involved now in quite a few cases where they are *utterly* unfounded claims ... To be blunt one of the reasons we didn't go ahead [with a case] also was that it was just so *ghastly* to have to witness [the claimant] being pulled apart by the ET because there was nothing in it ... We didn't settle it for a huge amount but the legal fees are huge. That's uppermost in my mind. You just think: 'This *can't* be right. It's not doing anyone any good.' SM7 (civil society/third sector, medium, lawyer)

In keeping with more senior lawyers' perception of personality as a significant factor in behavioural conflict, most likely reflecting the fact that the situations they witness or advise about tend to be extreme, there were statements about quite how destructive some individual litigants can be. One analysed their own experience of this to say:

The causal patterns that I see in these difficult claims that come to me are that the claimant has a lack of insight coupled with a lack of fear. It's a funny thing to say. I would say that in these difficult conflicts you've got an individual who is not very good at perceiving how they fit into a work context and who doesn't give a damn, who isn't frightened about their personal position. SL2 (solicitor, employer side)

This phenomenon was described as sometimes going to the lengths of people having 'no perception of the underlying realities of the case' and continuing 'to fight over a bone which isn't worth fighting over and where there can be no objective benefit'.

There is a lot in these observations, suggesting that the subset of really destructive conflicts, often in workplaces that prioritize consensual, participative decision-making,

---

[30] See the text to n 91 in Ch 2 on perceptions of the strength needed even to speak up.

involves individuals who cannot see where they fit into the collective, communal endeavour and who are impervious to the negative personal consequences of speaking out. The analysis is premised on the general propositions I extracted in Chapter 2, first, that individual challenges might fit very uncomfortably with the inherently collective nature of work, and, second, that employer-dominated constructions of legitimate workplace concerns will often exert a powerful force to stop working people doing anything much about problems they encounter. It seems to me that this comment hit the nail on the head of what can happen when individuals do not respond predictably to those forces and instead take the path of adversarial, individualized conflict towards which modern law arguably pushes them. Still, the relative scarcity of this phenomenon needs to be kept firmly in mind.[31] I return in the conclusion to the negative impact that this can have on the emancipatory capacity of individual labour and equality rights, not least in distracting public and political debate from the far greater reality of workplace problems going unacknowledged and unresolved.

Another senior lawyer described how bad things can get, recounting recurrent experiences of one person causing havoc for their union as much as for their employer:

What was quite common was to find a person who would suck the life out of their workplace by being difficult, and who would at some point make life very difficult for their employer and their union (if they were unionized), but who would portray themselves as a victim in proceedings. Of course there must be very many cases where people are badly treated and have a good case. If a case is simple and straightforward it wouldn't come to me. Still, I had that impression even as a junior. SL10 (barrister, mixed practice)

It is appropriate also to note that correspondingly extreme managerial conduct may in a different way result in major litigation, illustrated by the following description of people being so damaged by the degraded conduct of their manager that they lose the capacity to walk away and 'claim risk' is thereby increased:

People spin out because they just can't bear to continue working for the person. Good people get up and walk out. There are also good people who stay and the danger then is that at a certain point their confidence is so eroded by the behaviour that they no longer have the ability to leave. That is where you get the claim risk increasing, because the person begins to feel very badly damaged. They know they are being harmed. It's a bit like that hostage syndrome where people can't get out. That's when it becomes quite serious. SL7 (solicitor, mixed practice)

We have seen, however, that employees in this situation may be independently harmed by the harrowing adversarialism of litigation.[32]

3. Complex Unease about Legal Intervention

The final set of related themes was that senior manager interviewees often first, saw a dichotomy between enlightened approaches to employment relations and legal requirements, and second, were ambivalent about modern legal interventions at work, being simultaneously supportive and critical. Both strands might be dismissed as stereotypical managerial hostility to outside intervention. My sense, however, is that this would oversimplify what was being expressed, especially since many of the individuals I interviewed

---

[31] See pp 34–35 in Ch 2 and pp 115–18 in Ch 4.
[32] See pp 231–34 above on litigation harms and Ch 4, esp p 117 on highly combative approaches from both employers and employees as litigants.

were personally committed to high workplace standards and their organizational experience was disproportionately of employers that were unionized and espoused commitment styles of management.

Rather, I would contend that these strands in the data illustrated senior managers struggling to make sense of the gap between what they perceived to be required of employers to act fairly, reasonably, and equitably, even if from a managerial, organizational perspective, and their experience of law's influence, most of all where matters escalated to litigation. If I am right we should expect very different accounts from senior managers with more cut-throat attitudes to employment relations and from the more hierarchical end of the organizational spectrum. My suspicion, drawing on what interviewees said about employer-dominated workplaces and from vignettes in my survey of case law, is that there would be much less, if any, agonizing about what just employment relations require and about how law fits into this. Instead we should expect a more straightforward concern to ensure the system enables inconvenient workplace challenges and demands to be neutralized and managerial dominance to thrive.

(1) Dichotomizing enlightened management and law

Almost every senior manager contrasted what they perceived as good management with what law requires of organizations. Sometimes this was nuanced in that the contrast was between what an effective managerial approach would entail and how legal influences were refracted through HR and organizational policies, at times with awareness that the underlying legal message might have been 'lost in translation'. Still, about two-thirds of my interviewees straightforwardly perceived law, at times at least, to obstruct 'good people practices'.

This dichotomy was drawn from many points of view and often richly expressed. Sometimes it was front-line managers who contrasted their attempts to sort out a problem with their sense of legal requirements, with perhaps unintended irony:

I have to say I didn't feel … when I was new in the job and I was really very naïve, that I was dealing with the law as such. I felt I was trying to resolve a situation. I was just trying to sort this out. I wasn't worrying about the law. I wouldn't deal with it differently now, but I have a better awareness that actually the policies and the mechanisms in place are, or at least I have a sense that they are, addressing certain legal requirements …. SM2 (public, large, lawyer)

Another answered my probing on the point by baldly stating: 'I certainly had no sense that the law was there actually to help me to sort out this difficult situation. It was there to make sure I didn't make legal mistakes in dealing with the problem.' SM13 (civil society/third sector, small, non-HR).

Tellingly, one of the interviewees with a background in employment law drew the same kind of contrast:

The advantage of being a lawyer is that I'm much clearer about what you need to do … In a way that was a bit of a liberation, because it did mean that I could concentrate on trying to bring staff with me … I think part of that is to do with the fact that, since I was reasonably confident about the procedures, I could really throw myself into the staff engagement stuff. SM7 (civil society/third sector, medium, lawyer)

Again, the implicit message was that someone without a relevant legal background might get bogged down in legal issues at the cost of concentrating on 'staff engagement stuff'. Another interviewee drew essentially the same distinction in relation to union members asking for help: 'People have become so obsessed with all of the different individual employment rights that we now have, that they think that's the ultimate thing …

It can stop them being really clear about what they want as an outcome.' SM16 (public and private, various, non-HR).

A further version of the dichotomy came from a straightforwardly business perspective:

Today if you recruit an HR manager, which is who you've got to recruit now, rather than a personnel manager, you have to recruit *someone who is only really interested in the law.* They're often *fairly hopeless at running a business* ... Yet the business skills we want are very people skills in fact ... It's all really about that a good personnel manager should know all their staff *very well* and be able to bring them in for a chat, find out what their problems are and hopefully then the individual can feel a release, go back to work and perform better. SM21 (private, large, manager)

I found this especially interesting because it came from an uncompromisingly managerial point of view, yet treated sophisticated ability to deal with people as inherent to running a successful enterprise. This meant that criticism of legal developments was not in the stereotypical form of deprecating how law constrains management; rather the concern was with the modern legal framework deflecting HR professionals from developing vital people skills.[33]

Another way in which the operation of law was dichotomized with enlightened management involved various criticisms of the limited frame within which lawyers and adjudication operate, arguably evoking the kind of disconnections I described in Chapter 8 between legal process and the justice norms underlying relevant law.[34] One senior manager argued that lawyers have a wider responsibility to use litigation to educate organizations:

In my view organizations have a duty, and the legal fraternity has more of a duty, *to educate.* I know this isn't really the case, but it *feels* as if lawyers sit in a bit of a box giving out diktats about the law rather than actually working with organizations about it. I would suggest that, at the point when you're taking a case, particularly when it's concluding, actually the lawyers are at a very powerful position in that relationship, and there are things that could be said and done that could have a much more positive effect rather than the road we now go down ... I'm saying that litigation could be a catalyst for change but it doesn't work that way at the moment; people just carry on making the same mistakes. SM11 (public and private, various sizes, HR)

Another version of this saw the law as concerned solely with meting out punishment, humorously articulated in this extract:

To be honest, I see myself as a bit more foot-soldierish in all this, more the nuts and bolts, getting your hands dirty, and I only see a negative, punitive influence from law. You're not rewarding anyone for being a good employer are you? You can give employers Investors in People, but the chap down the chip shop has got Investors in People. There is the stick, but not the carrot. SM19 (public and private, various, HR)

While many senior lawyers expressed generally negative opinions about legal process, they also saw a division between the law's perspective on workplace issues and

---

[33] Again, another interviewee reported an analogous process for union officials: 'But I can see that one of the problems is that the focus on individual employment rights as the solution to anything—the idea that for any problem that arises at work the answer is to create a new employment right to deal with it—has weakened the collective focus sometimes and made some union reps struggle to keep on top of what the individual employment rights are and really constantly worry about that aspect of their role and hence focus on just representing individuals. That seems like a big issue for some. The growth of individual rights without the development of collective rights in recent years has led to this emphasis on problems at work being individual, isolated incidents and it's taken away the focus on collective solutions and collective action on certain problems.' SM16 (public and private, various, non-HR).

[34] See Ch 8, esp 212.

forward-thinking managerial approaches. One challenging meditation was expressed by SL12 observing that litigation 'very often appeals to that playground sense we have as children, when there are sides and we want somebody to come and tell us we're right and he's wrong'. This led the same interviewee to observe that lawyers were missing the point of the public sector equality duty's (PSED) attempt to use the law in a more constructive, creative way, expressed as follows:

But all that lawyers talking about the PSED discuss is litigation. They talk about how you could use it to found a case. I think: '*That's not what it was about*'. It's not meant to be like that. It's not about us, about whether we can add a ground into a J[udicial] R[eview]; it's about whether public sector employers can really use this to influence big change. They can use it in that way but that's how they need to see it. They've really got to take it on. SL12 (barrister, mixed practice)

(2) Ambiguity about law's influence

SL12's musings about legal process and the PSED gave rise to the rather wistful conclusion, at least for a barrister, that 'I do see the law as a very positive thing, but not the law I'm kind of working in I suppose. I don't think litigation is a very healthy aspect of the law.' This was a motif that ran through the comments of about two-thirds of the senior managers, simultaneously welcoming the existence of legal interventions at work and specifically individual rights while doubting their ultimate value. This was particularly because of perceived slips between the cup of theory and the lip of practice.

This point of view was articulated in various ways, for example with exasperation about ET litigation and comments on the failure of law to promote and encourage good practice. The following provides a good sense of the complicated appraisals I heard:

What worries me about the law is that you get compliance. You don't get the heart and mind. And the law stops any debate because people are frightened. So the law has a positive and a negative effect all at the same time … People almost become frightened of the law, wary of the law. I think they think the law is there, it has to be considered, it's something that's part of whatever they have to do, but it's not prompting them to do positive things. SM1 (public, large, HR)

Another involved a quite agonized attempt to make sense of a change in perception associated with an individual moving from professional legal practice to a purely managerial role:

Coming from the background that I do I've tended to sympathize with the employees rather than the idea of red tape being burdensome … But I do see that a lay person who might have some leadership role, so somebody who's not a lawyer but running an organization … can't just necessarily rely on their ability to think well … It may be that given the complexity of human relationships that you can't just rely on an individual's sense of fairness … But if anyone has this idea that in order to be an effective and fair leader all you need is a developed sense of fairness, then perhaps I've realized that's not enough in and of itself to enable you to comply with the law. SM12 (civil society/third sector, small, lawyer)

We have seen that senior lawyers expressed a similar kind of ambivalence. In a way, however, some of their attitudes were emblematic of how peculiar the legal system in operation can be and perhaps help to explain the perplexity managers expressed. In particular, almost all the senior lawyers were relaxed about the jurisdictional oddities discussed in Chapters 3 and 5. It was not that they did not acknowledge technical peculiarities; they just did not see them as a problem.

Moreover, this was despite some senior lawyers giving further examples of the weird system effects of jurisdictional differentiation. For example, there was discussion of the routine separation by claimants, organizations, and lawyers of similar fact situations into, on the one hand, an employment and equality law track and, on the other, a personal injury track. Further practical consequences for the conduct of cases than I observed in the judgments analysed in Chapter 5 were pointed out to me, often turning on employers being statutorily required to have liability insurance for personal injury only. As one senior lawyer stated:

Within corporate structures the reason why you'd get people saying that PI cases go to one part of the organization and are referred to insurers, and ET cases go to HR and aren't referred even if they include claims for compensation for PI, is that to that extent the system is clear. If a claim comes in that is in the CC or HC it will just immediately go off, the insurers will deal with it, there will be separate solicitors and the claim will kind of run its own life with the organization hardly being involved at all. But for claims in the ET it's all dealt with in-house. It feels much closer to the organization even though the HR team will instruct lawyers. When I talk about employment cases being more personal, perhaps that is just because there isn't that routine outsourcing of the litigation so the organization is more involved. Maybe that is part of it. SL12 (barrister, mixed practice)

Another senior lawyer explained how very complicated the associated practicalities can become:

Some employment cases should be brought as PI actions and the PI element in the damages is probably covered by compulsory employers' liability insurance. Most insurers think that too. The big difficulty usually comes not with the general damages. If the ET awards £30,000 for psychiatric illness, the insurer knows he's picking that up. The big problem is the loss of earnings claim. Is that covered by the employers' liability policy or not? Discrimination would not be an insured loss but PI may well be and it's quite difficult to work out what should be attributed to the PI. Some bits are obvious. Others are not. SL9 (barrister, mixed practice)

My suspicion is that many pure employment and equality law practitioners would not think of compulsory employers' liability insurance potentially covering any personal injury element in ET compensation and hence would not consider involving the insurers in the litigation. Be that as it may, this aspect of my data shows that this area of practice is ripe for further investigation and analysis.

For present purposes, what was clear was that practitioners who are closest to the system rarely saw jurisdictional boundaries as an issue. This was in a sense even more remarkable because a decent proportion of those I spoke to commented on specialism affecting their approach.[35] Some interviewees were also, as we have seen, perceptive about the implications more generally of seeing a skewed sample of workplace problems. In those circumstances it was astonishing to me that lawyer interviewees were, by and large, comfortable with what this book suggests are pointless, incoherent, and damaging legal divisions and distinctions. The implication was that their experience had somehow enured them to the negative aspects of this legal fragmentation.

4. Summary and Discussion

This chapter explained, first, how I extracted the hypothesis that individual labour and equality rights, at least as regards behavioural conflict and probably more generally, have variable impacts according to an employer's adherence to managerial versus pluralist ideas about working life. At one pole of the spectrum are organizations in which

---

[35] Specific practical effects of specialism on jurisdictional choices appeared to be that, first, only a few saw a claim under the PHA 1997 as potentially viable and, second, it was especially employment/equality practitioners who perceived that claimants are steered towards discrimination actions. See Ch 5, esp pp 119–20 and 132–37 on the variability of litigation choices and p 188 in Ch 8 on the latter issue.

employer concerns are straightforwardly dominant. My suggestion is that these work-places are likely to be least affected by individual legal entitlements, even if law and litigation impose after-the-fact costs when claims eventuate. At the other end are workplaces in which there is deep acceptance that multiple perspectives on working life, including those of the work force, individually and collectively, ought to be heard, debated, and reconciled. I contend that the latter organizations are most likely to be influenced by the standards contained in individual legal rights, yet at the same time are at risk of notable disruption from associated disputes and especially litigation. There are then multiple positions between these two extremes, particularly corresponding to experience with the law in organizations that adopt some form of unitarism. I also posit that there is increasing pressure on managers as a group to reconcile individual claims and entitlements with divergent ideas, however constructed, about the collective organizational good, in the manifold situations in which tension between these cause problems across all kinds of organizations.

The data suggested that the lesser challenge to how things are done in more employer-dominated workplaces derives from various individualized mechanisms by which legal influence on organizational life can be 'denatured', in the sense that its most potent emancipatory properties are neutralized. Most importantly there is the suppression internally of complaint and dissension. If claims nonetheless somehow emerge, it then seems quite easy to avoid any wider organizational impact, not least by buying claimants off. The more positive influence in less hierarchical workplaces came from organizations in different ways committing themselves to high labour standards, with adherence to law being more or less enthusiastically connected to that general approach. Some therefore spoke of law prescribing standards that organizations would adopt anyway, while others perceived employers to build on the law in the norms they adopted.

Even so, particular vulnerability to damaging individualized disputes and conflicts, arguably increasing with an organization's good intentions, was the result of the opposite tendencies in pluralist workplaces compared to employer-dominated ones. Instead of silencing and suppressing complaint, this was constructed as acceptable. Third party support for employees facing problems was often institutionalized, generally but not exclusively through trade unions, and there were indications of this aiding the effective resolution of problems in keeping with other evidence to this effect.[36] There were also, however, the problematic effects that proceduralization and formality could bring. Finally, instead of litigation tending to be brought to an end, disputes seemed to have more chance of proceeding, for example, because of external support and the lesser use of settlement. Looked at in the round, it becomes apparent that law's paradoxical organizational effects are partly produced by the various ways, both within organizations and in the context of litigation, that employers' concern to solve problems as well as focus on basic norms underlying legal interventions both seem to lose purchase in the context of particular individual disputes, the unfolding of which can instead take on a combative and adversarial logic of their own. A corollary is that this pattern entailed the sidelining of communal, collective means of regulating working life and of sorting out problems.

This second part of the story is critical to perceiving how things can go horribly wrong in legal terms without that meaning either that there is wholesale disrespect for the law in a given workplace or that a situation has, at least initially, been mishandled. At the same time, it further exemplifies the mismatch between the collective experience of working life and dissent being individualized. These insights come from analysing

---

[36] See p 51 in Ch 2.

the data about who comes forward when problems occur and which employers and employees fight claims to the bitter end. In some sense this brings to life how individual rights enforcement has been designed to be necessarily and profoundly conflictual, as opposed to constructive and even capable of delivering organizational and societal benefits. Convoluted attitudes to law that my senior managers described arguably supported this impression. Much as they had generally seen and experienced working life from an employer's perspective, it appeared that they were struggling to reconcile the sympathy they typically had for legal protections for working people with their experience of these in operation.

This is in a context, as Chapter 2 explained, in which very few workplace problems result in litigation, while a great many working people try and fail to resolve issues they encounter. Even where individuals pursue a matter to some degree, this can fall away at many stages without coming before lawyers, let alone courts. The extent to which working people are deterred from raising or pursuing complaints even when problems persist, and even more discouraged from litigating, in addition to the use of settlement to neutralize legal challenge, begs questions about how far litigants on both sides either have to be, or are steered into becoming, adversarial, combative, and uncompromising in fighting individualized legal battles.[37] The variable legal effects that I perceived on workplaces would also suggest that this kind of dynamic poses a particular risk for organizations that are more hospitable to individual legal entitlements at work, with an important part of the picture lying in the way that communal, collective means of solving problems, perhaps long established, are marginalized where conflict is individually framed. This also points to another important means, following on from the discussion in Chapter 8, by which the attitudes of lawyers, judges, and indeed anyone with an 'inside track' on law and legal process, derive from a partial view of how law functions. In turn, development of relevant law must be affected, as well as surrounding public and private discussion.

The urgent need that emerges from this analysis is for legal intervention to be adapted to the reality of different organizational experiences. The only possibility I perceive for achieving this is to find ways to integrate non-managerially constructed ideas about the communal, collective nature of working life into the implementation of individual rights within workplaces and their enforcement outside them. A critical aim in doing so is to be more successful at incorporating basic justice norms that underlie individual rights, for example of fairness, reasonableness, and equality, in the day-to-day working of all kinds of organizations, as opposed only to sometimes giving after-the-fact individual vindication through compensation.

The collective dimension that I think is missing, certainly regarding behavioural conflict and with implications for other kinds of problems, is the kind that challenges the pre-eminence of managerial and unitaristic ideas about how working life ought to unfold and that integrates the reality that individual interests at work are inevitably in some kind of balance with collective workplace concerns. The embedding of increased participation, whether based on trade unionism or otherwise, into the implementation and enforcement of individual entitlements is the only thing that can achieve the twin effects of rendering the challenge of individual rights more incisive in workplaces, especially at the employer dominated end of the spectrum, and more supportive of basic justice norms, especially at the more collectivist end. This kind of innovation would also

---

[37] Recall some of the more extreme instances of litigation that came through from the case law analysis, reported at pp 115–17 in Ch 4.

counteract the risk that arises from individual entitlements appearing easier to manage in employer-dominated workplaces, of laws in this form operating as another spur to greater managerial dominance at work, including of extreme kinds.

Whatever is done, it is plain that the law needs to be relevant not only to the variety of workplaces but also to the range of individuals within them. The interview data showed that managers struggling to deal with problems and employees stoically putting up with issues can be the same people.[38] My sense is that legal influences on these overlapping constituencies, including as mediated by HR,[39] will be central to law's effects on working lives in current conditions. It is surely as much the conversations, exchanges, and debates that law engenders, as opposed to the particular outcomes it produces, that matter to whether hierarchies at work are scrutinized and challenged, as I would contend is demonstrated by the case law analyses in Chapters 6 and 7. If it was clear to everyone that legal intervention is fundamentally, consistently about solving problems through the contextual application of fairness, reasonableness, and equality norms, I suspect that, day to day, it would become much more difficult for any employers to sideline individual rights at work and that law's influence, such as it is, would become more unequivocally constructive across all of working life.

[38] See pp 224–25 and 227 above and p 188 in Ch 8.
[39] See p 48 in Ch 2 on the importance of such mediating effects.

10

Conclusions

This chapter draws out the implications of my findings methodologically, theoretically, and for the design of individual labour and equality rights in the UK. I argue that the primary research I undertook has in a range of ways filled out the claim that law and legal process simultaneously challenge and support established power relations, structures, and ways of being. Furthermore, this research was conducted at the heart of legal interventions that on their face pursue emancipatory, socially transformative goals, demonstrating the salience of the legal shift to an individualized framing of working life and how ideological struggle over individualism is bound up with this process.

The first section explores the findings that may be relevant to understanding how law functions where it is not in the form of individual rights and does not concern work. The second section explains how the data support more specific theorizing about the impact and meaning of individual labour and equality rights in the UK. This leads to suggestions for improving the deployment of legal intervention at work in pursuit of justice goals. These aspects of the chapter may also have resonance for other countries in which law and industrial relations are on comparable trajectories.

1. Excavating the Two Faces of Law and Legal Process

(1) The challenge of law

(a) Enforcement

On the side of the legal equation that bears out the transformative potential of law, my findings pinpoint various ways in which UK individual labour and equality rights challenge established patterns of managerial dominance at work. The starting point is the large number of relevant legal interventions. The main ones were outlined in Chapter 3 albeit not exhausting the laws available to contest workplace conduct. Taken together, these impose considerable obligations on employers to act fairly, reasonably, and in keeping with equality norms. My examination of higher court enforcement in turn evidenced immense care and conscientiousness on the part of judges to unpack the factual background to specific conflicts and to apply basic justice norms where jurisdictional complexity permitted this.

The fact that my research design provided only indirect consideration of lower court adjudication, however, needs to be kept in mind. The oblique view this provided and the hierarchical superiority and legal authority of the judgments analysed suggest the decision-making approach I found is probably emulated in lower courts. Additional investigation would be necessary, however, to be sure of this. Moreover, this further research would be particularly valuable in regard to Employment Tribunal (ET) analyses of employer responses to problems, given the gap between what emerged about this issue from higher court judgments and interviewees' comments on procedural legal influence.[1] Nonetheless,

---

[1] See Ch 7, esp pp 180–82, pp 197–200 and 209 in Ch 8, and further the text to ns 44–45 below.

the nature of higher court decision-making about what is legally acceptable and unacceptable at work in itself makes good on the promise of individual rights to challenge background distributions of power.

My specific findings on adjudicative style when litigation reached the stage of elaborating the legality of workplace behaviour and employer reactions reinforced this conclusion. I consistently observed nuanced analyses that guided employers, explicitly and implicitly, first, about when behaviour is treated by law as a fact of working life and when it is legally proscribed, and second, about when employers' handling of situations is and is not legally acceptable. There was a notable consistency of approach to drawing these two sets of legal lines across courts and causes of action, much as deep contextualization caused substantive requirements to vary. In relation to behaviour itself, there was repeated emphasis on events having happened in a sequence and a recurrent strain of conduct being condemned outright. With respect to employer responses, judgments displayed more of a tendency to balance employer, employee, and societal interests, albeit that this was not entirely absent from evaluations of conduct, for example in judges' characterizing some bad workplace behaviour as being lawful. The normative message overall was that employers ought to treat employees fairly, reasonably, and in keeping with equality norms, both procedurally and substantively, taking account of the difference that the particular context and set of circumstances make to what that general stance entails.

Crucial to the challenge this presented was that judicial reasoning was intelligibly expressed. While non-lawyers (and indeed, many lawyers) are uncomfortable with legal technicality, the substantive musings about lawfulness in the judgments were in terms that would quite easily translate to other contexts in which people debate the acceptability of what goes on in the workplace. Contributing to this were instances in which judges smuggled in the balancing of individual claims, as protected by legal entitlements, with other points of view, of employers, other employees, and society at large, echoing more plural, collective modes of regulating working life. I see this form of expression as part of the challenge to managerial power because the user-friendliness of the language made it much harder, in theory at least, to dismiss legal interference as alien, abstract, and irrelevant. At the same time, such expression makes legal discourse more accessible to those seeking to make organizational life more just. That can even be argued regarding judges' multifaceted analyses about employer responses, in that these honoured individual rights while confronting the difficulty there can be, identified in Chapter 2, in accommodating them in the essentially communal context of working life.[2] This implicitly acknowledged the legitimacy of competing workplace interests, individual and collective, and modelled how they might be reconciled in a regulatory landscape in which legal protection of working people's interests increasingly takes an individualized form.

Perceiving a genuine challenge in this aspect of adjudicative practice, however, does not deny that what judges think and do is structured by who they are and their institutional vantage point. Indeed, the data also show that how judges and other legal insiders think about a given topic, and hence how the law and surrounding discourse develop, is influenced by the particularities of the sample of cases that come before lawyers and courts.[3] More generally, judges form a highly distinctive epistemic community, with in many ways homogeneous social, economic, and educational backgrounds, all of which, however inscrutably, affect how they adjudicate. The standards judges perceive as

---

[2] See pp 55–58 in Ch 2.   [3] See pp 117–18 in Ch 4, pp 212–13 in Ch 8, and pp 239–40 in Ch 9.

appropriate at work, the workplace interests they recognize as requiring balancing and how they determine their relative importance, are all framed by who these individuals are and the context in which they operate.

In some sense that makes the consistency I observed in higher court judicial approaches to substantive reasoning all the more interesting. The usual contention is that commonality amongst lawyers and judges is likely to produce consistency that undermines law's emancipatory power, although there is much more to be discovered about how this works. The findings here suggest that enquiry is also needed to discover what produces adjudicative consistency that reinforces legal challenge to existing power structures. The particular research questions this work points to are first, whether the presence of lay judges in ETs and employment appeal tribunals (EATs) over the years has made a difference, and second, whether the distinctive experience of judging employment and equality cases accounts for the consistency I found and if so, whether this has had any wider impact on adjudication.[4] Whatever the outcome to those enquiries, it may already be concluded that this form of legal discourse would be enhanced by being exposed to and building on a more participatory conversation within workplaces about what effective implementation and enforcement of legal rules requires.

(b) Implementation

Turning to organizational implementation of individual rights and the adjudicative outcomes to which they give rise, there were clear indications that the law makes a difference. My findings about the law's effects on employers do not claim to be capable of direct generalization but instead document legal influence in the workplaces that my interviewees described and support theorizing on which to base further investigation. Even so, the range of workplaces covered, the long cumulative experience of my interviewees, and their expertise increase confidence in the reliability of what emerged, reinforced by similarities with other research findings. First, there was attribution of internal proceduralization and formality to legal influence. This was in keeping with findings over the years, including the expression of ambivalence about the practical effect of procedural responses to law.[5] Second, there were widespread reports of equality law having an impact, again reflecting other research findings.[6] Overall, the message was that law in the form of individual labour and equality rights has shifted what organizations do, pushing them to subject managerial authority to procedural and substantive limits. Whatever else law and legal process stimulate, this shows that they can, to some extent, unsettle and alter workplace hierarchy.

(2) The acquiescence of law

On the darker side of the legal equation, however, there was depiction of phenomena that systematically undercut the transformative potential of individual labour and equality rights. These showed the law ultimately to leave existing power relations fundamentally untouched. The net effect was for established hierarchies to be bolstered and their legitimacy increased because they had endured in the face of emancipatory legal challenge.

---

[4] See S Corby and PL Latreille, 'Employment Tribunals and Ordinary Courts: Isomorphism Exemplified' (2012) 41 ILJ 387, 396, and 404–05 using the theory of 'professional isomorphism' to explain ETs becoming more like ordinary courts.
[5] See pp 48–49 in Ch 2.   [6] See pp 48–50 in Ch 2.

(a) *Enforcement*

The dizzying array of relevant legal interventions again provides the starting point here. In stark contrast to substantive judicial decision-making about the acceptability of behaviour and of employer reactions to problems, adjudication about the links between different causes of action has undermined the potential for individual rights to ameliorate workplace standards. Instead of consistency and accessibility, in this context multiple distinctions have been made between legal regimes that make little sense. The net enforcement effect of legal variety has therefore been to produce arbitrariness and artificiality in the handling of individual claims, resulting both from deliberate litigation choices, good and bad, and the vagaries of case law development. The scope for further surprising twists also remains, exemplifying the significant unpredictability, even for insiders, of legal evolution in the field. This strand in the case law muddles the normative implications of individual rights at work, complicating law's overall demands of employers to construct more just workplaces.

My data additionally uncovered specific mechanisms that uncouple the emancipatory dimensions of individual labour and equality rights from the organizational outcomes they deliver, both where complaints stay inside organizations and in the tiny proportion that result in litigation.[7] In terms of litigation, first there was disjuncture between motivations that senior lawyers reported for compromising claims and concern to resolve the underlying problem, let alone to do so by applying legally inspired fairness, reasonableness, and equality norms.[8] Second, senior lawyers spoke as if it was entirely obvious that judgments have minimal impact within workplaces, if any at all. This chimed with the extensive harm that both manager and lawyer interviewees ascribed to involvement in litigation, often associated with adversarialism and negative overall views about the value of legal intervention given its narrow focus. The standard-setting and guidance in higher court judgments appeared not only to have limited direct organizational influence, but not even to affect workplaces that were involved in the litigation. In this way, a prominent aspect of the challenge to workplace hierarchy from individual rights seemed to be dissipated, perhaps lost entirely.

(b) *Implementation*

When attention is turned to implementation of individual labour and equality rights at work, considerable patchiness of influence was found, in some sense mirroring the dislocation present in legal sources and their adjudicative development. Eclecticism about the organizational impact of the law, however, did not track jurisdictional technicalities, of which managerial interviewees seemed to be entirely unconscious. Rather, there was considerable straightforward ignorance of substantive behavioural norms aside from equality rules. This was marked to such a degree that several interviewees appeared confounded by questions premised on the existence of laws that regulate workplace conduct other than through equality law. I found this all the more remarkable given that my senior manager interviewees were a sophisticated, experienced group, with a disproportionate number of lawyers in their number. This aspect of the data was, however, confirmed by careful probing and was supported separately by senior lawyer interviewees.

---

[7] This chimes with the qualitative evidence discussed at pp 45–46 in Ch 2 about employee litigants' dissatisfaction that sight had been lost of justice issues.
[8] See n 110 in Ch 2 for classic US observations of like effects.

I contend that this adds the kind of detailed data about legal influence and its absence that Dickens and Hall argued are in short supply.[9] While organizations may react procedurally to individual rights in general and respond substantively to equality rules, the implication of my research is that they are not coming 'to accommodate and live with' law by perceiving that behaviour at work is regulated other than by equality law. Recent research from the Department for Business, Innovation and Skills (BIS) about private employers further supports this observation. Private employers generally eschewed legal influence but there were instances of equality and dismissal law being acknowledged to have an impact. It was spelled out, however, that law has very little effect on working practices when managing staff.

The BIS evidence also pointed to the deleterious organizational consequences of law being experienced as complex. Negative views were attributed to this, with particularly problematic effects for smaller businesses from an odd resulting combination of anxiety and passivity. Nonetheless, there was recognition overall of the need for legal intervention to ensure employees are treated fairly. My findings reinforce that there is concern about legal complexity amongst senior managers, about three-quarters of my sample commenting on this. Senior lawyers, however, seemed wholly untroubled by jurisdictional complexity in this area. This was despite them describing consequent practical problems that are not apparent from case law and being conscious that their specialisms limited what they saw of how relevant law functions.

The last specific mechanism which appeared to uncouple outcomes from the justice norms underlying the law came from the problematic effects that proceduralization and formality were described as having. This was strongly backed up by comments made by senior lawyers, probably reflecting their disproportionate experience of situations that had gone wrong. One must remember, however, that a substantial minority of senior managers had positive perceptions of proceduralization within workplaces and that law was seen as interacting with other pressures to produce this. This contrasted with many depictions of procedural legal influence impeding problem solving and specifically deflecting focus from basic ideals of fairness, reasonableness, and equality.

Finally, the uneven pattern of legal influence that my data revealed takes on another dimension from comparing how senior managers described their reasoning processes about behavioural issues and what emerged from judgments. First, nearly all senior managers, whatever influence they attributed to law, saw workplace attitudes about acceptable conduct as deriving essentially from personal values and the contextualized judgments these enabled people to make. Second, there were parallels, also independent of perceptions of legal influence, between how senior managers reported analysing the acceptability of workplace conduct and how judges appeared to do this. This apparently natural overlap with judicial approaches was not present, however, in respect of employer responses to problems. Instead, senior managers were often troubled by organizational reactions, frequently attributing workplace dysfunction of this type to procedural legal influence.

Irregularity in legal influence therefore emerged as producing some organizational effects, especially procedural ones, but not the penetration of law's overarching requirements, expressed both in written law and adjudication, that working people be treated fairly, reasonably, and equitably, both procedurally and substantively. Individual labour and equality rights therefore did not appear in practice to be supporting the contextualized, morally grounded thinking about workplace problems that many senior manager

---

[9] See the text to n 6 in Ch 1.

interviewees appeared to believe in. Indeed, managers frequently saw themselves as only free to approach problems in this way where they mistakenly thought the law was irrelevant. Ironically, however, these 'non-legal' reflections in many ways echoed the general normative stance I discerned in judgments.

(3) General methodological and theoretical implications

The richness of patterns in the data vindicated the decision to combine qualitative case law analysis inspired by American Legal Realism with more modern socio-legal mapping of how legal influence plays out in regulated spaces.[10] Undertaking the latter entailed sociological study of organizations with the potential for learning amplified by literature from other fields. What I extracted bore out Edelman's observation that '[t]he socio-legal field overlaps with the fields of regulated organizations'. The odd patterns of perceived legal influence and of decision-making approaches were inconsistent, however, with her vision of freely flowing ideas of rationality, morality, and legality.[11] It seems likely that the exchange of ideas between legal and organizational worlds played a part in producing the influences and overlaps I found, but the significant disconnections I also uncovered point to a more complicated set of causal patterns than this theorization suggests.

My findings departed from the contrasting premise of autopoietic theory that communication between systems requires translation.[12] Instead, there were discursive parallels between organizations and case law independent of any process of translation, and some legal notions appeared to transfer relatively easily to the organizational realm. My sense is that this reflects criticisms of the depiction and delineation of social systems in systems theory.[13] Certainly, 'law stuff' happens in so many sites and speaks in so many different ways that it is difficult to conceive of one legal 'system', let alone to identify its limits. My analysis of judgments even suggested that variety in the language and conceptualization of law is internal to quite particular adjudicative discourses.

Accordingly, neither Edelman's idea of legal endogeneity nor systems theory helped to make sense of my data as regards the relationship between UK individual rights and the organizational lives these laws seek to regulate. The most challenging aspect to systematic theorizing came across as the variety of interactions with law and legal process, including where there was little or no explicit engagement with law.[14] This supported the need for legal intervention to articulate itself to organizational reality, as theories of responsive or reflexive regulation advocate.[15] But it also underscored the difficulty of devising interventions that are both general and adaptable to the wide range of working environments. Certainly, it suggested that no single approach would be effective to bring

[10] See pp 4–6 in Ch 1.
[11] LB Edelman and MC Suchman, 'The Legal Environments of Organizations' (1997) 23 Annual Review of Sociology 479, 502.
[12] See generally A Lourenco, *Autopoeitic Social Systems Theory: The Co-Evolution of Law and the Economy*, Centre for Business Research, Cambridge University, Working Paper 409 and on this point at 3–5.
[13] R Baxter, 'Autopoiesis and the "Relative Autonomy" of Law' (1998) 19(6) Cardozo Law Review 1987, 2067–2075.
[14] See AJS Colvin, 'American Workplace Dispute Resolution in the Individual Rights Era' (2012) 23 International Journal of Human Resource Management 459, concluding the US individual rights era has produced 'a divergence between different workers and workplaces in the ability to access and mobilize these rights and sources of power'.
[15] See, eg, C McCrudden, 'Equality Law and Reflexive Regulation: A Response to the Discrimination Law Review's Consultative Paper' (2007) 36 ILJ 255, 259–60 and B Hepple, 'Enforcing Equality Law: Two Steps Forward and Two Steps Backwards for Reflexive Regulation' (2011) 40 ILJ 315, 320–23.

about the desired organizational change, such as the problem-solving method Sturm advocates for the regulation of workplace equality issues.[16]

The central overall messages I gleaned were first, that an inherent feature of law is confirmed by these data to be simultaneously to uphold and to undermine existing divisions of power, and second, that what matters to constructing legal interventions that strike a different balance is to locate and counteract the precise mechanisms in a given sphere that bring about law's dual outcomes, with special attention to how and why law works variably in different environments. Those conclusions, moreover, have potential relevance beyond laws that overtly seek transformative justice goals, that take the form of individual rights, and that relate to work.

The specific phenomena that I identified also have a generic quality. This is true of law and legal process having erratic effects on those to whom they are directed and, at the same time, there being independent overlap and dissonance in reasoning about the subject matter of regulation within enforcement processes and in regulated settings. The same can be said of authoritative decision-making that both consistently, accessibly elaborates legal standards and produces arbitrary and incomprehensible distinctions. Finally, there could easily be reproduction elsewhere of mechanisms internal and external to legal process, either the ones I saw or others, which disconnect outcomes from goals that the law on its face is designed to achieve. These processes could operate perfectly well in other contexts to produce the contradictory effects I argue are inherent to law.

In some ways it is the ultimate proof of law's Janus-like nature that this quality is present whether legal intervention is overtly emancipatory or repressive. My findings support that it is only the means by which power is simultaneously questioned and legitimated that alter between instruments that emphasize either the justice or the coercive dimensions of law. In respect of apparently socially progressive measures, legitimation comes from devices that further overt legal challenges to existing structures. For repressive laws, legitimation results from legally grounded constraints, as Thompson's classic study of the Black Acts demonstrated.[17] By the same token, mechanisms that undercut apparent justice goals, such as those I observed, must always be expected to limit law's capacity to alter the status quo, while the fact that law is itself an embodiment of state power means the preservation of existing hierarchies is its default setting.

It follows that maximizing law's transformative capacity is especially challenging where the object of regulation is a key site in which power is contested, like the labour market. In the next section, I turn to the detailed implications of my findings for working life and legal regulation in the UK, but the general argument may already be made that the use of law to *individualize* employment relations, combined with the influence of *individualism* on that process, are central to the duality I found. This combination of process and ideology evoke different elements in Thompson's account of law:

But all that is entailed in 'the law' is not subsumed in these institutions [(the courts ... the judges, the lawyers, the Justices of the Peace)]. The law may also be seen as ideology, or as particular rules and sanctions which stand in a definite and active relationship (often a field of conflict) to social norms: and finally, it may be seen simply in terms of its own logic, rules and procedures—that is, simply *as law*.[18]

---

[16] S Sturm, 'Race, Gender, and the Law in the Twenty-First Century Workplace: Some Preliminary Observations' (1997) 1 UPaJLab & EmpL 639, 'Second Generation Employment Discrimination: A Structural Approach' (2001) 101 ColumLRev 458, and 'Law, Norms and Complex Discrimination' in C Estlund and B Bercusson (eds), *Regulating Labour in the Wake of Globalization, New Challenges, New Institutions* (CUP, 2008).
[17] EP Thompson, *Whigs and Hunters: The Origin of the Black Act* (Pantheon, 1975).
[18] ibid, 260.

Struggle over the demands of liberal individualism and its societal influence is present throughout the design, enactment, and operation of individual rights at work. The more this results in law and legal process being individualized, however, the more legal intervention at work is tilted towards upholding existing power structures irrespective of any potential for rights to help enshrine a rich, positive liberty-inspired notion of individualism, or indeed a more communitarian idea of society. This follows from individualization at work necessarily pitting collective employer power against individual working people. The precise means by which individual workplace entitlements are enshrined in law is therefore itself an outcome of struggle over what is owed to individuals in society, while both legislative design and surrounding ideological battles are central to the balance ultimately struck between furthering transformative justice goals and legitimizing existing hierarchy.[19]

The outcome in the UK has been for individual rights at work to symbolize the acceptable face of liberal individualist ideology but in a form that ensures they can deliver only limited gains for working people. This legislative shift thereby entrenches the move from collectivism to individualism as the lens through which divisions of power and resources at work are conceived,[20] but at the same time curtails the emancipatory possibilities of individualist ideology. The consequence is that managerial power has been legitimated by legal emancipation 'on the books' at little cost in terms of symbolic or material rebalancing of interests at work. The ultimate irony is that opposing the collective power of management against isolated individual employees has along the way reduced the capacity of collective workplace institutions and activity to resist managerial domination of working lives.

Before turning more fully to how this dynamic has operated in the UK, it is important to make the methodological point that the features of law the research exposed could never be seen, let alone accurately documented and analysed, entirely from the inside. This became apparent from unearthing in Chapter 2 that which conflicts at work are authoritatively adjudicated is structured by background conditions, bringing into focus how far the insider legal perspective reflects only partial experience.[21] My interview data further unearthed the reality that lies behind a legally constructed world view, enabling hypotheses to be developed about the overall functioning of the law and what would have to change for it to have greater effect. The limited vantage point that legal process provides could not produce such an overall assessment; rather leading to serious mistakes in how law's failures are conceived and potential solutions are analysed.

---

[19] Compare the account of American legal process at M Galanter, 'Why the Haves Come Out Ahead' (1974) 9 Law and Society Review 1, 57: 'Thus its unreformed character articulates the legal system to the discontinuities of culture and social structure; it provides a way of accommodating cultural heterogeneity and social diversity while propounding universalism and unity; of accommodating vast concentrations of private power while upholding the supremacy of public authority; of accommodating inequality in fact while establishing equality at law; of facilitating action by great collective combines while celebrating individualism. Thus "unreform"—that is, ambiguity and overload of rules, overloaded and inefficient institutional facilities, disparities in the supply of legal services, and disparities in the strategic position of parties—is the foundation of the dualism of the legal system. It permits unification and universalism at the symbolic level and diversity and particularism at the operating level.' (notes omitted)

[20] My argument is that individualism is the critical ideological construct (and battleground) in this context, as ideas about property were depicted to be in Thompson, *Whigs & Hunters* (n 17) and racism in K Crenshaw, 'Race, Retrenchment and Reform: Transformation and Legitimation in Anti-Discrimination Law' (1988) 101 Harvard Law Review 1331, notably at 1370. It may also be inferred that the impact of individualism on the enactment and operation of individual rights is more negative for groups that are in other ways disadvantaged, including ethnic minority communities.

[21] See n 3 above and accompanying text.

An important further consequence is that the way law functions is ultimately dependent on the tools the political process provides. Wide-ranging, external analyses may well be of intellectual interest only if legislatures are not prepared to act on what this kind of enquiry reveals. Even putting aside the constitutional limits on what can properly be done within adjudication, the transformative capacity of law, for good or ill, emerges as significantly dependent on legislators being willing and able first, to inoculate legal intervention against the different means by which outcomes are in practice disconnected from emancipatory aims, and second, to engage in the ideological struggle this would require. I return below to the unlikelihood of this happening in current political conditions.

2. Individual Labour and Equality Rights and the Variety of Working Lives

(1) Managerialist evasion, unitarist ambiguity, and pluralist struggles

In this section I draw out the implications of these propositions for hypothesizing how individual labour and equality rights affect organizational life in the UK, explaining the interaction with my theory of law. In doing so I take account of data from interviewees about what lies behind different experiences that working people and organizations have of law and legal process, bringing more fully into the frame situations in which individuals do little or nothing about workplace problems.

The hypothesis the data support, foreshadowed in Chapter 9, is that the more dominant employers and managerial perspectives are at work, the less individual rights—certainly those that are relevant to behavioural conflict and probably others—are likely to affect how things are done, notwithstanding that they can impose after-the-fact costs for breach. By the same token, the more organizations espouse pluralist ideas about how working life ought to be regulated, the more guidance they are likely to take from individual rights, even building on them in the workplace standards they adopt.[22] Ironically, however, this kind of workplace appears to be at particular danger of disruptive, damaging individual conflicts, including those that escalate to litigation.

Across the board, moreover, the data suggested that line managers, who may be relatively low in organizational hierarchies, are being positioned as 'shock absorbers' for the tension and difficulty that were argued in Chapter 2 to result from divergences between collective interests at work, however constructed, and individual claims, including those backed up by law.[23] The position of line managers in this regard seems to some extent to mirror that of individuals facing problems at work, which are in any event overlapping constituencies. This is not in any sense to deny that people who encounter workplace difficulties are frequently under immense pressure and that this may well be caused or exacerbated by management, as amply demonstrated in this project. It is, rather, to notice parallels in the experience of managers.

Most crucially, I would argue that the pressure in both instances comes from the absence, increasingly, of organizational mechanisms for the expression and balancing

[22] Compare E Heery, B Abbott, and S Williams, 'The Involvement of Civil Society Organizations in British Industrial Relations: Extent, Origins and Significance' (2012) 50 BJIR 47, 67–8 about employer acceptance of non-governmental regulation likely being 'highly skewed'.
[23] See pp 55–58 in Ch 2.

of different points of view, collective and individual, about what ought to happen at work. In my contention it is not only employees encountering problems who feel the absence of more pluralist means within workplaces for raising and resolving difficulties, but also managers who are left to handle the fall-out. The casting of so many employee entitlements in individual rights is part of this landscape, given the inherent difficulty for individuals on their own of asserting entitlements in relation to an essentially collective activity and the corresponding challenge, perhaps also lonely, that managers face to reconcile such claims as do arise with other workplace interests.[24] In these circumstances it is predictable that managers are liable to respond in unconstructive ways, ignoring problems, turning on those who speak out, and resorting to crudely authoritarian measures. Indeed, the logic of my model is that an incentive has to some degree been set up for organizations to employ people with the capacity to act in precisely this way.

It is in this context that it matters so much that law and legal process create mechanisms with which employers can quite easily minimize, sideline, and defuse the emancipatory potential of individual labour and equality rights. The suggestion here, as conveyed by my interviewees, is that these devices will have most effect in organizations that are characterized by managerial dominance. Given that individual rights were depicted as having limited influence on the practices of organizations that my senior manager interviewees had experienced, which were no doubt disproportionately more receptive, how much more erratic is law's organizational implementation likely to be where it falls on unfertile ground? One can only imagine quite how irrelevant legal entitlements are to the construction of day-to-day working lives in the most hierarchical workplaces that senior lawyers and case law described. There is then the unlikelihood of complaints being made, evidenced by vivid depictions from managers and lawyers of some organizations being extremely effective at shutting down dissent. In addition, in the unusual situations in which individual enforcement is attempted, any wider impact this might have seems to be quite easy to neutralize, especially through settlement practice.

By contrast, in organizations at the pluralist, collectivist end of the range, it is more probable that greater acceptance of legal interference in general, and individual labour and equality rights in particular, will lead to higher labour standards.[25] The interview data suggested, however, that the virtuous circle the law might create is liable to be broken by the undercutting features identified, albeit within a different dynamic and with different net effects. The backdrop to this is that more expression of dissatisfaction is likely where complaint is tolerated and employees are assisted. When conflict emerges, however, the failure of law to infiltrate general normative messages, allied with legally influenced proceduralization and formality that is centered on individuals, can result in focus being lost on solving problems, and specifically on adhering to justice norms to do so. It is also more likely that individuals will turn to law, especially given external sources of support in such workplaces, while disputes have more chance of progressing to court hearings and appeals. This in itself increases the risk of wasteful adversarialism in which the potential is squandered for adjudication to deliver deep organizational learning.

I am positing a theory here about two poles in the organizational spectrum with, at one end, employer dominance, and at the other, wholehearted commitment to pluralist collectivism. This implies that many other positions exist along the spectrum. I would

---

[24] See further J Purcell, 'Line Managers and Workplace Conflict' in WK Roche, P Teague, and AJS Colvin (eds), *The Oxford Handbook of Conflict Management in Organizations* (OUP, 2014), 238–42 and p 52 in Ch 2.

[25] See pp 51–52 in Ch 2.

expect various versions of unitarist thinking to appear between the two extremes with overall tendencies first, to implement standards that the law endorses while denying legal influence, and second, for what happens when problems escalate to combine experience in the most and least employer-dominated environments. There are in particular likely to be multiple configurations of procedural reaction, settlement practice, and litigation combining to undermine legal normativity. Still, vignettes of organizational interaction with law are neatly schematic in a way that reality is not. Indeed, different parts of the same organization may correspond to different places along the spectrum.

This overall taxonomy was still supported by my data regarding what lies behind working people's variable engagement with the law and legal process. So many reasons emerged for individuals either to do nothing or to give up on initial efforts at resolution. These ranged from natural reluctance, reflecting perhaps the kind of professional commitment that Fevre and colleagues documented,[26] to organizational suppression of opposition. There are also the effects of perceiving, witnessing, and experiencing deleterious consequences from speaking out and litigating. A corollary is that securing authoritative adjudication will often in practice be conditional on employees and employers either being or becoming combative, uncompromising, and adversarial to a significant degree. This is important in itself, suggesting that law constructs individual rights enforcement as fundamentally conflictual rather than organizationally constructive and conducive to wider societal benefits. It may also be that the deleterious consequences of this fall disproportionately on well-intentioned employers. This picture additionally fills in particulars about the skewed nature of the legal insider's point of view.

Finally, standing back from the detail of how the individualization of law and legal process has produced dual outcomes, it is arguable that the variation in workplace influences itself exemplifies that it is in the nature of law simultaneously to support and undermine social transformation. First, my theory posits that the emancipatory dimension of individual labour and equality rights has the most impact where commitment already exists to the dismantling of traditional workplace hierarchy and has the least effect in organizations that espouse opposing ideologies. Second, laws in this form support the status quo in more plural, collectivist workplaces through the individualization of employee relationships and dispute resolution. This makes individual workplace rights a Trojan horse undermining plural broad involvement in the regulation of working life and strikes at critical means for evening out the balance of power and resources at work. Such employers are being legally steered into dealing with their workers one by one although, as Chapter 2 suggested and my findings bear out, adaptation to this shift in the landscape seems to be imperfect and potentially troublesome.[27] Third, support for existing structures in more employer-dominated workplaces is obvious in the manifold possibilities that individually focused law and legal process provide for shutting down appeals to emancipatory legislation and for minimizing its organizational effects.

Considering these factors together, the net outcome is for individual rights, at least the wide range that are implicated in my study and probably more generally, ultimately to support a good deal of traditional workplace hierarchy. Legitimation then follows from surviving the challenge presented by such measures intact and even strengthened. At the same time, there is implicit encouragement to move to a managerially dominant approach to reap its apparent benefits. In the final analysis, therefore, the ideology of individualism that permeates these workplace interventions translates into the interests

---

[26] See pp 22–23 in Ch 2.   [27] See pp 25 and 56 in Ch 2.

of working people being undermined and those of employers, ironically often in the form of collectives, being elevated.

My findings nevertheless suggest that the preservation, perhaps reinforcement, of established power relations at work is at some cost even to its beneficiaries. Silencing and marginalizing workplace problems do not mean that they have no negative effects, as comments by several interviewees showed. More broadly, there is the waste of effort and energy that suboptimal, sometimes dysfunctional, legal intervention provokes, piquantly captured by the mismatch between the seriousness with which adjudication is undertaken and the reported dismissiveness of those most closely involved.

The complex unease that senior managers expressed about individual labour and equality rights is illuminating in this context. Plainly this was not a representative sample, with disproportionate experience of workplaces with at least enlightened unitarist approaches to employee relations, and often embedded pluralist structures. The manager interviewees also tended personally to express commitment to high workplace standards. Their doubts about the interactions between law and work did not therefore generally come across as stereotypical, knee-jerk hostility that, on my hypothesis, might more routinely be expected of managers from the employer-dominated end of the spectrum. Rather, the way senior managers dichotomized legal approaches and what they perceived good management to entail, as well as their simultaneous endorsement and concern about current legal protections at work, arguably bore out that there is a broad constituency with interests in workplace rights being more effective.[28]

Most fundamentally, the failure in working lives to realize the emancipatory dimension of law represents a loss to many people. It is not only employers and employees who are directly concerned that suffer, but anyone who hopes for more just distributions of power at work. This does not presume that there is widespread agreement about a desirable end point for the construction of working lives, let alone about the balance between individual and collective interests. Rather, it contends that there is extensive disquiet about the depth of inequality, unfairness, and unreasonableness that exists in the modern labour market. The problem is not only that hierarchical workplace regimes have endured from earlier periods, but also that this form of organizational life appears increasingly entrenched and pervasive, especially as traditional forms of collective power are being dismantled.

(2) Discursive obstructions to the emancipatory potential of individual labour and equality rights

The discursive effects of law and legal process in this area provide a final expression of law's two-faced quality. They operate at the level of ongoing ideological struggle over the meaning and significance of liberal individualism as an organizing principle for society. This in fact seems to me the most significant duality in terms of ensuring that nothing fundamentally alters. The ideas presented in the next section for doctrinal development need therefore to be read against my view that there is highly unlikely to be purposeful effort to improve the capacity of individual rights at work, whether about behavioural conflict or anything else, to achieve their overt aims.

Starting with the necessarily partial nature of the legal insiders' perspective, this must affect ideas about what is wrong with the law, yet it misses entirely the reality of many working people trying and failing to resolve problems without resort to law and courts,

---

[28] See the citation from Purcell in the text to n 318 in Ch 2 on the importance of managerial attitudes.

as the empirical research discussed in Chapter 2 carefully documented. Instead, dysfunction associated with adversarialism naturally looms large, in turn tending to locate particular difficulties in organizations where complaint and litigation emerge and progress, as senior lawyers' ideas about public sector workplaces showed.

Noticing this kind of effect, however, does not deny that the dimensions of legal experience that worry legal insiders constitute real problems. The issue is that these are only the tip to an iceberg of working people being silenced and law's transformative potential neutralized. Furthermore, this world view is ironically liable to direct reforming zeal at organizations that are more receptive to what emancipatory workplace laws are trying to achieve and to deflect it from nefarious goings on where this kind of interference is rejected.

Turning to wider debate on this topic, we should not be surprised if the internal legal perspective is influential. Lawyers and judges especially have a privileged, expert status in discussion of legal development, speaking from intimate experience of the system in operation. The conflicts they witness act out the most direct encounters between individual rights and working life. Work-related battles that reach lawyers and courts, and the way they are talked about and reported, are therefore likely to construct and support myths about individuals easily turning to law and, in turn, of legal rules having direct effects, sometimes problematically. The messy reality of patchy legal influence, and of individuals facing problems struggling on with little or no resources to address them, may well be more resonant with actual workplace experience. It does not, however, translate into familiar narrative tropes of heroism and baseness in courtroom battles. Viewed in this light, common mischaracterizations of law's interaction with working lives start to appear natural.

It is an easy step from here to condemning individual labour and equality rights for being too easily invoked and because litigation about them can take convoluted, destructive paths, including in the hands of claimants bringing unmeritorious complaints. For those who are hostile to constraints, legal or otherwise, this pattern provides important tools for political contestation and resistance. The two-faced nature of law reappears in emancipatory gains from individual rights being won at another cost, this time giving supporters of existing distributional effects, often based on narrow liberal individualist ideology, easy arguments against the law intervening to protect working people. It is not only that it is easier for employer-dominated organizations to neutralize challenge from individual rights at work, but also that the law's functioning provides discursive, ideological means to forestall development that might make this form of legal intervention more transformative.

It is illuminating in this context to consider political evolution in the UK over the decades covered by this study. We saw from Chapters 2 and 3 that there has been proliferation of individual workplace rights, combined with successive attempts to deter individuals from enforcing them. Importantly, it was neither that only Labour administrations legislated and implemented individual rights, nor that measures to obstruct ET enforcement were only adopted by the coalition government after the 2010 election. The startling degree to which the most recent changes have succeeded in deterring individual enforcement also suggests that the patterns outlined in this work are set to heighten.

This leads to an argument that this political trend represents a further instance of law's contradictory nature. This time it is that politicians of all hues have made ideological use of individual labour and equality rights to garner legitimacy and popularity amongst some sections in society at the same time as they have limited the difference that these measures can make. This also enabled governments to make political gains through concessions to employer lobbies, including some who both make political capital from the dysfunctional elements of legal interventions at work and are adept at avoiding their direct influence. I cannot meaningfully surmise how far this has been deliberate, but the status-quo enhancing effects remain either way. In any event, this pattern fits the narrow ideological range within which political struggles over the structure of society are increasingly played out, reflecting growing attachment worldwide to reductionist versions of liberal individualism and to associated economic neo-liberalism. In a globalized economic system this involves a shift of power away from nation states that seems to leave little scope for reacting differently even for political actors who might sincerely want to rebalance power and resources at work.[29]

There has undoubtedly been little sign of UK political parties facing up to the profound challenge of making legal intervention at work more effective, whether through individual labour and equality rights or using some other technology of law. They have not even addressed the most obvious problems resulting from the proliferation of causes of action. Instead, as Chapter 2 explained, policy debate and related research have ignored the existence of common law relevant to working life.[30] This neglect has also endured despite other collateral damage from the current system, analysed in the section above, including sometimes for the powerful. The irresistible conclusion is that the current approach, for all its fragmentation, complexity and duality, in some sense plays well for governing parties across the political range. None of this leaves any cause for optimism about the chances of worthwhile legislative change.

The final inhibiting discursive effects I perceive concern the language and premises of individual workplace rights and this time operate on those who might agitate for reform. It is that it is incredibly difficult to find a language to criticize individual rights for not sufficiently delivering emancipatory goals or, in other words, to condemn their failure to bring about an enlarged version of what is owed to working people. Any criticism can so easily be heard as deprecating the underlying rights rather than the inadequate deployment of legal tools to realize the ideals they express.[31] In circumstances where established power structures and inequalities appear so entrenched, indeed ascendant, the temptation is to cling to any countervailing legal discourse and to keep quiet about its limitations. This is arguably yet another way that the duality of law expresses itself, this time limiting the argumentative, ideological resources available to those fighting for a fairer settlement at work.[32] Allied to this is the risk that finding such a language will become harder the more individualism takes hold ideologically and work relations become individualized. The less we think about and understand ourselves at work as engaging in an essentially collective, communal endeavour, the more difficult it will become to apply that frame of reference, including to secure effective implementation of existing individual legal entitlements and the more ambitious use of law to recast power relations.

---

[29] See also n 117 and accompanying text in Ch 2 about the growth of private equity being arguably set to heighten this tendency.

[30] See further L Barmes, 'Common Law Confusion and Empirical Labour Law' in A Bogg, C Costello, A Davies, and J Prassl (eds), *The Autonomy of Labour Law* (Hart, 2015), 108 generally, and especially on this point at 111–12.

[31] See Thompson, *Whigs and Hunters* (n 17), 266 on this dichotomy in relation to the idea and practice of the rule of law.

[32] See further, L Barmes, 'Individual Rights at Work, Methodological Experimentation and the Nature of Law' in A Blackham and A Ludlow (eds), *New Frontiers in Empirical Labour Law Research* (Hart, 2015).

(3) The missing collective dimension and using law to relocate it

The essential challenges for the design of individual labour and equality rights disclosed by this analysis are to infiltrate law's restraints on managerial power into the range of UK organizations and to ensure that this influence remains effective at realizing emancipatory goals. The only hope for meeting these challenges that I can perceive is for implementation and enforcement to draw on pluralist, collective involvement within workplaces, ideally with access to external support,[33] whether through trade unionism or other institutional forms. The central theoretical point is that this would address the mismatch between the lived reality of working lives as a collective, communal endeavour, and the individualization of employee interests, claims, and entitlements, at the same time counteracting the narrow ideology of individualism in the existing framework of rights. In practice this would mean trying legally to embed consideration of unheard, particularly employee-side points of view into the day-to-day implementation and enforcement of workplace standards.

The practical need this creates is for the design of individual rights to build in resistance first, to being easily translated into collective employer dominance over isolated individual workers, and second, to being experienced as unsettling collective, plural means of ordering working lives. Generally the goal would be to inscribe legally inspired justice norms into the routine operation of organizations such that they simultaneously challenge employer dominance of extreme kinds and help more receptive organizations to arrive at just solutions to multifaceted conflicts.

I have two sets of ideas for how this might be achieved, one concentrating on the messages law gives and the other on how these are received into workplaces. In a sense, the first responds especially to the findings in my qualitative study of judgments and the second to my interview data about the organizational impact of law. I put these forward, however, with scant hope that any UK government would take them forward.

(a) Normative accessibility as an emancipatory legal device

The first axis on which I contend change is needed is to make the general norms that underlie the current UK framework of individual rights more easily accessible to the range of people whose conduct they are meant to guide. Achieving this would require some legislative intervention to remove the arcane technicality associated with overlapping causes of action. Furthermore, it would arguably be desirable for Parliament to go further to clarify, where this is not obvious, the overarching norms it means legal intervention at work to convey. Equally, every conceivable opportunity should be taken in official guidance, judgments, and associated communications to get across the basic normative underpinnings of the law.

I argue for this while fully appreciating that the ideals that animate legal interventions can be hard to pin down, if they are present consistently at all. Equally, as argued in relation to what emerged from substantive adjudication of behavioural conflict cases, law's justice commitments will be differently perceived from different points of view. This ideological slipperiness and contestability are also perhaps especially issues in relation to individual labour and equality rights that address problems like behavioural conflict as opposed to rules that prescribe more determinate standards.

I contend, however, that it matters that immersion in judgments about behavioural conflicts, backed up by primary legal texts and what senior managers told me about their

---

[33] See n 200 and accompanying text in Ch 2.

reasoning processes, show certain recurrent justice concerns operating at a comprehensible level of generality and that could be extracted in accessible language. Beyond this, if legislatures and judges exerted themselves to make the law's essential requirements clearer and more digestible, this would in itself be legally authoritative.

The way I see this as helping to relocate the missing collective dimension to individual legal disputes is that related law would thereby become more useful in pursuing workplace justice for the range of people with a stake in working life, within and beyond organizations. In some sense I am advocating cutting through the mechanisms by which law's requirements of working people and of their employers are currently mystified, obfuscated, and complicated. Instead the goal would be for law directly, consistently, and straightforwardly to communicate its demands in language that is intelligible to those affected. Apart from anything else, this would make it easier for a wider range of people than managers and human resources (HR) personnel to influence the practical effect given to legal standards within particular workplaces and regarding specific situations. Such an approach might even enable guidance in the course of adjudication to make it through to those to whom it is addressed, conceivably assisting organizational actors to make sense in legal terms of highly complex problems that working life gives rise to, as shown in Chapter 4.

My cautious hope is that this would help people at work, whether in management, HR, or themselves experiencing and witnessing problems, to draw on legal standards to challenge employer dominance and to sort out problems by working through law's demands in a given context. This might equally facilitate groups doing the same, building on the hints from my interview data of new forms of collectivism, and from Pollert's work of informal group action.[34] Provision of external support may also become easier for having more accessible standards to draw on. In addition to trade unions, such help might come from other entities, work by Abbott, Heery, and Williams having begun to document and construct theories about non-governmental organizations (NGOs) and other external actors taking on a supportive role in securing the implementation of labour standards within UK workplaces.[35]

Nonetheless, simplification would remain incomplete and piecemeal if peculiar distinctions between different workplace legal rules remain. Removing these, however, presents fiendish technical and political challenges. If there was the will to take these on, the obvious starting point would be to standardize the remedial options for different courts deciding the same cause of action. In the current system, that would mean extending common law powers fully to ETs, especially the award of unlimited damages, including for personal injury, and the grant of injunctive relief. A more radical alternative would be to bring employment and equality adjudication entirely into the ordinary court system, hopefully still in the hands of specialist judges including non-lawyers with industrial experience. This no longer seems as unthinkable as it once did because ETs increasingly resemble ordinary courts and recent changes have taken them further in this direction.[36]

---

[34] See, respectively, p 224 in Ch 9 and p 36 in Ch 2.

[35] S Williams, E Heery, and B Abbott, 'The Emerging Regime of Civil Regulation in Work and Employment Relations' (2011) 64 Human Relations 951, S Williams, B Abbott, and E Heery, 'Civil regulation and HRM: the impact of civil society organizations on the policies and practices of employers' (2011) 21 Human Resource Management Journal 45, E Heery, S Williams, and B Abbott, 'Civil Society Organizations and Trade Unions: Cooperation, Conflict and Indifference' (2012) 26 Work, Employment and Society 145, and Heery et al, 'The Involvement of Civil Society Organizations in British Industrial Relations' (n 22).

[36] Corby and Latreille (n 4).

Even this adjustment would, however, leave significant remedial anomalies in place between common law and statutory entitlements. That sets up a case to standardize remedies across all causes of action. Achieving this would entail a higher level of challenge: not only would the technical issues be more difficult but any proposed solution would provoke intense political opposition. On the statutory side alone, politicians would need to opt for one remedial model, taking account of restrictions from EU law on reducing legal protections. As regards the relationship between overlapping statutory and common law rights, it would be necessary to clarify if it really is Parliament's ongoing intention to restrict employers' common law liabilities in respect of dismissal and, if so, to rationalize the exceptions to this.

Ultimately it appears that seriousness about removing the doctrinal oddities in this area would require some form of legal codification. This is the most obvious and perhaps the only way clarity could be achieved about the basic underlying norms that legal intervention at work is intended to embed, the particular legal entitlements that different categories of working people have, the available remedies, and when, if ever, alteration by agreement is permissible. This would evidently be a large task and seems particularly unlikely for any government to take on.

(b) *Widening participation in implementation and enforcement as an emancipatory legal device*

This leads naturally to my second set of ideas, which builds on and to some degree overlaps with those outlined earlier. Up to this point I have made the case for legislators and judges articulating what the enactment of individual rights positively asks of employees and organizations, as opposed to what it prohibits. To some extent this is easier where standards concern determinate entitlements although even here it can be challenging. In respect of more diffuse issues, this possibility naturally evokes what has been done in the equality field with successive positive duties on public sector employers in the UK.[37]

The point is that this is a legal technology that could encompass workplace obligations more generally, at the same time helping to communicate law's fundamental justice commitments. This might help those inside and outside workplaces to use law both to challenge and to guide problem-solving based on justice norms, conceivably even if some peculiar jurisdictional boundaries remained in place. Indeed, it would be possible for such a duty specifically to encourage participation in implementation and dispute resolution. This would emulate the participation requirement in the 2006 gender equality duty[38] and create a specific means of encouraging the missing collective dimension to be expressed.

This kind of approach would also provide the opportunity to make clear when balancing analyses of organizational reactions to problems are acceptable, perhaps specifying the various collective and individual interests that ought to be taken into account.[39]

---

[37] With antecedents going back further, particularly in Northern Ireland, the Race Relations (Amendment) Act 2000 created a public sector race equality duty by inserting s 76 into the Race Relations Act 1976, the Disability Discrimination Act 2005 created a public sector disability equality duty by inserting s 49A into the Disability Discrimination Act 1995, the Equality Act 2006 did the same for gender equality by inserting s 76A into the Sex Discrimination Act 1975 and these were all replaced and extended by the single public sector equality duty contained in s 149 of the EqA 2010. See that s 3 of the EA 2006 gives an account of society, the development of which the EHRC is required to exercise its functions 'with a view to encouraging and supporting'.

[38] See Hepple (n 15) generally and on the failures of the EqA 2010 in this regard.

[39] See Ch 7, esp pp 180–82.

Some may find this last suggestion a problematic, unjustifiable thing to argue for, viewing individual rights as sacrosanct. I contend, however, that some balancing of workplace interests in the adjudication of individual rights is perfectly reconcilable with the notion that some actions straightforwardly breach such standards and ought to be legally proscribed in the most trenchant way. The point is that when an employer is reacting to difficult situations, including horizontally between colleagues, they ought to consider the interests, individually and collectively, of more than the particular claimant, while the organization's aims and objectives are also relevant. Solutions, and the procedure followed to reach them, need to work not only for the individual concerned but also for other employees and for the organization.

In any event, the problem this proposal addresses is not that seriously wrongful behaviour can go unaddressed. Indeed that outcome seemed more likely where organizations, often at the employer-dominated end of the spectrum, were effective at shutting down and diverting complaint. The issue this idea responds to is rather that just resolution of initial difficulties, whether serious or less so, is apt to get lost in highly individualized procedures. My contention is that law needs to find ways to help organizations and individuals within them to resolve problems, large or small, in ways that intelligently reconcile the different interests in play and with consistent regard to substantive justice norms.

A crucial final aspect of legal development along these lines would be that it would open up enforcement and remedial possibilities to others than individuals who allege specific wrongful acts.[40] The existing positive equality duty enforcement model involves first, judicial review by individuals and groups, and second, institutional enforcement by the Equality and Human Rights Commission (EHRC). Judicial review would not work as a cause of action here because it is the means by which the lawfulness of public exercises of power are challenged, whereas the change advocated would apply to both public and private employers. Still, the current positive equality duty suggests innovative possibilities for remediation of workplace wrongs.

It shows that it is perfectly possible for legal design to empower a range of litigants, to provide for institutional enforcement, and to move the focus away from post hoc analysis to forward-looking evaluation of organizational practice. Such changes should logically also trace through to available remedies. These need not involve compensation but rather might address what needs to be altered. For example, remedies like injunctive relief could require organizational or group-based change. Courts might therefore require adoption of specific standards, whether procedural or substantive, and impose participation obligations, perhaps in working out the local implications of standards or in dispute resolution procedures, informally and formally. This would make demands of the legal process by requiring some mechanism for checking compliance. There are possibilities already in place, however, for example contempt of court proceedings and EHRC enforcement. The key in all circumstances would be for remedial design to concentrate on securing performance of legal obligations within workplaces.

This analysis highlights something of an irony in the recent innovation to redirect remedial attention to organizations by empowering ETs to impose fines. The worry is that this will turn out to be another means by which legal process disconnects enforcement activity from adherence to legal standards. That the measure is linked to discouraging individual enforcement, including by reducing available compensation, only adds

---

[40] Compare also the suggestions in Galanter, 'Why the Haves Come out Ahead' 1 (n 19), 58–60.

to the chances that it will misfire.[41] In effect it appears likely merely to add a bargaining chip to the settlement table.

The hardest question about legal design is whether there should instead be greater rewards for good practice built into the framework of individual labour and equality rights, conceivably linked to the enforcement of positive duties, to litigation about specific situations, or to both. The idea would be to increase the extent to which legal design, aside from deterring breach of legal standards, creates incentives for organizations to implement them effectively. The most controversial version of this approach involves employers avoiding liability entirely because of compliance efforts, while it is less contentious for remedies to be adjusted in light of workplace practice. The former is represented in UK law by employers having a defence to vicarious liability for unlawful discrimination if they have taken reasonable steps to avoid their employees engaging in unlawful conduct.[42] The most recent UK version of the latter was introduced by the Employment Act 2008. This gave ETs discretionary power to adjust compensation awards by up to 25 per cent if either an employee or employer acted unreasonably in not following the principles enunciated in the newly issued Advisory, Conciliation and Arbitration Service Code of Practice on Disciplinary and Grievance Procedures.[43]

Arguably, therefore, UK law already sufficiently encourages good practice by employers (and indeed employees). Balancing analyses in case law to decide on the legal acceptability of organizational reactions also seem to work in this way. A complicating factor, however, is that my interview data suggested that none of these features of law and legal process are well understood within organizations. Instead we have seen that the attribution of procedural influence to law was linked to a significant proportion of the managers I interviewed, and a higher proportion of the senior lawyers, perceiving organizations being pushed to act counter-productively and unfairly.[44] One consequence for me is that this is an area in which it would be highly useful to know more about ET adjudication. This would illuminate whether something is happening at that stage to interfere with legislative incentives getting through to workplaces and to contradict higher court judgments that law's procedural requirements depend on contextualized analysis of what was just in a given situation.[45]

The implication for present purposes is that there does not seem to be anything that can be gained from increasing the formal legislative incentives to improve organizational implementation of individual rights. Rather, it appears that what matters most is that the essence of legal standards infiltrates working life. There is also a strong comparative argument not to innovate in this way. The extent to which US employers are shielded from liability for legally wrongful conduct, either where they have institutionalized grievance procedures or in deference to private arbitration systems, has significantly supported, enhanced, and entrenched managerial dominance in the US and there is little realistic possibility of legislative reversal.[46] This points to a serious danger that going further

---

[41] See text to n 54 in Ch 3.   [42] See p 75 in Ch 3.

[43] EA 2008, s 3. These replaced provisions in the EA 2002 providing for increases and reductions to awards where statutory procedural requirements had not been complied with. (See n 33 in Ch 3.)

[44] See pp 197–200 in Ch 8.

[45] See n 1 above and accompanying text. Ideally this would be linked to finding out if there are consistent mediating effects, for example from HR and lawyers, that are producing this outcome, as the US literature suggests have operated in that context (on which see p 48 in Ch 2).

[46] See KVW Stone, 'Mandatory Arbitration of Individual Employment Rights: The Yellow Dog Contract of the 1990s' (1995–96) 73 Denver Univ LR 1017, M Finkin, 'Privatization of Wrongful Dismissal Protection in Comparative Perspective' (2008) 37 ILJ 149, and C Estlund, 'Employment Rights and Workplace Conflict' in Roche et al (eds), *Oxford Conflict Management Handbook* (n 24).

down this road in the UK would simply create another, notably powerful, means by which employers could avoid the potentially emancipatory impact of legal norms.[47]

(c) Experimentation as an emancipatory legal device

There is evidently something uncomfortable about putting forward ideas for improving the capacity of individual labour and equality rights to deliver justice goals when it is central to my theory of the nature of law and of how it functions in this context that those ideas will not be adopted. If an important means by which individual UK rights at work support existing distributions of power is through discursive, ideological effects that obstruct thoroughgoing reform, it is arguably incoherent, and certainly somewhat pointless, to make suggestions for reconstructing this form of law. To do so in some sense defaults back into assuming that society can be changed and made better if only those in charge find the right legal formula. It also ignores deeper battles that are intertwined with law in its various guises.

There is no way out of this bind. That law simultaneously transforms and secures the structure of society is the reality that anyone working with this medium, consciously or not, must hold in uneasy balance.[48] It follows that reasoning about what might technically help to rebalance legal effects towards emancipation is as much an argument about how those committed to that end ought to engage with the current law and take up the ideological struggle surrounding it. This leads me to the thought that there is nothing to stop individuals and groups within and beyond workplaces already orienting their response to individual rights to extracting these laws' basic normative implications and using that discourse to work towards improved organizational implementation and dispute resolution. In other words, the arguments made earlier suggest possibilities, even without legislative change, for counteracting the mechanisms by which law and legal process undermine the achievement of workplace justice, and for imbuing individual rights implementation with more positive conceptions about the appropriate balance of power and resources.

Indeed, the existing positive equality duty has arguably created a regulatory petri dish that is ideally suited to trying out this approach. Further, Heery and colleagues' work on the emergent UK experience of civil society organizations pursuing higher labour standards, called 'civil regulation', suggests that there are relevant practical developments and, intriguingly, that these are rooted in state action. Their research found legal innovation has given civil society actors leverage in workplace activism, opportunities to connect with employers, legitimacy in doing so, and ideological encouragement for the cooperative approach they tend to take in promoting change.[49] To some extent this suggests a more hopeful assessment of the political convenience of individual rights is possible from the potential for new actors to become involved in the quest for justice at work. From this perspective these legal tools might be seen as enabling the state to stimulate workplace change in the new ideological and labour market landscape.

---

[47] See LB Edelman and MC Suchman, 'When the "Haves" Hold Court: Speculations on the Organizational Internalization of Laws' (1999) 33 Law and Soc'y Rev 941, and LB Edelman, C Uggen, and HS Erlanger, 'The Endogeneity of Legal Regulation: Grievance Procedures as Rational Myth' (1999) 105 Am J Sociol 406, 448–49.

[48] As Crenshaw (n 20) put it at 1368–69: '[I]t might just be the case that oppression means ... that there are risks and dangers involved both in engaging in the dominant discourse *and* in failing to do so.' (emphasis in the original)

[49] Williams et al, 'The Emerging Regime of Civil Regulation' (n 35), 966–67, and Heery et al, 'The Involvement of Civil Society Organizations in British Industrial Relations' (n 22), 69–70.

Still, that civil regulation evidently has serious limitations[50] strongly supports the contention that using law in this way should be viewed as an experiment. The chimerical quality of law as a transformative medium means it is impossible to know in advance how any intervention will work and vigilance is needed about new status-quo-enhancing effects. It is vital, therefore, to find out more about existing capacity to reintegrate the missing collective dimension into the implementation and enforcement of individual rights. Evidently there is already some research[51] but much more is required to learn about first, more broadly based current uses of legal resources within workplaces, and second, if there are means by which working people might be stimulated, with or without external help, to do more in this regard. A methodological implication of this book is that this enquiry needs to draw both on industrial relations and socio-legal expertise.

An obvious specific area for research concerns the positive equality duty. There were so many alterations before the single duty was enacted in 2010 that it is still early days for mapping what has been done with it. However, initial signs have not been that encouraging,[52] making a particular case for empirical work that can inform both further enactments of this kind and the way the existing law is deployed. Equally, much as each system of employment and equality regulation has deep local roots, experience elsewhere is an important potential source of inspiration about uses to which law might be put by its subjects and how legislative innovation could stimulate this.[53]

There are further many legal topics, in the UK and elsewhere, in relation to which my theory about individual labour and equality rights might be tested and extended. As mentioned at the start, there are particular questions about how far what I found applies to more determinate legal interventions.[54] In each case, I would argue that such research itself could be a resource for the more effective use of law to achieve emancipatory workplace goals.

3. Individualism, Individualization, and Solidarity

At its most general level this work has exposed one way that law has in recent decades supported established power structures through the contemporary ideological power of individualism. Crucial to this process in the work context was the individualization of law and legal process, given the poor fit this framing has in relation to an essentially communal activity. Yet, against a backdrop of seemingly unstoppable, wider pressures

---

[50] ibid, respectively, 967 and 65–69.   [51] See pp 28–53 in Ch 2 and ns 22 and 35 above.

[52] See Audit Commission, *The Journey to Race Equality—Delivering Improved Services to Local Communities* (2004). J Ferrie, J Lerpiniere, K Paterson, C Pearson, K Stalker, and N Watson, *An In-Depth Examination of the Implementation of the Disability Equality Duty in England* (ODI, 2008), Schneider Ross, *The Public Sector Equality Duties, Making an Impact* (2007), Schneider Ross, *Assessing the Costs and Cost Effectiveness of the Specific Race, Disability and Gender Equality Duties* (GEO and Schneider Ross, 2009), H Conley and M Page, 'The Gender Equality Duty in Local Government: Prospects for Integration' (2010) 39 ILJ 321, and *Gender Equality in Public Services: Chasing the Dream?* (Routledge, 2014), and, finally, S Arthur, M Mitchell, J Graham, and K Beninger, *Views and Experience of the PSED, Qualitative Research to Inform the Review* (NatCen, 2013).

[53] The US is an obvious place to look for innovative organizational approaches to dispute resolution notwithstanding the problematic treatment of these in formal law. Eg, see Sturm, (n 16) on problem-solving, and JW Budd and AJS Colvin, 'The Goals and Assumptions of Conflict Management in Organizations' in Roche et al (n 24), 26 on peer review and ombudsperson procedures in non-union firms. As to regulatory interventions, recent history in Australia, including of the Fair Work Ombudsman system, creates scope for productive comparison. See T Hardy, '"It's Oh So Quiet?" Employee Voice and the Enforcement of Employment Standards in Australia' in A Bogg and T Novitz, *Voices at Work, Continuity and Change in the Common Law World* (OUP, 2014).

[54] See p 259 above and p 6 in Ch 1.

towards individualism and away from solidarity, legal contributions to this change, at work or anywhere else, might be regarded as relatively minor.[55] The message of this book is that it is an error to neglect the multiple ways that law embeds and extends existing hierarchies, even those it appears to challenge. Instead, the need is for ground-up collective engagement with any tools at society's disposal, individual legal rights and the emancipatory norms that underlie them included, that can help relocate the ties that bind, at work and beyond.

[55] E Heery, 'Debating Employment Law: Responses to Juridification' in P Blyton, E Heery, and P Turnbull (eds), *Reassessing the Employment Relationship* (Palgrave, 2010).

Sample of Judgments 1995 to 2010
(Chronological Order by Judgment)

1995–99

Burton v Rhule De Vere Hotels Ltd [1997] ICR 1 (EAT)
Prison Service and Others v Johnson [1997] ICR 275 (EAT)
Jones v Tower Boot Co Ltd [1997] ICR 254 (CA)
British Telecommunications v Williams [1997] IRLR 668 (EAT)
Parchment v The Secretary of State for Defence (QB, 23 February 1998)
Smith v Gardner Merchant Ltd [1999] ICR 134 (CA)
Reed & Bull Information Systems Ltd v Stedman [1999] IRLR 299 (EAT)
Sheriff v Klyne Tugs (Lowestoft) Ltd [1999] EWCA Civ 1663, [1999] ICR 1170
Rorrison v West Lothian College [2000] SCLR 245 (CSOH)
Harvest Press Ltd v McCaffrey [1999] IRLR 778 (EAT)
Stafford v National Westminster Bank (EAT, 10 November 1999)
Driskel v Peninsula Business Services Ltd [2000] IRLR 151 (EAT)
Bonna v Oxford CC (EAT, 17 December 1999) (13)

2000–04

Smith v Zeneca (Agrochemicals) Ltd [2000] ICR 800 (EAT)
Leavers v The Victoria University of Manchester (EAT, 21 February 2000)
Harris v The Post Office (Royal Mail) (EAT, 25 February 2000)
Moores v Bude-Stratton Town Council [2001] ICR 271
London Borough of Camden v Pullen (EAT, 27 March 2000)
Mather v British Telecommunications plc [2001] SLT 325
Waters v Commissioner of Police of the Metropolis [2000] UKHL 50, [2000] 1 WLR 1607
Fraser v State Hospitals Board for Scotland [2001] SLT 1051
Derby Specialist Fabrication v Burton [2001] ICR 833 (EAT)
Abbey National Plc v Robinson (EAT, 20 November 2000)
Levy v Allied Dunbar Assurance Plc (QB, 14 December 2000)
Greater Manchester Passenger Transport Executive v Sands (EAT, 11 January 2001)
Garrett v LB of Camden [2001] EWCA Civ 395
Long v Mercury Communications [2002] PIQR Q1 (QB)
Unwin v West Sussex CC (QB, 13 July 2001)
D Watt (Shetland) Ltd v Reid (EAT, 25 September 2001)
Wong v Parkside Health NHS Trust [2001] EWCA CIV 1721, [2003] 3 All ER 932
Sandwell MBC v Jones [2002] EWCA Civ 76, [2002] ICR 613
Cook v Tower Hamlets LBC (EAT, 1 April 2002)
Yeboah v Crofton [2002] EWCA Civ 794, [2002] IRLR 634
Ellis v Eagle Place Services Ltd [2002] EWHC 1201 (QB)
Zaiwalla & Co v Walia [2002] IRLR 697 (EAT)
Ahuja v Inghams (Accountants) [2002] EWCA Civ 1292, [2002] ICR 1485
Walton v Image Creative Ltd (EAT, 16 August 2002)
Santamera v Express Cargo Forwarding [2003] IRLR 273 (EAT)

Vento v CC of West Yorkshire Police [2002] EWCA Civ 1871, [2003] ICR 318
Mullins v Laughton [2002] EWHC 2761, [2003] Ch 250
Barlow v Broxbourne BC [2003] EWHC 50 (QB)
Yellow Pages Limited v Garton (EAT, 13 March 2003)
Ree v Redrow Homes (Yorkshire) Ltd (EAT, 9 April 2003)
Kopel v Safeway Stores [2003] IRLR 753 (EAT)
Johnson v Bank of England (EAT, 10 April 2003).
Smith v Martin & Co (Marine) Ltd (EAT, 4 June 2003)
MacDonald v AG for Scotland & *Pearce v Governing Body of Mayfield School* [2003] UKHL 34,
  [2003] ICR 937.
Horkulak v Cantor FitzGerald International [2003] EWHC 1918 (QB), [2004] ICR 697 &
  [2004] EWCA Civ 1287, [2005] ICR 402
Armstrong v Newcastle Upon Tyne MBC (EAT, 17 November 2003)
Virgo Fidelis School v Boyle [2004] ICR 1210 (EAT)
Essa v Laing Ltd [2004] EWCA Civ 2, [2004] ICR 746
Swift v CC of Wiltshire Constabulary [2004] ICR 909 (EAT)
Foster v Somerset CC [2004] EWCA Civ 222
Hyam v Havering NHS PCT [2004] EWHC 2971 (QB)
Dunnachie v Kingston upon Hull CC [2004] UKHL 36, [2005] 1 AC 226.
Eastwood v Magnox Electric plc & McCabe v Cornwall CC [2004] UKHL 35, [2005] 1 AC 503.
Brumfitt v MoD [2005] IRLR 4 (EAT)
Bahl v Law Society [2004] EWCA Civ 1070, [2004] IRLR 799
Omilaju v Waltham Forest LBC [2004] EWCA Civ 1493, [2005] ICR 481
Lambeth LBC v Owolade (EAT, 30 November 2004) (47)

2005–09

Moore v Welwyn Components Ltd [2005] EWCA Civ 6, [2005] ICR 782
Blackburn with Darwen Borough Council v Stanley (EAT, 20 January 2005)
Marks and Spencer Plc v Laneres [2005] CSIH 19
Bristol United Press Ltd v Beckett (EAT, 4 February 2005)
Banks v Ablex Ltd [2005] EWCA Civ 173, [2005] ICR 819
Spirit Group Ltd v Bell (EAT, 30 March 2005)
Crossland v Wilkinson Hardware Stores Ltd [2005] EWHC 481 (QB)
Premier International Foods Ltd v Dolan (EAT, 14 April 2005)
First Global Locums Ltd v Cosias [2005] EWHC 1147 (QB), [2005] IRLR 873
Riley v Nick Base t/a Gl1 Heating (EAT, 19 July 2005)
Smiths Detection Watford Ltd v Berriman (EAT, 9 August 2005)
Perkin v St George's Healthcare NHS Trust [2005] EWCA Civ 1174, [2006] ICR 617
Herbert Smith Solicitors v Langton (EAT, 10 October 2005)
Dike v Rickman [2005] EWHC 3071
Mark Warner Ltd v Aspland [2006] IRLR 87 (EAT)
Kircher v Hillingdon PCT [2006] EWHC 21 (QB), [2006] Lloyd's Rep. Med. 215
Pakenham-Walsh v Connell Residential [2006] EWCA Civ 90
Villalba v Merrill Lynch and Co Inc [2007] ICR 469 (EAT)
Spencer v Primetime Recruitment Ltd (EAT, 2 March 2006)
National Probation Service for England and Wales (Cumbria Area) v Kirby [2006] IRLR 508 (EAT)
Miles v Gilbank [2006] EWCA Civ 543, [2006] ICR 1297
Maclellan v Co-operative Group (CWS) Ltd (EAT, 11 May 2006)
Merelie v Newcastle PCT [2006] EWHC 1433 (Admin)
Sayers v Cambridgeshire CC [2006] EWHC 2029, [2007] IRLR 29

Majrowski v Guy's and St Thomas's NHS Trust [2006] UKHL 34, [2007] 1 AC 224
Daniels v Commissioner of Police for the Metropolis [2006] EWHC 1622 (QB)
Islam v Dunedin Housing Association Ltd (EAT, 8 August 2008)
Green v DB Group Services [2006] EWHC 1898 (QB), [2006] IRLR 764
Clark v CC of Essex [2006] EWHC 2290 (QB)
Thornett v Scope [2006] EWCA Civ 1600, [2007] ICR 236
Madarassy v Nomura International Plc. [2007] EWCA Civ 33, [2007] ICR 867
Cumbria CC v Carlisle-Morgan [2007] IRLR 314 (EAT)
Abbey National Plc. v Fairbrother [2007] IRLR 320 (EAT)
Daw v Intel Corp (UK) Ltd [2007] EWCA Civ 70, [2007] ICR 1318
Nageh v Southend University Hospital [2007] EWHC 3375 (QB)
Islamic Cultural Centre v Mahmoud (EAT, 27 June 2007)
Royal Bank of Scotland v McAdie [2007] EWCA Civ 806, [2008] ICR 1087
Luke v Stoke on Trent City Council [2007] EWCA Civ 761, [2007] ICR 1678
HM Prison Service v Johnson [2007] IRLR 951
GMB Trade Union v Brown (EAT, 16 October 2007)
Birmingham CC v Samuels (EAT, 24 October 2007)
Jocic v LB of Hammersmith & Fulham (30 October 2007)
Sunderland CC v Conn [2007] EWCA Civ 1492, [2008] IRLR 324
Robertson v The Scottish Ministers [2007] CSOH 186
Hammond v International Network Services UK Ltd [2007] EWHC 2604 (QB)
Geary v Amec Logistics & Support Services Ltd (EAT, 1 November 2007)
Royal Mail Letters v Muhammad (EAT, 20 December 2007)
RDF Media Group Plc v Clements [2007] EWHC 2892 (QB), [2008] IRLR 207
Lipscombe v The Forestry Commission [2008] EWHC 3342 (QB)
GAB Robins (UK) Ltd v Triggs [2008] EWCA Civ 17, [2008] ICR 529
Al Jumard v Clwyd Leisure Ltd [2008] IRLR 345 (EAT)
B v A (EAT, 17 June 2008)
Cumbria Probation Board v Collingwood (EAT, 7 August 2008)
Watson v Durham University [2008] EWCA Civ 1266
Saini v All Saints Haque Centre [2009] IRLR 74 (EAT)
Ormsby v CC of Strathclyde Police [2009] CSOH 143, 2008 SCLR 783
Live Nation (Venues) UK Ltd v Hussain (EAT, 22 October 2008)
English v Thomas Sanderson Blinds Ltd [2008] EWCA Civ 1421, [2009] ICR 543
Richmond Pharmacology v Dhaliwal [2009] ICR 724 (EAT)
Stafford and Rural Homes Ltd v Hughes (2009) 107 BMLR 155 (EAT)
West Coast Trains Ltd v Tombling (EAT, 2 April 2009)
St Christopher's Fellowship v Walters Ennis (EAT, 5 May 2009)[1]
London Probation Board v Lee (EAT, 20 May 2009)
Cheltenham BC v Laird [2009] EWHC 1253 (QB), [2009] IRLR 621
MoD v Guellard (EAT, 1 September 2009)
Dickie v Flexcon Glenrothes Ltd [2009] GWD 35-602 (Sheriff Court)
Doherty v The Training and Development Agency for Schools (EAT, 29 October 2009)
Veakins v Kier Islington Ltd [2009] EWCA Civ 1288, [2010] IRLR 132
Johnson v The Governing Body of Coopers Lane Primary School (EAT, 1 December 2009)
UPS Ltd v Sammakia (EAT, 3 December 2009)
Cartamundi UK Ltd v Worboyes (EAT, 4 December 2009) (71)

---

[1] There was a successful appeal to the Court of Appeal outside the period from which my sample was taken, for which the citation is [2010] EWCA Civ 921. This was against the finding in the Employment Tribunal, upheld in the Employment Appeal Tribunal, of race discrimination (but not against the upheld finding of constructive unfair dismissal).

2010 (to May 2010)

Munchkins Restaurant Ltd v Karmazyn (EAT, 28 January 2010)
Daley v Serco Home Affairs Ltd (EAT, 7 January 2010)
Rayment v MoD [2010] EWHC 218 (QB), [2010] IRLR 768
Aberdeen CC v McNeill (EAT, 9 February 2010)[2]
South London Healthcare NHS Trust v Rubeyi (EAT, 2 March 2010)
Sarkar v West London Mental Health NHS Trust [2010] EWCA Civ 289, [2010] IRLR 508
Marinello v Edinburgh CC [2010] CSOH 17, 2010 SLT 349[3]
M and L Sheet Metals Ltd v Willis (EAT, 12 March 2010)
Connor v Surrey CC [2010] EWCA Civ 286, [2011] QB 429
Cleveland Police Authority v Francis (EAT, 10 March 2010)
Bashir v Sheffield Teaching Hospital NHS Foundation Trust (EAT, 27 May 2010) (11)

---

[2] There was a successful appeal to the CSIH outside the period from which my sample was taken, reported at [2013] CSIH, [2015] ICR 27. As a result the ET's finding that there had been a constructive unfair dismissal was reinstated.

[3] There was a successful appeal to the CSIH outside the period from which my sample was taken, reported at [2011] CSIH 33, 2011 S.C. 736, such that Mr Marinello was allowed to proceed with his claim under the PHA 1997.

Research Interviews with People in Organizations

Definition of Behavioural Conflict

By a behavioural conflict at work I mean a dispute about how colleagues have behaved towards one another (whether or not the dispute is also about a particular workplace practice or decision, for example, allocation of work or disciplinary action).

Research Questions

How are people within organizations affected by law and legal process when either they are involved in, or required to respond to, behavioural conflict at work?
What causes behavioural conflict at work, first, to become litigious at all and, secondly, to become litigious to different degrees?

Interview Guide

My interest is not in specific behavioural conflicts but in the general conclusions that can be drawn from your experiences. In particular, please be careful only to use examples to illustrate your points if you can do so without explicitly or implicitly identifying anyone involved. The use of imaginary, hypothetical examples to make a point would be preferable.

- Do you have any formal organizational role in dealing with behavioural conflict at work?
- Have you any overall sense of how often there is conflict of this kind at your workplace? Do you have any overall sense or impression of how often behavioural conflict leads to, for example, informal complaints, formal complaints, lawyers becoming involved, settlements before or after proceedings, proceedings that go to court or proceedings that go on appeal?
- What is the approach in your workplace to behavioural conflict? Do you have a sense of how people at different places and levels in the organization react when there is a conflict?
- Are there written policies about behavioural standards? What do you know about them? Do you know how they define or understand unacceptable behaviour at work? What do you know about the procedures they put in place? Do you think the written policies are consistently adhered to? May I have copies?
- What is your direct experience of behavioural conflict at your workplace, whether involving yourself or others? For example, how have you been involved? How often and in what ways has this kind of conflict affected you?
- How (if at all) have you been affected by law or legal processes (eg settlements, litigation, appeals, etc) in dealing with behavioural conflict at work? Can you describe any specific legal influences on you personally? For example, has law affected what you think of as unacceptable behaviour at work? Has law affected what you think should be done in response either to the fact, or to allegations, of unacceptable behaviour at work?
- Are there ways in which you see either colleagues or the organization as a whole being affected by legal influences? What are the mechanisms by which you see this happening? What are the effects you perceive?

- Have you any ideas about what it is in different employees, employers, work situations, etc that leads, first, to behavioural conflict at work and secondly, to such conflict that becomes litigious to different degrees?
- What do you think is good and bad about the legal influences you perceive first, on behavioural conflict at work and, secondly, on how colleagues respond to the fact of unacceptable behaviour or to allegations of this? How does law's influence, for good or ill, compare with other influences (if any)?
- Is there anyone else you think I should be speaking to either in your organization or elsewhere?

Research Interviews with Practising Lawyers

Definition of Behavioural Conflict

By a behavioural conflict at work I mean a dispute about how colleagues have behaved towards one another (whether or not the dispute is also about a particular workplace practice or decision, for example, allocation of work or disciplinary action).

Research Questions

How are people within organizations affected by law and legal process when either they are involved in, or required to respond to, behavioural conflict at work?
What causes behavioural conflict at work, first, to become litigious at all and, secondly, to become litigious to different degrees?

Interview Guide

My interest is not in specific behavioural conflicts but in the general conclusions that can be drawn from your experiences. In particular, please be careful only to use examples to illustrate your points if you can do so without explicitly or implicitly identifying anyone involved. The use of imaginary, hypothetical examples to make a point would be preferable.

- Could you outline your experience of dealing with behavioural conflict at work? For example, what kinds of clients have you advised about this kind of dispute? What sorts of issues have they brought to you for advice and representation? Roughly speaking, what proportion of the disputes about which you have been consulted have settled, either pre or post proceedings being issued? How often have the matters you've dealt with ended up either in court or on appeal? How often are multiple claims pursued?
- Do you have ideas about what it is in different employees, employers, work situations, etc that lead to:
  - behavioural conflicts at work?
  - behavioural conflicts becoming litigious but only to the point of a settlement either pre or post proceedings?
  - behavioural conflicts being litigated to the point of a full-blown trial?
  - behavioural conflicts being litigated beyond a first instance trial?
  - behavioural conflicts being litigated by multiple routes?
- How do you see organizations dealing day to day with behavioural standards and conflicts? What do you think influences them? Do you see law playing a part in what they do? Do your answers differentiate between sectors?

- How (if at all) do you see the law interacting with the other influences that you perceive on behavioural conflicts at work and on how employees and employers respond to them? For example, do you regard the law as tending to reduce, to limit or otherwise to steer conflicts? Do you perceive the law as tending to escalate conflicts? Do you feel able to offer any general observations from your experiences?
- How are litigants affected, in your perception, by behavioural conflicts that end up in court and on appeal? How, for example, do they respond: to your advice, to the litigation experience, to the court's findings, to the court's reasoning and ultimate decision and to the court's remedial decision?
- Is there anyone else you think I should be speaking to, either another practicing lawyer or from within an organization?

Index

Tables, figures, and boxes are indicated by an italic t, f, and b following the page/paragraph number.

anti-discrimination, *see* discrimination

behavioural conflict at work; *see also* bullying
author's analytical approach to 6–10
definitional issues 6, 12
definition of 6
perceptions of, *see* interview study
use of term 11–13, 59–62, 103–4,
185–88, 271–72
behaviour rules, application of
arbitrariness and technicality, trend of 9,
59–61, 100–101, 119–37, 168,
248, 251
consistency in substantive application, trend
of 139–41, 167–69, 180–82, 243,
246–47, 251, 259–60, 263–64
contract and tort claims
arbitrariness etc 119–20, 128–37
consistency 140, 160–67, 177–80
discrimination claims
arbitrariness etc 122–28, 131–37
consistency 140, 142–50, 173–76
non-discriminatory harassment claims
arbitrariness etc 119–20, 131–37
consistency 151–60, 169, 181
unfair dismissal claims
arbitrariness 119–22, 124–25,
131–32, 134–37
consistency 140–42, 170–73
Blackstone, A 17, 29 n 121
British Workplace Behaviour Survey (BWBS),
see surveys
bullying
conceptual and definitional
approaches 13–14
judicial analyses 128–29, 131–32, 149–50,
161–68, 170–73, 177–79
psychological studies, and
conceptual and definitional
approaches 13–14
generally 13
incidence measurement 14–18
'latent class cluster analysis' 14
negative acts questionnaire (NAQ), *see*
negative acts questionnaire
references in judgments 6–8, 103–105,
109–12, 136
reporting to surveys of 15–16, 19–22, 36,
45, 53–54
socio-legal studies, and 35–36, 45,
53–54, 57–58
sociological studies, and
conceptual and definitional approaches 18
incidence measurement 19–25
use of term 6, 13, 15–16, 103–14, 185–86

case law qualitative analysis
actions of colleagues and
management 110–12, 169–82
author's approach to 103–106
behaviour rules, *see* behaviour rules,
application of
characteristics of sample judgments 105t
courts issuing sample judgments 105t
detailed narratives in
judgments 112–15, 118
extreme adversarialism 117, 150–51
factual complexity of cases 107–12, 117
group identity, influence of 109–110
the legal 'insiders' perspective 117–18
litigation commenced, where 105t
litigation process imposing costs 115–17
optimal direction of adjudicative
effort 118, 168
overlapping rights, *see* overlapping rights
Charlwood, A 29 n 128, 36–37
civil regulation 260, 264–65
claims, *see* complaints and claims
collective approaches
application to individual rights, need for 10,
55–58, 169, 180–83, 217–18, 242–43,
252, 259–66
danger to from individual rights 10, 56,
195–96, 241–43, 252, 255–56, 258
employer dominance, and 10, 50–52,
56, 216, 220–21, 241–43,
252, 254–56
government's attitude to reform 10, 26–28,
253, 256–58, 261, 264
individual employment rights, and 4, 9–10,
51–52, 55–58, 192–93, 215–20,
222–24, 229–31, 234–36, 240–43,
251–56, 259–66
large organizations 49, 52, 185,
223–24, 229
managers' perceptions 50–52, 192–93,
208, 216–20, 222–24, 229–231,
238, 241
movement towards individualism, and 1–2,
10, 25, 42, 55–58, 181–82, 216–17,
219, 223, 234–36, 245, 251–52,
255–59, 265–66
new versions of 224, 260, 264–65
pluralism, meaning of 215
recovery by use of law 259–66
strengths and limitations of 51–52, 192–93,
208, 218–19, 229–31, 240–43
tensions between collective nature of
work and assertion of individual
rights 9–10, 55–58, 181–82, 224–36,
241–42, 253–54

Colling, T 51
complaints and claims; *see also* litigation
  claiming behaviour
    individual employment rights, as to 31–37
    reluctance to complain 17, 22–23,
      44–46, 227–34
    studies of 28–37
  claimants as 'difficult' 190–91, 208, 234–36
  employee experiences of exercising rights 1,
    11–12, 28–47, 53–54, 57–58, 217,
    227–36, 241–42, 253–55
  organizational culture, and 191–92, 208,
    228–31, 241, 254–55
  personal costs as disincentive 57–58, 217,
    227, 231–34
  potential legal claims 61*t*
  silencing of 22, 53–56, 189, 195, 207–208,
    216–17, 227–36
conduct, *see* behaviour rules, application of
constructive dismissal
  behaviour rules, application in claims of
    contract claims 119–20, 131–35,
      139–41, 164–66
    discrimination claims 139–41, 143, 150
    generally 140
    unfair dismissal claims 119–22, 124–25,
      131–32, 135, 139–42, 170–73
  tests 60–62, 64–67, 94–95, 98
contracts of employment
  behaviour in breach of, application of
    rules 119–20, 131–35, 139–41,
      164–69, 178–82
  definition of 'contract of employment' 63
  duty of mutual trust and confidence 64–67,
    94–95, 97–99, 100–101
  duty to take reasonable care 93–97, 100–101
  potential actions for breaches
    of 60–62, 92–100
  primary liability 92
  remedies 98–100
  vicarious liability 92–93
Cooper, CL 12–16, 104
costs
  behavioural conflict generally 10, 53–56,
    106–107, 115–18, 137, 188–89,
    207–208, 224–27, 231–36, 241–42, 256
  funding for litigation costs 26–28
  litigation process imposing 115–17,
    231–34, 241–42
courts
  courts in which sample judgments
    given 105*t*
  litigation commenced, where 105*t*
  optimal direction of adjudicative effort 118,
    137, 168, 182
Coyne, I 15
Crenshaw, K 2, 252 n 20, 264 n 48
Critical Legal Studies movement 5

Deakin, S 6 n 27
Dickens, L 3, 11 n 2, 48–50, 52 n 327,
  58, 249
discrimination; *see also* victimization

  behaviour rules, application in
    claims of 109–10, 117, 122–28,
    131–37, 139–50, 167–70, 173–76
  complaints, organizational acceptability
    of 44, 216–17
  direct discrimination, definition of (pre and
    post Eq A 2010) 71–74, 82–87
  discriminatory harassment
    behaviour rules, application in claims
      of 126–28, 131–32, 134–40, 142–48,
      167–69, 173–74, 180–82
    legal approach before 2003 71, 72–77
    legal definitions from 2003 77–82
    employer responsibility (pre and post 2003
      and EqA 2010) 75–77, 81, 85
  remedies
    pre EqA 2010 72, 87–89
    EqA 2010 provisions 72, 89
  statutory wrongs of, introduction to 71
dismissal, *see* constructive dismissal; statutory
  right not to be unfairly dismissed
Dobbin, F 48
duty of mutual trust and confidence, general
  law on 64–67, 94–95, 97–99, 100–101
duty to take reasonable care, general law
  on, 93–97, 100–101

Edelman, LB 5 n 19, 48, 250
employees, *see* complaints and claims;
  individual employment rights
employer dominance
  individual employment rights, and 10, 50–52,
    57, 216–17, 220–21, 241–43, 252–56
  lawyers' perceptions 216–17, 221
  managers' perceptions 220–21
  meaning of 215
employment contracts, *see* contracts of
  employment
employment law, *see* law
employment rights, *see* individual
  employment rights
Employment Tribunal (ET)
  proportion facing workplace problems who
    make a claim to 35–36
  case for further research into ET
    adjudication 245–46, 263
  choice of ET or ordinary courts 27–28, 54,
    60–62, 100–101, 105*t*, 125, 132–37,
    139–41, 167–69, 180–82, 239–40
  claimants' experiences, qualitative study
    of 46–47
  difficulty enforcing awards 47
  diversion of claims to ordinary courts 28, 54
  exclusion of ET judgments from my
    sample 103
  impact of procedural rules and recent
    changes 25–27, 57, 257
  interview study findings, *see* interview study
  judicial mediation of claims in 44 n 261
  nature of disputes before 41–42, 57
  numbers of claims
    generally 26–27
    organizational factors affecting 51

organizational impacts of claims in 41, 50, 53 n 334
race discrimination claims, qualitative study of 42–43
sexual harassment claims, qualitative study of 43–44
steering claimants to ET equality claims 125
Surveys of Employment Tribunal Applications (SETA), *see* surveys
equality legislation, impact of, *see also* **interview study; law** 49–50
equality norms, *see* norms
equality rights, *see* individual employment rights

fairness, *see* norms
Fair Treatment at Work Survey (FTWS), *see* surveys
'FARE' questions 20–21, 24
Fevre, R 13, 15, 18–25, 35–36, 42, 45, 56–57, 107, 189, 216, 224, 234, 255
Freedland, M 65 n 24

Galanter, M 26 n 110, 104 n 5, 252 n 19, 262 n 40
Genn, H 25 n 108, 29–35, 37–40, 55 n 340, 190
Gross, C 16
group identity, case law qualitative analysis, *see* behaviour rules, application of; discrimination

Hall, M 3, 11 n 2, 48–50, 249
Handy, J 17
harassment; *see also* sexual harassment
discriminatory harassment, *see* discrimination
non-discriminatory harassment
behaviour rules, application to claims of, *see* behaviour rules, application of
employer responsibility 89, 135–36, 152–53
liability 89–92, 151–60
remedies 92, 156–57, 159–60
overlapping rights, and 135–37
psychological studies, and, *see* bullying
socio-legal studies, and 32–33, 35–36, 43–48, 53–54
sociological studies, and, *see* bullying
Heery, E 253 n 22, 260, 264–65
Hoel, H 12–6, 24 n 103, 104
human resources (HR), *see* interview study
importance to improving the functioning of law 143, 260
interview study 185, 193, 196–200, 208–209, 217, 218–20, 224–27, 237–39
mediating legal influence 48, 51–53, 185, 197–200, 209, 237, 226–27, 263 n 45
sample of manager interviewees, and 185

individual employment rights
collective approaches, and, *see* collective approaches
current overall effect of 1, 9–10, 251–56
employers and, *see* organizational context

exercise of, *see* complaints and claims
experimentation as transformative force 10, 264–65
government's attitude to reform 10, 26–28, 253, 256–58, 261, 264
increased risk of individualized conflict in more receptive workplaces 1, 9–10, 53–54, 191–92, 197, 208, 212–13, 216–24, 227–36, 240–43, 253–56
labour law scholarship, and 3–4
Legal Realism, and 4–6, 250
need for redesign of 1, 10, 58, 242–43, 256–67
origins of 1–4
overlapping rights, *see* overlapping rights
paradoxical effect of 1, 9–10, 251–58
reinforcing existing power structures, as 1, 9–10, 252, 255–56
socially transformative effect
obstructions to 1, 9–10, 211–12, 247–52, 256–58
potential for 1, 9–10, 101, 118, 139–41, 167–69, 180–83, 209–12, 245–47, 251, 259–67
systemic inequality, and 2
trend towards 1–4, 37, 41–42, 57, 59–62, 100–101, 251–53, 257–58
wider participation in implementation and enforcement as transformative force 1, 10, 58, 217–18, 242–43, 259–67
individualism
reinforcing existing power structures, as 216–17, 245, 251–53, 255–58, 265–66
trend towards 1–2, 10, 25, 41–42, 55–58, 219
individualization at work
individualized conflict
emergence and escalation 190–97, 234–36, 242
harm from 53–54, 57–58, 216–17, 231–37, 241–42, 262
increased risk in more receptive workplaces, *see* individual employment rights
pressure on managers 1, 23, 52, 220, 224–27, 253–54
relationship to collective conflict 23–25, 57, 262
legal support for 1–2, 4, 10–11, 37, 50, 245, 251–53, 265–66
reinforcing existing power structures, as 1–2, 10, 55–58, 216, 241, 251–53, 255–58, 265–66
relationship to workplace collectivism 1, 4, 9–11, 24–25, 37, 55–58, 195–96, 216–17, 241–42, 246, 251–53, 258–59, 265–66
traditions of labour law scholarship, and 2
interview study
findings
hypothesizing the differential organizational impact of individual employment rights 216–18, 240–43

interview study (*cont.*):
findings (*cont.*):
legal insider perspective giving incomplete insight on law's interaction with working life 183–84, 186–87, 207, 211–13, 217, 227, 239–40, 242
patterns of legal influence, as to 183, 197–204, 209–12
socially transformative effects of individual employment rights, *see* individual employment rights
lawyers' perceptions
advice to clients, influence of 205–206, 210–11
applicability of norms to workplace conduct 204, 210
claimants as 'difficult' 190–91, 194, 208, 234–36, 241–42
content of disputes 186–88, 207
emergence and escalation of conflict 190–91, 193–94, 196–97, 208–209
employees' reluctance to complain 228, 231–32
employer dominance and rights 221
employer responses to judgments 205, 207, 211–12
formal organizational policies and procedures 183, 196–200, 209
impact of conflict 189, 196–97, 209, 232–34, 241–42
impact of equality law rules 183, 201–202, 210–12
impact of law and legal process 183, 198–200, 200–202, 204, 205–207, 209–12
impact of legal rules outside equality law 202, 204, 210–12
impact of substantive legal rules 200–202, 204–207, 210–12
individualized causes of conflict 190–91, 208
organizational causes of conflict 193–94, 208–209
relaxed attitude towards effects of overlapping rights 217, 239–40
settlement practice, influences on 205–207, 210–11
managers' perceptions
applicability of norms to workplace conduct 204, 210
claimants as 'difficult' 190, 208, 234–35
collective approaches to rights 218, 222–24
compared with judges' reasoning 204–205
content of disputes 187, 207
dichotomizing good management and legal requirements 237–38
emergence and escalation of conflict 19–26, 208
employees' reluctance to complain 227–29, 231–32
employer dominance and rights 220–21
formal organizational policies and procedures 194–98, 209
impact of conflict 188–89, 207–208, 231–32

impact of equality law rules 183, 201–202, 210–12
impact of law and legal process 183, 197–98, 200–201, 201–205, 209–12
impact of legal rules outside equality law 183, 202–204, 210–12
impact of organizational culture 192–93, 198, 208–209, 221–24, 227–36, 241–42
impact of substantive legal rules 183, 200–205, 210–12
individualized causes of conflict 190, 208
organizational causes of conflict 191–93
reporting negative behaviour directed to them 188, 227, 243
trend towards individualism 219
unawareness of effects of overlapping rights 211, 248
unitarist approaches to rights 221–22
methodology 184–86

judgments, *see* behavioural rules, application of; case law qualitative analysis

Kelly, EL 48

labour and equality rights, *see* individual employment rights
labour rights, *see* individual employment rights
law
complexity in the field of 52, 59–62, 100–101, 135–37, 168, 185, 226–27, 239–40, 249, 258–61
duality of 2, 9–10, 245–58
factors reducing emancipatory influence in the field of 1, 9–10, 211–12, 247–52, 256–58
impact of equality law rules relevant to behaviour
lawyers' perceptions 183, 201–202, 210–12
managers' perceptions 183, 201–202, 210–212
impact of non equality legal rules relevant to behaviour
lawyers' perceptions 202, 204, 210–12
managers' perceptions 183, 202–204, 210–12
impact of substantive legal rules relevant to behaviour
lawyers' perceptions 200–202, 204–207, 210–12
managers' perceptions 183, 200–205, 210–12
individualization at work, support from 1–2, 4, 10–11, 37, 50, 245, 251–53, 265–66
influence in the field of
lawyers' perceptions 183, 198–202, 204, 205–207, 209–12
managers' perceptions 183, 197–98, 200–205, 209–12
researcher and wider perceptions 11–12, 25, 54.
legal background to the field, introduction to 59–62
legal insider perspective gives incomplete insight on law's interaction with working life 117–18, 183–84, 186–87, 207, 211–13, 217, 227, 239–40, 242

norms, *see* norms
paradoxical nature of 2, 9–10, 245–58
patterns of legal influence in the field,
    perceptions as to 183, 197–204,
    209–12, 257
reform, government's attitude to 10, 26–28,
    253, 256–58, 261, 264
variety of means for exerting
    influence 3–4, 8–9, 11–12, 45,
    48–58, 183–84, 198–200, 205–207,
    209–13, 239–40, 251–52, 256–58,
    260, 262, 265–66
lawyers
advice to clients, influence of 205–207, 210–11
interview study of, *see* interview study
legal insider perspective gives incomplete
    insight on law's interaction with
    working life, *see* law
Legal Realism 4–6, 250
Lewis, SE 17
Liefooghe, APD 16, 25
litigation; *see also* behaviour rules, application of;
    case law qualitative analysis
choice of Employment Tribunal or ordinary
    courts, *see* Employment Tribunal
examples of behavioural conflict
    litigation 7–8, 106–107
funding for costs of, *see* costs
litigation process imposing costs, *see* costs
strategy, choice of 119–20, 124–28, 132–37
studies on experience of 38–47, 150
Llewellyn, K 5, 106 n 6, 141 n 2
Lloyd-Bostock, S 29

Mackenzie Davey, K 16, 25
management
responses of, case law qualitative
    analysis 110–12, 117–18, 169–82
attitudes to labour standards of 10, 48–58,
    236–37, 239, 254, 256
different styles of 51–2, 191–92, 204, 215–17
empirical evidence relevant to behavioural
    conflict, and 16–18, 20–25, 35–37,
    44–45, 48–58
interview study of, *see* interview study
pressure on 1, 23, 52, 220, 224–27, 253–41
mutual trust and confidence, *see* duty of mutual
    trust and confidence, general law on

negative acts questionnaire (NAQ) 13–16,
    19–22, 103–104
negative behaviour at work, *see* behavioural
    conflict at work; bullying
negligence, *see* duty to take reasonable care,
    general law on
Niedl, K. 16
norms; *see also* duty of mutual trust and
    confidence; duty to take reasonable care,
    general law on
conflict generally over those governing
    working life of 24, 32, 189
difficulty in practice of applying to workplace
    conduct 204, 210
generally of workplace fairness,
    reasonableness, and equality

deployment of as means for more effective
    implementation of rights 10,
    242–43, 259–66
within relevant law and legal process 8–10,
    167–68, 180–82, 202, 211, 245–47
influence of personal values on managerial
    ideas about workplace versions
    of 203–204, 210, 249–50

Olafsson, R 16
Orford, J 17
organizational context; *see also* complaints
    and claims; employer dominance; HR;
    interview study; management; norms
acceptability of complaints 55–58, 216–17,
    227–36, 241, 254–55
comparing legal and organizational
    decision-making 183, 204–205,
    210–12, 249–50
formal organizational policies and
    procedures 16, 23–24, 41, 45 n 263,
    48–53, 76, 142, 170–74, 180–83, 191,
    194–200, 202–204, 209–13, 223–24,
    226, 229, 231–32, 241, 247, 249, 254
impact of individual rights 48–53, 183,
    197–204, 205–207, 209–13, 218–24,
    240–43, 245–58
law and legal process, and emancipatory
    organizational change
    supporting 9, 101, 118, 139–141, 180–82,
        183, 197–202, 209–12, 245–47
    undermining 1, 9–10, 53–58, 60–62,
        100–101, 117–18, 119–20, 132–37,
        183, 197–201, 202–204, 205–207,
        209–13, 247–50, 252, 255–56, 258
legal advice, influence of 11, 25–26, 34,
    36–37, 48, 50 n 313, 125, 188,
    198–201, 205–207, 209–13, 219,
    226–27, 230–31, 237–40, 249, 263
organizational causes of
    conflict 191–94, 208–209
responses to disputes 1, 48–53, 55–58,
    110–12, 117–18, 169–82, 191–200,
    202–13, 215–36, 240–43, 247,
    249–50, 253–56
responses to judgments 205, 207, 211
tensions between collective nature of work
    and assertion of individual rights,
    see collective approaches
overlapping rights
causing arbitrariness in the determination of
    liability 122–29, 130–32, 133*t*
causing arbitrariness in the determination of
    remedy 120–22, 129–30, 131–32, 134*t*
managers unawareness of effects of,
    see interview study
overview of 61*t*
problem of 119–20, 132–37, 167–68,
    180–82, 248–50
senior lawyers relaxed attitude towards effects
    of, *see* interview study

Paterson, A 29–30, 34 n 164, 39 n 213,
    55 n 340
pluralism, meaning of, *see* collective approaches

Pollert, A 29 n 128, 36–37, 57–58,
117 n 83, 260
psychological studies of bullying, *see* bullying
Purcell, J 50–51, 256 n 28

racial harassment, *see* harassment
realism, *see* Legal Realism
reasonable care, *see* duty to take reasonable care,
general law on
reasonableness, *see* norms
reporting of negative workplace experiences,
statistics for 14–16, 19–22, 32–36, 53–54

sexual harassment, *see also* Employment
Tribunal; harassment
emergence of term 72
women's responses to 17, 44, 45 n 262, 147,
sociological and socio-legal studies; *see also*
bullying
claiming behaviour 28–37
collaborative socio-legal and industrial
relations research, need for 4
individual employment rights
claiming, and 31–37
litigation, and 38–47
organizations, and 48–53
New Legal Realist literature, *see* United States
statutory right not to be unfairly dismissed
behaviour rules, application in claims
of 119–22, 124–25, 131–37, 139–42,
167–73, 180–82
liability for 63–68
main elements 62
origins 62
remedies 68–71
surveys
British Workplace Behaviour Survey
(BWBS) 13, 18–25, 42, 56–57,
189, 212,
Fair Treatment at Work Survey
(FTWS) 18–20, 21, 35–37, 57, 190
Surveys of Employment Tribunal
Applications (SETA) 39–41, 51
Unrepresented Worker Survey
(URWS) 36–37
Workplace Employment Relations Surveys
(WERS) 48–49, 51

Thompson, EP 2, 4 n 15, 9 n 35, 251–52
torts
behaviour rules, application in claims
of 119–25, 128–41, 160–64,
166–69, 177–82
liability
intentional wrongs, of 93
negligence 93–97
remedies 98–100
trade unions; *see also* collective approaches;
individualization; interview study
advice or representation in ETs 40
change regarding 192–93, 208, 218–19

definitions of bullying 14
influence on organizational responses to
individual employment rights 49, 51,
57–58, 192–93, 215–16, 222–24,
229–30, 241
legal advice, and 34 n 164, 213, 219, 230–31
legislative undermining of 3–4, 11 n 2
members reporting workplace problems 20
organizational attitudes to 51–52,
192–93, 218–19
reduced ET claim rates in presence
of 42, 229
responses to workplace problems 35–36, 17,
51, 57, 208, 219, 230, 241

unitarism
commitment-style management,
and 216, 222
engagement HR practices, and 51, 216
flattened hierarchy, and 221–22
individual employment rights, and 221–22,
241, 254–55
meaning of 215
United States
American law and legal process
general analyses 252 n 19, 6 n 25
individual rights era, effect of 250 n 14
American Legal Realism, *see* Legal Realism
employers' protection from liability for legally
wrongful conduct 263
escalation of individual workplace conflict,
evidence about 29 n 29, 31–32
innovation in dispute resolution 265 n 52
New Legal Realism 5, 45 n 263, 48, 250
'sexual harassment', emergence of term,
see sexual harassment
Unrepresented Worker Survey (URWS),
see surveys

victimization
behaviour rules, application in claims of 140,
148–50, 173, 176
liability
EqA 2010 87
pre-EqA 2010 85
remedies
EqA 2010 89
pre-EqA 2010 87–99
violence at work
in public-facing work
preponderance in 22
stoic reactions 22
incidence measurement 18, 20–22

work, culture of, *see* organizational context
workplace bullying, *see* bullying
Workplace Employment Relations Surveys
(WERS), *see* surveys
Wright Mills, C 18

Zapf, D 16